The Hongzhou School of Chan Buddhism in Eighth- through Tenth-Century China

The Hongzhou School
of Chan Buddhism
in Eighth- through
Tenth-Century China

Jinhua Jia

STATE UNIVERSITY OF NEW YORK PRESS

Published by

STATE UNIVERSITY OF NEW YORK PRESS, ALBANY

© 2006 State University of New York

For information, address State University of New York Press,
194 Washington Avenue, Suite 305, Albany, NY 12210-2384

Production, Laurie Searl
Marketing, Michael Campochiaro

Library of Congress Cataloging-in-Publication Data

Jia, Jinhua.
   Hongzhou school of Chan Buddhism in eighth- through tenth-
century China / Jinhua Jia.
      p. cm.
   Includes bibliographical references and index.
   ISBN 0-7914-6823-2 (hardcover : alk. paper)
    1. Hongzhou (Sect)–History.   2. Mazu, 709-788   3. Zen Buddhism–
China–History.   I. Title.
BQ9550.H652 J53 2006
294.3'92709510902–dc22

                                     2005025465

10 9 8 7 6 5 4 3 2 1

To my father Jia Maozhi 賈茂芝

and mother Lin Jinxuan 林金瑄

who raised and educated me in very difficult circumstances.

CONTENTS

ACKNOWLEDGMENTS

This book grew out of the Ph.D. dissertation I submitted to the University of Colorado at Boulder in 1999. The dissertation, as suggested by its title, "The Hongzhou School of Chan Buddhism and the Tang Literati," is an interdisciplinary study comprising two parts, the first of which examines the Hongzhou school, and the second the interrelationship between the Hongzhou school and the Tang literati and literature. This new work greatly enhances the first part, but omits the second due to the limitation of space. Thus, it becomes a pure study of Chan Buddhist history.

The revision and enhancement do not diminish my debt to my mentors at the University of Colorado. I am most grateful to Professors Paul W. Kroll, Victoria B. Cass, Terry Kleeman, Yan Haiping, Stephen Miller, and Madeline K. Spring for their inspiring teachings in my doctoral study and insightful suggestions on draft versions of my dissertation. I should also like to express my deep gratitude to Professors Robert M. Gimello, Donald K. Swearer, Miriam L. Levering, John R. McRae, Chen Jinhua, and Mr. Mikael Bauer for kindly taking the time to read all or parts of the manuscript. Their invaluable comments and suggestions greatly enhanced the final product.

Although I majored in Chinese literature in my undergraduate and M.A. studies, my mentors in China have always encouraged me to follow the academic tradition that literature, history, and philosophy are of the same family. I am immensely indebted to Professors Cheng Qianfang, Zhou Zuzhuan, Zhou Xunchu, Fu Xuancong, Yu Xianhao, Luo Zongqiang, and Chen Yunji for guiding me to expand the scope of study and open myself to the broad fields of Chinese studies.

My sincere thanks are also due to the two anonymous reviewers for their incisive comments and criticisms that helped to strengthen many arguments in this work; to Professor Kim Youcheol and my colleagues Ms. Han Ji-yeon and Karen Kim for their help in Romanizing Korean titles and names; to Professor Chen Shangjun for his generosity in allowing me to read and use the proofs of his forthcoming book, *Quan Tangwen bubian;* to Mr. James Glasscock for his valuable suggestions on draft versions of this book; and to editors Nancy Ellegate, Laurie Searl, and Allison B. Lee, and manager Michael Campochiaro of the State University of New York Press, who made the publication of this book possible. I must acknowledge the City University of Hong Kong for a grant supporting this research, my colleague Professor Randy LaPolla for his help in the preparation of my application for the grant, and the staff of Interlibrary Loan at the Library of City University of Hong Kong for their assistance in acquiring many research materials.

Finally, my special gratitude goes to Professors Li Zehou, Liu Zaifu, Mrs. Chen Feiya, Mr. Ni Yingda, Professors Qian Nanxiu, Shen Zhijia, and Liu Jianmei for their unfailing help and friendship; and to my parents, brothers, and sisters, whose ever-lasting love and support enable me to persevere through all the adversities in my life.

TABLES

ABBREVIATIONS AND CONVENTIONS

CDL	*Jingde chuandeng lu*, ed. Daoyuan
Chan Chart	*Zhonghua chuan xindi chanmen shizi chengxi tu*, by Zongmi
Chan Preface	*Chanyuan zhuquanji duxu*, by Zongmi
GDL	*Tiansheng guangdeng lu*, ed. Li Zunxu
P.	Numbered Paul Pelliot manuscripts from Dunhuang in the Bibliothèque National, Paris.
QTW	*Quan Tangwen*, ed. Dong Gao et al.
S.	Numbered Aurel Stein manuscripts from Dunhuang in the British Museum, London.
SBCK	*Sibu congkan*
SGSZ	*Song gaoseng zhuan*, by Zanning
SKQS	*Siku quanshu*
T.	*Taishō shinshū daizōkyō*
XXSKQS	*Xuxiu Siku quanshu*
XZJ	*Xu zangjing*, reprint of *Dai Nihon zokuzōkkyō*
ZJL	*Zongjing lu*, by Yanshou
ZTJ	*Zutang ji*, ed. Jing and Yun

Citations from the *Taishō* canon and *Xu zangjing* are listed in the following fashion: title; *T.* or *XZJ*; volume number; *juan* (fascicle) number; page, register (a, b, or c)—for example, *Huayan jing tanxuan ji*, *T.* 35: 16.405a; *Yuanjue jing dashu chao*, *XZJ* 14: 3.557b. The *Taishō* serial number of each text is given in the Bibliography.

Since most of the Sanskrit terms used in this study have been accepted as English words, all these terms are set in roman with diacritical marks for consistency.

INTRODUCTION

The Hongzhou school of Chan Buddhism in eighth–tenth century China, with Mazu Daoyi (709–788) and his successors as its central figures, represents a crucial phase in the evolution of Chinese Chan Buddhism. It inherited and creatively developed the abundant legacy of Sinitic Buddhism and the early Chan movement and exerted great influence in later developments of Chan Buddhism with its doctrinal, practical, genealogical, and institutional paradigms. This work aims to present a comprehensive study of this school, including its literature, formation, doctrine and practice, transmission and spread, road to orthodoxy, and final schism and division.

To examine Chinese Chan Buddhism in terms of specific schools, we first need to clarify three interrelated concepts—school, lineage, and orthodoxy. Scholars of Chinese Buddhism have noted that the widely used English term "school" is the conventional translation of the Chinese word, *zong*. *Zong* originally denoted ancestral temple (*zumiao*) and later evolved into many different meanings, including "ancestor," "lineage," "leading personage," "principle doctrine or theory," and so forth.[1] Tang Yongtong was the first to discern the different senses of *zong* in Chinese Buddhist texts, and he was followed by Mano Shōjun, Hirai Shun'ei, Stanley Weinstein, and others. According to these scholars, *zong* is used in three main senses in Chinese Buddhist texts: (1) a specific doctrine or an interpretation of it; (2) the theme or theory of a text, or an exegetical tradition of it; (3) a group or tradition that traces its origin back to a founder and shares some common doctrines and practices among its lineal successors.[2] Whereas scholars in general agree that *zong* as in the third sense can be translated as "school," recently some scholars suggest an alternative term "lineage."[3]

"Lineage" is surely one of the basic connotations of *zong*, and there is evidence that the Chinese Buddhist concept of lineage, especially that of Chan Buddhism, was strongly influenced by the tradition of ancestor cult.[4] Under the Chinese patriarchal clan system of legitimate and collateral lineages, lineage was closely associated with notions such as identity, legitimacy, and orthodoxy.

1

As a matter of fact, the original meaning of the term "orthodoxy," *zhengzong* or *zhengtong*, refers to "orthodox lineage." However, lineage has also always been an important organizational framework in the Buddhist tradition. In Indian Buddhism, as early as about one century after the Buddha's nirvāṇa, there were already accounts of different lineages descending from immediate disciples of the Buddha, and these were considered to be sacred issues for monks because tracing a lineage back through a series of preceptors and disciples was an acknowledged way of proving the orthodoxy of a person's ordination.[5] During the period of schism, lineage further became a means of sectarian disputation, as various schools developed lineages tracing back ficti-tiously to immediate disciples of the Buddha in order to claim legitimacy and authority for their doctrines.[6] In Chinese Buddhism, the Tiantai tradition was the first to create a lineage of "sūtra-transmission" tracing back to twenty-three (or twenty-four) Indian patriarchs based on the *Fu fazang yinyuan zhuan* (Biographies of the Circumstances of the Transmission of the Dharma Collection).[7] However, it is in the Chan tradition that lineage became a central concern, because, as Bernard Faure indicates, it represents the desire of the marginal group to become the party of the orthodox.[8] According to the *Xu Gaoseng zhuan*, from the early sixth century to the mid-seventh century, there were at least six meditation groups active in China. While the other five groups were brought to the capital during the Sui dynasty, the group in the line of Bodhidharma-Huike was excluded from the national meditation center.[9] In the early Tang, the Dongshan/Northern group connected itself to the Bodhidharma-Huike line, which was marginal in the Sui, and eventually to the Buddha. This genealogy helped them to advance from marginal to orthodox. Then, the Heze, Niutou, Baotang, and Hongzhou groups further revised and recreated the genealogy in order to become the party of orthodox.[10]

Historically, from both the broader cultural and specifically Buddhist contexts, *zong* in the sense of Buddhist group, with its actual or fictitious founder(s) and lineal successors, may indeed be most correctly translated as "lineage." However, there were two major types of lineage: (1) some major and influential, not only comprising founder(s) and lineal successors, but also having their own distinctive doctrines and practices; (2) others small and subordinate, forming only master-disciple or monastery-abbotship successions, without setting up their own doctrinal system. To classify the different types of lineage more exactly and to define research scopes more clearly, the modern term "school" is still applicable to the fully fledged lineages of the first type.[11] Thus, in this work, the Hongzhou tradition/lineage, as well as other fully fledged lineages such as the Northern, the Heze, the Niutou, or the Baotang, is regarded as a school, though in its early stage of formation when the Hongzhou lineage was not yet fully fledged, "community" or "lineage" is used to designate it, whereas any other group that was derived from the Hongzhou school and not yet or never fully developed is referred to as a "lineage" or "house."[12]

In the traditional Chan genealogy, Mazu, literally "Patriarch Ma," was connected to the six great patriarchs of early Chan, from Bodhidharma to Huineng (638–713), via his mentor Nanyue Huairang (677–744). Discourses attributed to Mazu and his major disciples and encounter stories about them remained the core of traditional Chan literature and were repeatedly read, performed, interpreted, and eulogized. Their images were idolized as representatives of Chan spirit and identity not only by the successors of Chinese Chan but also of Korean Sŏn, Japanese Zen, and Vietnamese Thiên.

The discovery of the Dunhuang manuscripts has greatly changed our view of Chan history. On the basis of interpretations of the Dunhuang texts, recent scholarship has rewritten the history of early Chan and reveals convincingly that the traditional Chan genealogy that erases the significant contributions of the Northern school and other early schools and lineages is historically inaccurate, and that the old paradigms of gradualism versus subitism and North versus South do not reflect the historical development of early Chan. Unfortunately, since there are few Dunhuang texts related to Mazu and his Tang successors, we must return to the traditional "discourse record" (yulu) texts and "transmission of the lamp" (chuandeng) histories, and thus face two methodological and hermeneutical dilemmas.

First, modern scholars' view of the Chan literature of the eighth to tenth centuries can be summarized as consisting of three types. (1) Earlier and some current historians often accept almost all the discourse records and "transmission of the lamp" histories at face value as historical fact and use the transmission framework of traditional genealogy as a base on which to construct a narrative history of "classical" Chan Buddhism. (2) Since the famous debate about Chan historicity between Hu Shi (1891–1962) and D. T. Suzuki (1870–1966) in the 1950s,[13] some scholars have assumed a more balanced stance toward the Chan literature. While noticing the ever ongoing "supplementarity" in Chan literature,[14] they also recognize that Chan historians' sense of history differs significantly from that of modern historians in areas such as their fervent concern for genealogical metaphors, their enlightenment and transmission experience, and the literary nature of the genres of Chan texts.[15] (3) Recently a number of scholars have adopted the view that texts attributed to the Tang Chan masters in the generations following Huineng, especially encounter dialogues and relevant stories that were the central content of Chan literature,[16] were the retrospective creations of Song-dynasty Chan monks.[17]

The second dilemma is closely related to the first. Modern scholarship has usually described the eighth to tenth century Chan centered on Mazu and his successors as the "golden age" or "classical" Chan, which represented a revolutionarily iconoclastic tradition, with the Song-dynasty Chan in decline. Recently, along with question of the validity of the Chan literature attributed to the Tang masters, scholars have also challenged the validity of these definitions and argue that the true "golden age" is the Song Chan tradition, and that Mazu and his Tang successors came to represent a "classical" age only after their time had passed, and were merely images created by the imaginations of their Song devotees.[18]

In order to deal with these two dilemmas, this work adopts a synthetic approach combining historical-philological and philosophical-hermeneutical studies. The author believes that the first important task facing modern students of mid-Tang to Five-Dynasties Chan studies is the discrimination between original or relatively datable materials and later layers of modification and recreation, and that no assertion of truth or fabrication can be made before a solid investigation of each text is completed. Therefore, we need to perform a thorough examination of the texts attributed to Mazu and his disciples to present credible texts for further study of the Chan doctrine and religious practice of the Hongzhou school. On the other hand, as many scholars have noted, fabrications and legends are also of historical and doctrinal value and should not simply be discarded. This is especially true of the literature attributed to the Hongzhou school, as the results of our examination reveal that the retrospective creation and updating did not begin with the Song-dynasty monks but was begun by the third- and fourth-generation disciples of Mazu in the late Tang. This project was then continuously repeated by Five-Dynasties and Song successors. Hence, the separate texts of original parts and later layers are all useful and serve different purposes in our philosophical analysis and historical reconstruction. With the identified original and relatively datable texts of the Hongzhou literature, we are able to observe the Hongzhou doctrine and practice through our own lens instead of the lens of the late-Tang, Five-Dynasties, or Song-dynasty Chan monks. From the identified layers of the late-Tang and Five-Dynasties creations, we can get the sense of the responses to and criticisms of the Hongzhou doctrine by their successors of that period and consequently find the reasons for the schism of the Hongzhou line and the rise of the Shitou line and various houses during that period.

The philological approach is applicable due to the existence of three bodies of reliably datable texts. The first body of texts is the extant stele inscriptions of Tang monks and monasteries written by contemporary writers. Scholars have made use of some common, well-known stele inscriptions, such as the epitaphs and stūpa inscriptions of Mazu Daoyi and his several disciples. However, there are still many inscriptions that have been insufficiently studied or almost totally ignored. For example, the stele inscriptions written for the Korean disciples of Tang masters contain much useful information but are rarely studied.[19] Many biographies in the *Song gaoseng zhuan* (Biographies of Eminent Monks Compiled in the Song Dynasty, comp. 988) are acknowledged by Zanning (919–1001) as based on original Tang stele inscriptions and thus reliably datable.[20] Many inscriptions included in the *Quan Tangwen* (Complete Tang Prose), *Tangdai muzhi huibian* (Collection of Tang Epitaphs), *Quan Tangwen bubian* (Supplement to the Complete Tang Prose), and so forth have not been examined. A thorough investigation of all extant inscriptions is very encouraging. We find in them information about the emergence and maturity of encounter dialogues, the transcriptions of encounter dialogues much older than the *Zutang ji* (Anthology of the Patriarchal Hall; 952),[21] *Jingde chuandeng lu* (Records of the Transmission of the Lamp Compiled during the Jingde Reign-Period; 1004),[22] and so forth.

The second body of texts consists of datable Buddhist texts such as Guifeng Zongmi's (780–841) works, Huangbo Xiyun's (d. 855) *Chuanxin fayao* (Essential Teachings of the Transmission of Mind), and the works and catalogs of visiting Japanese scholars. Although Zongmi depicted the vision of his own Heze school as superior, modern scholars in general agree that Zongmi's works are valuable in that they offer a contemporary, basically accurate account of the various factions of Chan during the mid-Tang and so provide a corrective to the traditional picture described by Song monks.[23] In archaeological studies, scholars utilize a few bronze wares whose dates are known as "standard ware" to determine the dates of similar wares. Since Zongmi was a younger contemporary of Mazu's immediate disciples, his works can be used as "standard texts" to determine the dates and authenticity of those texts attributed to Mazu and his disciples. For example, because the main themes and even some expressions from Mazu's sermons are seen in Zongmi's summaries and criticisms of the Hongzhou doctrine,[24] we can determine that those sermons in general represent Mazu's ideas, though they may contain certain editorial modifications by his immediate disciples who were the recorders and compilers of those sermons. Huangbo's *Chuanxin fayao*, compiled by Pei Xiu (ca. 787–860) in 857, can also serve as a "standard text" in the same way, although certain modifications by Pei Xiu and Huangbo's disciples are also possible.[25] The works and catalogs of the visiting Japanese monks during the mid-Tang such as Saichō (767–822), Ennin (794–864), Eun, and Enchin (814–891) are all datable and can serve the same function.

The third body of reliably datable texts comprises the works of the Tang literati, such as Bai Juyi's (772–846) collected works, Duan Chengshi's (d. 863) *Youyang zazu* (Assorted Records from Youyang), and other relevant poems and essays, which also contain much valuable information about the development of Chan.

Equipped with these three bodies of texts, we are able to perform a thorough examination on the lives of Mazu and his disciples and the texts attributed to them. The first chapter provides a complete biography of Mazu Daoyi, which clarifies many previous misunderstandings of the sources and therefore more accurately describes the various stages of training, teaching, and establishment of the Hongzhou community in Mazu's life. Chapter two examines Mazu's immediate disciples who comprised the main body of the Hongzhou lineage and pushed it toward its maturity as a religious school. It focuses on solving the controversies over three second-generation masters of the mid-Tang Chan, Tianhuang Daowu (727–808), Danxia Tianran (739–824), and Yaoshan Weiyan (744–827), who were traditionally ascribed as disciples of Shitou Xiqian (700–790). Our new studies in this chapter demonstrate that all three actually learned from both Mazu and Shitou, and that Yaoshan even had a much closer relationship with Mazu. On the basis of Yanagida's studies, this chapter further produces a new list of Mazu's disciples with relevant data such as dates, native places, locations and foundations of monasteries, and sources. The third chapter and some parts of the fifth are dedicated to one of the major concerns of this work—a thorough examination of the Hongzhou literature. First, according to stele inscriptions and other reliably datable Tang texts, during the mid-Tang period when Mazu and his immediate disciples were active, encounter dialogue emerged in two forms, one being the vogue of witty, paradoxical phrases, and the other the fictionalized account of enlightenment dialogue. Then during the late Tang and Five Dynasties, encounter dialogue achieved full maturity in multiple forms and styles. Second, with reference to this background of the evolution of encounter dialogue, the Hongzhou literature is carefully examined and some original or relatively datable texts and discourses are identified: Mazu's six sermons and four dialogues, the *Extended Records of Baizhang, Pang Yun's Verses,* the *Extended Discourses of Dazhu Huihai* (fl. 788), Yaoshan Weiyan, Fenzhou Wuye (760–821), and Nanquan Puyuan (748–834) in *Juan* 28 of the *CDL,* sixteen discourses of Mazu's disciples, three fragments of Li Fan's (d. 829) *Xuansheng qulu* (Inn of the Mysterious Sages), the *Baolin zhuan* (Chronicle of the Baolin Monastery), the Chan verses attributed to the Liang-dynasty monk Baozhi (ca. 418–514), and the "Song of Realizing the Way" attributed to the early-Tang monk Yongjia Xuanjue (665–713).

The reader will then see that these original or relatively datable materials make feasible a philosophical-hermeneutical study of the Hongzhou doctrine and practice, free of the views and mythologies of later times. Like early Chan, the doctrinal foundation of the Hongzhou school was mainly a mixture of the tathāgata-garbha thought and prajñāpāramitā theory, with a salient emphasis on the kataphasis of the former. Despite the iconoclastic image depicted by his successors of the late Tang to early Song, Mazu was well versed in Buddhist scriptures. He followed the early Chan tradition to claim Bodhidharma's transmission of the *Laṅkāvatāra-sūtra,* and applied this sūtra and the *Awakening of Faith,*[26] as well as other *tathāgata-garbha* texts, to construct the doctrinal framework of the Hongzhou school and introduce some new themes and practices into the Chan movement. His proposition that "this mind is the Buddha" or "ordinary mind is the Way" followed the fundamental belief of early Chan in the existence of Buddha-nature within all sentient beings, and further identified the ordinary, empirical human mind with Buddha-nature, with the equivalence of tathāgata-garbha and ālayavijñāna in the *Laṅkāvatāra-sūtra,* and the two inseparable aspects of one-mind in the *Awakening of Faith* as scriptural support. He simplified the enlightenment cycle of "original enlightenment"-"non-enlightenment"-"actualized enlightenment" illustrated in the *Awakening of Faith* by directly highlighting immanent or original enlightenment. He also utilized the tathāgata-garbha notion of non-origination to advocate that "the Way needs no cultivation." Inspired by the Huayan theory of nature origination from the Tathāgata, which was an interpretation of the essence/function paradigm of the two aspects of one-mind in the *Awakening of Faith*, Mazu proposed that the ultimate reality of enlightenment was manifested in function, and consequently affirmed that the entirety of daily life was of ultimate truth and value. These new doctrines provided a theoretical underpinning for the emergence and maturity of encounter dialogue, a rhetoric style that germinated in early Chan and became an important feature of Chan practice after Mazu. These doctrines and practices represented a major development from early Chan and constructed the theoretical framework for the later Chan movement, which has been regarded as the most Chinese-style Chan. Yet these doctrines remained genuinely Buddhist,[27] as they were not revolutionarily iconoclastic innovations that repudiated the beliefs and doctrines of early Chinese Buddhism, as their admirers among Song Chan monks thought, but rather drew out some of the ramifications of the ambiguous tathāgata-garbha theory and made explicit those that were implicit.

After Mazu passed away, his immediate disciples strove for the self identity of the Chan movement and the orthodoxy of their own lineage. Chapter five depicts their rough road toward these aims. They first revised and completed the century-long project of Chan genealogy with the *Baolin zhuan*, which implies a propagandistic, polemical claim of Chan movement as a "separate" and "mind-to-mind" transmission tracing back to the Buddha(s) and superior to other scholastic teachings of Buddhism, and which sets their own lineage as the orthodox one after the sixth patriarch, Huineng, in order to legitimize their new doctrines and practices and elevate their lineage from marginal to orthodox. Because of the inseparable relationship between lineage and orthodoxy in both Chinese culture and Buddhist tradition, this twofold polemical claim was validated and eventually became the doctrinal background for the late-Tang to Song-dynasty Chan movement, from which a new kind of Chan—the Patriarchal Chan—emerged. At the same time, those second-generation masters of the Hongzhou school created more texts and attributed them to mythologized or famous monks such as Baozhi and Yongjia Xuanjue in order to legitimize and disseminate their doctrinal teachings. They established and administered sixteen monasteries as centers of development. They expanded gradually from remote, regional Jiangxi to the whole nation and the two capitals to obtain official, imperial recognition and authority. Thus, through the nearly forty-year cooperative effort of these masters, the Hongzhou lineage grew from a regional community to a fully fledged and national school and assumed a dominant position in the Chan movement. This chapter also identifies that the true author of the *Baolin zhuan* was Zhangjing Huaihui and determines that Baizhang Huaihai (749–814) did not create a set of monastic regulations but his immediate disciples led by Baizhang Fazheng (d. 819) did.

The new doctrine and practice of the Hongzhou school brought serious criticism from contemporaries of Mazu and his disciples, such as Nanyang Huizhong (683–769) and Zongmi. After the Huichang persecution of

Buddhism, Mazu's third- and fourth-generation successors further reflected on and debated the Hongzhou doctrine. However, intriguingly, just as Mazu's disciples created or updated the images of their real or fictitious patriarchs in the *Baolin zhuan*, most of the reflections and controversies of the late-Tang masters appeared in retrospectively created encounter dialogues and stories attributed to their mid-Tang or earlier predecessors, such as the famous debate about the two propositions, "this mind is the Buddha" and "neither mind nor Buddha," and the two metaphors, "genuine-gold store" and "convenience store." Yet these controversies engendered new lineage assertions. Dongshan Liangjie (807–869), Deshan Xuanjian (782–865), Shishuang Qingzhu (807–888), and Touzi Datong (819–914), successors of Tianhuang, Yaoshan, and Danxia who were students of both Mazu and Shitou, broke away from the Hongzhou line and attached themselves exclusively to the Shitou line. As a result, the tradition of the two great lineages after Huineng was retrospectively created. From the late Tang to Five Dynasties, during the dynamic process of this division, various lineages/houses sprang up due to the striving for orthodoxy and the establishment of numerous new monasteries headed by Chan masters. Among those were eight major houses—Gui-Yang, Linji, Cao-Dong, Deshan, Xuefeng, Shishuang, Yunmen, and Fayan. The designation of the Five Houses—Gui-Yang, Linji, Cao-Dong, Yunmen, and Fayan—was not fixed until the mid-Northern Song, and represented the current state of the Northern-Song Chan after the rise and fall of the various houses. Thus, this study eventually deconstructs the traditional Chan genealogy of two lines and five houses, which has not only been passed on within the Chan tradition for more than a thousand years, but also constituted the basic framework for presenting historical narratives in modern historiography of Chan Buddhism for nearly a century. The deconstruction of this traditional genealogy calls for new frameworks of narration in the study of Chan history.

An annotated translation of Mazu's authentic or relatively datable discourses, including six sermons and four dialogues, is found in the Appendix. Many relevant, reliably datable discourses of Mazu's disciples and comments by Zongmi and other contemporaries are cited in the annotations.

The study of this work demonstrates that the Hongzhou school is neither a revolutionarily iconoclastic tradition representing a sharp break with early Buddhist tradition, nor a mere mythology of a "golden age" created by the Song-dynasty Chan monks, but rather a vibrant, significant tradition that stood firmly in the middle phase of Chan history. On the one hand it inherited and creatively developed the abundant legacy of Sinitic Buddhism and early Chan; on the other it exerted great influence in late Chan development with its doctrinal, practical, genealogical, and institutional paradigms. Indeed, all later houses, branches, and offshoots from the Song dynasty onward were derivations of this school.

To recognize the Tang dynasty as the "golden age" of the Chan tradition, as well as of the whole Sinitic Buddhist tradition, does not mean that one has to declare the Song dynasty as an age of decline, or vice versa. If we observe the two eras from a comprehensive horizon, we will see that both periods deserve to be recognized as parts of the same "golden age." As for the designation "classical" Chan used by some scholars, since both the original and recreated discourses attributed to Mazu and his successors, produced during the eighth to tenth centuries, were regarded as "classics" by Chan monks of Song dynasty onward, and Mazu and his successors of mid-Tang to Five Dynasties actually provided doctrinal, practical, genealogical, institutional paradigms for later Chan development, this designation may still be used. However, it seems more proper that we adopt the phase designations regarding Chan movement during the Tang-Song period suggested by some scholars, namely, early Chan (early seventh to mid–eighth centuries), middle Chan (mid-eighth to mid-tenth centuries), and Song-dynasty Chan.[28] While on the one hand there was an unbroken current of evolution in doctrine, practice, rhetorical style, and genealogical construction in the Chan tradition of the Tang and Song; on the other the three phases represent specific developmental stages of the Chan tradition. In the early Chan phase, the various branches of the Chan movement loosely based their doctrines on the belief of the existence of Buddha-nature within all sentient beings and exhibited a variety of Chan practice that grew out of the meditation tradition. They also achieved a sense of identity and orthodoxy through the continuing construction of Chan genealogy. During this phase, however, the term "Chanzong" (Chan lineage/ school) did not appear,[29] and different designations were used, such as "Dharma-gate of Dongshan" (Dongshan famen), "Subitic Teaching of Mahāyāna" (Dasheng dunjiao),[30] "Bodhidharma Lineage" (Damo zong),[31] and "Chan-gate" (Chanmen).[32] This reveals that they had not yet reached a coherent self-identification. In the middle Chan phase, the Hongzhou-school doctrine of "ordinary mind is enlightenment" gradually came to dominate the Chan movement, and the practice of encounter dialogue formally emerged and matured. The construction of a Chan genealogy was finally completed, and the institutional establishment of Chan monasteries was initiated. During this phase, the term Chanzong or Chanmen zong (Chan-gate lineage/school) was widely applied,[33] which indicates the general acknowledgment of the Chan tradition as an independent lineage/school, or, in its own words, a separate transmission. By the Song dynasty, the Chan school reached high maturity and coherence—its genealogies, doctrines, practices, and institutions were perfected, its texts were compiled, canonized, and interpreted, and it dominated the mainstream of Chinese Buddhism.

CHAPTER ONE

BIOGRAPHY OF MAZU DAOYI

Mazu Daoyi (709–788), who was acknowledged as the founding patriarch of the Hongzhou school of Chan Buddhism by his successors, is generally regarded as a key figure in Chan tradition. During his eighty years, Mazu witnessed almost all of the important events of the eighth century. His two training periods as novice monk and Chan practitioner fell in the Kaiyuan reign-period (713–741) of Emperor Xuanzong (r. 712–756), a time marked by political stablility, economic prosperity, and military expansion. His career as a Chan teacher began with the Tianbao reign-period (742–756) of the same emperor, a period that still looked powerful and prosperous on the surface but gradually developed potential crises. During the seven-year turmoil of the An Lushan rebellion (755–763), Mazu continued to teach in the remote mountains of Jiangxi and was therefore less affected by wars. He successfully gathered a large community in Hongzhou during the early post-rebellion period and enjoyed the patronage of local political and military magnates, who became more and more powerful and independent after the rebellion as the central government gradually lost its control.

Although modern scholars have made significant efforts toward reconstructing Mazu's biography,[1] it remains incomplete. Many important events in his life have not been clearly or accurately described. In this chapter, based on other scholars' studies and drawing upon a variety of available sources, I provide a new, complete biography of Mazu, which describes the various stages of training and teaching in his life, in order to facilitate further studies of the Hongzhou school.

The most important sources for Mazu's life are three Tang stele inscriptions. The first is the epitaph written by Bao Ji (ca. 727–792) in 788, when Mazu had just passed away. Although the original text is no longer extant, it is almost completely preserved in the hagiography of Mazu in the SGSZ.[2] The second is the "Tang gu Hongzhou Kaiyuansi Shimen Daoyi chanshi taming bingxu" (Stūpa Inscription and Preface for Daoyi, the Deceased Chan Master of Kaiyuansi and Shimenshan in Hongzhou; hereafter cited as "Daoyi Stūpa") written by Quan Deyu (761–818) in 791, three years after Mazu's

11

death.[3] The third is a short inscription inscribed on the stone case of Mazu's relics in 791, which was unearthed in 1966 underneath Mazu's stūpa in the Baofengsi in Jing'anxian. This text will be cited as "Stone Case Inscription."[4]

Other reliable but scattered references to Mazu are found in stele inscriptions and biographies of his disciples, as well as Zongmi's (779–841) works. The entries on Mazu in the *ZTJ* and *CDL* contain some events that do not appear in other sources.[5] The compilers of these two texts seem to have relied on sources other than the inscriptions, possibly the *Yuben* (Discourse Text) or *Yulu* (Discourse Record) attributed to Mazu and the *Baolin zhuan*, which was compiled by Mazu's disciple(s) in 801.[6] Because of the fictitious nature of these sources, they are used with caution and critical restraint.[7] The *Jiangxi Mazu Daoyi chanshi yulu* (Discourse Records of Chan Master Mazu Daoyi in Jiangxi, hereafter cited as *Mazu yulu*) compiled by Huinan (1002–1069) in the mid-Northern Song dynasty contains no new biographical information,[8] and therefore will not be used in this chapter.

MAZU'S YOUTH IN SICHUAN (709–CA. 729)

Mazu's family name is Ma, from which the appellation Mazu (Patriarch Ma) is derived. He was born in the third year of the Jinglong reign-period (709) in Shifangxian of Hanzhou (also called Deyangjun in the Tang, in present-day Sichuan).[9]

The two inscriptions describe Mazu as having an unusual appearance: "He was stalwart like a standing mountain, deep and clear like a still river. His tongue, broad and long, could cover his nose. On the soles of his feet, there were marks which formed characters";[10] "he had the walking gait of a bull, and the gaze of a tiger."[11] Later sources add more extraordinary features, such as wheel-signs on his soles. A broad and long tongue and wheel-signs on the soles are among the thirty-two physical marks of the Buddha.[12] This kind of hagiographic feature is a convention of biographies of eminent monks and should not be taken as accurate historical description.

Mazu entered monastic life at the Luohansi located in his hometown when he was still a child. Later, he had his head shaved by the Chan master Chuji (669–ca. 736) at the Dechunsi in Zizhou (in present-day Sichuan) and received plenary ordination from the Vinaya master Yuan in Yuzhou (in present-day Sichuan) at the age of twenty-one.[13] Chuji was a disciple of Zhishen (609–702), one of the major disciples of the fifth patriarch, Hongren (601–674). According to the *Lidai fabao ji*, Chuji stayed at the Dechunsi in Zizhou from 702 to 732 or 736.[14] This time period coincided with Mazu's youth. Mazu's lifelong career as a Chan practitioner may have been decided by his noviceship with Chuji.

No information regarding the Vinaya master Yuan has been found. As for the year in which Mazu received his ordination, the "Daoyi Stūpa" says that when he died in 788 he had spent sixty years as a monk,[15] but the *SGSZ* gives a period of fifty years.[16] According to the former, Mazu was ordained in 729 when he was twenty-one, and according to the latter, he was ordained in 739 when he was thirty-one. Since those Tang monks who became novices in childhood were usually ordained at the age of twenty or a few years later, and also judging from what we know of Mazu's life after ordination (see next section), the earlier date seems more plausible.

Zongmi, however, told a different story: "Formerly, Daoyi was a disciple of Reverend Jin (Kim) in Jiannan."[17] This statement is problematic. "Reverend Jin" refers to Wuxiang (Mu-sang, 684–762),[18] who came from Silla to Chang'an, the capital of Tang, in 728.[19] He later went to Zizhou and became a disciple of Chuji. When Chuji died, the Dharma was passed to Wuxiang, but the latter remained alone on Tiangushan for a long period. He came to Chengdu around 740 and began to teach only after Zhangqiu Jianqiong, the Military Commissioner of the Jiannan xidao from 739 to 746, paid his respects to him.[20] Since Mazu left Sichuan about 730, became Nanyue Huairang's (677–744) disciple about 732, and started his own teaching in 742 (see next section), he did not have the chance to study with Wuxiang.[21]

In addition, Zongmi said that among the major disciples of Wuxiang there was a "Ma of Changsongshan."[22] The *CDL* also records a "Chan Master Ma of Changsongshan in Yizhou" who was Chuji's disciple.[23] Yanagida believes that this Chan master was Mazu, and he cites the *Yuanwu xinyao* (The Mind-Essence of Yuanwu) and *Wujia zhengzong zan* (Encomium to the Five Houses of Orthodox Genealogy) to suggest that after learning from Huairang, Mazu came back to Sichuan and stayed on Changsongshan for a short time.[24] Suzuki Tetsuo agrees with Yanagida, and further cites a record from the *Sichuan tongzhi* (General Gazetteer of Sichuan), which states that Mazu built the Changsongsi during the Kaiyuan reign-period.[25] These assertions are not well founded. First, in an expression such as "Chan Master Ma of Changsongshan," Changsongshan usually refers to the place in which this Chan master stayed for a long or important period of his teaching or the last years of his life. None of the early sources mentions that Mazu ever stayed in such a place for a long or important period of teaching. Second, the *Yuanwu xinyao* and *Wujia zhengzong zan* tell the story that when Mazu came back to Sichuan, local people called him by his old humble name, the son of Ma Boji ("boji" means winnowing fan), so he again left Sichuan.[26] However, not only do none of the earlier sources mention this event but also these two later texts state that Mazu left Sichuan immediately after being called by his humble name. Hence, even if this story were true, Mazu would not have been called "Ma of Changsongshan" because he stayed there only briefly. Third, since the *Sichuan tongzhi* is a Qing text, it is not applicable without any earlier textual support. Fourth, because the *CDL* never places one person under the lines of two masters, Daoyuan must have considered Ma of Changsongshan to be another monk.[27] Considering Mazu's life after his ordination (see next section), regardless of who his master was, this Chan master Ma was certainly not Mazu.

WANDERING AND TRAINING IN HUBEI AND HUNAN (CA. 730–742)

In about 730, soon after his ordination, Mazu left Sichuan and began a period of "wandering and learning," as many Tang monks did. He set off from Yuzhou, where he received ordination, traveling along the Yangzi River, and arrived at southwestern Hubei. He then resided for a long time on Mingyueshan in Songzixian of Jingzhou (in present-day Hubei). In a stele inscription, Li Shangyin (ca. 813–858) states, "[Daoyi] directly went out of Sanba."[28] Sanba refers to the southeastern area of Sichuan. Zongmi wrote: "[Daoyi] resided for a long period on Mingyueshan in Jingnan."[29] Jingnan refers to Jingzhou which was also called Nanjun in the Tang.[30] Mingyueshan was located seventy *li* west of Songzi.[31] None of the other early sources mentions Mazu's wandering in Hubei. However, since Hubei is located between Sichuan and Hunan, Mazu's next place of travel and residence, it is reasonable to believe that he first traveled in this region.[32]

Zongmi said that before meeting Huairang, Mazu "was a wandering monk with high principles and the supreme Way, and he practiced seated meditation wherever he stayed."[33] The Song monk Qisong (1007–1072) also said, "When [Mazu] became a monk, at first he learned precepts and meditation, on either of which he was able to concentrate."[34] In Sichuan Mazu first studied with the Chan master Chuji, then received plenary ordination from Vinaya master Yuan. Hence, his practice of seated meditation must have been a legacy of Chuji, while his observation of precepts derived from Yuan. Chuji's master was Zhishen, a disciple of Hongren. Seated meditation was one of the major practices of the Dongshan teaching; hence, Mazu's early practice can be seen as a legacy of this school.

In about 732, Mazu left Jingzhou, going south to enter Hunan and arriving at Hengshan (in present-day Hunan). He built a hermitage beside the Boresi on Tianzhufeng. There he met Huairang and became his disciple. The stele inscriptions pertinent to the Hongzhou masters written during the Zhenyuan-Yuanhe period (785–820), such as the "Daoyi Stūpa" and Huairang's epitaph written by Zhang Zhengfu (752–834), which was under the request of Mazu's two major disciples, Xingshan Weikuan and Zhangjing Huaihui,[35] claim that Huairang studied with Huineng. Hu Shi suspects that Huairang was not Huineng's disciple, but the only evidence he gives is that he was once a Vinaya master.[36] Although Huairang's apprenticeship with Huineng is not without question, Hu's reason is not convincing, as many Chan masters in the Tang were Vinaya masters or masters in other Buddhist trends before they affiliated themselves with the Chan line. Huairang's epitaph and a fragment of the *Baolin zhuan* state that he also learned from Dao'an (ca. 584–708; also known as Hui'an or Lao'an), Huineng's confrere.[37] It was quite common that Chan monks of early to mid-Tang visited and studied with several famous masters, without acknowledging who their main mentors were. For example, Jingzang (675–746), Huairang's contemporary, actually studied with both

Dao'an and Huineng.[38] Hence, it is not impossible that Huairang also visited and learned from both masters.

Huairang's epitaph states that he went to Hengshan in about 721 and built a hermitage on the Guanyintai north of the Boresi.[39] The *Nanyue zongsheng ji* records that when Mazu arrived at Hengshan, he also built a hermitage beside the monastery. The hermitage later became a part of the monastery and was named Chuanfayuan, which still existed during the Song dynasty.[40]

Huairang's entry in the *CDL* states that Mazu attended him for ten years.[41] Although this record is not supported by other sources, it is roughly in accord with the known course of Mazu's life. Mazu left Huairang to begin his own teaching in 742 (see next section), so he might have arrived at Hengshan in about 732. His possible itinerary involved setting off from Jingzhou, going south to enter Hunan, and finally arriving at Hengshan.

Both the *ZTJ* and *CDL*, as well as later texts, tell the famous story of Mazu's first meeting with Huairang: the teacher pretended to make a mirror by polishing a brick, and used this action as a metaphor to tell the student that he could not become a Buddha by sitting in meditation. The student was enlightened, and the teacher passed on a verse of mind transmission to him.[42] It is impossible that this kind of highly mature encounter dialogue appeared in Huairang's time.[43] Two parts of this story are seen in the extant fragments of the *Baolin zhuan* with some textual variations:

> The *Baolin zhuan* records: "If learning to sit like a Buddha, the Buddha is neither sitting nor lying. If learning to sit in meditation, meditation has no fixed form."

> The *Baolin zhuan* records: "[Daoyi asked:] 'How should I apply my mind to accord with the formless samādhi of meditation?' The master replied, 'Your learning of the formless samādhi is like planting a seed.'"[44]

Huairang's verse also agrees with *Baolin zhuan*'s feature that every patriarch composed a verse of mind transmission. Thus, we can assume that this story first appeared in the *Baolin zhuan*, which was created by Mazu's disciple(s) in 801.[45]

TEACHING ON THE MOUNTAINS OF FUJIAN AND JIANGXI (742–772)

In the first year of Tianbao (742), Mazu left his teacher and went to northern Fujian. He settled on Fojiling in Jianyangxian of Jianzhou (in present-day Fujian), and began to receive disciples. Ganquan Zhixian, who was a native of Jianyang, attended Mazu on Fojiling in 742.[46] In the same year, Ziyu Daotong (731–813) became a monk in Nan'anxian of Quanzhou (in present-day Fujian), and "at that time, the Chan master Daoyi began to gather and teach disciples on Fojiling in Jianyang, so [Dao]tong went there."[47] Quanzhou was close to Jianyang. Another follower of Mazu at Fojiling was Qianqing Mingjue (d. 831), who was also a native of Jianyang.[48]

Mazu did not stay at Fojiling at length. The next year (743) he moved to Shigong on Qishan in Chongrenxian of Fuzhou (in present-day Jiangxi), and taught there at least until 750. The *SGSZ* records that, in 743, Chao'an, who was a native of Danyangxian in Runzhou (in present-day Jiangsu), "went to a monastery in Fuzhou and was awakened by Daji [Great Quiescence, Mazu's posthumous title]."[49] According to the stele inscription for Xitang Zhizang (738–817) by Tang Ji, Zhizang was born in Qianzhou (in present-day Jiangxi); in the ninth year of Tianbao (750) when he was thirteen years old he first attended Mazu at a mountain in western Fuzhou.[50] Hence, Mazu was still in Fuzhou in 750.[51] The "Daoyi Stūpa" also states that Mazu taught at a mountain in western Fuzhou,[52] while the *SGSZ* gives the name of the mountain as Qishan.[53] The *Fuzhoufu zhi* records that during the reign of Emperor Xuanzong, Mazu built a hermitage in Shigong, and there was still a square brick inscribed with four characters, "Mazu faku" (Dharma Cave of Mazu). The gazetteer also records several poems on Mazu's sojourn in Shigong by poets of the Song, Ming, and Qing dynasties.[54] Shigong was located in the southwest of Fuzhou; hence, it was highly possible that it was the site of the western mountain or Qishan mentioned in the "Daoyi Stūpa" and *SGSZ*. Another new follower of Mazu in Fuzhou was Shigong Huizang, who was most likely a native of Shigong.[55] After Huairang died at Hengshan on the tenth day of the eighth month in the third year of Tianbao (10 August 744), Mazu returned to the mountain to build a stūpa for his master.[56]

It is still unknown when Mazu left Fuzhou, but it is possible that during the Zhide reign-period (756–758), he was already at Gonggongshan in Ganxian of Qianzhou. He was certainly in Qianzhou in the second year of the Dali reign-period (767) and stayed there until 772, when he moved to Hongzhou. Zhaoti Huilang's (738–820) epitaph, written by Liu Ke (*jinshi* 819), says that after Huilang accepted ordination at age twenty, he visited Mazu at Gonggongshan.[57] When Huilang was twenty, it was the second year of Zhide (757). In addition, the "Daoyi Stūpa" says: "[Daoyi] recited Chan . . . at Gonggongshan in Qianzhou. . . . Prefect Pei, who is now Prefectural Governor of Henanfu, attended him for a long time and placed great faith in him."[58] According to Yu Xianhao, Prefect Pei is Pei Xu, who was Prefect of Qianzhou in 767 and also Prefectural Governor of Henan in 791 when Quan Deyu wrote the inscription.[59] The administrative center of Qianzhou was located in Ganxian.[60] The *Ganxian zhi* records that Mazu first stayed on Forifeng, east of the city, and later moved to Gonggongshan, to the north.[61] Since all other sources mention only Gonggongshan, Mazu might have stayed on Forifeng only for a short time.

Huilang was from Qujiangxian of Shaozhou (in present-day Guangdong).[62] Other new followers of Mazu in Qianzhou included: Baizhang Huaihai (749–814), from Changlexian of Fuzhou (in present-day Fujian);[63] Funiu Zizai (741–821), from Huzhou (in present-day Zhejiang);[64] Ezhou Wudeng (749–

830), living in Qianzhou;[65] and Yanguan Qi'an (d. 842), from Hailingxian of Yangzhou (in present-day Jiangsu).[66]

Zongmi stated that after leaving Hengshan Mazu stayed in Qianzhou, Hongzhou, and Huzhou.[67] There were two Qianzhou during the Tang. One was a subordinated prefecture (*jimizhou*) on the northwest border of Sichuan, established in 768.[68] Hu Shi supposes that Mazu might have taught in this prefecture before he left Sichuan;[69] He Yun surmises that he wandered there.[70] However, Mazu could not have taught or wandered in a subordinated prefecture governed by the chief of a minority group (Qiang in this case), and was already on Gonggongshan in 768. The other Qianzhou belonged to Jingzhao superior prefecture (in present-day Shaanxi), but it was not established until 894.[71] Both Mazu and Zongmi, who died before that year, could not have known this prefecture. Thus, Qianzhou is probably a phonetic error of Jianzhou. There was no Huzhou in the Tang; this is obviously a graphic error for Qianzhou.[72] In another instance, Zongmi misread Qianzhou as Chuzhou.[73]

For three decades Mazu arduously undertook his Chan mission in the mountains of Fujian and Jiangxi, experiencing a gradual development from obscurity to reputation. When Mazu stayed on Fojiling, the three disciples whose names are known were all natives of this region. When he moved to Shigong, his new followers were again three in number, of whom one was from remote Runzhou. On Gonggongshan, Mazu had more followers who came from other places, and he also obtained support from the Prefect. Both facts indicate his growing fame and influence.

ESTABLISHING THE HONGZHOU COMMUNITY (772–788)

In the seventh year of Dali (772), Lu Sigong (711–781), then Surveillance Commissioner of Jiangxidao, invited Mazu to stay at the Kaiyuansi in Zhonglingxian of Hongzhou, which was the provincial capital of Jiangxi. Mazu taught in Hongzhou until he died in 788. During the sixteen years, under the patronage of successive commissioners, he attracted a great number of followers and gathered a large community.

Both the "Daoyi Stūpa" and the *SGSZ* state that during the Dali reign-period, Jiangxi Commissioner Lu Sigong invited Mazu to stay in "the place where his administrative center was located" (*lisuo* or *fu*). "The place where the administrative center was located" refers to Zhonglingxian, where the administrative centers of both Hongzhou and Jiangxidao were situated.[74] According to Yu Xianhao, Lu Sigong was Prefect of Hongzhou and Surveillance Commissioner of Jiangxi from the first month of the seventh year to the eighth year of Dali (772–773).[75] In addition, the *SGSZ* reads as follows:

> During the Dali period, because of the broad imperial grace, Daoyi's name was registered at the Kaiyuansi. . . . While he stayed there for merely ten years, he was like the sun rising from the *fusang* tree. . . . During the Jianzhong reign-period [780–783], there was an

imperial edict that all monks return whence they had come. Daoyi was going to return to his hometown, but Commissioner Bao secretly let him stay, without dismissing him.[76]

Commissioner Bao is Bao Fang (723–790), who was Surveillance Commissioner of Jiangxi from the fourth month of the first year to the third year of Jianzhong (780–782).[77] From the seventh year of Dali (772) to the third year of Jianzhong (782) was ten years. Hence, 772 can be fixed as the date of Mazu's arrival to Hongzhou.[78]

According to the previous citation, we also know that in about 782, after Mazu stayed in Hongzhou for ten years, Emperor Dezong issued an edict ordering all monks return to their native places,[79] but Bao Fang secretly protected Mazu, without dismissing him. Bao Fang's action of disobedience was not extraordinary at that time. As is well known, after the rebellion local commissioners gained more and more power and often ignored orders from the capital. Bao Fang's protection was surely very important to Mazu's teaching career and to the Hongzhou community. If Mazu had been sent back to his hometown in remote Sichuan, the gathering and development of the Hongzhou community would probably have been interrupted.

The *SGSZ* again states: "At that time, Buddha-dharma was flourishing to the extreme in Hongzhou, and no place under heaven could surpass it"; "There were more than eight hundred disciples under Daji."[80] This is the period during which Mazu gathered a large community that later developed into a full-fledged lineage/school. As Zongmi later said, "[Daoyi] transmitted Huairang's teaching in the Kaiyuansi in Hongzhou, therefore contemporaries called [Daoyi and his followers] the Hongzhou lineage/school."[81] Since Mazu's disciples were important components of the Hongzhou lineage, and there have been some complicated questions and controversies regarding some of them, they will be discussed in detail in the next chapter.

Mazu passed away in the fourth year of Zhenyuan (788), at the age of eighty.[82] The "Daoyi Stūpa" says that Mazu died on *gengchen* (the first day) of the second month (3 March 788),[83] and the *ZTJ* gives the same day,[84] but the *CDL* records his death on the fourth day of the month.[85] Since the stūpa inscription uses the heavenly-stem and earthly-branch way of numbering days, which is less likely to cause scribal errors, it is more reliable. The "Stone Case Inscription" unearthed in 1966 also convincingly states: "The great master died on the first day of the second month in the fourth year of Zhenyuan."[86]

Before Mazu died, when the abbot of the Kaiyuansi asked about his health, he humorously replied, "Sun-face Buddha, Moon-face Buddha."[87] Many people attended Mazu's funeral, which was described as being as grand as those of Puji (651–739) and Shandao (613–681).[88] Li Jian, who was Surveillance Commissioner of Jiangxi from 785 to 790, and who was also devoted to Mazu, helped to build his stūpa on Shimenshan in Jianchangxian of Hongzhou, which was completed in 791.[89] A portrait-hall of Mazu was also built in Jianchang, which still existed at the beginning of the Song dynasty.[90]

During the Yuanhe reign-period (806–820), possibly between the third and twelfth years (808–817), Emperor Xianzong (r. 805–820) conferred upon Mazu the posthumous title "Daji chanshi."[91] In 827, because of the petition of Li Xian, then Surveillance Commissioner of Jiangxi, Emperor Wenzong (r. 826–840) conferred upon Mazu's stūpa the title "Yuanzheng" (Perfect Realization).[92] After the Huichang persecution of Buddhism, in the fourth year of the Dazhong reign-period (850), Emperor Xuanzong (r. 846–859) ordered Pei Chou, then Surveillance Commissioner of Jiangxi, to rebuild Mazu's stūpa and the Letansi that was located next to the stūpa, and also conferred upon the new stūpa the title "Dazhuangyan" (Grand Adornment) and the new monastery the name "Baofeng." Pei Chou wrote the *zhuan* (seal-script) characters for the title of the stūpa.[93]

CHAPTER TWO

MAZU DAOYI'S DISCIPLES

Mazu Daoyi was a successful teacher with the largest number of disciples whose names are known in the history of Chinese Chan Buddhism. The *ZTJ* states that Mazu had more than one thousand followers,[1] while the *SGSZ* records a number of more than eight hundred.[2] These numbers must have included both religious followers and lay devotees who attended Mazu's sermons but were not necessarily his disciples. The "Daoyi Stūpa" records the names of eleven of his disciples: Huihai, Zhizang, Gaoying, Zhixian, Zhitong, Daowu, Huaihui, Weikuan, Zhiguang, Chongtai, and Huiyun.[3] They can be regarded as having become either the most important or most senior disciples by the time Mazu passed away. The *ZTJ* states that Mazu had eighty-eight close disciples, while the *CDL* puts the number at 139.[4] The latter actually lists 138 names. Based on this list and other early sources, Yanagida Seizan compiled a new list with a total number of 153.[5]

During the early post-rebellion period, in the extensive area of south China, the relationships between Chan masters and lineages were harmonious and interactive. Many disciples of Mazu also learned from other Chan masters such as Jingshan Faqin (714–792), Niutou Huizhong (683–769), and Shitou Xiqian, and the earliest biographies of these disciples did not usually state who their main teachers were. This fact indicates a lack of sectarian color and lineage affiliation during this period. Nevertheless, three of these disciples, Tianhuang Daowu, Danxia Tianran, and Yaoshan Weiyan, unfortunately became the targets of later sectarian contention, and controversies over the question of whether their true master was Mazu or Shitou have continued since the Song dynasty.

The period during which Mazu Daoyi's immediate disciples were active began approximately with the reign of Emperor Dezong (r. 780–805), when the Tang government began to recover from the rebellion and put forward a series of economic, political, and military reforms, and ended in the reign of Emperor Wenzong (r. 824–840), just before the Huichang persecution of Buddhism—that is, roughly from the last two decades of the eighth century through the first four decades of the ninth century. It was through the successful spread of these disciples throughout the nation and their cooperative efforts of striving for orthodoxy that the Hongzhou lineage developed from a local, southern community to an officially acknowledged, full-fledged school.

In this chapter, I first examine Tianhuang, Danxia, and Yaoshan individually in order to resolve the controversies over their masters and lineages. The results of this study not only determine their apprenticeship with Mazu, but also provide a significant prerequisite for a new investigation of the division of the Nanyue-Mazu line and the Qingyuan-Shitou line and the rise of the various houses during the late Tang and Five Dynasties, and consequently for a deconstruction of the traditional Chan genealogy, which will be the focus of chapter six. I then examine Yanagida's list to add and delete some names according to early sources, and consequently produce a new list of Mazu's disciples with relevant data.

TIANHUANG DAOWU

The case of Tianhuang is the most complicated. It involves not only the question of his mentor and lineage but also the controversy over the alleged existence of another Tianwang Daowu. During the mid-Northern Song there appeared a "Tianwang Daowu chanshi bei" (Epitaph of Chan Master Tianwang Daowu) that was attributed to Qiu Xuansu and said that this Daowu was Mazu's disciple exclusively. From the Song to the Qing, controversies have continued about whether there were two Daowu in Jingzhou at the same time of the mid-Tang and also about the Yunmen and Fayan houses descended from which Daowu. Modern scholars have also focused on these controversies. Nukariya Kaiten, Chen Yuan, and Ui Hakuju summarize in detail the discussions among premodern scholars, and all speculate that the epitaph attributed to Qiu Xuansu was a Song forgery.[6] Ge Zhaoguang tries to protect this epitaph, but he does not provide any supporting evidence.[7] Based on those scholars' studies, I carefully examine early sources in order to present a convincing conclusion.

Early sources of Tianhuang contradict each other in an intricate way. Both the *ZTJ* and *CDL* place Tianhuang in the genealogical diagram of the Shitou line.[8] The hagiography of Shitou in the *SGSZ*, which is based on the epitaph written by Liu Ke, also lists Tianhuang as Shitou's disciple.[9] However, we do find Tianhuang's name among the eleven major disciples of Mazu listed in the "Daoyi Stūpa." In Nanyue Huairang's epitaph written by Gui Deng, Tianhuang was again listed as Nanyue's second-generation disciple.[10] Moreover, Zongmi indicated that Tianhuang was the common disciple of Mazu and Jingshan Faqin.[11] The hagiography of Tianhuang in the *SGSZ*, which is based on his epitaph written by Fu Zai (b. 760),[12] records that Tianhuang studied with and was enlightened by all three masters, Jingshan, Mazu, and Shitou, and does not differentiate between them.[13] However, the *QTW* version of the same epitaph says that after learning from Jingshan and Mazu, Tianhuang "visited Shitou and was thoroughly enlightened."[14] Thus, according to the first three sources, Tianhuang was Shitou's disciple, while according to the other three, Tianhuang was Mazu's disciple, as well as Jingshan's. Based on the *SGSZ* version of Tianhuang's epitaph, he was the common disciple of Jingshan, Mazu, and Shitou, while based on the *QTW* text, he was enlightened by Shitou, so Shitou was his true teacher, and the first three sources seem to be reliable.

Since the *QTW* version of the epitaph has been considered an authentic Tang text, modern scholars in general agree that, although Tianhuang learned from the three masters, his main teacher should be Shitou. Here I present a new, important discovery. A careful examination of early sources shows that Tianhuang's epitaph in the *QTW* is actually not the original text by Fu Zai, but was copied word by word from the *Fozu lidai tongzai* (General Records of Buddhist Patriarchs through the Ages) compiled by Nianchang in the Yuan dynasty.[15] In the *Fozu lidai tongzai*, before the beginning of the epitaph, Nianchang states, "Chan master Tianhuang Daowu in the eastern part of the Jingzhou city: Chief Musician Fu Zai wrote the epitaph for him. An abridged version of the epitaph is as follows." This clearly states that the text had been abridged by Nianchang. Moreover, comparing with the *SGSZ*, Nianchang not only greatly abridged the epitaph, but also inserted three phrases into it and adapted one sentence. First, he added the phrase "then he was thoroughly enlightened," which was based on the *ZTJ* and *CDL*,[16] to the line "[Tianhuang] paid his respects to Shitou in the second year of Jianzhong reign-period." Second, he added "the teaching of Shitou became popular in this place," which was based on the *CDL*,[17] to the paragraph about Tianhuang's residence at Tianhuangsi. Third, he inserted an encounter dialogue about throwing a pillow, which was taken from the *ZTJ* and *CDL*,[18] as Tianhuang's deathbed words. The application of body language such as the throwing of a pillow in encounter dialogue had not emerged during the time of Mazu and his immediate disciples;[19] hence, it is impossible that this kind of dialogue would appear in Fu Zai's writing. Fourth, he changed the sentence "Monks Huizhen, Wenbi and others are quiet and easy Chan descendents, all of whom have crossed his threshold and are enlightened" into "the three generations of [Tianhuang's] dharma heirs are named Huizhen, Youxian, and Wenbi." This is a misinterpretation of Fu Zai's text. Fu meant that the disciples Huizhen, Wenbi, and others were of a quiet and easy nature. Nianchang misread "youxian," quiet and easy, as the name of a disciple, and also absurdly changed Tianhuang's immediate disciples to "three generations."[20] The compilers of the *QTW* copied the epitaph from the *Fozu lidai tongzai* verbatim, not only mistaking the abridged version as a full text, but also following all four falsifiers. Thus, neither of these texts is original and should not be used in the study of Tianhuang.

Tianhuang's entries in the *ZTJ* and *CDL* are also questionable. The *ZTJ* records three encounter dialogues: the first his first meeting with Shitou, the second a dialogue between him and an anonymous monk, and the third his deathbed dialogue about throwing a pillow. None of these three dialogues is found in the biography in the SGSZ. In the first dialogue, Shitou asked, "I wonder when you left that place?" Tianhuang answered, "I did not belong to that place." "That place" refers to Mazu's place. This eager expression of lineage affiliation exposes the trace of forgery. As mentioned, during the early post-rebellion period in the southern region, the sectarian atmosphere was very thin, and Chan students freely visited different masters. Shitou especially emphasized the compatibility of various Chan lines and branches, as he said in his famous verse "Can tong qi" (Inquiry into Matching Halves): "Though the capacity of men may be sharp or dull, / In the Way there are no Northern and Southern patriarchs."[21] Moreover, as previously noted, the inclusion of the body language of throwing a pillow could not have happened at Tianhuang's time. Hence, those dialogues must be later creations. Tianhuang's entry in the CDL copies all three dialogues, and does not supply any new information.

According to these studies, the hagiography of Tianhuang in the SGSZ was based on his epitaph written by Fu Zai; it is the earliest and most reliable source about his life. The epitaph in the QTW is not an original text but a copy of the text in the Fozu lidai tongzai, which was abridged and rewritten by Nianchang, and is therefore not authentic. The encounter dialogues recorded in the ZTJ and CDL, which indicate Tianhuang's sole affiliation with Shitou, are all later creations. As Fu Zai tells us, Tianhuang studied with Jingshan, Mazu, and Shitou, "meeting great masters three times," without attaching himself to any single mentor.

This conclusion, however, has not yet solved the question of Tianhuang's mentor if we do not solve Tianwang Daowu's case as well. The key issue for this case is whether the "Epitaph of Chan Master Tianwang Daowu" attributed to Qiu Xuansu is authentic or not. The first appearance of this epitaph was in the Linjian lu (Record of the Forest; 1107–1110) by Huihong, who said that he found the epitaph in Tanying's (989–1060) work titled Wujia zongpai (Genealogies of the Five Houses) and believed its authenticity.[22] At about the same time, Shanqing also mentioned the same epitaph in his Zuting shiyuan (Collected Events of the Ancestral Court).[23] Later, the "Chongjiao wujia zongpai xu" (Preface to the Re-collated Genealogies of the Five Houses) by Juemengtang, states that the scholar-officials Zhang Shangying (1043–1122) and Lü Xiaqing (jinshi 1072) got a copy of the epitaph from Tanying.[24] In the stūpa inscription he wrote for Chongxian (980–1052), Lü Xiaqing attributed Chongxian to Mazu's lineage.[25] As Chongxian actually belonged to the Yunmen house that traced its origin to the Shitou-Tianhuang line, Lü's reattribution obviously followed the epitaph of Tianwang Daowu. Thus, almost all early sources about the epitaph point to Tanying, who seems to be the earliest owner of this text.[26]

The Wudeng huiyuan, Fozu lidai tongzai, and QTW, respectively, keep a copy of the epitaph.[27] The version of the QTW resembles verbatim that of

Fozu lidai tongzai; hence, it must have been copied from this text, not that it had other early origins.

From the Song to the Qing, controversies over this epitaph continued. However, almost all arguments, whether supporting or denying, came out of sectarian bias with little reliable evidence.[28] The only exception is the Yuan monk Zhiyou's opinion. In his "Da Yuan Yuanyou chongkan *Rentian yanmu* houxu" (Postscript to the *Eyes of Humans and Gods*, Reprinted in the Yuanyou Reign-Period of the Yuan Dynasty), he put forward two important arguments: first, there was no Tianwangsi recorded in the new or old gazetteers of Jingzhou that were extant in the Yuan dynasty; second, the encounter dialogues recorded in the epitaph were originally Tanzhao's stories, which were seen in the old gazetteer and the *CDL*.[29] The gazetteer did not exist, while Tanzhao's entry in the *CDL* is as follows:

> Chan master Tanzhao in the Baimasi in Jingzhou often said, "Happy! Happy!" When he was dying, he cried, "Painful! Painful!" He said again, "King Yama comes to get me." The abbot asked, "When you were thrown to the river by the commissioner, you were calm and peaceful. Why did you become so now?" The master held up the pillow and asked, "Do you think I was right then or I am right now?" The abbot was answerless.[30]

These encounter dialogues were copied almost word for word into the epitaph. Furthermore, there are two more records about Tanzhao. The first is found in the *ZTJ*, which says he was a disciple of Nanquan Puyuan, one of Mazu's major disciples;[31] this agrees with the lineage in the *CDL*. The second is found in the *Duyi zhi* (Exclusively Extraordinary Records) by Li Kang (fl. 846–873) and *Nanbu xinshu* (New Book from the South) by Qian Yi (*jinshi* 999), which relates that Tanzhao was a monk in Jingzhou and had a close relationship with several local commissioners;[32] this is also in accord with Tanzhao's entry in the *CDL*. According to Zhiyou, Tanzhao's story was not only recorded in the *CDL*, but was also found in the old gazetteer of Jingzhou. Thus, it seems that the epitaph copied the *CDL* or the gazetteer, and not the reverse.

Apart from the possible copying of Tanzhao's story, two more doubts exist about the epitaph. First, as mentioned earlier, the body language of holding up a pillow should not have appeared during the time of Mazu and his disciples. Second, the epitaph was attributed to Qiu Xuansu with the official title of "Jingnan Military Commissioner." Although Qiu was a scholar-official during the mid-Tang,[33] he never held this post.[34] With these three flaws, the epitaph can be assumed as a later forgery. As previously discussed, all the early appearances of the epitaph were related to Tanying, who was a successor of the Mazu-Linji line; hence, he was probably the one who forged it.[35]

The forged epitaph lists Longtan Chongxin as Tianwang Daowu's disciple, while the epitaph for Tianhuang by Fu Zai does not mention Chongxin at all. Since Chongxin later became an influential figure, some scholars take this as a reason to confirm that the epitaph is genuine.[36] However, it is easy to guess why Tianhuang's epitaph does not mention Chongxin: he was a junior disciple when Tianhuang passed away, as if among the eleven major disciples mentioned in the "Daoyi Stūpa," we could not find the names of Baizhang Huaihai, Nanquan Puyuan, and so forth.

DANXIA TIANRAN

Both the *ZTJ* and *CDL* ascribe Danxia Tianran as solely Shitou's disciple.[37] However, Danxia's hagiography in the *SGSZ*, which was based on his epitaph written by Liu Ke, states that he studied with Shitou, Mazu, and Jingshan, without indicating who his main mentor was, quite similar to the case of Tianhuang.[38] Thus, Danxia's mentor and lineage also became a problem. Based on the *SGSZ*, Du Jiwen and Wei Daoru suppose that it may have been his successors' idea to ascribe Danxia to the Shitou line exclusively, but they do not prove it further.[39] I agree with them and further verify this supposition.

A careful comparison of the *SGSZ* text with the other two texts will help us to discern the truths from the fabrications. All three texts can be divided into four sections: (1) Danxia's background; (2) his training period; (3) his experience in Luoyang; (4) his late years in Danxiashan.

In the first section, the *SGSZ* simply says that Danxia entered monastic life when he was still a child. But the *CDL* narrates a story that he grew up as a Confucian student and was traveling to Chang'an for the imperial examination, but a Chan monk guided him to visit Mazu in order to "be selected as a Buddha." The *ZTJ* further adds some embellishments to this story: Danxia was accompanied by the famous lay Buddhist Pang Yun on his way to the capital, and had an encounter dialogue with a Chan monk, in which the body language of raising a teacup was applied. This story not only contradicts Danxia's experience of entering monastic life at an early age, but also is full of fictitious color with at least two layers of forgery. Although the *CDL* was compiled later then the *ZTJ*, the story it states seems to have been based on an earlier forgery.

In the second section, the *SGSZ* states that Danxia first attended Shitou for three years, by whom he was given the Buddhist name and had his head shaved. Then Danxia received plenary ordination from the Vinaya master Xi in Hengshan. The Vinaya master Xi should be Xicao, who resided in the Hengyuesi in Hengshan from the late Tianbao to Dali reign-periods.[40] Two other disciples of Mazu, Xingguo Shencou (744–817) and Yaoshan Weiyan, also received plenary ordination from Xicao during the Dali.[41] The biography further states that after receiving ordination, Danxia visited Mazu and then stayed at Tiantaishan for three years. He later visited Jingshan Faqin. Thus, just like Tianhuang, Danxia studied with the three masters without recognizing his main teacher. During the Tang dynasty, monks who became novices in their youth usually received plenary ordination at the age of twenty or a few years later. Tianran died in 824, so he was twenty in the first year of the Qianyuan reign-period (758). Hence, his training experience after the ordination happened in the early post-rebellion period.

Both the *ZTJ* and *CDL* picked the events of Danxia's visit to the three masters from the epitaph, but each of them added some forged plots favorable to either the Shitou or Mazu line. The *ZTJ* follows the records that Danxia was named and shaved by Shitou, but adds some fictitious details and also three new encounter-dialogue stories. In the first story, Mazu recommended Danxia to visit Shitou, implying that he was not as good as Shitou. In the second story, Danxia rode on a statue of Buddha, and this behavior was admired by Shitou. The third story says that after he was enlightened by Shitou, Danxia returned to Mazu to show off. In the *CDL*, the event of riding on a Buddha statue is moved to the place of Mazu, and Danxia was named by Mazu. These layered, contradictive fabrications reveal the competition of the two lines during the late Tang and Five Dynasties.

According to the third section of the *SGSZ*, during the Yuanhe reign-period (806–820) Danxia stayed in Xiangshansi in Luoyang and became a close friend of Funiu Zizai, another disciple of Mazu. It then relates two anecdotes: first, on a very cold day, Tianran burned a wooden Buddha statue to fight the cold in the Huilinsi. Someone scolded him, and he answered: "I am cremating it for *śarīram* (Buddha's remains)"; second, in the third year of the Yuanhe, one morning he went to the Tianjin bridge and lay on it. Just then Regent Zheng passed by. The soldiers scolded Danxia, but he did not move. Slowly raising his head, he said, "I am just an idle monk." During this period, the burning of wooden Buddha statues by monks did occur from time to time; for example, the *Youyang zazu* records two similar cases.[42] Thus, the account of Danxia's burning of a statue must be authentic. Regent Zheng should be Zheng Yuqing (746–820), who was Regent of the Eastern Capital from the sixth month of the third year to the tenth month of the sixth year of the Yuanhe reign-period (808–810).[43] The second anecdote matches Zheng's experience; hence, it is authentic as well. The *ZTJ* and *CDL* also relate these two anecdotes, which must have been copied from the epitaph.[44]

The fourth section of the *SGSZ* recounts the late years of Danxia. He went to stay at Danxiashan in Nanyangxian (in present-day Henan) in 820 and died in 824 at the age of eighty-six. He was conferred the posthumous title of "Zhitong chanshi" (Chan Master of Penetrating Wisdom), and his stūpa was conferred the title "Miaojue" (Marvelous Enlightenment). The *CDL* says that he had three hundred disciples. The *ZTJ* records that he died in 823; this might be a scribal error.

Apart from these four sections, the *ZTJ* records five more encounter dialogues, and the *CDL* takes two out of the five and adds another. None of these dialogues is found in the *SGSZ* and all display the radical, mature style of the late Tang and Five Dynasties; hence, they must have been created by late Chan monks.

In addition, the *ZTJ* attributes six Chan poems to Danxia, and the *CDL* includes two of them. P. 3597 of the Dunhuang document also copies one of the poems.[45] However, the *SGSZ* mentions neither that Danxia was gifted in poetry nor that he had poetic works, so the true author of these poems is questionable.

In conclusion, Danxia's hagiography in the *SGSZ*, which was based on his epitaph written by Liu Ke, is the most reliable source. According to it, Danxia studied with the three great masters, Shitou, Mazu, and Jingshan, without differentiating any one of them as his main mentor. Danxia's entries in the *ZTJ* and *CDL* draw many elements from the epitaph, but the events that they added to it were all created by later monks. Except for the two encounter dialogues recorded in the *SGSZ* (viz., "burning wooden Buddha statue" and "idle monk"), all the dialogues are unauthentic. It is also doubtful that he wrote the six poems attributed to him.

YAOSHAN WEIYAN

Yaoshan Weiyan was traditionally regarded as Shitou's disciple as well. All the three early sources, the *ZTJ*, *SGSZ*, and *CDL*,[46] are consistent at this point. Nevertheless, the "Lizhou Yaoshan gu Weiyan dashi beiming bingxu" (Stele Inscription plus Preface for Weiyan, the Deceased Chan Master of Yaoshan in Lizhou) written by Tang Shen says that Yaoshan followed Mazu for nearly twenty years.[47] Thus, his master and lineage have also become a controversy. The *Mazu yulu*, compiled by Huinan in the mid-eleventh century, includes an encounter dialogue in which Yaoshan first visited Shitou and could not be enlightened; consequently he went to see Mazu and was awakened, then said, "When I was in Shitou's place, I was like a mosquito on an iron cow."[48] This is obviously meant to disparage Shitou. Other Song monks of the Mazu line, such as Dahui Zonggao (1089–1163), took delight in repeating this story.[49] However, perhaps because of the orthodoxy of the *CDL*, they were not able to change Yaoshan's lineage. Modern scholars have in general regarded the epitaph as a forgery,[50] but recently some scholars have tried to verify its authenticity.[51] In this section I follow this new argument and provide further evidence to support it.

First, the epitaph is included in the *Tangwen cui* (The Quintessence of Tang Writings) anthologized in 1011 by Yao Xuan (968–1020), just seven years after the *CDL*. Yao Xuan had no relationship with any Chan line, and he was famous for his serious attitude in the selection of works for the anthology. Thus, this epitaph must have been picked up from original Tang texts, and the compilers of the *ZTJ*, *SGSZ*, and *CDL* would have had the chance to see it as well. This must be the reason for the presence in the three texts of some elements that are in accord with the epitaph. Tang Shen, author of the epitaph, was a famous scholar in the mid-Tang, who passed the imperial examination on the subject of Virtuous and Upright, and Capable of Straight Remonstration in 825,[52] just nine years before the epitaph was written.

Second, Yaoshan's life as stated in the epitaph is the most complete and reasonable among all early sources, and the other sources actually took many elements from it (with certain scribal errors). The epitaph states that Yaoshan died on the sixth day of the twelfth month in "the next year after His Highness ascended the throne." "His Highness" refers to Emperor Wenzong (r. 826–840), who ascended the throne in the twelfth month in the second year of the Baoli reign-period (826); hence, Yaoshan died in the first year of the Dahe reign-period (827). The *SGSZ* states that he died in the second year of Dahe; this could be the mistake of taking the first year of Dahe as the year in which the Emperor ascended the throne. Both the *ZTJ* and *CDL* state that Yaoshan died in the eighth year of Dahe (834); this is probably mistaking the year in which the stele was erected as the year of his death,[53] as original stele inscriptions of the Tang often indicate the years in which they were constructed. The epitaph was written eight years after Yaoshan died; if including the year of his death, as ancient Chinese people often did, the epitaph was written in the eighth year of Dahe.[54] The epitaph says that Yaoshan died at the age of eighty-four, along with a Buddhist age of sixty, and the *CDL* records the same. The *ZTJ* records his secular age as eighty-four, Buddhist age sixty-five; the latter may be a scribal error. The *SGSZ* records an age of seventy; according to this age, Yaoshan would have received plenary ordination before twenty, which is obviously impossible. As the epitaph mentions a "Kuanjing in the Xingshansi," Yinshun doubts that this was a fictitious figure,[55] but it may be a miswriting of Xingshan Weikuan, who was summoned to the capital and stayed in the Xingshansi during the Yuanhe reign-period.[56]

The epitaph states that Yaoshan was born in the Xinfengxian of Nankangjun, while the *ZTJ*, *SGSZ*, and *CDL* say his family was originally from Jiangzhou or Jiangxian and later moved to Nankang, and his secular surname was Han. Jiangzhou belonged to Hedongdao, which was one of the places from which the Han families originally came.[57] Therefore, the four texts do not actually contradict each other: Yaoshan's secular surname was Han, his family origin was Jiangzhou (in present-day Shanxi), and he was born in Xinfeng of Nankang (in present-day Jiangxi).

According to the epitaph, Yaoshan became a novice monk at the age of seventeen (760), and attended Chan master Huizhao at the western mountain of Chaozhou. Then the epitaph states that he received plenary ordination in the eighth year of Dali (773) from the Vinaya master Xichen. This must be a mistake; according to the fact that he died in 827 with a Buddhist seniority of sixty, he must have received ordination in the third year of Dali (768). The other three texts follow the epitaph's mistake. The name of the Vinaya master, Xichen, was a scribal error misrepresenting Xicao, who was also Danxia's Vinaya master, as discussed earlier.

The epitaph further states: "At that time, there was Qian at the South Marchmount [i.e., Hengshan], Ji in Jiangxi, and Hong at the central Marchmount [i.e., Songshan]; Yaoshan was awakened by the mind doctrine of all the three masters." Qian refers to Shitou Xiqian, and Ji refers to Mazu whose posthumous title was Daji. We do not know who Hong at Songshan was, but there had been many successors of the Northern school who resided at that mountain, so Hong may have been one of them.[58] According to this paragraph, Yaoshan did study with Shitou for a while.

The epitaph continues to state that Yaoshan "stayed in Daji's place for nearly twenty years." From 768 to 788, when Mazu passed away, is twenty years; deducting the years of Yaoshan's visiting to Shitou and Hong and also his traveling to several places before Mazu's death as seen in the epitaph is just nearly twenty years. The epitaph then says that he went to Yaoshan in the early Zhenyuan reign-period and stayed there for almost thirty years. If we count from the fifth year of Zhenyuan (789) to 827 when he died, the total is thirty-eight years; hence, the epitaph may just list a rounded number and not specify an exact number of years. Yaoshan was located in Liyangxian of Lizhou (in present-day Hunan).[59]

Third, the epitaph describes Yaoshan's teaching career at Yaoshan as follows:

> After that time, the master always ate a few vegetables with meals. As soon as he finished his meal, he preached the *Fahua jing* (*Saddharmapundarīka-sūtra*), *Huayan jing* (*Avatamsaka-sūtra*), or *Niepan jing* (*Mahāparinirvāṇa-sūtra*) at his seat. Day or night, he did consistently thus for almost thirty years. . . . From the beginning, the master always used a large white cloth to make his dress and bamboo to make shoes, and he shaved his own head and prepared his own meals.

The epitaph describes the image of a conservative Chan master who preached sūtras and led a self-disciplined life.[60] This image is completely different from that described in the *ZTJ* and *CDL*, of which Yaoshan discarded the precepts (śīla), concentration (sāmadhi), and wisdom (prajñā) as useless furniture, and "always forbade others to read scriptures."[61] In addition, the epitaph records his teaching as thus: "The numinous mind is pure by itself, but it is obscured by phenomenal appearances. If you can dismiss all phenomena, there will be no dual things." This teaching emphasizes the pure mind of self nature, which had been a general concept since the early Chan. Yin Yaopan, a contemporary of Yaoshan, says in his poem "To Master Weiyan" (Zeng Weiyan shi):

> Talking Dhyāna, he has kept the perpetual lamp since long,
> Protecting Dharma, he has rewritten treatises with marvelous ideas.[62]

Yin also depicted Yaoshan as a conservative Chan master, protecting Buddhist Dharma and writing treatises to interpret scriptures. Yaoshan's conservative image and concept as shown in the epitaph and this poem tell us two things: first, this epitaph was not forged by Chan monks of the Hongzhou line during the late Tang and Five Dynasties, otherwise it would have contained the iconoclastic concepts and encounter dialogues of that time; second, none of the iconoclastic and highly mature encounter dialogues related to Yaoshan in the *ZTJ* and *CDL* is authentic. Among these encounter dialogues, some famous ones are related to Li Ao (774–836), who was said to have been awakened by Yaoshan, and consequently composed several poems to express delight in his enlightenment. However, the epitaph says, "Some high officials paid respects to the master's teaching, but none of them crossed his threshold"—that is, none of them understood his teaching well. Therefore, Yaoshan's relationship with Li Ao must be a later creation.[63]

To sum up, the epitaph for Yaoshan written by Tang Shen is an authentic text. All the other three early sources, the *ZTJ*, *SGSZ*, and *CDL*, take biographical elements from the epitaph and mix them with encounter-dialogue stories created by Chan monks of the late Tang and Five Dynasties. According to the epitaph, Yaoshan did once study with Shitou, but because he attended Mazu for nearly twenty years, he had a closer relationship with the Hongzhou school.

NEW LIST OF MAZU'S DISCIPLES

Of the 153 names of Mazu's disciples in Yanagida's list, there are three repetitions: Guiyang Wuliao appears twice,[64] Dayang Xiding and Dayang heshang must be the same person,[65] and likewise Jingzhao Zhizang and Zhizang in Jingzhao Huayansi.[66] Moreover, Guiyang Wuliao was born in 787 and died in 867;[67] when Mazu died in 788, Guiyang was only one year old and could not have been Mazu's disciple.[68] In addition, seven other names should be removed from the list. The first is that of Baizhang Weizheng (d. 819).[69] In the stūpa inscription for Baizhang Huaihai, Chen Xu mentions Fazheng as the leading disciple of Baizhang.[70] The *Jinshi lu* records an epitaph for Niepan heshang written by Wu Yihuang and copied by Liu Gongquan (778–865).[71] This epitaph is recorded as "Fazheng chanshi bei" (Epitaph of Chan Master Fazheng) in the *Yudi bei jimu*.[72] The *QTW* includes a fragment of this epitaph but attributes the authorship to Liu Gongquan;[73] this attribution must be a mistake, as Liu was only the inscriber. The Song monk Huihong, who had the chance to read the whole inscription, said that Fazheng, Weizheng, and Niepan heshang were the same person who followed Baizhang to become the second abbot of the Baizhangsi.[74] Thus, Fazheng/Weizheng was Baizhang's disciple, not Mazu's. The second name that ought to be removed is Wangmu Xiaoran,[75] who was actually Ehu Dayi's disciple.[76] The third name is Quanzhou Huizhong,[77] who was actually Guiyang Wuliao's disciple.[78] The fourth is Longya Yuanchang,[79] who was actually a disciple of Helin Xuansu (668–752), one of the patriarchs of the Niutou school. Xuansu's family name was Ma, and he was also called Masu or Mazu; this may be the reason for the listing of Yuanchang as Mazu's disciple in the *CDL*.[80] The fifth is Bimoyan heshang.[81] According to the *CDL*, Bimoyan was Yongtai Lingrui's disciple, that is, Mazu's second-generation disciple.[82] The sixth is Beishu heshang.[83] The *ZTJ* says that Beishu heshang was Yaoshan's disciple,[84] and the encounter dialogues recorded in both the *ZTJ* and *CDL* are said to have happened between Beishu and Daowu Yuanzhi (769–835), who was also Yaoshan's disciple. The last is Quan Deyu.[85] Quan paid his respects to Mazu and wrote the stūpa for him, but he was not necessarily Mazu's disciple. Thus, the list should be reduced to 142.

On the other hand, there are three names that can be added to the list. The first is Danyuan Yingzhen, who first followed Mazu, then became Nanyang Huizhong's (683–769) disciple.[86] The second is Langrui. In Zhaozhou Congshen's entry in the *ZTJ*, a certain disciple of Mazu named Langrui was mentioned.[87] The third is Li Fan (d. 829), who studied with Mazu and even wrote a work titled *Xuansheng qulu* (Inn of the Mysterious Sages) to elucidate the Hongzhou doctrine.[88] Hence, the names of Mazu's known disciples reach a total of 145.

Table 1 beginning on page 33, is the new list of Mazu's disciples with relevant data about their dates, native places, monastery locations, foundations of monasteries, Chan teachers other than Mazu, and biographical sources. Of course, this list is still tentative, as many names are related to unauthentic encounter dialogues only.

TABLE 1. Mazu Daoyi's Disciples with Relevant Data

No.	Name	Dates	Native Place	Monastery Location	Monastery Founder	Other Chan Teacher(s)	Sources
1	Anfeng Huaikong 安豐懷空	697–784	Langzhou 閬州 (Sichuan)	Xuzhou 徐州 (Jiangsu)	Yes		SGSZ 20, CDL 8
2	Baihu Faxuan 白虎法宣			Shaozhou 韶州 (Guangdong)			CDL 7
3	Bailing heshang 百靈和尚						CDL 8
4	Baizhang Huaihai 百丈懷海	749–814	Fuzhou 福州 (Fujian)	Hongzhou 洪州 (Jiangxi)	Yes		"Huaihai Stūpa," SGSZ 10, CDL 6
5	Baiyan Changche 柏岩常徹			Taizhou 台州 (Zhejiang)			CDL 7
6	Baiyan Mingzhe 柏岩明哲			Dingzhou 定州 (Hebei)			CDL 7
7	Beilan Rang 北蘭讓			Hongzhou 洪州 (Jiangxi)[a]			CDL 6
8	Benxi heshang 本溪和尚						CDL 8
9	Caotang heshang 草堂和尚			Jingzhao fu 京兆府 (Shanxi)			CDL 8
10	Caoyi Fengchu 草衣奉初		Shu 蜀 (Sichuan)	Hengzhou 衡州 (Hunan)			Yongyuan Jishi heshang yulu[b]
11	Changzhou Minggan 常州明幹			Changzhou 常州 (Jiangsu)			CDL 6

TABLE 1. *Continued*

No.	Name	Dates	Native Place	Monastery Location	Monastery Founder	Other Chan Teacher(s)	Sources
12	Chao'an 超岸		Runzhou 潤州 (Jiangsu)				SGSZ 11
13	Chongtai 崇泰						"Daoyi Stūpa"
14	Cibei Liangjin 慈悲良津			Jinzhou 金州 (Shaanxi)			CDL 7
15	Dadi heshang 打地和尚			Xinzhou 忻州 (Shanxi)			"Dadi heshang Stūpa Court,"[x] CDL 8
16	Dahui Daowu 大會道晤						CDL 6
17	Damei Fachang 大梅法常	752–839	Xiangzhou 相州 (Hubei)	Mingzhou 明州 (Zhejiang)	Yes		ZTJ 15, SGSZ 11, CDL 7
18	Datong Guangdeng 大同廣燈			Lizhou 澧州 (Hunan)			ZTJ 15, CDL 8
19	Dayang Xiding 大陽希頂			Yingzhou 郢州 (Hubei)[d]			CDL 8
20	Dazhu Huihai 大珠慧海	fl. 788	Jianzhou 建州 (Fujian)	Yuezhou 越州 (Zhejiang)			ZTJ 14, CDL 6
21	Danxia Tianran 丹霞天然	739–824		Dengzhou 鄧州 (Henan)	Yes	Jinshan Faqin, Shitou Xiqian	ZTJ 4, SGSZ 11, CDL 14

	Name	Native place	Dates	Place of activity		Teacher	Sources
22	Danyuan Yingzhen 耽源應真					Nanyang Huizhong	*ZTJ* 4, *CDL* 5
23	Deng Yinfeng 鄧隱峰	Jianzhou 建州 (Fujian)		Daizhou 代州 (Shanxi)		Shitou Xiqian	*ZTJ* 15, *SGSZ* 21, *CDL* 8
24	Dongsi Ruhui 東寺如會	Shaozhou 韶州 (Guangdong)	744–823	Tanzhou 潭州 (Hunan)		Jingshan Faqin	*ZTJ* 15, *SGSZ* 11, *CDL* 7
25	Dong'an heshang 洞安和尚						*CDL* 8
26	Dongquan Weixian 洞泉惟儼			Yuezhou 越州 (Zhejiang)			*CDL* 7
27	Ehu Dayi 鵝湖大義	Quzhou 衢州 (Jiangxi)	746–818	Xinzhou 信州 (Jiangxi)	Yes		"Dayi Epitaph," *ZTJ* 15, *CDL* 7
28	Hongtang heshang 洪潭和尚			Ezhou 鄂州 (Hubei)			*CDL* 6
29	Ezhou Wudeng 鄂州無等	Bianzhou 汴州 (Henan)	749–830	Ezhou 鄂州 (Hubei)	Yes		*SGSZ* 11, *CDL* 7
30	Fenzhou Wuye 汾州無業	Shangzhou 商州 (Shaanxi)	760–821	Fenzhou 汾州 (Shanxi)			*ZTJ* 15, *SGSZ* 11, *CDL* 8
31	Fengshan Hongjun 封山洪俊			Huzhou 湖州 (Zhejiang)ᶜ			*CDL* 7
32	Fo'ao heshang 佛嶴和尚			Wenzhou 溫州 (Zhejiang)			*CDL* 8
33	Foguang Ruman 佛光如滿		752–846	Luoyang 洛陽 (Henan)			*CDL* 6
34	Funiu Zizai 伏牛自在	Huzhou 湖州 (Zhejiang)	741–821	Luoyang 洛陽 (Henan)		Jingshan Faqin	*ZTJ* 15, *SGSZ* 11, *CDL* 7

TABLE 1. *Continued*

No.	Name	Dates	Native Place	Monastery Location	Monastery Founder	Other Chan Teacher(s)	Sources
35	Fuqi Ce 伏棲策			Huazhou 華州 (Shaanxi)			CDL 6
36	Furong Taiyu 芙蓉太毓	747–826	Shengzhou 昇州 (Jiangsu)	Changzhou 常州 (Jiangsu)		Niuton Huizhong	SGSZ 11, CDL 7
37	Fubei heshang 浮杯和尚						CDL 8
38	Fuxi heshang 福溪和尚						CDL 8
39	Ganquan Zhixian 甘泉志賢		Jianzhou 建州 (Fujian)	Taiyuan 太原 (Shanxi)			SGSZ 9, CDL 6
40	Gaocheng Fazang 高城法藏						ZTJ 14, ZJL 18, 44, 48
41	Gaoying 鎬英						"Daoyi Stūpa"
42	Gusi heshang 古寺和尚			Quzhou 衢州 (Jiangxi)			CDL 8
43	Guangming Puman 光明普滿						CDL 7
44	Guizong Zhichang 歸宗智常		Chenzhou 陳州 (Henan)ᵍ	Jiangziou 江州 (Jiangxi)			ZTJ 15, SGSZ 17, CDL 7
45	Hailing Qingyun 海陵慶雲			Yangzhou 揚州 (Jiangsu)			CDL 6
46	Hangwu Zhizang 杭烏智藏	741–849	India	Yuezhou 杭州 (Zhejiang)	Yes		SGSZ 6

	Name	Dates	Hongzhou	Location	Stele	Sources
47	Hangzhou Zhizang 杭州智藏			Hangzhou 杭州 (Zhejiang)		CDL 6
48	Hezhong Baoqing 河中寶慶			Puzhou 蒲州 (Shanxi)		CDL 6
49	Hezhong Fazang 河中法藏			Puzhou 蒲州 (Shanxi)		CDL 7
50	Hezhong Huaize 河中懷則			Puzhou 蒲州 (Shanxi)		CDL 6
51	Heijian heshang 黑澗和尚			Luoyang 洛陽 (Henan)		ZTJ 15, CDL 8
52	Heiyan heshang 黑眼和尚					CDL 8
53	Hongluoshan heshang 紅螺山和尚			Youzhou 幽州 (Hebei)		CDL 8
54	Hongshan Shanxin 洪山善信	d. 827		Suizhou 隨州 (Hubei)	Yes	"Record of Lingfengsi," CDL 8
55	Hualin Shanjue 華林善覺			Tanzhou 潭州 (Hunan)		CDL 8
56	Huayan Zhizang 華嚴智藏	d. 835	Hongzhou 洪州 (Jiangxi)	Chang'an 長安 (Shaanxi)		SGSZ 11, CDL 8
57	Huishan Tanji 灰山曇覬			Chizhou 池州 (Anhui)		CDL 7
58	Huiyun 金鵝惠雲					"Daoyi Stūpa"
59	Jinku Weizhi 金窟惟直					CDL 7
60	Jinniu heshang 金牛和尚			Zhenzhou 鎮州 (Hebei)		ZTJ 15, CDL 8

TABLE 1. *Continued*

No.	Name	Dates	Native Place	Monastery Location	Monastery Founder	Other Chan Teacher(s)	Sources
61	Jingzhao Chong 京兆崇			Jingzhaofu 京兆府 (Shaanxi)			CDL 7
62	Jingzhao Huaitao 京兆懷韜			Jingzhaofu 京兆府 (Shaanxi)			CDL 6
63	Jingnan Baozhen 荊南寶貞			Jingzhou 荊州 (Hubei)			CDL 7
64	Jiujing Xuance 九井玄策	d. 854	Yuezhou 越州 (Zhejiang)	Huangzhou 黃州 (Hubei)	Yes		SGSZ 11
65	Kaiyuan Xuanxu 開元玄虛			Hongzhou 洪州 (Jiangxi)			CDL 6
66	Kulsan Towŏn 崛山道元		Silla	Silla			CDL 7
67	Kunshan Dingjue 崑山定覺			Suzhou 蘇州 (Jiangsu)			CDL 8
68	Langrui 朗瑞						ZTJ 18[i]
69	Letan Changxing 泐潭常興			Hongzhou 洪州 (Jiangxi)			CDL 7
70	Letan Fahui 泐潭法會			Hongzhou 洪州 (Jiangxi)			CDL 6
71	Letan Weijian 泐潭惟建			Hongzhou 洪州 (Jiangxi)			CDL 6

						Junzhai dushuzhi houzhi 2
72	Li Fan 李繁	d. 829	Jingzhaofu 京兆府 (Shaanxi)			CDL 8
73	Lishan heshang 利山和尚					CDL 6
74	Licun Ziman 酆村自滿			Xinzhou 忻州 (Shanxi)		CDL 7
75	Lianshan Shenwan 練山神翫					
76	Lushan Fazang 廬山法藏	ca. 745–826	Qianzhou 虔州 (Jiangxi)	Jiangzhou 江州 (Jiangxi)	Yes	SGSZ 20, CDL 8
77	Luzu Baoyun 魯祖寶雲			Chizhou 池州 (Anhui)		ZTJ 14, CDL 7
78	Lufu Farou 潞府法柔			Luzhou 潞州 (Shanxi)		CDL 6
79	Lühou Ningbi 呂後寧賁	754–828	Bozhou 亳州 (Anhui)	Yuezhou 越州 (Zhejiang)		SGSZ 29, CDL 8
80	Luofu Daoxing 羅浮道行	ca. 731–825	Yuezhou 越州 (Zhejiang)	Guangzhou 廣州 (Guangdong)		SGSZ 20, CDL 8
81	Magu Baoche 麻谷寶徹			Puzhou 蒲州 (Shanxi)		ZTJ 15, CDL 7
82	Matou Shenzang 馬頭神藏			Cizhou 磁州 (Hebei)		CDL 8
83	Mengxi heshang 濛溪和尚					CDL 8
84	Miling heshang 米嶺和尚			Hongzhou 洪州 (Jiangxi)		ZTJ 20, CDL 8
85	Mingxi Daoxing 茗溪道行			Lizhou 澧州 (Hunan)		CDL 6

TABLE 1. *Continued*

No.	Name	Dates	Native Place	Monastery Location	Monastery Founder	Other Chan Teacher(s)	Sources
86	Nanquan Puyuan 南泉普願	748–834	Zhengzhou 鄭州 (Henan)	Cizhou 池州 (Anhui)	Yes		*ZTJ* 16, *SGSZ* 11, *CDL* 8
87	Nanyuan Daoming 南源道明			Yuanzhou 袁州 (Jiangxi)			*CDL* 6
88	Nanyue Zhizhou 南嶽智同			Hengzhou 衡州 (Hunan)			*CDL* 7
89	Pangshan Baoji 盤山寶積			Youzhou 幽州 (Hebei)			*ZTJ* 15, *CDL* 7
90	Pang Yun 龐蘊			Xiangzhou 襄州 (Hubei)		Shitou Xiqian	*ZTJ* 15, *CDL* 8
91	Qiling Zhitong 棲靈智通			Yangzhou 揚州 (Jiangsu)			"Daoyi Stūpa," *CDL* 6
92	Qifeng heshang 齊峰和尚			Hangzhou 杭州 (Zhejiang)^k			*CDL* 8
93	Qizhou Daoyan 齊州道岩			Qizhou 齊州 (Shandong)			*CDL* 7
94	Qianqing Mingjue 千頃明覺	d. 831	Jianzhou 建州 (Fujian)	Hangzhou 杭州 (Zhejiang)	Yes	Jingshan Faqin	*SGSZ* 11, *CDL* 8
95	Qianzhou Fazang 虔州法藏			Qianzhou 虔州 (Jiangxi)			*CDL* 6
96	Qianyuan Hui 乾元暉			Fuzhou 福州 (Fujian)^j			*CDL* 7

97	Qinglian Yuanli 青蓮元禮	Luzhou 潞州 (Shanxi)	CDL 6
98	Ruyuan heshang 乳源和尚	Shaozhou 韶州 (Guangdong)	CDL 8
99	Sanjiao Zongyin 三角總印	Tanzhou 潭州 (Hunan)	CDL 7
100	Shanshan Zhijian 杉山智堅	Chizhou 池州 (Anhui)	CDL 6
101	Shigong Huizang 石鞏慧藏	Fuzhou 撫州 (Jiangxi)	ZTJ 14, CDL 6
102	Shijiu heshang 石臼和尚		CDL 8
103	Shilin heshang 石林和尚		CDL 8
104	Shishuang Dashan 石霜大善	Tanzhou 潭州 (Hunan)*	CDL 8
105	Shuangling Daofang 雙嶺道方	Hongzhou 洪州 (Jiangxi)	CDL 7
106	Shuilao heshang 水老和尚	Hongzhou 洪州 (Jiangxi)	CDL 8
107	Shuitang heshang 水塘和尚	Tingzhou 汀州 (Fujian)	CDL 8
108	Shongshan heshang 松山和尚		CDL 8
109	Songzi Zhicong 松滋智聰	Lizhou 澧州 (Hunan)	CDL 6

TABLE 1. *Continued*

No.	Name	Dates	Native Place	Monastery Location	Monastery Founder	Other Chan Teacher(s)	Sources
110	Tianhuang Daowu 天皇道悟	727–808	Wuzhou 婺州 (Zhejiang)	Jingzhou 荆州 (Hubei)	Yes	Jingshan Faqin, Shitou Xiqian	"Daoyi Stūpa," ZTJ 4, SGSZ 10, CDL 14
111	Wangwu Xingming 王屋行明			Henanfu 河南府 (Henan)			CDL 8
112	Wujiu heshang 烏臼和尚						CDL 8
113	Wuxie Lingmo 五洩靈默	747–818	Changzhou 常州 (Jiangsu)	Wuzhou 婺州 (Zhejiang)		Shitou Xiqian	ZTJ 15, SGSZ 10, CDL 7
114	Xishan Liang zuozhu 西山亮座主			Hongzhou 洪州 (Jiangxi)			ZTJ 14, CDL 8
115	Xitang Zhizang 西堂智藏	738–817	Qianzhou 虔州 (Jiangxi)	Qianzhou 虔州 (Jiangxi)		Jingshan Faqin	"Zhizang Epitaph," ZTJ 15, SGSZ 10, CDL 7
116	Xiyuan Tanzang 西園曇藏	758–827		Hengzhou 衡州 (Hunan)		Shitou Xiqian	SGSZ 11, CDL 8
117	Xiantong Jueping 咸通覺平			Chang'an 長安 (Shaanxi)			CDL 6
118	Xianshan Dingqing 峴山定慶			Xiangzhou 襄州 (Hubei)			CDL 7

No.	Name	Dates	Place	Native place		Teacher	Sources
119	Xiangzhou Changjian 襄州常堅		Xiangzhou 襄州 (Hubei)				CDL 7
120	Xiangyuan Huaitan 象原懷坦						CDL 6
121	Xiaoyao heshang 逍遙和尚		Fuzhou 撫州 (Jiangxi)"				CDL 8
122	Xinsi Baoji 新寺寶積		Jingzhou 荊州 (Hubei)				CDL 7
123	Xingguo Shencou 興果神湊	744–817	Jiangzhou 江州 (Jiangxi)	Jingzhaofu 京兆府 (Shaanxi)			"Shencou Stūpa," SGSZ 16
124	Xingping heshang 興平和尚		Jingzhaofu 京兆府 (Shaanxi)				ZTJ 20, CDL 8
125	Xingshan Weikuan 興善惟寬	755–817	Chang'an 長安 (Shaanxi)	Quzhou 衢州 (Jiangxi)			SGSZ 10, CDL 7
126	Xiuxi heshang 秀溪和尚		Tanzhou 潭州 (Hunan)				CDL 8
127	Xunzhou Xiuguang 循州修廣		Xunzhou 循州 (Guangdong)				CDL 7
128	Yanguan Qi'an 鹽官齊安	ca. 752–842	Hangzhou 杭州 (Zhejiang)	Yangzhou 揚州 (Jiangsu)	Yes	Shitou Xiqian	"Qi'an Stūpa," ZTJ 15, SGSZ 10, CDL 7
129	Yangqi Zhenshu 楊岐甄叔	d. 820	Yuanzhou 袁州 (Jiangxi)				"Zhenshu Epitaph," SGSZ 10, CDL 8
130	Yaoshan Weiyan 藥山惟儼	744–827	Lizhou 澧州 (Hunan)	Qianzhou 虔州 (Jiangxi)	Yes	Shitou Xiqian	"Weiyan Epitaph," ZTJ 4, SGSZ 17, CDL 14

TABLE 1. *Continued*

No.	Name	Dates	Native Place	Monastery Location	Monastery Founder	Other Chan Teacher(s)	Sources
131	Yixing Shengbian 義興勝弁			Changzhou 常州 (Jiangsu)			CDL 6
132	Yinshan heshang 隱山和尚			Tanzhou 潭州 (Hunan)			ZTJ 20, CDL 8
133	Yongtai Lingrui 永泰靈瑞	761–829	Hengzhou 衡州 (Hunan)	Jingzhou 荊州 (Hubei)			ZTJ 15, SGSZ 11, CDL 7
134	Yutai Weiran 玉台惟然						CDL 7
135	Yuandi chanshi 元提禪師			Lianzhou 連州 (Hunan)			CDL 8
136	Yunshui Jingzong 雲水靖宗						CDL 7
137	Yunxiu Shenjian 雲秀神鑒	d. 844		Tangzhou 唐州 (Henan)			SGSZ 20, CDL 6
138	Zechuan heshang 則川和尚						CDL 8
139	Zhangjing Huaihui 章敬懷暉	757–816	Quanzhou 泉州 (Fujian)	Chang'an 長安 (Shaanxi)			"Huaihui Epitaph," ZTJ 14, SGSZ 10, CDL 7
140	Zhaoti Huilang 招提慧朗	738–820	Shaozhou 韶州 (Guangdong)	Tanzhou 潭州 (Hunan)		Shitou Xiqian	ZTJ 4, CDL 14
141	Zhiguang 智廣						"Daoyi Stūpa"

142	Zhongyi Hong'en 忠邑洪恩		Langzhou 朗州 (Hunan)				CDL 6
143	Zhujing Qinghe 渚逕清賀		Shaozhou 韶州 (Guangdong)				CDL 7
144	Ziyin Weijian 紫陰惟建						CDL 7
145	Ziyu Daotong 紫玉道通	731–813	Luzhou 廬州 (Anhui)		Yes	Shitou Xiqian	ZTJ 14, SGSZ 10, CDL 6

Sources: In addition to Yanagida's list, Suzuki's *Tō Godai no zenshū* and *Tō Godai zenshūshi* and Poceski's table titled "Data about Mazu's Disciples" ("Hongzhou School," 520–22) were also consulted in the preparation of this table.

[a] Beilansi was in Hongzhou; see Suzuki, *Tō Godai no zenshū*, 139.
[b] *T.* 81: 1.110b.
[c] Zhang Shangying, "Xinzhou Dingxiangxian xinxiu Dadi heshang tayuan ji," *Shanyou shike congbian,* XXSKQS, 15.26a/b.
[d] Dayangshan was in Yingzhou; see *Wudeng huiyuan,* 8.494, 12.748, 14.856.
[e] Fengshan was in Huzhou; see Li Jifu, *Yuanhe junxian tuzhi,* 25.606.
[f] Gusi was in Quzhou; see *Wudeng huiyuan,* 10.581.
[g] See the entry of Shuitang heshang in *CDL,* 8.14b.
[h] The *CDL* only mentions a Master Hongshan in Suizhou (8.1b). According to an inscription written by Zhang Shangying, this Master Hongshan's name was Shanxin. See Zhang, "Suizhou Dahongshan Lingfengsi Shifang chanyuan ji," in *Zimen jingxun,* ed. Rujin, *T.* 48: 10.1096a–97a.
[i] Langrui was mentioned in the entry of Zhaozhou Congshen.
[j] Miling is in Hongzhou; see *Wudeng huiyuan,* 9.548.
[k] Qifengsi was in Hangzhou; see *Wudeng huiyuan,* 9.544.
[l] Qianyuansi was in Fuzhou; see *Wudeng huiyuan,* 20.1374, 1392.
[m] Shishuangshan was in Tanzhou; see *Wudeng huiyuan,* 5.286, 12.699.
[n] Xiaoyaoshan was in Fuzhou; see *Wudeng huiyuan,* 6.321.

CHAPTER THREE

EXAMINATION OF THE HONGZHOU
SCHOOL LITERATURE

As mentioned at the beginning of this study, modern scholars have presented
three stances toward the Chan literature of the eighth to tenth centuries: first,
to accept almost all the discourse records and "transmission of the lamp" histories at face value as historical fact; second, to recognize certain fabrications
in Chan literature while at the same time emphasizing Chan historians' distinctive sense of history; third, to assert that the whole body of the middle
Chan literature was the retrospective recreation of the Song-dynasty Chan
monks. In this chapter, I take a new stance that no assertion can be made
before a case-to-case examination of relevant texts is done, and apply a philological approach to discriminate the original materials from later layers of
addition and recreation. I first do a general investigation on the emergence
and evolution of encounter-dialogue practice based on stele inscriptions and
other reliably datable Tang texts. I then draw upon all relevant sources to
perform a detailed, accurate investigation of the texts and discourse records
attributed to Mazu Daoyi and his disciples. This will help identify the original
parts for our next discussion of Chan doctrine and religious practice of the
Hongzhou school, and the layers of the late Tang and Five Dynasties for
further study of this school's impact and of its schism during that period.

EMERGENCE AND MATURITY OF
ENCOUNTER DIALOGUE

John McRae has thoroughly examined the antecedents of encounter dialogue
and depicted an eightfold path toward the emergence of this dialogue rhetoric:
(1) the image of the Chan master responding spontaneously to his students;
(2) the "questions about things" in the Northern school; (3) the Chan style
of explanation; (4) doctrinal bases for the social orientation of early Chan
practice; (5) the use of ritualized dialogue between teachers and students;
(6) the widespread use of anecdote and dialogue in teaching; (7) the fabrica-

tion of enlightenment narratives; and (8) the genealogical structure of Chan dialogue.[1]

Most of these antecedents developed before or during the first half of the eighth century, and were preparatory to the emergence of formal encounter dialogue. As a matter of fact, a few dialogues among these antecedents, such as Huizhen's (673–751) use of metaphorical, poetic phrases, and Xuanlang's (673–754) use of witty phrases,[2] exhibit germs of encounter dialogue. McRae's excellent study evinces that encounter dialogue did not appear suddenly in its fully mature form but rather represented a continuing search for a new rhetorical style, pedagogical device, and religious practice within the Chan tradition.

Masters of middle Chan continued and developed this search. Setting aside temporarily the texts of discourse records and "transmission of the lamp" histories, and relying solely on stele inscriptions and other reliably datable Tang texts, we find that the mid-Tang period, roughly from mid-eighth century to mid-ninth century—the period during which Mazu Daoyi, Shitou Xiqian, Jingshan Faqin, and their immediate disciples were active—witnessed the emergence of formal encounter dialogue. Then, during the period of the late Tang and Five Dynasties, from mid-ninth century to mid-tenth century, encounter dialogue achieved its full maturity.

In the first period, the emergence of formal encounter dialogue is marked by two major developments. The first is the vogue of witty, indirect, and paradoxical phrases in Chan dialogues between masters and students. For example, the epitaph for Jingshan Faqin, written by Li Jifu (758–814) in 793, records a dialogue between the master and a student. The student asked whether, if two messengers knew the station master was slaughtering a sheep for them, and one went to save the sheep, but the other did not, they cause different results of punishment and blessing. Jingshan answered, "The one who saved the sheep was compassionate, and the one who did not save the sheep was emancipated."[3] By applying witty and paradoxical phrases, Faqin avoided giving a direct answer to the dilemma concerning the Buddhist commandment against killing and expounded the Mahāyāna creed of compassion and emancipation. In addition, the *Youyang zazu xuji* records a dialogue: Liu Yan (ca. 716–780), then the Prefect of Zhongzhou, once begged Jingshan for a mind-verse. Jingshan replied, "Do not do any evil thing, and practice every good thing." Liu said that even children knew this. Jingshan answered that although all children knew it, an old man of one hundred years might not practice it.[4] Later this anecdote was remolded to become an encounter dialogue attributed to the Chan master Niaoke and Bai Juyi.[5]

Mazu and his disciples also frequently applied such witty, indirect, and paradoxical phrases. Fenzhou Wuye's hagiography in the *SGSZ*, which is based on the epitaph written by Yang Qian in 823,[6] describes the first meeting between Wuye and Mazu. Wuye was eager to find an answer to his question about "this mind is the Buddha," while Mazu smiled and joked at his large stature: "What a lofty Buddha hall! But no Buddha is inside it."[7] Mazu humorously used the Buddha hall as a metaphor to refer to Wuye's body and to guide him to look into the Buddha/mind inside himself. This dialogue was later remolded into a more mature style of encounter dialogue (see next section). Ehu Dayi's epitaph written by Wei Chuhou (773–829) in 818 records a dialogue between Dayi and Emperor Shunzong (r. 805) during the Zhenyuan reign-period (785–804) when the latter was the Crown Prince: the prince asked, "What is Buddha-nature?" Dayi answered, "It does not leave that which Your Highness is asking." Then the prince silently understood the mysterious teaching.[8] The question about Buddha-nature that the prince asked is the same as the question about "the first patriarch's intention in coming from the west" repeatedly asked in later Chan encounter dialogues. Dayi used an indirect answer to inspire the prince to look back into his own inherent nature and therefore attain awakening. In the two datable encounter-dialogue anecdotes of Danxia Tianran that were told in his epitaph written by Liu Ke, "burning wooden Buddha statue" and "idle monk," Danxia's replies also belong to this kind of witty, paradoxical, and terse language.[9]

The popularity of this kind of dialogue can be seen more clearly in Zongmi's *Chan Preface*, which records a dialogue between a questioner and himself. When the questioner asked why he included so many Chan dialogues in his Chan collection, Zongmi answered that Chan masters' mission was to awaken their students suddenly by mysterious resonance without leaving any trace of language. He then cited the following examples:

> When someone asked how to cultivate the Way, [the master] answered there was no need for cultivation. When someone sought liberation, [the master] asked who bound him. If someone asked the path of attaining Buddhahood, [the master] said there was no ordinary man. If someone asked how to pacify mind when dying, [the master] said there was originally not a thing. . . . In a word, they just followed the conditions and responded to the encounters at the given moments.[10]

Following the conditions and responding to the encounters at the given moments are salient features of encounter dialogue. All the examples include witty, interrogational, or paradoxical phrases applied to clear various kinds of attachments presented by the students, in order to push them back to themselves. From Zongmi's statement we can infer that he included a large amount of this kind of dialogue in his *Chanyuan zhuquanji* (Collected Works on the Source of Chan).[11] It should be noted that, among the encounter dialogues cited by Zongmi, two were actually from Mazu, Shitou, or the *Baolin zhuan*. The first, "when someone asked how to cultivate the Way, the master answered there was no need for cultivation," is found in one of Mazu's sermons.[12] The second, "when someone sought for liberation, the master asked who bound him," is found in both Shitou's hagiography in the *SGSZ*, which is based on the epitaph written by Liu Ke,[13] and in the forged dialogue between the third patriarch Sengcan and the fourth patriarch Daoxin in the *Baolin zhuan*.[14] This intertextuality of Zongmi's work and the discourses of Mazu, Shitou, and the *Baolin zhuan* further testifies to the vogue of this kind of encounter dialogue. On the other hand, because Zongmi did not mention any illogical, iconoclastic vocal or physical exchange, and also Huangbo Xiyun's *Chuanxin fayao* compiled by Pei Xiu in 857 contains only sermons and regular or witty, paradoxical dialogues,[15] we can infer that the highly mature type of encounter dialogue was not actually practiced before the mid-ninth century.

The second development that marks the emergence of formal encounter dialogue in the mid-Tang period is the fictionalized accounts of enlightenment experiences in the *Baolin zhuan* and other texts, which display the mature styles of encounter dialogue. As discussed in chapter one, the encounter-dialogue story of Mazu's enlightenment by Huairang first appeared in the *Baolin zhuan*. Another fragment of the *Baolin zhuan* states that when young Huairang visited Dao'an, the master opened and closed his eyes to display a kind of "esoteric function," and the young student was enlightened by this body language.[16] In addition, ten more encounter stories of enlightenment experience of the Indian and Chinese patriarchs are found in the *Baolin zhuan*.[17] It is also notable that in the Dunhuang version of the *Platform Sūtra*, there is an encounter story about Shenhui's first meeting with Huineng, in which the patriarch beat the new student.[18] Since Zongmi cited this story in his *Chan Chart*,[19] it is certain that the story was current in the mid-Tang period, though the date of the Dunhuang manuscript is still debated. These made-up encounter dialogues were almost the same as the later mature, "classical" ones and were obviously their immediate forerunners.

Then, by the period of the late Tang and Five Dynasties, encounter dialogue developed into multiple forms and achieved full maturity. The stūpa inscription for Yangshan Huiji (807–883) written by Lu Xisheng in 895 states:

> [Yangshan] intended to guide the students by interrupting [their train of thought] directly, and nobody could do so as well as he could. However, the students often lost the point. Raising eyebrows, twinkling eyes, knocking with a wooden stick, and pointing to objects, they imitated each other, little short of making fun. This was not the Master's fault.[20]

A salient feature of encounter dialogue is "to guide the students by interrupting their train of thought"; "raising eyebrows, twinkling eyes, knocking with a wooden stick, pointing to objects" are applications of body language. According to this datable statement, Yangshan Huiji, a third-generation successor of Mazu, seems to have been one of the forerunners of mature encounter dialogue. This inference can be further supported by the stūpa inscription of Yangshan Guangyong (850–938) written by Song Qiqiu (887–959) in 938. After Guangyong received plenary ordination, he visited Yangshan. Yangshan asked him: "Do you think I look like a donkey?" Guangyong answered, "I think you do not look like a Buddha."[21] Guangyong received his plenary ordination in 867, and Yangshan died in 883; hence, this mature encounter dialogue with absurd and illogical phrases must have happened between 867 and 883, and was transcribed at the latest in 938.

In addition, in 884 Yunming wrote the stūpa inscription for his master Xiyuan Da'an (793–883),[22] who was also Guishan's major disciple. In about the same year, Cui Yin (854–904) wrote the epitaph for Da'an, which is preserved in the SGSZ.[23] The former records that when Da'an first met Shigong Huizang, Mazu's disciple, Huizang drew the bow to test him, and Da'an passed the test. The latter gives a more detailed account of this encounter anecdote: "At the beginning of each discourse, Huizang always drew the bow and aimed it at the students. While Da'an was bowing, not yet rising from his knees, Huizang shouted, 'Look at the arrow!' Da'an was calm and undertook proper reply. Shigong threw away the bow, saying, 'For the first time in many years I hit at half a man.'" It is doubtful that Huizang, who was Mazu's immediate disciple, could have performed such highly mature encounter dialogue, and the same incident was also said to have happened between Huizang and Sanping Yizhong;[24] thus, this anecdote was more likely a later retrospective creation. If this is the case, we know that in the late Tang period encounter dialogues attributed to the mid-Tang masters began to be created retrospectively. This inference can be supported by the content of the Shengzhou ji (Collection of the Sacred Heir) compiled in 898–901. The Song-dynasty Dazangjing gangmu zhiyao lu (Annotated Essential Records of the Catalog of the Tripiṭaka) states, "During the Guanghua reign-period, Chan master Xuanwei in Huashan collected the encounter dialogues of the masters who had emerged since the Zhenyuan reign-period, and used the verses of the patriarchs as a basis to compile the Xuanmen shengzhou ji (Collection of the Sacred Heir of the Mysterious School)."[25] The masters since the Zhenyuan reign-period (785–805) began with Mazu's disciples. Thus, we know that this text compiled by the end of the Tang contained encounter dialogues attributed to Mazu's disciples, many of which must have been retrospectively created by late-Tang monks. Another text titled Xu Baolin zhuan (Sequel of the Chronicle of the Baolin monastery) compiled by Weijin in 907–910, during the beginning of the Five Dynasties, contained encounter dialogues of Chan masters since the Guanghua reign-period (898–901), which was a continuation of the Shengzhou ji.[26] According to the Dazangjing gangmu zhiyao lu, the three texts, Baolin zhuan, Shengzhou ji, and Xu Baolin zhuan, were the major sources for the compilation of the CDL.[27]

In the epitaph for Yungai Huaiyi (847–934) written by Ouyang Xi in 934, Huaiyi is said to have been enlightened by his master, Guanxi Zhixian, who was Linji Yixuan's disciple, through the couplet, "In the ancient Buddha hall on the mountain of Five Aggregates, / The Vairocana Buddha shines with perfect light day and night."[28] Zhixian died in 895;[29] thus, this encounter dialogue must have happened before that year, and was transcribed at the latest in 934. The Korean monk Chŏljung's (826–900) stūpa inscription written by Ch'oe Ŏnhwi (868–944) in 924 also transcribes an encounter dialogue.[30] In the stūpa inscription that Xuefeng Yicun wrote for himself and the Military Commissioner Wang Shenzhi inscribed on a stone in 903, an illogical, non-conceptual verse is included.[31]

So far we have seen that from the 880s to 930s, Chinese or Korean writers transcribed lively or created encounter dialogues in stele inscriptions of Chan monks and the two "transmission of lamp" histories, the *Shengzhou ji* and *Xu baolin zhuan*. By the middle of the tenth century there were many more Chinese or Korean stele inscriptions that transcribed encounter dialogues.[32] Apart from stele inscriptions, many other kinds of Chan texts were current in the Tang and Five Dynasties, such as *yuben* (discourse text), *bielu* (separate records), *xinglu* (biographical records), *xingzhuang* (biographical outline), *yaojue* (essential oral teaching), *yaoyu* (essential discourses), *fayao* (essential teaching), and *guangyu* (extended discourses), some of which were recorded in the catalogs of the Japanese monks Ennin and Enchin.[33] As is well known, all the compilers of the four works that contain large amounts of encounter dialogues and were compiled from 952 to 1004, the *ZTJ*, *ZJL*, *SGSZ*, and *CDL*, declared from time to time that their compilations were based on various kinds of earlier texts. There is an obvious intertextuality among these four works, a fact that indicates the existence of a large body of earlier texts on which these compilations were based. Those earlier texts were originally transcribed or created during the Tang and Five Dynasties. Then, after the great vogue of the *CDL*, these original materials were lost, and the reproduced *ZTJ* survived purely by chance. Therefore, it is incorrect to say that the encounter dialogues contained in the *ZTJ* and *CDL* were created completely by Chan monks of the Song dynasty, though they may have actually edited, polished, or added a great deal to the original materials.

In conclusion, during the mid-Tang period when Mazu, Shitou, Jingshan, and their immediate disciples were active, encounter dialogue emerged in two forms, the first involving the vogue of indirect, paradoxical phrases, and the second the fictionalized accounts of enlightenment dialogues that already displayed the highly mature style of "classical" encounter dialogue. Then, from the late Tang to Five Dynasties, beginning with Mazu's third-generation successors, encounter dialogue achieved full maturity with multiple forms, including illogical, nonconceptual phrases and physical actions. Chan monks also created encounter anecdotes retrospectively for their mid-Tang or earlier masters. During this period, lively oral encounter dialogues or retrospectively created encounter anecdotes were transcribed in various kinds of texts, and some of them are preserved in stele inscriptions. These facts that are derived from stele inscriptions and other reliably datable Tang texts will effectively help us to set criteria for distinguishing original texts from late layers in the discourse records and "transmission of the lamp" histories pertinent to Mazu and his disciples.

DISCOURSE RECORDS ATTRIBUTED TO MAZU

According to Yanagida's study, soon after Mazu passed away his discourse texts (*yuben*) were in circulation, and were likely edited based on the notes of his disciples.[34] It is hard to determine the contents of those original texts, but the *Extended Discourses of Chan Master Daji Daoyi* (Jiangxi Daji Daoyi chanshi [guang]yu) preserved in *Juan* 28 of the *CDL*, which contains a long sermon of Mazu, is probably one of them.

The extant *Mazu yulu* was first compiled in the Northern Song by Huinan, who was a successor of the Hongzhou-Linji line and the patriarch of the Huanglong branch. It was edited together with the discourses of Baizhang Huaihai, Huangbo Xiyun, and Linji Yixuan to form a text titled *Sijia lu* (Records of the Four Masters), which was also named *Mazu sijia lu* in the Song,[35] and renamed as *Sijia yulu* (Discourse Records of the Four Masters) in the Ming Dynasty.[36] The Qing bibliophile Ding Bing (1832–1899) recorded a Yuan edition of *Sijia lu* in two *juan*.[37] This text is preserved in the Nanjing Library, but the editors of the *Zhongguo guji shanben shumu* (Catalog of Chinese Ancient Rare Books) re-identify it as a Ming edition.[38] However, this text differs from other Ming editions of *Sijia yulu* in five ways. First, it keeps the Song title *Sijia lu*, and none of the four masters' discourses is titled with "Yulu." Second, at the beginning of each *juan* there is a line: "Compiled by Huinan, the abbot and monk of transmitting dharma at Huanglongshan in Hongzhou." This is not found in other editions. Third, at the first page of the text there is a preface by Yang Jie dated 1085, which is also not found in other Ming editions. Fourth, the beginning of the first *juan* is a hagiography of Nanyue Huairang that was copied verbatim from the *GDL*, while other editions do not contain such biography, but rather the story of Mazu's awakening by Huairang inserted into the biographical part of Mazu's record. Five, at the end of the text there is a postscript written by the Yuan monk Shiqi in 1363. Based on these five differences, we can assume that even if this text is a Ming edition, it still keeps the appearance of Song and Yuan editions.[39] Since the *GDL* was compiled in 1029, the compilation of the *Sijia lu* must have taken place between 1029 and 1069,[40] about a half-century after the compilation of the *CDL*.

Like most recorded discourse texts, *Mazu yulu* comprises three parts: biographical sketch, sermons, and encounter dialogues.[41] The first part, the biographical sketch of Mazu's life, is copied verbatim from Mazu's entry in the *CDL*, with only two additions from the *ZTJ*—one about Mazu's entrance to monastic life in the Luohansi in his hometown, and the other a dialogue between him and the abbot of the Kaiyuansi in Hongzhou, which occurred the night before Mazu died.[42]

The second part of *Mazu yulu* contains the transcripts of three sermons. Yanagida compares these with earlier sources such as the *ZJL*, *ZTJ*, *CDL*, and *GDL*, and draws two more sermons from the *ZJL* to form a total of five. He then reorders them as follows:

Sermon 1: *ZJL*, *T.* 48: 1.418b/c, 24.550c.
Sermon 2: *ZJL*, *T.* 48: 14.492a.
Sermon 3: *ZJL*, *T.* 48: 49.707b.
Sermon 4: *CDL*, *SBCK*, 28.6b–7b.
Sermon 5: *GDL*, *XZJ* 136: 8.652a–53b.

In addition, Yanagida cites Zongmi's works and discourses of Mazu's disciples to justify the reliability of these sermons.[43] Based on Yanagida's study, I add one more sermon from the "Daoyi Stūpa" by Quan Deyu, and further adduce stele inscriptions and other datable Tang texts to verify the reliability of these sermons (for detailed verifications and an annotated translation of Mazu's six sermons, see the Appendix). As previously mentioned in the Introduction, Zongmi's works can be used as "standard texts" to determine the dates and authenticity of Mazu's sermons because the main themes and many expressions of these sermons are seen in Zongmi's summaries and criticisms of the Hongzhou doctrine. The opposite view, that these sermons were retrospectively created based on Zongmi's accounts by Mazu's successors, is definitely unlikely, because not only could they not have fabricated texts to cater to Zongmi's fierce criticisms, but also these sermons are filled with scriptural quotations and allusions, thirty-five in total,[44] a conservative style that was not seen in the discourses of Mazu's successors in the late Tang to Five Dynasties.[45] It is possible that certain modifications were made by later successors, but these sermons are essentially datable.

The third part of *Mazu yulu* consists of thirty-four encounter dialogues.[46] While most of these dialogues show the fictitious color and traces of later creation, a few of them seem to have had reliable provenances. Below is a case-to-case examination of these dialogues.

Dialogue 1: Mazu and three disciples played with the moon. This encounter story demonstrates most clearly the traces of layered fabrications. In Baizhang Huaihai's entry in the Song and Yuan editions of *CDL*, only Xitang Zhizang and Baizhang attend Mazu. In the *GDL* and the Korean and Ming editions of *CDL*, Nanquan Puyuan's name is added to the party. Iriya indicates insightfully: "Among Mazu's disciples, at first Xitang's position was most important. Later, because of the active roles of Baizhang's successors, Baizhang's position was elevated, and consequently the story of two great disciples competing with each other' and 'playing with the moon' was produced. Then, during the Northern Song period, because the Linji line appreciated Zhaozhou Congshen very highly, his master Nanquan was added to the story and given the highest appraisal."[47] Iriya is correct. Among the eleven major disciples listed in the "Daoyi Stūpa," Xitang is the second, while Baizhang's name does not even appear. It is left to Baizhang's stūpa, written by Chen Xu, to cover this fact for him: "He always humbled himself in daily life, so that his master's stele inscription conceals his name."[48] Obviously, when Mazu was alive, Baizhang was only a marginal disciple, so the situation of "the two great disciples competing with each other" definitely did not exist. Thus, this story was first created by Baizhang's successors to elevate his position, and then, during the early Song, some Linji monks added Nanquan's name to create "three great disciples." This addition must have happened between 1004, when the *CDL* was compiled, and 1029, when the *GDL* was compiled.

Dialogue 3: Dialogue between Mazu and Baizhang about the essence of Buddha-dharma. In Mazu's entry in the *ZTJ*, the question is raised by an anonymous monk,[49] whereas in Mazu's entry in the *CDL* the anonymous monk is replaced by Baizhang.[50] The *Mazu yulu* follows the latter. This later replacement was also aimed at elevating Baizhang's position in the Hongzhou school.

Dialogue 4: Dazhu Huihai's first visit to Mazu. This discourse came from Dazhu's entry in the *CDL*.[51] When Dazhu told Mazu the purpose of his visit was to seek Buddha-dharma, Mazu said, "Without looking at your own treasure, why do you abandon your home and wander about? Here I do not have a single thing." Dazhu then asked what his own treasure was, and Mazu replied, "That which is asking me right now is your treasure. It is perfectly complete and lacks nothing. You are free to use it. What is the need to seek outside?" Dazhu was enlightened by these words. Later, when he returned to his home monastery in Yuezhou, he wrote the *Dunwu rudao yaomen lun* (Treatise on the Essential Doctrine of Suddenly Entering onto Enlightenment). After reading the treatise, Mazu told the assembly, "In Yuezhou, there is a great pearl, whose perfect brilliance shines freely without any obstruction." In this dialogue, Mazu applied metaphorical phrases to enlighten Dazhu, which was a common practice during that time. Dazhu's secular surname was Zhu, and he later was called Dazhu (Great Pearl). The *Extended Discourses of Dazhu Huihai* also records, "I, the poor priest, heard that the Reverend in Jiangxi said, 'Your own treasure is perfectly complete; you are free to use it and do not need to seek outside.' From that moment onward, I have ceased [from my seeking]."[52] This text is relatively datable (see next section). Therefore, we have reason to assume that this encounter dialogue is authentic.

Dialogue 6: Letan Weijian sat in meditation. This story came from Weijian's entry in the *CDL*.[53] It relates that while Weijian was sitting in meditation, Mazu first blew twice in his ear and then had a bowl of tea sent to him. The implied meaning is a ridicule of the practice of seated meditation. In the *Linji lu*, there is a quite similar story, in which Huangbo Xiyun knocked both Linji and the Head Monk on their heads with a stick, when he saw the former was sleeping and the latter was sitting in meditation.[54] This kind of story must have been popular in the late Tang and Five Dynasties.

Dialogue 9: Black hair and white hair. This dialogue is first seen in Mazu's entry in the *ZTJ* and Xitang's entry in the *CDL*.[55] An anonymous monk asked the meaning of Bodhidharma's intention to come to China, and Mazu directed him to ask Xitang. Xitang said he had a headache and directed the monk to see Baizhang, who said he did not know anything about it. The story ends with Mazu's comments that Xitang's hair was white and Baizhang's hair was black. Clearly, this is another story of "two great disciples competing with each other," which must again have been forged by Baizhang's successors.

Dialogue 10: The dialogue about nirvāṇa between Mazu and Magu Baoche. This dialogue came from Magu's entry in the *CDL*.[56] However, in Danxia Tianran's entry in the *ZTJ*, the same dialogue happened between Danxia and Magu.[57] Iriya believes the *ZTJ* version is the original,[58] but if we look at Danxia's life as studied in chapter two, this version is also not authentic.

Dialogue 11: "The plum is ripe." The plum refers to the Chan teaching of Damei Fachang because Dameishan, where he stayed, literally means Mt. Great Plum. There are three different versions of the story. The first is from Fachang's hagiography in the *SGSZ*, which was based on his epitaph written by Jiang Ji in 840, in which an anonymous monk told Yanguan Qi'an about Fachang.[59] The second is from Fachang's entry in the *ZTJ*, in which the commentator became Yanguan.[60] The third is from Fachang's entry in the *CDL*, in which the commentator became Mazu.[61] Since the *SGSZ* version is authentic, the other two must be later modifications.[62] According to the *SGSZ* biography, Fachang moved to Dameishan in 796, eight years after Mazu's death; hence, it was not possible for Mazu to make the comment. In addition to the replacements of the commentator, both the *ZTJ* and *CDL* stories append a vivid plot: a monk sent by Yanguan or Mazu came to tell Fachang that Mazu had changed his proposition from "this mind is the Buddha" to "neither mind nor Buddha" (*feixin feifo*), whereupon Fachang replied, "You can have 'neither mind nor Buddha,' but I would insist on 'this mind is the Buddha.'" In Dialogue 21, these propositions are again discussed as different expedients used by Mazu. However, the proposition "neither mind nor Buddha" is not found in Mazu's sermons. According to the remolding of Fachang's story, this dialogue was also a later creation.

Dialogue 12: Fenzhou Wuye's first visit. As previously mentioned, Wuye's hagiography in the *SGSZ*, which is based on the epitaph written by Yang Qian in 823, recounts that during the first meeting of Wuye and Mazu, Mazu applied both witty, metaphorical phrases and doctrinal instructions to awaken him. However, this event was recreated into two versions during the late Tang and Five Dynasties. The first is seen in Mazu's entry in the *ZTJ*, in which he used the method of calling Wuye's name to awaken him.[63] In the second version, which is seen in the *ZJL*, Wuye's entry in the *CDL*, and *Mazu yulu*, in addition to the formula of calling his name, Wuye's question became the cliché, "Why did Bodhidharma come from the West to transmit the mind-seal mysteriously?"[64] Clearly the account of Wuye's visit to Mazu was remolded at least twice during the late Tang and Five Dynasties.[65]

Dialogue 13: "Shitou's path is slippery." This dialogue came from Mazu's entry in the *CDL*.[66] In the encounter story, Deng Yinfeng said good-bye to Mazu before he set out to visit Shitou, but Mazu reminded him, "Shitou's path is slippery." "Path" refers to teaching method, and "slippery" implies that Shitou's encounter discourse was sharp and difficult for students. When Yinfeng arrived at Shitou's place, he walked around the Chan seat once and then struck his staff on the ground, asking, "What is the Chan doctrine?" Shitou answered, "Heaven! Heaven!" Yinfeng failed to respond to Shitou, so he returned to ask help from Mazu. Mazu taught him to hiss twice at Shitou, but it turned out that Shitou acted the same way before Yinfeng could do so. This story praises Shitou's teaching under the guise of Mazu's name, and hints that Mazu was not as good as Shitou. The body language of walking around the Chan seat, striking a staff on the ground, and hissing are also not likely to have appeared at that time. The story must have been created by later monks of the Shitou line.

Dialogue 18: Pang Yun's enlightenment. This story came from Pang Yun's entries in both ZTJ and CDL.[67] Pang asked Mazu, "Who was the one parting from all phenomenal-appearances?" The master answered, "I'll tell you if you can dry the water of the Western River in one drink." Pang was enlightened by this reply. This kind of mature, illogical dialogue could not have been generated during this period. Furthermore, in the Pang jushi yulu, Pang asked the same question to Shitou and was enlightened by him as well.[68] This is obviously a recreation of the first story.

Dialogue 20: Pang Yun's inquiry about water and boats. In both the ZJL and the Extended Discourses of Nanquan Puyuan in Juan 28 of the CDL,[69] this inquiry was made by an anonymous scholar. In Mazu's entry in the CDL, this scholar became Pang Yun,[70] and the Mazu yulu follows this change. Thus, the modification might have happened in the early Song.

Dialogue 23: "I am not in harmony with the Way." This dialogue came from Mazu's entry in the CDL, in which Mazu replied to an anonymous monk with these words.[71] However, in Deng Yinfeng's entry in the same text, it is Shitou who replied to Yinfeng with these words.[72] These conflicting stories reveal the traces of the competing fabrications created by monks of the two lines.

Dialogue 29: Taking wine and meat. This dialogue came from Mazu's entry in the CDL, which recounts: "The pure-handed commissioner in Hongzhou asked, 'To take wine and meat or not to do it, which is correct?' Mazu replied, 'If you, the Vice Censor-in-Chief, take them, it is [the use of] your salary. If you don't, it is your blessing.'"[73] Mazu's witty answer to the dilemma concerning the Buddhist precept of alcohol and meat is quite similar to Jingshan's "the one who saved the sheep was compassionate, and the one who did not save the sheep was emancipated." It is highly possible that this pure-handed commissioner with the title of Vice Censor-in-Chief was Bao Ji, the author of Mazu's epitaph. From 779 to 780, Bao Ji was the Prefect of Jiangzhou and Probationary Transport and Salt-Iron Monopoly Commissioner. Jiangzhou was next to Hongzhou, and the office of the probationary commission was located in Hongzhou. The designation "pure-handed commissioner" (lianshi) usually referred to a commissioner who was in charge of money, while the unofficial term to a provincial surveillance commissioner was "aggregation leader" (lianshuai). In the Tang dynasty, after the An Lushan rebellion, it became a convention that all commissioners carried official titles of the censorate.[74] Bao Ji then also bore the title Vice Censor-in-Chief. For example, in the first month of 780, Jiaoran (ca. 720–ca. 793), the famous monk-poet, wrote the "Letter to Vice Censor-in-Chief Bao [Ji]," in which he introduced another monk-poet, Lingche (746–816), who was going to visit Bao in Jiangxi.[75] Judging from the fact that he later wrote the epitaph for Mazu, Bao Ji must have had a close relationship with Mazu during his two-year stay in Jiangxi. The position of Probationary Transport and Salt-Iron Monopoly Commissioner with the title of Vice Censor-in-Chief was temporary for a short time in Jiangxi, and it is not possible for later monks to have forged it; hence, the dialogue is likely an original one.

Dialogue 30: Yaoshan Weiyan's visits to Shitou and Mazu. In this story, because Yaoshan could not be enlightened by Shitou, he visited Mazu and was awakened; then he said, "When I was in Shitou's place, I was like a mosquito on an iron cow." This story was obviously intended to disparage Shitou. Since it is not found in the ZTJ, SGSZ, and CDL, it must have been created after 1004.

Dialogue 31: The designation of Danxia Tianran's Buddhist name. This encounter story came from Danxia's entry in the CDL, which was forged by monks of the Mazu line. It conflicts with the story narrated in Danxia's entry in the ZTJ, which was forged by monks of the Shitou line, as discussed in chapter two.

Dialogue from the biographical part: "Sun-face Buddha and Moon-face Buddha." This dialogue came from Mazu's entry in the ZTJ, which records: "The master was going to pass away tomorrow. That evening, the abbot asked, 'The Reverend's health has not been in good condition. How is the Reverend feeling these days?' The master replied, 'Sun-face Buddha, Moon-face Buddha.'"[76] Before the mid-Tang, Chan monks usually registered in official monasteries. The Kaiyuansi of Hongzhou, where Mazu stayed for sixteen years, was also a major official monastery. Then, beginning with Mazu's disciples, increasing numbers of Chan masters established and administered their own monasteries and cloisters.[77] This dialogue between Mazu and the abbot of the Kaiyuansi reveals the fact that, although he attracted many followers and was supported by provincial commissioners when he stayed at the monastery, Mazu had never been appointed abbot. This fact is unlikely to have been distorted by later Chan monks, and Mazu's reply was a witty phrase typical of the encounter dialogues emerging in that period.

In Dialogues 5, 17, and 24, Letan Fahui, Shuilao heshang, and an anonymous monk asked about the purpose of Buddhidharma's intention of coming to China, and Mazu slapped, kicked, or beat them respectively. In Dialogue 14, Deng Yinfeng pushed a cart to run over and hurt Mazu's foot. In Dialogue 15, Mazu asked Shijiu to beat Wujiu with a stick. In Dialogue 19, Pang Yun visited Mazu, and the latter blinked his eyes. In Dialogue 25, Danyuan Yingzhen drew a circle. In Dialogue 27, Mazu also drew a circle and mailed it to Jingshan, whereupon Jingshan put a dot in the center of the circle and sent it back to Mazu. In Dialogue 28, Mazu hissed out a lecture master. The physical actions of beating, drawing, and hissing were not likely to appear in Mazu's time. Therefore, these sharp, radical, and iconoclastic encounters must have been created by monks of the late Tang, Five Dynasties, and even early Song.

Besides the twenty-eight dialogues mentioned, there are six more in the *Mazu yulu*: Dialogue 2, about Nanquan Puyuan's pail; Dialogues 7 and 8, Shigong Huizang stopped hunting and herded cows; Dialogue 18, Pang Yun's enlightenment; and Dialogue 32, Zhaoti Huilang looked for Buddha's knowledge and insight. These dialogue stories are full of fictitious color, and their reliability is also in doubt.

In addition to *Mazu yulu*, Iriya Yoshitaka finds twenty-two more dialogues from the "transmission of the lamp" histories and discourse records compiled from the Five Dynasties to the early Song, including the *ZTJ, CDL, GDL, Zheng fayan zang, Liandeng huiyao, Zongmen zhiying ji, Mingjue yulu, Chanmen niansong ji,* and *Wujia zhengzong zan.*[78] The last six texts appeared later than the *Mazu yulu*, and all the five dialogues collected from these texts use physical actions and iconoclastic, illogical words. Therefore, they must have been created by Song monks. Of the other seventeen dialogues, three involve mysterious and supernatural events, and seven involve either sectarian competition between the Mazu and Shitou lines or the use of body language; hence, these are also all later creations. All the remaining seven dialogues focus on extolling Baizhang. For instance, the famous encounter story of wild ducks came from Baizhang's entry in the *GDL.*[79] It narrates that one day, as Baizhang accompanied Mazu on a walk, they heard the cries of wild ducks. In replying to the master's question about the sounds, the student said they were gone. Then the master grabbed the student's nose, and the latter was awakened. The next day the student rolled up the bowing mat in front of the master's seat, while the master gave him a loud shout to approve his awakening. However, in Wuxie Lingmo's entry in the *ZTJ*, the story of wild ducks happened between Baizhang Weizheng (i.e., Fazheng) and Mazu.[80] Since Weizheng was Baizhang's disciple,[81] the story in the *ZTJ* is necessarily a fake, and the *GDL* further reworked the story to fit into Baizhang's discourse records and combined it with another forged story of rolling the mat. To make things worse, later the *Liandeng huiyao* added a detail that after being enlightened, Baizhang cried and laughed in turns.[82] The other six encounter dialogues are as follows: The *ZTJ* records that Baizhang prepared a meal for a monk who turned out to be the Pratyeka-Buddha and Mazu foretold that Baizhang would be greatly blessed;[83] both the *ZTJ* and *CDL* include two encounter stories, in which Baizhang rolled up the mat in front of Mazu's seat and held up a whisk in reply to Mazu;[84] in the *GDL*, the second story adds the detail that Mazu issued a loud shout and Baizhang became deaf for three days;[85] the *GDL* also includes three more encounter stories—Mazu foretold that Baizhang would become everybody's master of "Great Silence," Baizhang replied to Mazu with the sharp phrase, "meeting nobody," and Baizhang broke the three sauce jars sent by Mazu.[86] Obviously, all these were created to elevate Baizhang's position in the Hongzhou lineage. Among them, the first three are found in the *ZTJ*, so they must have been created during the late Tang to Five Dynasties; the last four are first seen in the *GDL*, so they must have been created in the early Song.

To sum up, among the extant discourse records attributed to Mazu, six sermons and four encounter dialogues—Dazhu Huihai's first visit, Fenzhou Wuye's first visit, taking wine and meat, and Sun-face Buddha and Moon-face Buddha—are authentic or relatively datable. All the other encounter dialogues can be determined or doubted as creations of Chan monks from the late Tang to the early Song, many of which even reveal traces of layered forgery.

TEXTS AND DISCOURSES ATTRIBUTED TO MAZU'S DISCIPLES

This section will examine the texts and discourses attributed to Mazu's disciples, including the *Dunwu rudao yaomen lun* (Treatise on the Essential Teaching of Suddenly Entering into Enlightenment, hereafter cited as *Dunwu yaomen*), the *Baizhang guanglu* (Extended Records of Baizhang), the *Pang Yun shiji* (Verses of Pang Yun), the *Mingzhou Dameishan Fachang chanshi yulu* (Discourse Records of Chan Master Fachang at Dameishan of Mingzhou, hereafter cited as *Fachang yulu*), *Lizhou Yaoshan Weiyan heshang [guang]yu* (Extended Discourses of Reverend Weiyan at Yaoshan in Lizhou), *Fenzhou Dada Wuye guoshi [guang]yu* (Extended Discourses of National Teacher Dada Wuye in Fenzhou), *Chizhou Nanquan Puyuan heshang [guang]yu* (Extended Discourses of Reverend Puyuan in Nanquansi in Chizhou), and many other discourses recorded in the texts of the late Tang to the early Song. Nevertheless, several texts created by or attributed to Mazu's disciples are related to their religious practice and sectarian activities of striving for orthodoxy, such as the *Baolin zhuan*, the *Zhengdao ge* attributed to Yongjia Xuanjue, the verses attributed to Baozhi, and the *Chanmen guishi* (Regulations of the Chan School) attributed to Baizhang. For the convenience of narrative structure, these texts will be discussed in chapter five.

Dazhu Huihai and the *Dunwu yaomen*

In the "Daoyi Stūpa" written by Quan Deyu, Dazhu Huihai's name is listed as the first among Mazu's eleven major disciples, who led other disciples in holding Mazu's funeral. This indicates that he was either the most senior or most important disciple of Mazu, and still alive in 788 when Mazu passed away.

The *Chongwen zongmu* attributes two texts to Dazhu: *Rudao yaomen lun* and *Dayun heshang yaofa* (Essential Teachings of Reverend Dayun).[87] The *Tong zhi* records the first text.[88] The *Song shi* records both, with the first text appearing twice under different titles, *Rudao yaomen lun* and *Dunwu rudao yaomen lun*.[89] According to Dazhu's entry in the *CDL*, his preceptor was Daozhi in the Dayunsi in Yuezhou; later, after studying with Mazu for six years, he returned to Dayunsi to take care of the aged Daozhi.[90] Therefore, the *Essential Teachings of Reverend Dayun* must be Dayun Daozhi's discourses recorded and compiled by Dazhu.

The current *Dunwu yaomen* attributed to Dazhu was first published by Miaoxie in 1374. It comprises two texts: the first is the *Dunwu yaomen* proper, which was rediscovered by Miaoxie; the second, titled *Zhufang menren canwen yulu* (Discourse records of Dazhu and Visiting Students from All Quarters), was taken by him from the *CDL*, including both Dazhu's entry in *Juan* 6 and the *Extended Discourses of Dazhu Huihai* in *Juan* 28.

According to Yanagida's study, the Kanazawa bunko possesses a manuscript equivalent to the first text of Miaoxie's edition, that is, the *Dunwu yaomen* proper, and older than it; moreover, this manuscript contains a completely different preface, though both prefaces are probably spurious.[91] Yanagida further indicates that the *Dunwu yaomen* discusses themes common to the Northern school and its opponent Shenhui, themes that antedate the *Mazu yulu*.[92] Suzuki Tetsuo carefully compares the *Dunwu yaomen* with Shenhui's discourses and finds that they contain many similar expressions, especially those of "seeing into the nature" (*jianxing*), "no-thought" (*wunian*), and "the three learnings [morality, concentration, and wisdom] are identical" (*sanxue deng*).[93]

Dazhu's entry in the *CDL* includes seven dialogues,[94] two of which are also found in the *ZTJ*.[95] The *Extended Discourses of Huihai* in the *Juan* 28 of the *CDL* contains thirty-one sermons and dialogues,[96] three of which are found in the *ZTJ*,[97] and two in the *ZJL*.[98] Among these sermons and dialogues preserved in the *ZTJ*, *ZJL*, and *CDL*, some contain witty phrases,[99] and others are in the relatively conservative style common to Chan literature of the early and mid-Tang, without any sign of the illogical, iconoclastic encounter dialogues of the later Tang and Five Dynasties. The themes discussed in these sermons and dialogues are in accord with Mazu's sermons and Zongmi's summary of the Hongzhou doctrine, befitting Dazhu's identity as Mazu's major disciple. Therefore, these sermons and dialogues are probably credible, especially those preserved in the *Extended Discourses of Dazhu Huihai* in *Juan* 28 of the *CDL*.

How do we then explain the contradiction between the *Dunwu yaomen* and the discourses of Dazhu, with the themes of the former in accord with early Chan, especially Shenhui's teaching, and the themes of the latter in accord with Mazu's teaching? One possible answer is that the titles of the two texts attributed to Dazhu, *Dunwu yaomen* and *Dayun yaofa*, were confused in later times. As mentioned earlier, Dazhu stayed with his preceptor, Dayun Daozhi, much longer than with Mazu, and even compiled Dayun's essential teachings for circulation. The current *Dunwu yaomen* is more likely to be the *Dayun yaofa*, and the extant discourses of Dazhu, especially the *Extended Discourses of Dazhu Huihai*, are likely the original *Dunwu yaomen*. Therefore, in this study I will cite only the discourses of Dazhu as his understanding of the Hongzhou doctrine.

Baizhang Huaihai's Discourses

Baizhang's stūpa inscription written by Chen Xu in 818 states that after Baizhang passed away, his disciples Shenxing and Fanyun collected the master's discourses and compiled a *Discourse Text* (Yuben), which was circulated along with a letter written by Baizhang in response to a question about Buddha-nature from a Vinaya master.[100] In Enchin's (814–891) catalogs, there is reference to a *Baizhangshan heshang yaojue* (Essential Teachings of the Reverend from Baizhangshan).[101] The *ZJL* cites a certain *Baizhang guangyu* (Extended Discourses of Baizhang) twice.[102] The *Chongwen zongmu* also records *Baizhang guangyu* in one *juan*.[103] During the early Song, the Chan master Daochang (d. 991) at Baizhangshan recompiled Baizhang's discourses and named it *Baizhang guanglu* (Extended Records of Baizhang), which is included first in the *GDL* and then in the *Sijia lu*.[104] The *Gu zunsu yulu* also includes this text, but divides it into two parts: "Guanglu" (Extended Records) and "Yulu zhi yu" (Supplement to Discourse Records). At the end of the "Guanglu," the *Sijia lu* text adds five more discourses collected from the *ZTJ* and *CDL* and, according to Huihong, this addition was probably done by Huinan when he compiled the *Sijia lu*.[105]

Yanagida believes that the *Baizhang guanglu*, which contains sermons and short addresses in a conservative style of rhetoric, was based on old sources and therefore authentic.[106] Some themes of this text are in accord with Mazu's sermons and Zongmi's account of the Hongzhou doctrine. However, one of its major themes is "penetrating the three propositions" (*tou sanju guo*).[107] The basic mode of this theme was a threefold negation—nonattachment to any beings or nonbeings, not dwelling in nonattachment, and not developing an understanding of nonattachment.[108] This radical apophasis of Mādhyamika dialectic is different from the more kataphatic stance of Mazu's sermons, and is not found in Zongmi's account of the Hongzhou doctrine. In the late Tang, beginning with Mazu's second-generation disciples, more apophatic expressions such as "no-mind" and "neither mind nor Buddha" appeared frequently in the controversies over the Hongzhou doctrine.[109] Hence, though the *Baizhang guanglu* may have been based on the original discourse text compiled by Baizhang's disciples, it seems also to have been supplemented with the ideas of Baizhang's successors.

In the *Sijia lu*, the "Guanglu" comprises only the second part of Baizhang's discourses, and the first part includes dialogues collected from the *ZTJ*, *ZJL*, *CDL*, *GDL*, and other early Song texts. A large portion of these dialogues involves Mazu and is unreliable as previously noted. The others also display the highly mature, iconoclastic features of the later Tang and Five Dynasties encounter dialogues. Thus, this part is not dependable and will not be used in this study.

Pang Yun's Verses and Discourses

The *Chongwen zongmu* records *Pang jushi ge* (Songs of Lay Buddhist Pang) in one *juan*.[110] The *Xin Tang shu* records *Pang Yun shiji* (Verses of Pang Yun) in three *juan* and more than 300 pieces.[111] The *Junzhai dushu zhi* records *Pang jushi yulu* (Discourse Records of Lay Buddhist Pang) in ten *juan*.[112] According to the *Xin Tang shu*, Pang Yun's courtesy name was Daoxuan; he came from the Hengyangxian in Hengzhou, and was active during the early Zhenyuan reign-period (785–805).[113]

The current *Pang jushi yulu* comprises two texts.[114] The first is *Yulu* (*Juan* 1), including more than twenty encounter dialogues collected from the *ZTJ*, *CDL*, and other early Song texts, most of which involve the use of physical action such as holding up or throwing something, beating, and shouting. Therefore, this part must be a later creation. The second text is *Shi* (Verses, *Juan* 2 and 3), including 189 verses.[115] These verses involve a broad range of themes, including Buddhist teachings such as "emptiness" and "eliminating the three poisons," early Chan ideas such as "no-phenomenal-appearance" and "no-thought," and teachings of Mazu and other contemporary masters, such as "no-thing," and "ordinary activities are the manifestation of the Way." No iconoclastic theme or style of encounter dialogue of late Tang and Five Dynasties is found in these verses. They are basically credible, and the main body must originally belong to the *Pang jushi ge* or *Pang Yun shiji* recorded in the Northern Song *Chongwen zongmu* and *Xin Tang shu*, though it is possible that they include certain later additions.

The *ZTJ* says that Pang Yun was Mazu's disciple,[116] while the *CDL* says he was enlightened by both Shitou and Mazu.[117] Although the encounter dialogues that state his enlightenment by the two masters are not genuine,[118] it was possible that he visited or studied with them, as they were contemporaries, and the idea that "ordinary activities are the manifestation of the Way" was one of Mazu's basic teachings.[119]

Damei Fachang's Discourses

As indicated earlier, Fachang's hagiography in the *SGSZ*, which was based on the epitaph written by Jiang Ji, is the most reliable source. According to this biography, Fachang was born into a Zheng family in the Xiangyangxian of Xiangzhou. He became a novice monk in the famous Yuquansi when he was a child, and received plenary ordination at the age of twenty in Longxingsi. From 796 on, he secluded himself at a mountain in the south of the Yuyaoxian of Mingzhou, which he named Dameishan. In about 836, he built a cloister at the mountain and enjoyed a large community of several hundred followers until he died in 839.[120] The biography does not mention his relationship with Mazu or any other Chan master; thus, his apprenticeship with Mazu is not certain.

The Kanazawa bunko possesses a text entitled *Mingzhou Dameishan Chang chanshi yulu*, and the compiler called himself "Disciple Huibao." This text contains seven encounter dialogues, five sermons, a verse, and a eulogy by Yanshou.[121] Three of the dialogues are found in both the *ZTJ* and *CDL*,[122] while two of the sermons are found in the *ZJL*.[123] Among those discourses, one dialogue is the famous "The plum is ripe" (no. 1), which was recreated by later monks. Another dialogue, which is said to have happened between Fachang and Pang Yun, repeats the phrase "The plum is ripe" (no. 3). One sermon, like the first dialogue, plays between the two propositions, "this mind is the Buddha" and "neither mind nor Buddha" (no. 11), a debate that was put forward during the late Tang period.[124] Four other dialogues or sermons involve the holding or knocking of something, shouting, looking back, or illogical words (nos. 3, 5, 7, 8). Therefore, this text is not authentic, though it seems to have appeared earlier than the *ZTJ*, *ZJL*, and *CDL*, and could have been their source. It may have been created during the late Tang period by Fachang's successors.

Discourses of Yaoshan Weiyan, Fenzhou Wuye, Nanquan Puyuan, and Others

The twenty-eighth *juan* of the *CDL* includes *Extended Discourses* of Mazu's other three disciples, Yaoshan Weiyan, Fenzhou Wuye, and Nanquan Puyuan. These discourses include sermons and short addresses, and in general are much more conservative than the encounter dialogues included in their entries in the same text or the *ZTJ*. Referring to the authenticity of the *Extended Discourses* of Mazu and Dazhu in the same text, these discourses can be considered relatively authentic, though it is also possible that there were remoldings and additions by these masters' successors.

In Enchin's catalogs, there is a *Xitang heshang ji* (Verses of Reverend Xitang).[125] Reverend Xitang is probably Xitang Zhizang, but unfortunately no trace of this text has been found. Whereas most of the encounter dialogues of Mazu's disciples preserved in their entries in the *ZTJ* and *CDL* display the iconoclastic characteristics of the late Tang and Five Dynasties, some genuine discourses can be unearthed from early stele inscriptions and biographies. These are as follows:

Wuye's discourse on his deathbed, recorded in his hagiography in the *SGSZ*, which is based on his epitaph written by Yang Qian.[126]
Yaoshan's discourse on his deathbed, recorded in his epitaph by Tang Shen.[127]
Yangqi Zhenshu's discourse, recorded in his epitaph written by Zhixian.[128]
The dialogue between Zhangjing Huaihui and a student, recorded in his epitaph written by Quan Deyu,[129] and a discourse of Huaihui cited by Muyŏm (800–888), Magu Baoche's Silla disciple, in his "Musŏlt'o ron" (Treatise on the Tongueless Realm).[130]
The encounter dialogue between Ehu Dayi and Emperor Shunzong (when he was the Crown Prince) and the debate between Dayi and some

monks at Emperor Dezong's court, recorded in Dayi's epitaph by Wei Chuhou.[131]

Yanguan Qi'an's discourse, recorded in his stūpa inscription written by Lu Jianqiu.[132]

Xingshan Weikuan's four dialogues with Bai Juyi, recorded by Bai in the "Chuanfatang bei" (Stele of the Hall of Transmitting the Dharma).[133]

Tianhuang Daowu's sermon, recorded in his hagiography in the *SGSZ*, based on the epitaph written by Fu Zai.[134]

Danxia Tianran's two encounter dialogues, recorded in his hagiography in the *SGSZ*, which is based on the epitaph by Liu Ke.[135]

Ganquan Zhixian's two sermons, recorded in the *ZJL*.[136] The themes and expressions of these sermons are very close to Mazu's sermons. One of Ennin's catalog records a *Ganquan heshang yuben* (Discourse Text of Reverend Ganquan).[137] Hence, we know during the first half of the ninth century, Ganquan Zhixian's *Discourse Text* was current.

Li Fan's *Xuansheng qulu* (Inn of the Mysterious Sages)

Li Fan was Mazu's lay disciple. The *Xin Tang shu* records this book in one *juan*.[138] The *Junzhai dushu zhi houzhi* records it in two *juan*, and states: "[Li] Fan studied with the monk Daoyi in Jiangxi. . . . During the Dahe reign-period [827–835], Shu Yuanyu framed a case of excessive slaughter against Li Fan. Li was wrongfully imprisoned. He knew that he was going to die, so he wrote a book of sixteen chapters to elucidate the Chan doctrine."[139] This book was still current in the Song dynasty, and though it is no longer extant, three fragments of the book are preserved in the *Fazang suijin lu* (Records of Golden Bits of the Buddhist Scriptures) and *Daoyuanji yao* (Essentials of the Collection of the Buddhist Court) compiled by Chao Jiong (951–1034).[140]

According to stele inscriptions and other reliably datable Tang texts, during the mid-Tang period when Mazu, Shitou, Jingshan, and their immediate disciples were active, encounter dialogue emerged in two forms, the first being the vogue of witty, paradoxical phrases, and the second the fictionalized accounts of enlightenment dialogues. Then, during the late Tang and Five Dynasties, encounter dialogue achieved full maturity with multiple forms, including iconoclastic, illogical, nonconceptual phrases and physical actions such as beating and shouting.

In reference to this background of the evolution of encounter dialogue, this chapter has thoroughly examined the Hongzhou literature. By distinguishing the original materials from later layers, I have identified some authentic or relatively datable texts and discourses: Mazu's six sermons and four dialogues, *Baizhang guanglu*, *Pang Yun's Verses*, *Extended Discourses* of Dazhu Huihai, Yaoshan Weiyan, Fenzhou Wuye, and Nanquan Puyuan, sixteen discourses of Mazu's disciples, and three fragments of Li Fan's *Inn of the Mysterious Sages*.

CHAPTER FOUR

CHAN DOCTRINE AND PRACTICE OF
THE HONGZHOU SCHOOL

As discussed in chapter two, Mazu's ability and commitment as a Buddhist teacher allowed him to attract the largest number of promising young students of Chan Buddhism during the period. After Mazu passed away, those talented disciples began to strive for the orthodoxy of their lineage and finally made it a fully fledged and dominant school of the Chan movement. The rough road of those disciples toward orthodoxy will be described in chapter five, and this chapter focuses on an analysis of the Chan doctrine and practice of the Hongzhou school based on the reliably datable discourses and texts of Mazu and his immediate disciples identified in chapter three.

Like early Chan, the doctrinal foundation of the Hongzhou school was mainly a mixture of the tathāgata-garbha thought and prajñāpāramitā theory, with a salient emphasis on the kataphasis of the former. Mazu was well versed in Buddhist scriptures. In the six sermons and four dialogues that are original or relatively datable, he cited more than fifteen sūtras and śāstras thirty-five times.[1] He followed the early Chan tradition to claim Bodhidharma's transmission of the *Laṅkāvatāra-sūtra*. He used mainly this sūtra and the *Awakening of Faith*,[2] as well as other tathāgata-garbha texts such as the *Śrīmālā Sūtra*, the *Ratnagotravibhāga*, and even the *Vajrasamādhi*,[3] to construct the doctrinal framework of the Hongzhou lineage and introduce some new themes and practices into the Chan movement. These new themes and practices marked a new phase of Chan development—middle Chan or the beginning of "classical" Chan.

"ORDINARY MIND IS THE WAY"

Earlier studies define the proposition "this mind is the Buddha" (*jixin shi fo*) as the core of Mazu's teaching.[4] Nevertheless, in his *Tō Godai zenshūshi*, Suzuki Tetsuo collects plentiful examples of the use of this proposition to show that it antedated Mazu's teaching.[5] Among these sources, however, the authenticity of some is problematic, such as the works attributed to Baozhi (ca. 418–514) and Fu Xi (497–569),[6] and the encounter dialogues recorded in the *ZTJ*, *ZJL*, and *CDL*, which involve the second patriarch Huike (487–593), Huineng (638–713), Sikong Benjing, Qingyuan Xingsi (d. 740), Nanyue Huairang (677–744), Niutou Huizhong (683–769), and Shitou Xiqian. Others are more reliable, including the *Rudao anxin yao fangbian famen* (Fundamental Expedient Teachings for Entering the Way and Pacifying the Mind) attributed to the fourth patriarch Daoxin and included in the *Lengqie shizi ji* (Record of Masters and Disciples of the *Laṅkāvatāra*), Heze Shenhui's (684–758) discourse preserved in the Dunhuang manuscripts, Nanyang Huizhong's *Extended Discourses* in *Juan* 28 of the *CDL*, and the decree attributed to Emperor Gaozong (r. 649–683) in the *Caoxi dashi [bie]zhuan* ([Separate] Biography of the Great Master of Caoxi;[7] though the attribution is not believable, the text was compiled in 781 and was probably a creation of the Heze line).[8] However, the expression "this mind is the Buddha" in the *Fundamental Expedient Teachings* is a citation from the *Sukhāvatīvyūha-sūtra (Guan Wuliangshoufo jing)*, which means that, by commemoration of the Buddha, the mind and the Buddha become identical.[9] This was somewhat different from the later idea of "this mind is the Buddha." Nanyang Huizhong was an older contemporary of Mazu, and it is not clear whether his use of this expression antedated Mazu's. Thus, Shenhui is the only one who can be determined to have used this expression earlier than Mazu. However, it appears only once in Shenhui's discourses, in which "this mind" refers to the pure, tranquil Buddha-nature inherent in all sentient beings, and it does not become a major theme in his theoretical framework.[10]

This proposition appears frequently in the reliably datable discourses of Mazu and his disciples, and, more important, "this mind" was changed to the ordinary, empirical human mind. Hence, it can still be regarded as a hallmark and new theme of the Hongzhou school. Mazu and his disciples sometimes used another proposition, "Ordinary mind is the Way," to express their new idea more clearly. As Mazu preached to the assembly:

> If you want to know the Way directly, then ordinary mind is the Way. What is an ordinary mind? It means no intentional creation and action, no right or wrong, no grasping or rejecting, no terminable or permanent, no profane or holy. The sūtra says, "Neither the practice of ordinary men, nor the practice of sages—that is the practice of the Bodhisattva." Now all these are just the Way: walking, abiding, sitting, lying, responding to situations, and dealing with things.[11]

The term "Way" designates both the Buddhist path and enlightenment. Ordinary mind is enlightenment itself, which means intellectual noncommitment to any oppositional thinking and discrimination, and also all the spontaneous activities of daily life. Moreover, when Fenzhou Wuye first visited Mazu and said that he could not understand the meaning of "this mind is the

Buddha," Mazu replied, "This very mind that doesn't understand is it, without any other thing."[12] The mind that does not understand is the mind of ignorance and delusion. Mazu directly identified it with the Buddha or Buddha-nature. Mazu further preached: "Self-nature is originally perfectly complete. If only one is not hindered by either good or evil things, he is called a man who cultivates the Way. Grasping good and rejecting evil, contemplating emptiness and entering concentration—all these belong to intentional action. If one seeks further outside, he strays farther away."[13] "Self-nature" or "ordinary mind" is perfect within its original state, and it is unnecessary to grasp good or reject evil intentionally. Mazu's "ordinary mind" represents the complete, empirical human mind of good and evil, purity and defilement, enlightenment and ignorance of ordinary people.[14] This interpretation is in accordance with Zongmi's (780–841) description of the Hongzhou doctrine: "The total essences of greed, hatred, and delusion, the performance of good and evil actions, and the corresponding retribution of happiness or suffering of bitterness are all Buddha-nature."[15]

As Buddhist doctrine in general regards ignorance as the root of all sufferings and rejects the three poisons—greed, hatred, and delusion—and other unwholesome activities, Mazu's unconditional identification of the complete, empirical human mind of good and evil, purity and defilement, enlightenment and ignorance with absolute Buddha-nature immediately provoked strong criticisms from more conservative quarters within the Chan movement. Nanyang Huizhong was the first to launch an attack. He criticized that "the south[ern doctrine] wrongly taught deluded mind as true mind, taking thief as son, and regarding mundane wisdom as Buddha wisdom."[16] Scholars in general agree that the target of this criticism was Mazu's teaching.[17] Huizhong himself advocated "this mind is the Buddha," but he could not tolerate that Mazu included deluded mind in "this mind," because he thought it betrayed and confused the basic teachings of Buddhism.

Zongmi's criticism followed shortly. He fiercely condemned the Hongzhou thought as representing the most serious challenge not only to the Huineng-Heze line but also to the whole Buddhist tradition:

> Now, the Hongzhou school says that greed, hatred, precepts (śīla), and concentration (samādhi) are of the same kind, which is the function of Buddha-nature. They fail to distinguish between ignorance and enlightenment, the inverted and the upright. . . . The Hongzhou school always says that since greed, hatred, compassion, and good are all Buddha-nature, there could not be any difference between them. This is like someone who only observes the wet nature [of water] as never changing, but fails to comprehend that, since water can both carry a boat or sink it, its merits and faults are remarkably different.[18]

Zongmi attacked the Hongzhou doctrine for equating greed and hatred with compassion and good, taking ignorance as enlightenment, and inverting right and wrong. The metaphor of water-nature implies a warning that the Hongzhou doctrine might sink the ship of Buddhism.

The critical stance of both Huizhong and Zongmi was basically ethical: what worried them was the possible tendency toward antinomianism caused by Mazu's "ordinary mind." However, they failed to see that Mazu did not intend to advocate deluded mind. He simply wanted to recognize the insepa-rable relationship of enlightenment and ignorance, purity and defilement in the ordinary human mind, which was not an iconoclastic innovation but drew out one of the ramifications of the ambiguous tathāgata-garbha theory and made explicit what was implicit in it.

In his sermons, Mazu clearly declared that what Bodhidharma and he transmitted was the "dharma of one-mind (yixin)" that was based on the Laṅkāvatāra-sūtra.[19] The dharma of one-mind refers to the tathāgata-garbha theory.[20] In the Sanskrit term tathāgata-garbha, "garbha" means both "embryo" and "womb," and the meaning of the term tathāgata-garbha varies depending on the context. It implies first that every sentient being possesses the germ or cause—the embryo of Tathāgata—to attain Buddhahood. In other contexts, it is also explained as the essence or effect of Buddhahood, and therefore becomes synonymous with Buddha-nature, bodhi, dharmakāya, Thusness (Zhenru), and so forth.[21] Like the masters of early Chan, Mazu preferred the second implication and recognized the inherent essence/Buddha-nature as "one's own original mind" (zijia benxin), "one's own original nature" (zijia benxing),[22] "one's own treasure" (zijia baozang),[23] or "maṇi pearl."[24]

The term tathāgata-garbha refers further to the sentient beings that possess the germ or essence of Buddhahood, as the Tathāgatagarbha-sūtra defines it thus: "All sentient beings are tathāgata-garbha"; or as the Chinese rendering "rulaizang" expresses it: "The storehouse which stores Tathāgata." It also indi-cates the existing state of all sentient beings: Buddha-nature is enwombed/ stored within defiled sentient existence, so that even its owners are not aware of it.[25] In order to explain the defiled aspect of the tathāgata-garbha, the Laṅkāvatāra-sūtra equates tathāgata-garbha with ālayavijñāna,[26] the storehouse consciousness that stores the seeds of both purity and defilement. Hence, tathāgata-garbha is described as the source of all pure and impure dharmas: "The tathāgata-garbha is the cause for both the wholesome and the unwhole-some; therefore, it can serve as the cause for birth and death in the six destinies."[27]

This complicated paradox of tathāgata-garbha that is at once immanently pure and yet appears to be defiled is explained by the famous "two aspects of one-mind" in the Awakening of Faith. The first aspect is the mind as Thusness (xin Zhenru) that neither is born nor dies, and the second aspect is the mind subject to birth and death (xin shengmie), which is the ordinary realm that is subject to continual life and death. Since the relationship of these two aspects of one-mind is "neither one nor different," their difference is a matter of per-ception. The sentient beings, in their delusion, perceive the tathāgata-garbha/ mind as being defiled. When they see it from the perspective of ultimate truth, they then realize that it is originally pure and perfect, none other than the dharmakāya.[28]

Mazu's unconditional identification of Buddha-nature/one-mind with the ordinary, empirical mind was grounded in this idea. Mazu preached:

> There are the aspect of the mind subject to birth and death and the aspect of the mind as Thusness. The mind as Thusness is like a clear mirror which reflects images. The mirror symbolizes the mind, and the images symbolize various dharmas. If the mind grasps various dharmas, it gets involved in external causes and conditions and is therefore subject to birth and death. If the mind does not grasp various dharmas, it is as Thusness. . . . The nature is without differentiation, but its functions are different. In ignorance it functions as [the storehouse] consciousness; in awakening it functions as [Buddhist] wisdom. To follow the absolute is enlightenment; to follow the phenomenal is ignorance. When ignorant, it is the ignorance of one's own original mind; when awakened, it is the awakening of one's own original nature.[29]

Mazu used the relationship between mirror and image as a metaphor to explain the two kinds of perceptions. The mind perceives things, just as a mirror reflects images. If the mind perceives things from a conventional perspective and intends to grasp them, it is in accord with conditions and causes, and therefore subject to birth and death, and functions as the storehouse consciousness—the ālayavijñāna. If the mind perceives things from the perspective of enlightenment and does not become attached to them, it does not accord with conditions and causes, and therefore is as Thusness and functions as Buddhist wisdom. In other words, when perceiving from the viewpoint of the absolute, the mind is enlightenment; when perceiving from the viewpoint of the phenomenal, the mind is ignorance. Therefore, "when ignorant, it is the ignorance of one's own original mind; when awakened, it is the awakening of one's own original nature." The mind remains the same forever; what needs to be transformed is not the mind itself, but the way that one perceives his own mind and the external phenomena.[30] When Mazu told Fenzhou Wuye that his mind of ignorance was Buddha-nature, he further explained, "When people do not understand, they are ignorant; when they understand, they are awakened. Being ignorant, they are sentient beings; being awakened, they are the Buddha." Wuye was awakened by these words and replied that he knew then "the true form of dharmakāya" was inherently complete in his mind.[31] Tianhuang Daowu also said, "Defilement and purity stay together, as water and wave share the same substance."[32] Tianhuang used the famous metaphor of water and waves in the Laṅkāvatāra and Awakening of Faith to explain the inseparable relationship between the pure, tranquil mind and the defiled, empirical mind. The Laṅkāvatāra says: "They are neither different, not nondifferent; the relation is like that between the ocean and its waves. So are the seven vijñānas (consciousnesses) joined with the citta (mind)."[33] The *Awakening of Faith* says, "Since the appearances of ignorance are not separate from the nature of enlightenment, they can neither be destroyed nor not be destroyed. It is like the water of a vast ocean: when it is stirred into waves by the wind, the motion of the water and the activity of the wind are not separate from one another."[34] Although there is a slight difference in the use of the metaphor between the two texts,[35] both emphasize that when the water of Thusness is stirred, the waves of discrimination arise, but the waves are not different in substance from the water.

In addition, Mazu and his disciples elucidated another major idea of the tathāgata-garbha theory, the eternality of tathāgata-garbha/dharmakāya. The *Śrīmālā Sūtra* and other tathāgata-garbha texts, including the *Awakening of Faith*, attribute some positive qualities to the tathāgata-garbha in its true aspect as the dharmakāya, among which are the famous four perfections of eternality, bliss, self, and purity.[36] Along with his identification of Buddha-nature with the ordinary mind, Mazu further endowed "this mind" with the perfection of eternality:

> This mind is as long-lived as space. Even though you transmigrate to multiple forms in the six destinies of transmigration, this mind never has birth and death. . . . The body of four elements currently has birth and death, but the nature of the numinous mind actually has no birth and death. Now you realize this nature, which is called longevity, and also called the longevity-measure of the Tathāgata and the motionless nature of fundamental emptiness.[37]

Mazu's disciples Dazhu Huihai, Fenzhou Wuye, and Yangqi Zhenshu also talked about the eternality of the mind.[38] A wandering Chan practitioner told Nanyang Huizhong that the Hongzhou masters taught that "the body has birth and death, but the mind-nature has never had birth or death throughout beginningless time. When a body is born or dies, it is like a dragon transforming its bones, a snake sloughing off its skin, or a man leaving his old house." Huizhong fiercely criticized that this teaching was the same as the immutable holy-soul advocated by the heretic Hindu Śrenika (*Xianni waidao*) or Brahminism.[39] Although the wanderer seems to have exaggerated the Hongzhou teaching, he conveyed Mazu's idea about the ontological, immutable aspect of ordinary mind/Buddha-nature, which was a development of the traditional Indian tathāgata-garbha theory, not the holy-soul of Hindu beliefs as Huizhong criticized. On the other hand, however, Huizhong's criticism was somewhat reasonable, as the assertion of the four perfections in the tathāgata-garbha theory has indeed caused some scholars to question whether this theory might involve a form of Hindu monism, in which case it might contradict fundamental Buddhist doctrines such as impermanence, no-self, suffering, and causality.[40]

ORIGINAL ENLIGHTENMENT AND NO-CULTIVATION

Corresponding to his identification of ordinary mind with Buddha-nature, Mazu advocated original or immanent enlightenment, a concept illustrated in the *Awakening of Faith*. Mazu preached:

> [The mind] originally existed and exists at present. It does not depend on the cultivation of the Way and seated meditation. Neither cultivation nor seated meditation—this is the pure Chan of Tathāgata.[41]

> This mind originally existed and exists at present, without depending on intentional creation and action; it was originally pure and is pure at present, without waiting for cleaning and wiping. Self-nature attains nirvāṇa; self-nature is pure; self-nature is liberation; and self-nature departs [from delusions].[42]

Although Mazu did not actually use the term "original enlightenment," the frequently used phrases "originally existed and exists at present" *(benyou jinyou)* and "originally pure and is pure at present" *(benjing jinjing)* clearly convey this idea. In the *Awakening of Faith*, the term "original enlightenment" is related to two other terms—"non-enlightenment" *(bujue)* and "actualized enlightenment" *(shijue)*, and the three together form a cycle of religious practice. All sentient beings innately possess original enlightenment; however, they do not realize this identity and entertain delusions ("non-enlightenment"). Through religious practices such as meditation they realize that deluded thoughts have no real status and therefore achieve "actualized enlightenment," which does not acquire any new elements but simply leads back to "original enlightenment."[43] Mazu's "originally existed and exists at present" simplifies this cycle and highlights only "original enlightenment." If the process of actualization is a cycle that presupposes its beginning and reaches its beginning only at its end, and if enlightenment is a matter of perception, one can simply stand at the beginning and perceive from this point of "original enlightenment." Then one will find that enlightenment "originally existed and exists at present" without depending on any religious practice. In this regard, Mazu can be seen as a forerunner of the "original enlightenment" doctrine of medieval Japanese Buddhism, even though he did not actually use this term. The imagery series of "original mind" *(benxin)*, "original nature" *(benxing)*, "original man" *(benlai-ren)*, and "original visage" *(benlai mianmu)*, which frequently appeared in later Chan discourses, were all used to illustrate this core doctrine (see later discussion on Chan imagery).

Furthermore, under Mazu's advocacy of original enlightenment, the gradual/sudden paradigm of Chan awakening became meaningless. Mazu said: "It is in contrast to ignorance that one speaks of awakening. Since intrinsically there is no ignorance, awakening also need not be established."[44] Zongmi indicated that though the Hongzhou school was close to the gate of sudden awakening, it totally "betrayed the gate of gradual cultivation."[45] However, Mazu ultimately denied any kind of awakening. Awakening presupposes a discrimination of enlightenment and ignorance; since the ordinary, complete mind is Buddha-nature and originally lacks any discrimination, awakening is nowhere to be found, no matter whether it is sudden or gradual.

Grounded on the notion of original enlightenment, Mazu inevitably "betrayed the gate of gradual cultivation" and argued that "the Way needs no cultivation."[46] Zongmi summarized the Hongzhou teaching of no-cultivation as follows:

> Since the principles of awakening are all spontaneous and natural, the principles of cultivation should accord with them. One should neither arouse his intention to excise evil, nor arouse his intention to cultivate the Way. The Way is the mind; one cannot use the mind to cultivate the mind. Evil too is the mind; one cannot use the mind to excise the mind. One who neither excises evil nor cultivates good, but freely follows his destiny and is spontaneous in all situations, is called a liberated man. There is no dharma which can bind, no Buddha which can be attained. The mind is like space which is neither increasing nor decreasing. How can we presume to supplement it? Why is this? There is not one dharma which can be found outside the mind-nature; hence, cultivation means simply to let the mind be free.[47]

The spontaneous state of human mind is the Way or the state of enlightenment. Chan practice involves nothing more than keeping the mind in a complete state and releasing it from all artificially imposed restraints, free to act naturally and spontaneously. As a result, the various forms of religious practice of early Chan, such as *nianfo*,[48] seated meditation, "pacifying the mind" (*anxin*), "maintaining the mind" (*shouxin*), "cultivating the mind" (*xiuxin*), and "contemplating the mind" (*guanxin*),[49] were no longer advocated. The story of Mazu's first meeting with his master, which was created by Mazu's disciple(s) in the *Baolin zhuan*,[50] strongly rejected seated meditation.[51] As Bernard Faure insightfully indicates, the disappearance of one-practice samādhi (*yixing sanmei*) was an indicator of the "epistemological split" that opened between early Chan and "classical" Chan.[52] According to two Korean stele inscriptions, the Silla monk Toūi (d. 825), who was Xitang Zhizang's disciple, brought back to Korea the Hongzhou doctrine of "following one's destiny freely and acting nothing" and "no-cultivation and no-certification," which was strongly rejected by the scholastic schools of early Korean Buddhism.[53]

Mazu's "no-cultivation" was supported by the tathāgata-garbha notion of "non-origination." Mazu preached: "If you understand the mind and the phenomenal appearance, deluded thought will not originate. If deluded thought does not originate, this is the acceptance of the non-production of dharmas."[54] Although Mazu did not indicate its scriptural provenance, this passage virtually combines two citations from the *Laṅkāvatāra-sūtra*, which state, "If you understand the mind and the phenomenal appearance, deluded thought will not originate";[55] "Departing from the deluded thought of discrimination in one's mind, one will attain the acceptance of the non-production [of dharmas]."[56] It is an important notion in the tathāgata-garbha texts that nirvāṇa should be understood as non-origination, rather than the extinction, of suffering and deluded thought. Suffering is the deluded product of mental activity. When one ceases to originate deluded thought of duality and discrimination, one ceases suffering. Hence, non-origination is the practice of indiscriminative wisdom, a practice that is not simply the means to liberation but also liberation itself. Since all sentient beings possess the tathāgata-garbha/ dharmakāya, they have the capacity to practice this wisdom.[57] Mazu clearly illustrated this idea in his sermon:

> Self-nature is originally perfect and complete. If only does one not get hindered by either good or evil things, he is called a man who cultivates the Way. . . . Just put an end to all mental calculations of the triple world. If one originates a single deluded thought, this is the root of birth and death in the triple world. If one simply lacks a single thought, then he excises the root of birth and death and obtains the supreme treasure of the dharma-king.[58]

The mind is originally perfect and complete, and cultivation involves nothing more than practicing indiscriminative wisdom and not originating deluded thought of duality and discrimination.

It should be noted that Mazu's "non-origination of deluded thought" was different from the "no-thought" (*wunian*) advocated by Shenhui and other early Chan masters. Shenhui's no-thought was based on the apophasis of Mādhyamaka theory, which emphasizes that deluded thought is intrinsically empty,[59] whereas Mazu's non-origination of deluded thought was based on the more kataphatic mode of tathāgata-garbha doctrine, which emphasizes the inherent capacity of non-origination of the mind.[60] By stressing this notion of tathāgata-garbha doctrine, Mazu sharply criticized Shenhui's equivalence of concentration and wisdom as an attachment to emptiness, "sinking into emptiness and clinging to quiescence, without seeing Buddha-nature," because "contemplating emptiness and entering concentration" belong to "intentional creation and action." Mazu denounced this kind of practice as that of the Śrāvaka (the Hearer) who does not know that the mind fundamentally has no differentiation of position, cause, fruition, or stage, and "abides in the samādhi of emptiness" to pass through numerous kalpas; "although he is awakened, his awakening is ignorant."[61]

"BUDDHA-NATURE MANIFESTS IN FUNCTION"

The core issues central to Chan Buddhism, as well as other schools of Sinitic Buddhism, are: (1) how it is possible for an ordinary individual to attain Buddhahood/enlightenment; (2) how enlightenment is attained; (3) how the ultimate realm of enlightenment manifests itself. As with his answers to the first two issues, Mazu again relied on the tathāgata-garbha theory to put forward his resolution on the third—"Buddha-nature manifests in function," or in other words, "function is identical with Buddha-nature."

Yanagida indicates that "the Buddhist standpoint of Linji is its absolute recognition of the fundamental value of the human being."[62] However, this recognition was initiated by Mazu, and Linji Yixuan was simply one of his most devoted followers. While identifying absolute Buddha-nature with the ordinary human mind, Mazu confirmed that the entirety of daily life was of ultimate truth and value.

> Since limitless kalpas, all sentient beings have never left the samādhi of dharma-nature, and they have always abided in the samādhi of dharma-nature. Wearing clothes, eating food, talking and responding, making use of the six senses—all these activities are dharma-nature.[63]

> If you now understand this reality, you will truly not create any karma. Following your destiny, passing your life, with one cloak or one robe, wherever sitting or standing, it is always with you.[64]

When a Vinaya master asked Dazhu Huihai how he cultivated the Way, Huihai answered, "When I feel hungry, I eat food; when I am tired, I sleep."[65] These words later became a remarkable slogan of the Hongzhou school. Zongmi also summarized the Hongzhou doctrine as "whatever one has contact with is the Way, and one should let the mind be free," and further described it as follows: "The idea of the Hongzhou school is that the arising of mental activity, the movement of thought, snapping fingers, or twinkling eyes, all actions and activities are the functions of the entire essence of Buddha-nature."[66] Daily activities of ordinary life, even those as seemingly trivial as the slightest movements of the eye or finger, are equated with the ultimate reality of dharma-nature. The ultimate realm of enlightenment manifests itself everywhere in human life, and Buddha-nature functions in every aspect of daily experiences. Ordinary people are liberated from their former karma in limitless kalpas; they spontaneously practice Chan in daily life and attain personal and spiritual freedom. Indeed, from early Chan's "pacifying the mind," "maintaining the mind," "cultivating the mind," or "contemplating the mind" to Hongzhou school's "letting the mind be free," a great change had undoubtedly happened. This is the true liberation of humanity in the development of Sinitic Buddhism, as Yanagida indicates: "After Mazu, the characteristics of Chan demonstrate the strong significance of life; it is a religion of humanity born in the vast expanse of the Chinese land."[67]

In order to verify this new view of the ultimate realm of enlightenment, Mazu applied the paradigms of absolute/phenomena and essence/function to lay an ontological foundation for it:

> The absolute (*li*) and the phenomenal (*shi*) are without difference; both are wonderful functions. All are because of the revolving of the mind, and there is no other principle. For example, though there are many reflections of the moon, the real moon is not manifold. Though there are many springs of water, the nature of water is not manifold. Though there are myriad phenomenal appearances in the universe, empty space is not manifold. Though there are many principles being spoken of, the unobstructed wisdom is not manifold. Whatever is established comes from the one-mind. One can construct it or sweep it away; either way is a wonderful function, and the wonderful function is oneself. It is not that there is a place to stand where one leaves the truth, but the very place where one stands is the truth. This is the essence of oneself. If it is not so, then who is one? All dharmas are Buddha-dharma, and all dharmas are liberation. Liberation is Thusness, and all dharmas never leave Thusness. Walking, abiding, sitting, and lying—all these are inconceivable functions, which do not wait for a timely season.[68]

Mazu first identified the phenomenal with the absolute. Their relationship is that of many and one, which is inseparable and unobstructed, many being one, and one being many. The absolute is manifested in each of the manifold phenomena, and each of the manifold phenomena possesses the value of the absolute. Mazu then assimilated this paradigm to the essence/function paradigm and identified function with essence in the same way. Finally, he attributed the essence to one-mind/Buddha-nature to affirm that all functions are of true value and liberation themselves. Since everything that occurs to the individual is a manifestation of the functioning of his intrinsic Buddha-nature, the daily life he experiences is identical to the ultimate experience of Buddhist enlightenment and liberation. In other places, Mazu further used the maṇi pearl as a metaphor. The maṇi pearl changes according to the colors it touches. When it touches the color blue, it becomes blue; when it touches the color yellow, it becomes yellow, though its essence lacks coloration. Hence, "seeing, listening, sensing, and knowing are inherently your original nature, which is also called original mind. There is no Buddha other than the mind."[69] In Bodhidharma's entry in the *CDL*, which must have been copied from the *Baolin zhuan*,[70] there is a dialogue between Boluoti, who is said to have been awakened by Bodhidharma, and an Indian king. The king asked, "Where is [Buddha-]nature?" Boluoti replied, "[Buddha-]nature manifests in function" (*xing zai zuoyong*).[71] As Buswell insightfully points out, here lies the conceptual divide between early and "classical" Chan: instead of contemplating and seeing the internal essence of the true mind, Mazu stressed that it is through the external functioning of the mind that its essence is seen.[72]

Although the application of the paradigms of absolute/phenomena and essence/function is a universal formulation of Chinese philosophy, Mazu seems to have been influenced directly by the Huayan theory of nature-origination from the Tathāgata. The Huayan master Fazang (643–712) held that all mundane and supermundane dharmas are the manifestations of Buddha-nature—the pure, perfect absolute (*li*), and all living beings can realize bodhi because of its origination.[73] How can the pure, perfect essence or absolute give rise to the impure, imperfect mundane dharmas? This paradox is resolved by the theory of the unobstructed interrelation of the absolute and the phenomenal. Following the essence/function paradigm of the two aspects of one-mind in the *Awakening of Faith*, Fazang further identified the absolute with the mind as Thusness and the phenomenal with the mind subject to birth and death. Since the interrelation of the absolute and the phenomenal is unobstructed and harmonious, the immutable Thusness can give rise to dharmas of birth and death when responding to conditions, as the absolute is manifested in the phenomenal. The dharmas of birth and death arising from response to conditions are, after all, without self-nature; hence, they are identical with Thusness, as the phenomenal is identical with the absolute.[74] Mazu used these paradigms of absolute/phenomena and essence/function to support his idea that "function is identical with [Buddha-]nature." As he said, "The absolute and the phenomenal are without difference, all of which are wonderful functions. All occur because of the revolving of the mind, and there is no other reality." On the other hand, while their theoretical frameworks are the same, the target and content of the Huayan nature-origination and Mazu's idea that function is identical with Buddha-nature are nevertheless different. In the Huayan theory, the pure Buddha-nature remains forever untainted, even though it gives rise to defiled phenomena and originates the realization of all sentient beings' enlightenment. In Mazu's doctrine, the spontaneous, ordinary state of human mind and life, which is a mix of purity and defilement, is identical with Buddha-nature.

Critics of the Hongzhou school did not overlook this new view of ultimate experience. Nanyang Huizhong was again the first to criticize it. He argued the necessity of differentiating the psychophysical functions from Buddha-nature: "If one practices seeing, listening, sensing, and knowing, then these are seeing, listening, sensing, and knowing, not seeking the Dharma."[75] Later, Zongmi further attacked Mazu on the basis of the essence/function paradigm. He picked up the metaphor of the maṇi pearl used by Mazu. The nature of the pearl is intrinsically perfect and luminous, but when it comes into contact with external objects, it reflects different forms and colors. When it reflects the color black or other colors, its entire surface appears black or as other colors. The Hongzhou school would assert that this very blackness, or blueness, or yellowness, was the pearl, and did not recognize that those colors were all delusory and empty. Zongmi countered that the Hongzhou school collapsed essence into function and did not realize the difference between them, and therefore they did not really see the essence of the true mind. The fact that they defined all activities of daily life, whether good or evil, as Buddha-nature represented a dangerous antinomianism. He further introduced a critical distinction between two levels of function, the intrinsic function of self-nature (*zixing benyong*) and the responsive function in accord with conditions (*suiyuan yingyong*), and related them to the teachings of the Heze and the Hongzhou schools, respectively.[76] Zongmi acutely perceived that in the essence/function theory of the Heze school, as well as of the Huayan school, the essence/Buddha-nature remains forever pure, whereas in the Hongzhou teaching, both the pure and impure mind and life of ordinary man are identical with Buddha-nature and enlightenment. Thus, what worried him most was not the ontological problem but its ethical tendency. Although Zongmi was biased against the Hongzhou school, his criticism was not entirely overreaction. Mazu did not intend to advocate an antinomianism but wanted to recognize the value of ordinary human life; however, his unconditional identification of Buddha-nature with ordinary human mind had actually caused certain confusion among Chan students. During the late Tang, questions such as whether the mind transmitted by the patriarchs was the mind of Thusness or the deluded mind were raised, and Huangbo Xiyun, Mazu's second-generation disciple, had to put forward a new proposition that "no-mind is the Way" to complement Mazu's "ordinary mind is the Way." These issues will be discussed in detail in chapter six.

NEW PRACTICE OF ENCOUNTER DIALOGUE AND NEW TERMINOLOGY AND IMAGERY

In early Chan, religious practice focused on various forms of meditation, such as *nianfo*, seated meditation, "pacifying the mind," "maintaining the mind," "cultivating the mind," "contemplating the mind," and "seeing the nature." Theoretically, Mazu and his disciples advocated spontaneous, original enlightenment and rejected all forms of meditation and cultivation. Their successors in the late Tang and Five Dynasties further described them as iconoclasts who abandoned scriptural recitation, worship of images, and so forth. These declarations and exaggerations, however, should not be taken at face value. Liturgically and practically, it is doubtful that the daily practices of traditional monastic life did not continue in Chan communities. For example, Mazu's sermons are full of citations from scriptures. His disciple Yanguan Qi'an preached once in every five days and always "cited scriptures to certify the mind."[77] Yaoshan Weiyan also preached Buddhist scriptures daily.[78] Guishan Lingyou, Mazu's second-generation disciple, advised his followers to read scriptures.[79] Dongshan Liangjie, Mazu's third-generation disciple, compiled a text titled *Dasheng jingyao* (Essentials of Mahāyāna Scriptures).[80] Li Fan, Mazu's lay disciple, emphasized the immobility of mind and body and "entering the quiescence of listening and meditation";[81] and Baizhang was said to advise his disciples on keeping the mind indifferent, like wood or stone;[82] these conditions were actually a kind of samādhi.[83]

As previously discussed, Mazu confirmed daily activities as the functioning of Buddha-nature and advocated non-origination as the practice of indiscriminative wisdom. In addition, Mazu and his disciples actually performed a new kind of religious practice—encounter dialogue. In chapter three, we have seen there were antecedents of encounter dialogue in the early Chan phase, and during the mid-Tang period when Mazu, Shitou, Jingshan, and their immediate disciples were active, formal encounter dialogue emerged in two forms, the first involving witty, paradoxical phrases, and the second fictionalized accounts of enlightenment dialogues. Then, during the late Tang and Five Dynasties, encounter dialogue achieved full maturity with multiple forms, including iconoclastic, illogical, nonconceptual phrases and physical actions such as beating and shouting.

It is not by chance that formal encounter dialogue emerged and matured during the period from the mid-eighth to the mid-tenth centuries. First, Mazu's advocacy of ordinary mind and original enlightenment provided the doctrinal framework for the emergence and maturity of encounter dialogue. Since enlightenment involves nothing more than changing one's perception, what one needs to do is simply to be inspired to relinquish his misperception that he is ignorant and acquire the right perspective to discover his own luminous mind and original enlightenment. This is the basic reason why momentary, situational evocation or inspiration becomes the salient feature of encounter dialogue. Second, the *Baolin zhuan*, which was created by Mazu's first-generation disciple(s), describes an unbroken genealogy of special transmission from the Buddha to Mazu. This transmission was fabricated for the polemical, pedagogical claim of the superiority of the Chan over other scholastic traditions and the Hongzhou lineage over other Chan branches. Nevertheless, Huangbo Xiyun and other second-generation disciples of Mazu interpreted this genealogy as a mind-to-mind transmission that was separated from scriptural teachings and also as a major doctrine and an actual practice of the Chan school.[84] This interpretation later became a theoretical underpinning for the iconoclastic, radical aspect of encounter dialogue.

As a result, encounter dialogue gradually became an effective means of Chan teaching and practice. Unlike the personal meditation and cultivation of early Chan, the encounter-dialogue practice was a spiritual exchange and mental contest, which happened not only between master and student, but also master and master or student and student. It was not used for cultivating one's mind-nature, but for inspiring, activating, revealing, and even competing for immanent enlightenment and wisdom. Based on the Hongzhou doctrine, encounter dialogue soon became an important and dynamic religious practice of middle Chan and even identified with Chan itself. Some scholars have assumed that encounter dialogue distinguishes the "classical" Chan of

Mazu from the "pre-classical" Chan of the Northern, Heze, and Niutou schools.[85]

During the time of Mazu and his immediate disciples, although actual practices of encounter dialogue had just emerged in its early form of witty, paradoxical phrases, they virtually produced a new set of Chan terminology along with their new doctrines and practices. Indeed, with some basic knowledge of Chan history one could easily distinguish the discourses and texts of middle Chan from those of early Chan. While many frequently used phrases of early Chan, such as "pacifying the mind," "maintaining the mind," "contemplating the mind," "no-thought," "no-abiding" (wuzhu), and "the equivalence of concentration and wisdom" (dinghui deng) almost completely disappeared, new terms such as "ordinary mind," "one's own original mind" (zijia benxin), "one's own original nature" (zijia benxing), "no-cultivation" (wuxiu), "no-certification" (wuzheng), "freely following one's destiny" (renyun), and "dharma-eye" (fayan) were to pervade all later Chan discourses and texts.[86]

More important, as encounter dialogue grew to maturity, Chan discourse relied more on figurative and poetic language, and finally constructed a large set of images with connotations exclusive to Chan. It is notable that several basic series of Chan images can be traced back to the reliable discourses of Mazu and his immediate disciples.

1. Pearl and treasure. The maṇi pearl used as a metaphor by Mazu, the "Great Pearl" he dubbed Huihai, and "one's own treasure" he used to indicate Huihai's originally enlightened mind, all soon became popular images in encounter dialogues and Chan verses for symbolizing the inherently pure, luminous, invaluable mind of enlightenment. For example, there were four songs about the pearl or mind-pearl attributed to Danxia Tianran in the ZTJ and CDL,[87] one attributed to Shigong Huizang in the ZTJ,[88] one to Shaoshan Huanpu in the CDL,[89] and one to Guannan Daochang in the same text.[90] These attributions may have some problems, but as they were all anthologized in the ZTJ or CDL, we can assume that they were created during the late Tang and Five Dynasties periods.

2. "Original man" (benlairen) and "original visage" (benlai mianmu). These images were derived from Mazu's frequent use of the terms, "one's own original mind" and "one's own original nature," and his emphasis that enlightenment/Buddha-nature "originally existed and exists at present" and that the mind "originally was pure and is pure at present."[91] This imagery series symbolizes the original, spontaneous enlightenment within all beings. In the encounter dialogues recorded in both the ZTJ and CDL, these images appear in great number.[92]

3. Buddha hall and statue. In Fenzhou Wuye's first visit, Mazu used the term "Buddha hall" to refer to Wuye's body and the Buddha statue within the hall to refer to his mind. These images soon became popular in the encounter dialogues of the late Tang and Five Dynasties. For example, Linji Yixuan's

disciple Guanxi Zhixian used the couplet "in the ancient Buddha hall on the mountain of Five Aggregates, the Vairocana Buddha shines with perfect light day and night" to awaken Yungai Huaiyi.[93] "Buddha hall" and "mountain of Five Aggregates" refer to Huaiyi's body, and the Vairocana Buddha to his mind.

4. Daily activities of wearing clothes, eating food, and sleeping. Mazu and Dazhu Huihai first related these daily activities to the function of Buddha-nature and Chan practice, and Linji Yixuan further spread this idea.[94] Later, more ordinary activities were added to this imagery series in encounter dialogues, such as "drinking tea," "washing bowl," "chopping wood and carrying water," and "getting warm by the fire when cold; relaxing in a cool place when hot."

The tathāgata-garbha theory in the Mahāyāna texts is very ambiguous and open to multiple interpretations.[95] Belying the image of an iconoclast depicted by his successors of the late Tang to early Song, Mazu immersed himself in the tathāgata-garbha texts and worked hard to draw out some of the ramifications of the theory to furnish new doctrines and practices for his Hongzhou school. These new doctrines and practices—ordinary mind is the Way, original enlightenment, no-cultivation, Buddha-nature manifests in daily activities, and encounter dialogue—represented a major development from early Chan and constructed a theoretical framework for "classical" Chan that has been regarded as the most Chinese-style Chan. Yet these doctrines and practices remained genuinely Buddhist as they were not revolutionarily iconoclastic innovations, but rather made explicit what was implicit in the tathāgata-garbha texts.[96] Although he disagreed with the Hongzhou doctrine, Zongmi had to acknowledge its scriptural provenance:

> They meant to follow the Laṅkāvatāra-sūtra which reads, "The tathāgata-garbha is the cause of both wholesome and unwholesome actions. It can produce all the [six] destinies and the [four kinds of] birth where the suffering or happiness which is received will be commensurate with the causes which were created." It also reads, "In the Buddha's discourses, the mind is the essence." The sūtra again reads, "There is a Buddha-realm where raising the eyebrows, shifting the eyes, laughing, yawning, coughing, and all other actions are all the activities of the Buddha."[97]

CHAPTER FIVE

ROAD TO ORTHODOXY

In the terminology of traditional Chinese military strategy, the formation of the Hongzhou community in the central-southern region during the early post-rebellion period catered to the three ideal conditions—favorable season (*tianshi*), geographical advantages (*dili*), and support of the people (*renhe*). After the destructive wars of the An Lushan rebellion, which were fought in and around the Chang'an and Loyang region, all the Buddhist scholastic traditions and schools that emerged in the Tang and centered in this region—the Faxiang, the Vinaya (Lü), the Huayan, the Esoteric, and the Northern Chan— were heavily stricken.[1] While those old traditions and schools were at low ebb, the early postwar period was a favorable time for the rise of new lineages and schools. In addition, under the influence of his three leading ministers, Wang Jin (d. 781), Du Hongjian (709–769), and Yuan Zai (d. 777), Emperor Daizong (r. 763–779) became the most devout of all the Tang rulers. His obsession with and support of Buddhism had a baneful influence on officials and people all over the country who increasingly "neglected the affairs of the world to serve the Buddha."[2] Geographically, Hongzhou was the administrative center of Jiangxidao—the rich central-southern region that was of increasing importance to the imperial court because of its economic, agricultural, and population growth. Furthermore, like other provincial governors of the post-rebellion period, the Jiangxi surveillance commissioners, who were Mazu's patrons and devotees, possessed increasingly military, political, and economic power and a certain degree of independence. For example, Bao Fang dared to disobey an imperial order and allowed Mazu to stay in Hongzhou, which was an important protection for the growth of the community.[3] Added to these favorable conditions were the new doctrine and practice that Mazu advocated and his great ability and commitment as a Buddhist teacher, which enabled him to attract almost all of the most promising young students of Chan Buddhism at that period, as well as a large number of lay followers.

Although he earned a great reputation and the community was prosperous during his sixteen-year stay in Hongzhou, Mazu seems to have concentrated on his mission of Buddhist teaching and paid no attention to the sectarian disputers within the Chan movement. Soon after Mazu passed away, however, his immediate disciples began to strive for the orthodoxy of their lineage. This task was carried out mainly by a quadruple strategy: the first was to revise and complete the century-long project of Chan genealogy, describing their lineage as the orthodoxy after the sixth patriarch Huineng; the second was to create some texts and attribute them to previously famous or mythologized monks in order to legitimize and disseminate their doctrinal teachings; the third was to establish their own monasteries and cloisters as institutional bases of development; and the fourth was to expand from Jiangxi to the whole nation and obtain official, imperial recognition and authority. Through the nearly forty-year cooperative effort of these disciples, the Hongzhou lineage arose from a regional community to a national tradition and evolved to become a full-fledged, dominant school of the Chan movement.

BAOLIN ZHUAN: ITS AUTHOR AND TWOFOLD CLAIM OF ORTHODOXY

Due to the excellent studies of Yanagida Seizan and other scholars, the *Baolin zhuan* (Chronicle of the Baolin Monastery) has been generally acknowledged as an important production of the Hongzhou school.[4] However, the author of this text remains an enigma. Traditionally the authorship is attributed to Zhiju.[5] Since there is no other source that mentions this name, Yanagida asserts that it is the pseudonym of a disciple of Mazu.[6] Following Yanagida's study, I further propose that this disciple was Zhangjing Huaihui, and then examine the Chan genealogy presented in the *Baolin zhuan* to reveal the main purpose of its author—a twofold claim of orthodoxy.

In the stele inscription for Huaihui, Quan Deyu tells us: "[Huaihui] wrote a text titled *Fayan shizi zhuan* (Biographies of the Masters and Disciples of the Dharma-eye), in which he truthfully elaborates on the masters from Great Mahākāśyapa on Mt. Cock's Foot to Huineng and Shenxiu."[7] The title of the text is obviously an imitation of the Northern school's *Lengqie shizi ji* (Record of the Masters and Students of the *Laṅkāvatāra-sūtra*) by Jingjue (683–ca. 750). None of the other sources mentions this text. However, it may exist under another title, namely, the *Baolin zhuan*, and there are several factors supporting this hypothesis.

First, the basic structure of the *Baolin zhuan* is as follows:

1. The twenty-eight patriarchs in India, from Mahākāśyapa to Bodhidharma.
2. The six patriarchs in China, from Bodhidharma to Huineng, including an account about Shenxiu.[8]

This is in complete accord with the content of the *Biographies of Masters and Disciples of the Dharma-Eye*, which "elaborates on the masters from Great Mahākāśyapa on Mt. Cock's Foot to Huineng and Shenxiu," as mentioned in Huaihui's stele inscription.

Second, the *Baolin zhuan* records that, before attaining nirvāṇa, Śākyamuni told Mahākāśyapa: "I entrust to you the pure dharma-eye, the marvelous mind of nirvāṇa, and the subtle true dharma, which in its authentic form is formless. You must cherish it."[9] Then, in every generation of the patriarchs, the dharma-eye was transmitted without exception. According to Śākyamuni's speech to Mahākāśyapa, we know that the dharma-eye, the insight able to penetrate all things, implies the formless essence of Buddhist dharma—the Buddha's mind/wisdom/enlightenment. Alhough this term is seen in various sūtras and earlier Chan texts, the *Baolin zhuan* was the first to use it as a kernel term to make up a complete system of "transmitting mind by mind" from masters to disciples.[10] This is in perfect harmony with the title of Huaihui's text, *Biographies of Masters and Disciples of the Dharma-Eye*. Indeed, this title is much more appropriate for the text than *Chronicle of the Baolin Monastery*.

Third, as Yanagida points out, in the *Baolin zhuan* the verses and teachings of the patriarchs and the *Sūtra of Forty-Two Sections* (which is different from other editions) contain the ideas of the Hongzhou school, and in the prophecy of the twenty-seventh patriarch Prajñātāra the orthodoxy of the Huineng-Huairang-Mazu line is acknowledged.[11]

Fourth, Zhiju is possibly Huaihui's *zi* (courtesy name). Huaihui, which means "embracing sunlight," is in semantic accord with the name Zhiju, meaning "torch of wisdom." Many monks had *zi* that accorded semantically with their names, as did secular people. For example, the famous monk-poet Jiaoran, whose name means "clear and bright," had the *zi* Qingzhou, which means "pure daytime."[12]

Fifth, Lingche, a famous monk-poet and the author of the preface to the *Baolin zhuan*,[13] visited Hongzhou during the years 781–786, when Mazu was still alive and Huaihui attended his master there.[14] Both Lingche and Huaihui knew Quan Deyu quite well,[15] so the two must actually have known each other. This increases the probability of the cooperation of Huaihui and Lingche in the creation of the text. In addition to the mind-verses of the patriarchs, the *Sūtra of Forty-two Sections* contained in the *Baolin zhuan* uses many more rhymed phrases than other editions.[16] This also points to the possibility of Huaihui's cooperation with one or more poets.[17]

Sixth, as scholars have noted, the *Shishi tongjian* (comp. 1270) records that the *Baolin zhuan* was completed in the seventeenth year of the Zhenyuan reign-period (801).[18] This date fits well with certain events in Huaihui's life. After Mazu died in 788, he went north to transmit Mazu's teaching. In 808, he was summoned to court.[19] The *Biographies of Masters and Disciples of the Dharma-Eye* or *Baolin zhuan*, compiled around 801, was obviously a preparation for gaining both imperial and social recognition for the orthodoxy of the Hongzhou lineage.

Seventh, Xingshan Weikuan, another major disciple of Mazu who was summoned to court in 809, just one year after Huaihui, also propagated the genealogy of Chan patriarchs in the capital. In Weikuan's account, from Mahākāśyapa to Weikuan, there were fifty-nine generations (fifty-one Indian patriarchs and nine Chinese).[20] Hu Shi asserts that this account followed the genealogy in the *Chu sanzang ji*, and is different from the one narrated in the *Baolin zhuan*.[21] This assertion has not been challenged until recently. Xu Wenming retorts that, in the fifth *juan* of the *Baolin zhuan*, where Li Chang asks Sanzang Qianna how many patriarchs were in India, the latter answers that there were forty-nine—from Mahākāśyapa to Prajñātāra twenty-seven patriarchs of direct line, and from Dharmada, another disciple of the twenty-fourth Patriarch Aryasimha, to his third-generation successors twenty-two patriarchs of collateral branches. Weikuan's account was actually based on this genealogy, except that he added Buddhasena, Bodhidharma's confrere, as the fiftieth patriarch.[22] Xu's explanation seems to be reasonable, as the description of forty-nine Indian patriarchs appears in the *Baolin zhuan* twice.[23] Thus, Weikuan's account of the Indian genealogy was virtually the same as the *Baolin zhuan*.

With those seven facts, we can conclude with certain assurance that the *Biographies of Masters and Disciples of the Dharma-Eye* compiled by Huaihui has not been lost but remains extant under another title *Baolin zhuan*; or, in other words, Huaihui may be the true author of this text.

The construction of a Chan genealogy can be traced back to the end of the seventh century, as seen in Faru's (638–689) biography written in 689.[24] During the eighth century, almost all Chan schools, the Northern, the Heze, the Baotang, the Niutou, and the Hongzhou, participated in the project of creating and perfecting their legendary history in order to establish the identity of their tradition and to progress from marginal to orthodox.[25] Mazu's disciples followed their predecessors in completing the genealogy and used the *Baolin zhuan* to produce an official version that was to be repeated in all the later "transmission of the lamp" histories. Yet this final version differs markedly from previous ones in two features.

The first is the change in what was being transmitted by the patriarchs. In the two Northern-school histories, the *Chuan fabao ji* (Record of the Transmission of Dharma-Treasure) and *Lengqie shizi ji*, the dharma-treasure being transmitted was the *Laṅkāvatāra-sūtra*. The latter even sets Gunabhadra, the first translator of the sūtra, as the first patriarch in China. Shenxiu's epitaph written by Zhang Yue (667–731) also emphasizes his devotion to this sūtra.[26] The Laṅkā tradition, which claimed an unbroken line from Bodhidharma to Shenxiu, has been called into question by many modern scholars,[27] and is still a debatable issue.[28] However, whether this tradition was credible or not, the successors of the Eastern Mountain teaching actually claimed it for two strong reasons: (1) All the Buddhist schools that arose in the Sui and early Tang legitimated their teachings by appealing to a scripture or scriptural corpus. The Chan school would also have done so in order to achieve the aura of legitimacy, especially after Shenxiu and his confreres and disciples entered the capital cities where scriptural studies had been dominant. As Faure indicates, the desire to legitimize Chan practice by scriptural tradition constituted one of the main differences between early and later Chan.[29] (2) In the texts attributed to the Chan patriarchs, from Bodhidharma to Shenxiu, the impact of the tathāgata-garbha theory, one of the major themes of the *Laṅkāvatāra-sūtra*, is obvious and central. As David Chapell points out, there was an "affinity of their spirit and essential teaching" with this sūtra.[30] Then, in the genealogies presented in Shenhui's discourses and the *Platform Sūtra*, the scripture being transmitted became the *Diamond Sūtra*,[31] and in addition to the sūtra were Bodhidharma's robe and even the *Platform Sūtra* itself. The replacement of the *Diamond Sūtra* for the *Laṅkāvatāra-sūtra* signaled Shenhui's polemical rejection of the Northern school. The fabrication of the robe transmission was a claim of orthodoxy since the robe was a symbol of intimacy with and authority of the Indian patriarchs. The *Platform Sūtra* indicates that a copy of the sūtra itself serves as a symbol of transmission.[32] In the Baotang-school history, the *Lidai fabao ji* (Record of the Dharma-Treasure through the Ages), the transmission of the *Diamond Sūtra* is not mentioned, but the robe transmission remains a central concern. The text even fabricates a strange story that Huineng presented the robe to Empress Wu (r. 684–704) upon her request, and the empress in turn bestowed it to Zhishen (609–702), Huineng's confrere and the Sichuan school's first patriarch.[33]

In the *Baolin zhuan*, Bodhidharma's transmission of the *Laṅkāvatāra-sūtra* to Huike remains a legacy of the tradition, but this is mentioned very casually. The robe transmission of Bodhidharma to Huineng is also a legacy, but the text hints in other places that this kind of transmission was used only for particular reasons.[34] What was being transmitted throughout was only the dharma-eye—the penetrating insight/mind/enlightenment of the Buddha and patriarchs,[35] which was expressed by the mind-verses.[36] Since each patriarch composed his own verse to represent his own enlightenment, no authoritative teaching or dharma was actually transmitted. Zhangjing Huaihui said, "For example, the space has formlessness as its form and nonaction as its action. Chan transmission is also like this: it has nontransmission as transmission; therefore, the transmission transmits nothing";[37] "The mind is away from writings."[38] The transmission that "transmits nothing" implies a polemical claim: the Chan movement was a special transmission of the Buddha's mind/enlightenment, a transmission that did not rely on scriptures.[39] Chan doctrine was utterly formless and essentially different from other teachings that were conveyed by the Buddha in the form of written scriptures. The Chan school transmitted the marrow of Buddhism, the Buddha-mind itself, while other schools were devoted to verbal understanding and interpretation.

This implied concept was then openly spelled out by Mazu's second-generation disciples. Muyŏm called the scholastic teachings the "tongued realm" and the Chan (Kor. Sŏn) transmission the "tongueless realm." "Tongueless realm" implies the formless, ineffable essence of the Buddha-mind. He argued that scholastic teachings were expedient means adapted to the capacities of inferior people, whereas the mind transmission of Chan patriarchs was the only true way of enlightenment. In other words, the scholastic teachings were the provisional explanations of truth, while Chan was truth itself.[40] Huangbo Xiyun, another second-generation disciple of Mazu, also interpreted the genealogical transmission of the *Baolin zhuan* as "since the Tathāgata transmitted the Dharma to Mahākāśyapa, [the patriarchs] have certified mind with mind, and all minds are the same."[41] The Chan transmission is the mutual certification of enlightenment, and the minds of the master and student are brought into harmony by each other's enlightenment. In his preface to the *Chuanxin fayao*, Pei Xiu says, "He carried only the seal of the highest vehicle which is apart from writings, and transmitted only the one-mind, without any other dharma."[42] This clearly states that in the Chan school transmission was by mind only, apart from any scriptures or doctrines.[43] According to early Korean sources, Toŭi (d. 825), Xitang Zhizang's Silla disciple, had already used the term "patriarchal Chan" (*zushi chan*);[44] and Pŏmil (810–889), Yanguan Qi'an's Silla disciple, had already used the phrase "special transmission outside the teaching" (*jiaowai biechuan*).[45] If these sources are reliable, these terms and concepts also represent the interpretation of the *Baolin-zhuan* genealogy by Mazu's second-generation disciples.

Paradoxically, when Mazu preached that Bodhidharma transmitted the dharma of one-mind to China, he actually cited scriptures as support: "The great master Bodhidharma came from South India to China to transmit only the Mahāyāna dharma of one-mind. He used the *Laṅkāvatāra-sūtra* to certify the minds of all sentient beings, lest they not believe in that dharma of one-mind. The *Laṅkāvatāra-sūtra* says: . . . ."[46] In Mazu's sermons, Buddhist scriptures were cited from time to time. Therefore, the special mind-transmission implied in the *Baolin zhuan* is more accurate as a polemical claim of the superiority of the Chan school over other scholastic schools than as an account of doctrinal advocacy and actual practice. The polemical stance and fictional account of the *Baolin zhuan* genealogy by Mazu's first-generation disciples were interpreted as major doctrine of the Chan school by Mazu's second-generation disciples. This interpretation was then accepted and practiced by successors of the Hongzhou line in the late Tang and Five Dynasties and became the theoretical framework for the iconoclastic, radical aspect of encounter dialogues.

Another new feature of the Hongzhou genealogy is that although the last *juan* of the *Baolin zhuan* is not extant, according to the prophecies of Prajñātāra and Narendrayaśas about Huairang and Mazu preserved in the *ZTJ* and the recently discovered biographical fragments of Huairang and Mazu from the *Baolin zhuan*,[47] the text emphasized the orthodoxy of the Huineng-Huairang-Mazu lineage within the Chan movement.[48] This claim was also clearly expressed in Weikuan's account of Chan genealogy as he said, "Down from the Fourth Patriarch, though [all successors] have followed the true dharma, there are heirs of legitimate line and descendants of collateral branches, just like the legitimate lineage and collateral branches [of secular families]." Weikuan applied the terminology and pattern of secular kinship to divide the Chan lineages into the legitimate line and collateral branches. Then he described his confreres Xitang Zhizang, Ganquan Zhixian, Baizhang Huaihai, Zhangjing Huaihui, and himself as brothers of the great family of the legitimate lineage from the patriarchs to Mazu Daoyi, and masters of the Niutou, Heze, and Northern as their grand-uncles, uncles, and cousins—that is, relatives of minor families of the collateral branches.[49] Thus, by using secular kinship terminology, Weikuan openly declared the orthodoxy of their lineage. Other disciples of Mazu also made the same claim. For example, both Silla Chan monks Toyun (780–868), who was Nanquan Puyuan's disciple, and Hyŏnuk (787–868), who was Huaihui's disciple, proclaimed that Nanyue Huairang was the "Heir-Apparent" of Huineng.[50] This concept must have come from their masters.

In conclusion, the Hongzhou genealogy presented in the *Baolin zhuan*, which was likely composed by Zhangjing Huaihui, completed the century-long project of Chan genealogy and implied a twofold polemical claim: the first argued that the Chan movement was a "separate transmission outside the teachings," which transmitted the Buddha's mind/enlightenment itself and was therefore superior to the scholastic teachings; the second argued that the Hongzhou school was the orthodox lineage within the Chan movement, and all the other schools and lineages were collateral branches. This twofold polemical claim was interpreted as a doctrinal tenet by Mazu's second-generation disciples, and then practiced by successors of the Hongzhou line during the late Tang and Five Dynasties.

CHAN VERSES ATTRIBUTED TO BAOZHI AND YONGJIA XUANJUE

The *CDL* attributes three series of verses to the Liang monk Baozhi, including ten pieces of "Encomium of Mahāyāna" (*Dasheng zan*), twelve pieces of "Eulogy of the Twelve Time-Periods" (*Shi'ershi song*), and fourteen pieces of "Eulogy of the Fourteen Classes" (*Shisike song*).[51] In addition to these three series, one more poem and six more couplets attributed to Baozhi are found in Zongmi's works, Huangbo Xiyun's discourses, and the *ZJL*.[52] The *CDL* also attributes the "Song of the Realization of the Way" (*Zhengdao ge*) to Yongjia Xuanjue, who was said to be Huineng's disciple. These verses and songs are replete with rhetorical formulations characteristic of Hongzhou style and doctrine, and a careful study reveals that they were probably created by Mazu's immediate disciples.

The earliest sources referring to Baozhi were his epitaph written by Lu Chui (470–526) and his hagiography in the *Gaoseng zhuan*.[53] According to these two texts, Baozhi's secular surname was Zhu, and he was a native of Jincheng (in present-day Jiangsu). He became a novice monk at an early age. At the beginning of the Taishi reign-period (465–472) of the Song, he suddenly began acting miraculously, uttering predictions, and appearing in different places at the same time. He was highly esteemed by Emperor Wu of Liang (r. 502–549). After Baozhi died in 514, more and more legends about him were generated. By the mid-Tang he had become the incarnation of the twelve-faced Avalokitesvara and was widely worshiped.[54]

The *Luoyang qielan ji* records that during the Northen Wei, there was a Master Bao (Bao gong) in the Baimasi who composed the "Song of the Twelve Time-Periods" (Shi'erchen ge).[55] Wang Zhongmin (1903–1975) connects this song with the "Eulogy of the Twelve Time-Periods" attributed to Baozhi in the *CDL*, but he also expresses some doubts about it. In his letters to Wang, Zhou Yiliang (1913–2001) indicates that the verses attributed to Baozhi were late forgeries, as those verses contain Chan ideas of the Tang and afterward; he also doubts that Baozhi and Master Bao were the same person.[56] According to the *Luoyang qielan ji*, *Wei shu*, and *Fayuan zhulin*, Master Bao in the Luoyang was still alive after 514 when Baozhi died;[57] thus, Baozhi and Master Bao were certainly two different people.[58]

Zhou Yiliang insightfully asserts that the three series of verses attributed to Baozhi contain Chan ideas of the Tang and afterward. When examining these verses more closely, we find a host of striking terminological and ideological similarities between them and the Hongzhou texts. Several major Hongzhou ideas appear in these verses. The first is the concept that ordinary psychophysical activities are the function of Buddha-nature, and the complete, ordinary mind of good and evil is Buddha-nature:

> At the *chen* time-period when dinner is ready,
> Ignorance is originally the body of Śākyamuni.
> If you do not know that sitting and lying are the Way,
> You suffer pains and toils at all time.[59]

Second, the Way needs no cultivation and the spontaneous state of the human mind is Buddha-nature:

> Buddha-nature is spontaneous and natural;
> There is no reason for cultivation.[60]

Third, Buddha-nature is ontologically immutable:

> At the *chou* time-period when cocks crow,
> There is a round pearl, bright and eternal.
> Looking internal and external, one cannot find it;
> When it functions in the realm, it is always there.
> No head, no hand, it is immutable even when the world extinguishes.
> Those who do not understand listen to my word—
> Don't speak, it is at present.[61]

Furthermore, Zongmi indicated that the Hongzhou school applied the metaphor of wheat flour and flour products to illustrate their idea that function was identical with Buddha-nature.[62] This metaphor appears once in the *Extended Records of Baizhang*.[63] It also notably appears twice in the verses attributed to Baozhi:

They only want to ask for cakes beside the flat pan,
But do not know to return to the essence to observe flour.
Flour is the essence of good and evil;
It can be made in multiple forms.[64]

The Hearer (Śrāvaka) loathes bustle and seeks tranquility,
Just like discarding flour and asking for cakes.
Cakes are always flour;
It can be made in multiple forms.[65]

According to this analysis, these verses are suffused with ideas, terms, and images of the Hongzhou school, and therefore must have been created by monks of that school.[66] One piece of evidence supporting this conclusion is the fictive role and function of Baozhi in the *Baolin zhuan*. In the story of Bodhidharma's meeting with Emperor Wu of Liang, Baozhi foretold this meeting and its consequence.[67] In the Twenty-seventh Patriarch Prajñātāra's prophecy, Baozhi was also mentioned.[68]

The *Extended Records of Baizhang* cites Baozhi's verses twice.[69] As previously mentioned, Zongmi's works and Huangbo Xiyun's discourses also cite Baozhi's verses. Zongmi was a younger contemporary of Mazu's immediate disciples, and Xiyun was Mazu's second-generation disciple. Eun's catalog dated 847 records the *Song of Master Zhi* (*Zhi gong ge*) in one *juan*,[70] and Enchin's catalog dated 854 has the same record.[71] Thus, the first appearance of these verses was in the first half of the ninth century, which is in accord with the time of Mazu's first-generation disciples, and these verses were possibly connected to the creation of the *Baolin zhuan*.

A close analysis of the rhymes of these verses further supports this conclusion. The rhyming scheme of these verses is in accord with that of mid-Tang poetry but different from that of Qi-Liang poetry. The most striking features are indicated in Table 2.

The "Song of the Realization of the Way" is not included in Yongjia Xuanjue's *Yongjia ji* (Collected Works of Yongjia), and the ideas and terms in this song differ completely from those in the text. As early as the Song, Zhipan already suspected that it was not Xuanjue's work.[72] In modern times, Hu Shi was the first to restate this doubt. According to a Dunhuang manuscript (P. 2140) in which this song is copied under the title *Chanmen miyao jue* (Formulas of the Secret Essential of the Chan Gate) and attributed to Zhaojue, Hu assumes that this song was not written by Xuanjue and there was not even such a Chan master.[73] Ui Hakuju rejects Hu Shi's doubts and affirms Xuanjue's authorship, though he admits there must be some later additions in the song, such as the genealogy of "transmission of twenty-eight generations in India" and "transmission of the robe through six generations," which did not appear in the early Tang.[74] Bernard Faure thinks that it is likely an apocryphal work.[75] Nie Qing corrects Hu Shi's assertion by pointing out that under the title

TABLE 2.   Comparison of the Rhyming Schemes of the Verses Attributed to Baozhi, Mid-Tang Poetry, and Qi-Liang Poetry

Verses Attributed to Baozhi	Mid-Tang Poetry	Qi-Liang Poetry
Hao 豪 is kept alone, occasionally rhyming together with *xiao* 肴, *xiao* 宵 and *xiao* 蕭	*Hao* 豪 is kept alone, while *xiao* 肴, *xiao* 宵, and *xiao* 蕭 rhyme together	*Hao* 豪, *xiao* 肴, and *xiao* 宵/*xiao* 蕭 belong to three separate subgroups, seldom rhyming together
Yu 魚 and *yu* 虞 are confused, and occasionally rhyme with *mo* 模	*Yu* 魚, *yu* 虞, and *mo* 模 rhyme together	*Yu* 魚 is kept alone, while *yu* 虞 and *mo* 模 rhyme together
Zhi 支, *zhi* 脂, *zhi* 之, and *wei* 微 rhyme together	*Zhi* 支, *zhi* 脂, *zhi* 之, and *wei* 微 are merged	*Zhi* 脂 and *zhi* 之 are merged, *zhi* 脂 and *wei* 微 are separate, and *zhi* 支 is kept alone
Ge 歌 and *ge* 戈 are confused, and occasionally rhyme with *ma* 麻	*Ge* 歌 and *ge* 戈 are confused, and rhyme more and more with *ma* 麻	*Ge* 歌 and *ge* 戈 are confused, while *ma* 麻 is kept alone
Zhi 職 and *de* 德 rhyme together	*Zhi* 職 and *de* 德 rhyme together	*Zhi* 職 and *de* 德 keep apart
Geng 庚, *qing* 清, and *qing* 青 rhyme together	*Geng* 庚, *geng* 耕, *qing* 清, and *qing* 青 rhyme together	*Geng* 庚 and *qing* 清 are confused, and occasionally rhyme with *qing* 青

Source: Jinhua Jia, "Chuanshi Baozhi chanji kaobian," *Zhongguo chanxue* 3 (2004): 129–132.

Chanmen miyao jue, the manuscript P. 2140 actually copies several texts of the Chan school. Therefore, it is a general title for Chan texts, not only for this song, and also the name Zhaojue must be a scribal error for Zhenjue, as seen in P. 3360 and S. 403. However, Nie's new conclusion that Shenhui was the author of this song does not seem well documented.[76]

A close reading of this song reveals that, like the verses attributed to Baozhi, it is full of Hongzhou tenets and terms. Apart from the "transmission of the twenty-eight generations in India," which is in accordance with the *Baolin zhuan* genealogy as noted by Ui and other scholars, there are some other examples:

> Have you not seen the idle man of the Way who learns and does
>   nothing,
> Neither discarding delusion nor seeking truth?
> The real nature of ignorance is Buddha-nature;
> The illusory empty body is the dharma body.
>
>   . . .
>
> Rejecting deluded mind and grasping true principle,
> This mind of rejecting and grasping becomes false.

These lines illustrate Mazu's teaching that "this very mind that does not understand is it (Buddha-nature),"[77] and "without grasping good and rejecting evil, one should not rely on either purity or defilement."[78] The song further reads:

> After realizing the dharma body, there is not a thing;
> The inherent self-nature is the spontaneous Buddha.
>
>   . . .
>
> Walking is Chan and sitting is Chan;
> Speaking or silent, moving or still, the essence is undisturbed.
>
>   . . .
>
> Not that I, a mountain monk, want to be presumptuous,
> But cultivation may make you fall into the pit of cessation and permanence.

Here we hear Mazu's preaching that "now knowing self-nature is the Buddha, at all time you just walk, abide, sit, and lie, without a single dharma to attain";[79] and Zongmi's summary of the Hongzou doctrine that "Knowing it is spontaneous and natural, one should not raise the mind to cultivate the Way."[80]

Mazu's use of the metaphor of maṇi pearl also appears:

> The maṇi pearl is unknown to people;
> You can find it in the Tathāgata-garbha.
> The functions of the six senses are both empty and not empty,
> One perfect light with colors, yet colorless.

Furthermore, Mazu's application of the paradigms of essence/function and absolute/phenomenal is expressed in these lines:

> One nature perfectly pervades all natures;
> One dharma contains all dharmas.
> One moon appears in all waters;
> The moon reflections in all waters are one moon.[81]

These lines are often explained as an expression of the Huayan tenet of unobstructed interrelation of the absolute and the phenomenal. However, we should remember that Mazu did apply this Huayan tenet and the image of the moon to illustrate his teaching that "function is identical with Buddha-nature." As he said: "The absolute and phenomenal are without difference; both are wonderful functions. . . . Though the reflections of the moon are many, the real moon is not manifold."[82]

As Ui has indicated, the earliest citations of this song are seen in Huangbo Xiyun's *Chuanxin fayao* compiled in 857.[83] This song is listed in the catalogs compiled by the visiting Japanese monks under different titles: "Song of Buddha-nature of the Most Superior Vehicle" (*Zuishangsheng foxing ge*) in

Ennin's catalog dated 838, "Song of Buddha-nature" (*Foxing ge*) in his catalog dated 840, "Song of Chan Master Caoxi's Realization of the Way" (*Caoxi chanshi zhengdao ge*) in his catalog dated 847, "Song of the Nature of the Way" (*Daoxing ge*) in Eun's catalog dated 847, and "Song of Seeing the Nature of the Way" (*Jian daoxing ge*) in Enchin's catalogs.[84] According to these records, we can be certain that this song was current in the 830s, and was very popular from the 830s to the 850s. Hence, its true author seems again to have been among Mazu's immediate disciples.

The *ZTJ*, *SGSZ*, and *CDL* record the famous encounter-dialogue story of Xuanjue's visit to Huineng and becoming enlightened in one single day.[85] Although Xuanjue might have visited or studied with Huineng,[86] this kind of highly mature encounter dialogue would not have happened in Huineng's time. It is probably a creation along with the song. According to a fragment of the *Baolin zhuan*, Xuanjue was listed as one of Huineng's disciples, and his biography was included in *Juan* 10 of the original text.[87] Thus, the creations of this song and the encounter-dialogue story of Xuanjue and Huineng also seem to have been connected with the compilation of the *Baolin zhuan*.

Furthermore, it is worthy of special attention that the phrase "there is not a thing" (*wu yiwu*) appears twice at both the beginning and end of the "Song of the Realization of the Way." In the *Chuanxin fayao*, this phrase appears three times, one being a citation from this song.[88] In the *Wanling lu*, the same phrase again appears twice, one also being a citation of this song, the other reading as "originally there is not a thing, so where is the dust?"[89] This couplet is from the mind-verse attributed to Huineng, which is said to be in competition with Shenxiu's verse, as seen in the *ZTJ* and *ZJL*,[90] and also all versions of the *Platform Sūtra* except the two Dunhuang manuscripts and the Western Xia translation of 1071. According to the Dunhuang versions of this text, there were two mind-verses attributed to Huineng.[91] The main difference between the original two verses and the later single verse is that the phrase "clean and pure Buddha-nature" was changed into "there is not a thing."[92] Considering the citations of this phrase in the "Song of the Realization of the Way," *Chuanxin fayao*, and *Wanling lu*,[93] and also the relationship between the song and the *Baolin zhuan*, we have reason to surmise that in the *Baolin zhuan* the two verses of Huineng's enlightenment had already been transformed and merged into one, and that this change was later adopted by the new versions of the *Platform Sūtra*.[94] This assumption can be supported by two citations in the *ZTJ*. In Bodhidharma's entry, the twenty-seventh patriarch Prajñātāra issued a prophecy about Huineng's enlightenment verse, saying: "He only wrote a verse of four lines." In the fifth patriarch Hongren's entry, there is only a quatrain of mind-verse attributed to Huineng.[95] As mentioned in chapter one, the biographies of the twenty-eight Indian patriarchs and six Chinese patriarchs in the *ZTJ* were based on the *Baolin zhuan*. It is likely that these two citations were copied from that text.

The associations with Baozhi and Xuanjue would have elevated the stature of the Hongzhou doctrine, and enabled the Chan monks of the

Hongzhou line to legitimize their doctrinal innovations by finding clear antecedents in the works of Baozhi, the mythologized Liang monk, and Xuanjue,
the alleged disciple of the Sixth Patriarch.

ESTABLISHMENT OF CHAN MONASTERIES AND MONASTIC REGULATIONS

Chan tradition claims that Baizhang Huaihai established the first monastic
code that marked the institutional independence of the Chan school. Baizhang's
image as a great monastic regulator and iconoclastic master has been widely
acknowledged by both traditional and modern scholars. Recently, however,
some scholars have questioned this image and assumed that it was merely a
myth created during the Song dynasty. They also related this issue with the
argument that the "golden age" of Chan Buddhism in the Tang dynasty was
a mythology created by Song Chan monks. In this section, I first use a generally ignored stele inscription, which contains a set of monastic regulations,
to determine that Baizhang definitely did not create any monastic code, but
his immediate disciples headed by Baizhang Fazheng established and codified
the first set of regulations for their monastery. I then discuss the content and
significance of these early regulations, as well as the impact of the continuing
development of many self-constructed and self-administrated monasteries by
Chan monks from the mid-Tang to the Five Dynasties.

Baizhang's entry in the *CDL* includes a sketch of the text titled *Chanmen
guishi* (Regulations of the Chan Gate),[96] and a quite similar but more abridged
version is seen in Baizhang's hagiography in the *SGSZ*.[97] The *Xin Tang shu*
also records a *Chanmen guishi* by Baizhang in one *juan*,[98] a fact that indicates
the actual circulation of the text during the Northern Song.

According to these accounts, Baizhang created the first set of Chan
monastic regulations for his community on Baizhangshan, which represented
the beginning of the institutional independence of the Chan school. Baizhang
was said to have deliberately established a "separate Chan monastery" that
would not follow Vinaya rules. The *Chanmen guishi* describes the structure,
administration, and regulations of this kind of Chan monastery: buildings
included an abbot's quarter, a dharma hall, ten offices, and a saṅgha hall; the
administration included an abbot and ten head monks; and the regulations
designated sermons and meetings, sleep, meals, communal labor, and punish-
ments.[99] The text emphasizes that no Buddha hall was built, and the most
honored individual was the current patriarch/abbot, and it does not mention
any practice of scriptural study or Buddhist ritual. As a result, it had been
interpreted as iconoclastic, and traditionally Baizhang's image as a great monastic regulator and an iconoclast master had been widely acknowledged since
the Song dynasty.

Modern scholars in general accept this image. Many believe that the
similarity of the accounts in the *SGSZ* and *CDL* indicates the existence of
a common source, which must be the set of regulations that Baizhang created

for his monastery. They agree with the Chan school's claim that those regulations signaled the institutional independence of the Chan school, and further regard it as a major reason for the school's singular prosperity after the Huichang persecution of Buddhism.[100]

Kondō Ryōichi is the first to adopt a critical stance toward this issue. Although he still believes that Baizhang created a set of monastic regulations, he suggests that since there is no evidence in pre-Song sources indicating Baizhang's authorship, those regulations were not codified but rather a body of oral instructions transmitted and modified among Chan communities until the early Song.[101] Recently, some scholars have raised further arguments against Baizhang's traditional image. Yifa agrees with the general opinion that Baizhang could have had a monastic text written for his order, as did many monks before him, but she argues that, whether or not Baizhang virtually created or codified those regulations, they did not represent the institutional independence of the Chan school because the monastic regulations described in the *Chanmen guishi* were based on traditional Buddhist codes explained in the Vinaya texts and practiced generally in medieval monasteries.[102] Ishii Shūdō speculates that Baizhang initiated some basic principles of the monastic code as seen in the *Chanmen guishi*, such as the practice of communal work and the integration of "the appropriate Mahāyāna and Hīnayāna precepts," but he did not actually create any regulations. Then during the time of the third abbot Baizhang Niepan (Baizhang Niepan was the second abbot, not the third; see later discussions), there was already a set of monastic regulations at Baizhangshan. Those regulations were transmitted from generation to generation, and by the tenure of the eleventh abbot, Baizhang Daochang (d. 991), those regulations were codified and used as a basis for the *Chanmen guishi*.[103] However, Ishii does not provide sufficient evidence for his interesting hypotheses, and therefore they are not very convincing. Foulk's argument is the most radical. He asserts that Baizhang neither created nor codified such a set of monastic regulations, and it is merely a myth forged by Song Chan monks. He further assumes that this myth helped to form the myth of the "golden age" of Tang Chan, which he again believes to have been created in the Song dynasty.[104] These novel assertions, however, are not well-documented.

These controversies call attention to the Baizhang puzzle and make it one of the central issues in the study of Buddhist monasticism and Chan history of the eighth to tenth centuries. In this section, I use a rarely noticed stele inscription to resolve this puzzle. The Yuan-dynasty *Chixiu Baizhang qinggui* includes Baizhang's stūpa inscription written by Chen Xu. Along with the inscription appear not only Chen Xu's specific official title but also the inscriber Wu Yihuang's name and official title,[105] a fact indicating that the inscription was likely copied from the original stele. The Song-dynasty *Baoke leibian* (Assorted Compilation of Precious Inscriptions) actually records that this inscription was written by Chen Xu and scribed by Wu Yihuang.[106] It should be noted that at the end of the inscription Dehui (fl. 1329–1336), the compiler of the *Chixiu Baizhang qinggui*, added these words: "On the back of the stele, the assembly [of the monastery] together wrote down five matters, which are now still extant. As those matters could be used as admonitions, I copied them as follows." Dehui stated clearly that on the back of Baizhang's stele was an inscription that contained five matters that were decided and written by the assembly of the Baizhangsi. This inscription was still extant during the Yuan dynasty, and Dehui copied it himself. Below is the complete inscription inscribed on the back of Baizhang's stele and copied by Dehui:

> During the period when the great master had just passed away and a new abbot had not been installed, the assembly discussed five long-term matters for reforming the monastery. (1). A fully ordained monk should be placed in charge of the court of [Baizhang Huaihai's] stūpa, and a novice should be appointed to sweep the floor. (2). Nuns' quarters, tombs, and stūpas should not be established within the boundaries of the monastery. Lay people are not allowed to dwell within the boundaries of the monastery. (3). Monks who come to reside in the monastery and young postulants who join the monastery must be required to attend the abbot only, and all other monks are not to be attended. (4). Beyond the boundaries the monastery should not possess any estate or land. (5). Resident members of the assembly are not allowed to accumulate personal money or grain inside or outside the monastery. If we want to make the stream clear, we must clean the origin. We hope later successors forever to follow these regulations with respect. The assembly notes together on the day when the stele is established.[107]

According to the *Baoke leibian*, Baizhang's stele was established on the thirteenth day of the tenth month in the thirteenth year of Yuanhe reign-period (14 November 818),[108] nearly five years after Baizhang passed away on the seventeenth day of the first month in the ninth year of Yuanhe (10 February 814).[109]

This precious inscription tells us several important facts. First, when Baizhang just passed away in 814, the assembly at the Baizhangsi, which must have included Baizhang's immediate disciples, agreed to establish five matters/regulations for the sake of reforming the monastery. Then, when Baizhang's stele was erected in 818, the assembly decided to inscribe those regulations on the back of the stele. Thus, the first set of monastic regulations at Baizhangshan was created in 814 and codified in 818 by Baizhang's immediate disciples.

Second, Baizhang definitely neither created nor codified any regulation for his monastery; otherwise what were inscribed on the back of the stele would have been his regulations, not those discussed and agreed on by the assembly, or at least the inscription should have mentioned Baizhang's contributions to those regulations.

Third, the five regulations were very simple and plain, without any sign of iconoclasm. They did not even mention any term or concept related to Chan. From the Song to the Yuan the *Chanmen guishi* had been augmented and altered to various forms of *Pure Regulations*, and Baizhang's image as Chan monastic legislator and great master of iconoclasm had long been established. Thus, it is impossible that Dehui or any other monk during the Song-Yuan period forged such a plain inscription. Dehui was the nineteenth abbot of the Baizhangsi and certainly had direct access to the Baizhang stele, which was regarded as sacred by successors of the monastery.[110] When Dehui said he copied the inscription from the back of the stele, he must have been telling the truth. In addition, the first regulation in the inscription was about appointing a monk to maintain the court of Baizhang's stūpa and a novice to sweep the floor. This internal evidence self-attests that the regulations were set soon after Baizhang passed away. Hence, this inscription is original and authentic.[111]

According to relevant sources, we can identify the figure who led Baizhang's disciples in the creation and codification of this set of monastic regulations. In the stūpa inscription for Baizhang, Chen Xu acknowledged Fazheng (d. 819) as Baizhang's leading disciple.[112] Fazheng was also called Weizheng or Niepan heshang, and the *Quan Tangwen* includes a fragment of his epitaph written by Wu Yihuang.[113] The Song monk Huihong, who had the chance to read the complete inscription, said Fazheng followed Huaihai to become the second abbot of the Baizhangsi and contributed greatly to the establishment and development of the monastery.[114] According to the extant fragment of Fazheng's epitaph, when Baizhang's stele was established in 818, Fazheng still held the abbotship; the epitaph also says that he was specialized in Vinaya teaching and observed Buddhist precepts strictly.[115] Thus, it can be inferred that the first set of regulations of the Baizhangsi was produced and practiced under his direction.

Baizhangshan (also named Daxiongshan) was located in the west of Xinwuxian of Hongzhou (in present-day Jiangxi).[116] According to Baizhang's stūpa inscription by Chen Xu, two lay Buddhists contributed their estates to Baizhang to build the monastery.[117] The time was possibly in the third year of the Yuanhe reign-period (808).[118] From the statement that "the assembly note together" in the inscription of regulations, we can assume that the Baizhangsi remained unofficial during Fazheng's tenure and was administrated by all the members of the assembly and the abbot elected by them. Baizhang, the founder of the monastery, naturally became the first abbot himself, whereas the second abbot, Fazheng, who was the leading disciple of Baizhang, was obviously elected by his fellow members. In the first year of the Changqing reign-period (821), Emperor Muzong (r. 820–824) conferred on Baizhang the posthumous title "Dazhi chanshi" (Chan Master Great Wisdom) and upon his stūpa the title "Da baosheng lun" (Great Wheel of Treasure and Superiority).[119]

The emperor might also have bestowed the name-tablet of "Dazhi chansi" or "Dazhi shousheng chansi" on the Baizhangsi at the same time.[120] According to Jacques Gernet's study, the bestowal of a name-tablet from the emperor signaled that the monastery had become an officially recognized establishment and was safeguarded against all future confiscations and even destruction.[121] However, the Baizhangsi might not have obtained the same status as the official monasteries established under imperial orders because all of its abbots seem to have continued to be Chan masters elected by the assembly.[122]

We can now examine in detail the five primitive regulations codified in the inscription. The first regulation required a fully ordained monk to be placed in charge of the court of Baizhang Huaihai's stūpa and a novice to be appointed to sweep the floor, while the third declared that only the abbot could be attended by visiting and younger monks. These two regulations highly honored the patriarch and abbot. Baizhang was the "opening-mountain patriarch" (*kaishan zushi*) and first abbot of the monastery. As previously discussed, the *Chanmen guishi* also holds their patriarchs/abbots in the highest esteem. This coincidence hints that this text may have had connections with the earliest regulations of the Baizhangsi. It is highly possible that, as Ishii has partly suggested, later generations of the Baizhangsi added to and altered the contents of the early regulations, and the *Chanmen guishi* recorded in early-Song texts was the result of an evolution over about two centuries. Therefore, Baizhang's authorship of the text was not a myth created by Song monks, but simply because the text came from the Baizhangsi, and as an accumulative, anonymous product, it was easy for later generations to trace the text all the way back to their great "opening-mountain patriarch."

In the second regulation, nuns' quarters, tombs, and stūpas were banned from being established within the boundaries of the monastery, and lay people were also not allowed to dwell there. Since the Vinaya strictly forbids sexual activities, and monks are not allowed to walk, sit, or have other close contact with nuns or lay women, this regulation might have been a precaution against breaking those precepts.

The last two regulations deserve close attention. The fourth decided that the monastery would not possess any estate or land beyond its boundaries, and the fifth prohibited all resident members of the monastery from accumulating personal wealth. This economic pattern was in accord with the Vinaya rule against accumulating and handling wealth, but was quite different from the economic pattern of the official monasteries in the Tang period. Those official monasteries often possessed a large amount of land, buildings, shops, orchards, and so forth, and Buddhist monks who resided in those monasteries freely accumulated personal property, with some even becoming very rich. Indeed, the excessive financial gain of Buddhist monasteries and monks was one of the major causes of the Huichang persecution.[123] Thus, the first set of monastic regulations at the Baizhangsi was actually stricter in observing Vinaya precepts than that of the official monasteries.

The fourth regulation can also be used to resolve the puzzle of whether communal labor was practiced at the Baizhangsi. As analyzed earlier, one of the regulations stated in the *Chanmen guishi* is the practice of communal labor. Many stories of encounter dialogues recorded in Chan texts such as the *ZTJ* and *CDL* and attributed to Baizhang and other masters of the mid-Tang period depict them as engaging in various forms of physical labor; Baizhang was even said to have formulated the famous slogan, "A day without work is a day without food."[124] According to these sources, many modern scholars believe that extensive and productive work was actually practiced at Baizhangshan and other Chan monasteries, and those monasteries were economically self-sufficient. Recently, Mario Poceski has opposed such conclusions and proposed that there is little evidence to show that Chan monks during the Tang widely engaged in physical work or strove to be economically self-sufficient.[125] Since the fourth regulation of the Baizhangsi clearly enjoined the monastery not to possess any estate or land beyond its boundaries, we can infer that no extensive agricultural labor was practiced at Baizhangshan during the tenures of Baizhang and Fazheng because, without the possession of large pieces of land,[126] communal agricultural labor was impossible. As a matter of fact, Baizhang's stūpa inscription states that, after the monastery was built, "provisions and alms heaped up."[127] This clearly indicates that at that time the monastery relied mainly on alms from lay devotees. Although large-scale communal labor was most likely not practiced, other chores such as collecting and chopping firewood, drawing water, cleaning, and cooking would have been inevitable for the routine maintenance of such a large monastery. About twenty years later, in 839, Ennin recorded that the Fahuayuan in Wendengxian of Dengzhou (in present-day Shandong) owned an estate with a farm rent of five hundred *shi* of rice each year, which provided food for the monastery. However, when the turnips and radishes that grew within the monastic boundaries were harvested, all of the monks worked to pick the leaves, and when the firewood was used up, all of the monks went out to gather firewood.[128] The "communal work" undertaken at the Baizhangsi was very possibly of the same kind. This kind of work, however, could not have made the monastery economically self-sufficient.

Some scholars have indicated that the creation of a monastic code for one's order was not a rare thing before or after Baizhang.[129] Other Chan monks who created regulations for their monasteries include Baizhang's disciple Guishan Lingyou (771–853), Baizhang's confrere Guizong Zhichang, Zhichang's disciple Furong Lingxun, and Lingxun's disciple Xuefeng Yicun (822–908).[130] Guishan Lingyou's "Guishan jingce" (Admonitions of Guishan) and Xuefeng Yicun's "Shigui zhi" (Regulations of the Master) are also extant.[131] There are noticeable similarities between the Xuefeng regulations and those of the Baizhangsi. In the introduction, Xuefeng emphasizes that "a family does not have two masters, and a country does not have two kings," and he specifies in the first rule that only the abbot could be attended by new resident members. He also indicates that this rule was a legacy of his master, Furong

Lingxun.[132] This rule resembles the third regulation of the Baizhangsi. Thus, we can infer that the early regulations of the Baizhangsi circulated to some degree and were appropriated by other Chan communities. These extant monastic regulations and admonitions show some distinct identities of each monastery, but none of them implies a rejection of the Vinaya or a break from the mainstream monastic traditions.[133] In contrast, Guishan's admonitions emphasized observance of Buddhist precepts, and the first set of Baizhang regulations were even stricter in following Vinaya rules than those of official monasteries.

The more important development in mid-Tang Buddhist monasticism, one that substantially affected the growth of the Chan school, was not the rejection of the Vinaya but the emergence of many new monasteries established and headed by Mazu's first-generation disciples. Besides Baizhang, there were fifteen more founders of monasteries or cloisters.[134] Contrasting with the fact that, before the mid-Tang, only a few monasteries had been created by Chan monks,[135] this sudden increase of self-constructed and self-administrated monasteries and cloisters was indeed remarkable. The impact of this event can be observed in three aspects.

First, following their mid-Tang predecessors, Chan monks and their patrons built numerous monasteries and cloisters during the late Tang and Five Dynasties, and most of the names of these establishments carried the specific denomination "Chan." In Guangdong, Yunmen Wenyan, Mazu's fifth-generation disciple, built the Guangtai chanyuan in 923, which later was promoted to Dajue chansi and became the base of the Yunmen house.[136] In Jiangxi, Shushan Kuangren, Mazu's fourth-generation disciple, built the Baiyun chanyuan in 890, on which an imperial name-tablet was conferred in 894;[137] a rich family in the Chongrenxian built the Dizang pu'an chanyuan for the Chan monk Shouxun in 904;[138] Huicong, Mazu's fourth-generation disciple, built the Yong'an chanyuan in 914;[139] Li Mengjun, the magistrate of Longquanxian, built the Shishan chanyuan for Yinwei, Mazu's fifth-generation disciple, in 929–935, and later his disciples Qiren and Xingchang successively held the abbotship.[140] In Fujian, the cloister created by Furong Lingxun was conferred the imperial name-tablet of Xiantong yanqing chanyuan in 867;[141] Xiyuan Da'an, Mazu's third-generation disciple, created the Yanshou chanyuan that was conferred the imperial name-tablet in 874;[142] the cloister built by Xuefeng Yicun was conferred the imperial name-tablet of Yingtian xuefeng chanyuan in 875.[143] In Zhejiang, Yuan Zhen (779–831) and Lu Gen (765–835), two commissioners of Zhedongdao, built the Wozhoushan chanyuan for the Chan master Jiran in 829–830;[144] Ren Jingqiu, the magistrate of Fenningxian, built the Dongjin chanyuan for Zanghuan, Mazu's second-generation disciple, in 858;[145] and Qian Yuanguan (887–941), the king of Wuyue, built the Qinghua chanyuan for Quanfu (882–947), Mazu's fifth-generation disciple, in 937.[146] In Anhui, Cui Yu, the commissioner of Xuanzhou, built the Shengrui chanyuan for Hengtong (834–905), Mazu's third-generation disciple, in 873;[147] Huijing built the Zhushan chanyuan during the Xiantong reign-period (860–

874), which was changed to Yong'an chanyuan in 900.[148] In Hunan, Judun
(835–923), Mazu's fourth-generation disciple, was invited to stay in the Miaoji
chanyuan by Ma Yin (852–930), the king of Chu, in about 915.[149] In Jiangsu,
two rich families in Huatingxian built the Fayun chanyuan in 860, which was
promoted to Fayun chansi by an imperial order in the same year;[150] Fayan
Wenyi (885–958), Mazu's seventh-generation disciple, was invited by Li Bian
(889–943), the first king of Nantang, to stay in the Bao'en chanyuan in 937–
942. In Shaanxi, the Changxing wanshou chanyuan was conferred the imperial
name-tablet in 932;[151] and the Guangci chanyuan was conferred the imperial
name-tablet in 953.[152] There were still many other Chan monasteries and
cloisters of the late Tang and Five Dynasties recorded in various early texts.
According to the sources previously cited, the ZTJ, the CDL, and other early
texts, most of these establishments were occupied and administered successively by monks of Chan lineage, many of which can be identified as descendents of Mazu. These regional Chan establishments and movements became
the major force through which the official institutionalization of Chan monasteries during the Northern Song was precipitated.[153]

Second, these monasteries became institutional bases for the further development and prosperity of the Chan school, making the transmission of the
genealogy not only spiritual but also institutional. For example, it is not by
chance that the traditionally acknowledged five major houses that emerged in
the late Tang and Five Dynasties traced their genealogies back to the three
masters, Baizhang, Tianhuang, and Yaoshan, who actually built their own monasteries. Furthermore, along with the succession of these Chan monasteries
from generation to generation, a new concept of monastery genealogy (shidai)
appeared. Each monastery of a certain tradition formed its own genealogy,
and the successive abbotship was counted in numerical order—the first-generation abbot (yishi), the second-generation abbot (ershi), and so forth.[154] For
example, by the late Five Dynasties and early Song, the Baizhangsi can be
counted down to the eleventh-generation abbot, Baizhang Daochang,[155] and
the Yaoshansi can be counted down to the ninth-generation abbot, Yaoshan
Keqiong.[156] Monastery genealogy was different from and subject to school/
line genealogy (zongxi or faxi). The abbots of one monastery might have come
from different lineages. For example, at the Baizhangsi, the tenth abbot,
Mingzhao, was a descendent of the Cao-Dong lineage, and the eleventh abbot,
Daochang, was a disciple of Fayan Wenyi.[157] Suzuki Tetsuo indicates that the
concept of monastery genealogy was connected only to monasteries created
and administered by Chan monks, and he further assumes that it first emerged
among successors of Dongshan Liangjie (807–869).[158] However, the germ of
this new concept can be traced back to the Baizhangsi, as Fazheng, the second
abbot of the monastery, was already called "Di'er Baizhang" (Baizhang the
Second, or the Second-Generation Abbot of Baizhangsi).[159]

Third, those self-administered monasteries provided relatively stable envi-
ronments for the compilation or creation of discourse records and encounter
dialogue texts by Chan monks. For example, Baizhang's discourse text was

first compiled by his disciples, Shenxing and Fanyun, and later recompiled by the eleventh abbot, Daochang, at the monastery he founded at Baizhangshan, and Damei Fachang's discourse text was created by his successor(s) in the cloister he founded at Dameishan.[160]

In conclusion, this section demonstrates that the first set of monastic regulations at Baizhangshan was created in 814 and codified in 818 by Baizhang Huaihai's immediate disciples led by Baizhang Fazheng. This set of regulations was stricter in observing the Vinaya than that of the official monasteries during the Tang, and no sign of iconoclasm is seen in them. The more important event that happened in Buddhist monasteries in the mid-Tang period, which substantially affected the development of the Chan school, was the emergence of many new monasteries and cloisters established and headed by Mazu's first-generation disciples. The *Chanmen guishi* recorded in early-Song texts was neither a creation of Baizhang Huaihai nor that of Song Chan monks, but rather the result of a continuing evolution over about two centuries at Baizhangshan.

EXPANSION OF THE HONGZHOU SCHOOL AND IMPERIAL RECOGNITION

After Mazu Daoyi passed away, from about the last decade of the eighth century to the first three decades of the ninth century, Mazu's disciples expanded their school from the south to the north, and from local, remote places to the two capitals, forming a large-scale and dynamic stream within the Chan movement. According to Table 1, among the one hundred and forty-five disciples whose names are known, seventy-nine spread to seven provinces in the south, including Jiangxi, Hunan, Hubei, Jiangsu, Anhui, Guangdong, and Fujian; thirty-five spread to five provinces in the north, including Shaanxi, Shanxi, Hebei, Henan, and Shangdong;[161] one returned to Korea; two were lay Buddhists; and twenty-five were unknown. Moreover, out of the seventy-nine disciples in the south, fourteen built their own monasteries; out of the thirty-five disciples in the north, two built their own monasteries. Thus, by that time, the school had taken root firmly across the vast extent of the empire.

During the Dali-Zhenyuan reign-periods (766–805), however, the influence of the Heze school was still very strong, especially in Chang'an and Luoyang, the two capital cities. Shenhui's disciple, Huijian (719–792), was summoned to the capital during the Dali reign-period (766–779). Emperor Daizong ordered him to build a memorial hall for Shenhui, and conferred the title "Hall of Transmision of the Dharma of True Prajñā" and a portrait of Shenhui on the hall. During the early Zhenyuan period (785–792), Huijian was also highly esteemed by Emperor Dezong and the Crown Prince, the later Emperor Shunzong.[162] According to Zongmi, Emperor Dezong conferred on Shenhui the title Seventh Patriarch, and wrote eulogies for all the seven patriarchs.[163] This event might have been one of the causes of the

competition of Mazu's disciples with the Heze line and of their bid for imperial support.

In 796–798, under the help of the powerful eunuch Huo Xianming
(d. 798), Mazu's disciple, Ehu Dayi, was summoned to court. He successfully
defeated masters of the Heze, Niutou, and Northern schools, and obtained
the support of Emperors Dezong and Shunzong.[164] In the seventeenth year
of Zhenyuan (801), Emperor Dezong ordered the eunuch, Wang Shize, to be
shaved and become Dayi's disciple. In the first year of the Yuanhe reign-period
(806), another eunuch, Li Chaozheng, built a stele for Bodhidharma and
wrote an inscription to note this event, in which he acknowledged the
Bodhiharma-Mazu line and highly praised Mazu's teaching.[165] Foguang
Ruman, another disciple of Mazu, was also summoned to court by Emperor
Shunzong (r. 805).[166] When Zhangjing Huaihui and Xingshan Weikuan were
in the capital during the Yuanhe reign-period, they again fought off the chal-
lenges of other schools, dispelled the doubts of scholar-officials, obtained
the support of Emperor Xianzong, and attracted hundreds and thousands of
followers.[167]

In the tenth year of the Yuanhe period (815), Emperor Xianzong conferred on Huineng the posthumous title "Chan Master Great Mirror" (Dajian
chanshi),[168] and on Mazu the posthumous title "Chan Master Great Quiescence"
at about the same time.[169] In the same year, at the request of Huaihui and
Weikuan, Zhang Zhengfu, the Surveillance Commissioner of Hunan, built a
stele for Huairang's stūpa on Hengshan, and wrote an inscription to com-
memorate the Huineng-Nanyue-Mazu line.[170] Gui Deng also wrote an epitaph
for Huairang at about the same time,[171] and Emperor Jingzong conferred on
him the posthumous title "Great Wisdom" (Dahui) and the title "Supreme
Wheel" (Zuisheng lun) on his stūpa in 825–827.[172] Soon after Huaihui died
in 815, several leading ministers, including Quan Deyu, Linghu Chu (766–
837), Zheng Yuqing (746–820), Gui Deng, and Zheng Yin (752–829), wrote
or inscribed epitaphs for him;[173] and Emperor Xianzong conferred on him
the posthumous title "Chan Master Great Propagator" (Daxuanjiao chanshi)
in 816.[174] When Weikuan died in 817, Emperor Xianzong conferred on him
the posthumous title "Chan Master Great Penetration" (Dache chanshi).[175]
Weikuan had more than one thousand followers in the capital, among
whom was the famous scholar-official Bai Juyi.[176] In 821, Emperor Muzong
conferred the posthumous titles "Chan Master Great Enlightenment"
(Dajue chanshi) on Xitang Zhizang and "Chan Master Great Wisdom"
(Dazhi chanshi) on Baizhang Huaihai.[177] These marked the imperial and
official recognition of the Hongzhou school.

In Ehu Dayi's epitaph written in 818, Wei Chuhou indicated there were
four current schools of the Bordhidharma line—the Northern, the Heze, the
Niutou, and the Hongzhou.[178] In Hualin Yuntan's epitaph written in 825, Jia
Su again acknowledged two schools of the Huineng line, the Heze and the
Hongzhou.[179] In Zongmi's works about Chan Buddhism, the Hongzhou or
Jiangxi was frequently mentioned as a major school opposing the Heze.[180] In

Zongmi's epitaph written in 841, Pei Xiu also marked the Heze and the Hongzhou as two major schools of the Huineng line.[181] Thus, through the concerted efforts of Mazu's disciples, the Hongzhou lineage became a full-fledged, dominant school and generally acknowledged during the first half of the ninth century.

CHAPTER SIX

SCHISM OF THE HONGZHOU SCHOOL DURING
THE LATE TANG AND FIVE DYNASTIES:
DECONSTRUCTING THE TRADITIONAL GENEALOGY
OF TWO LINES AND FIVE HOUSES

Since the Song dynasty, all historians of Chan Buddhism have described a genealogical diagram of two lines and five houses after the sixth patriarch Huineng. This genealogical diagram has not only been passed on within the Chan school for more than a thousand years, but also constituted the basic framework for presenting historical narratives in modern studies of Chan Buddhism for nearly a century.

Some scholars have questioned the historical reliability of this traditional lineage. In a letter to Yanagida Seizan in 1961, Hu Shi proposed that during the mid-Tang, Huineng's successors divided into two lines—the Heze and the Hongzhou; the Shitou line did not arise until much later, and Qingyuan Xingsi's apprenticeship with Huineng may have been a later creation.[1] Du Jiwen and Wei Daoru suggest that the rise of the Shitou line may have started from the *ZTJ* with its obvious sectarian inclination toward this school.[2] Suzuki Tetsuo points out that during the late Tang and Five Dynasties various houses arose, but it was not until the mid-Northern Song that the designation of the Five Houses became fixed.[3] Other scholars have challenged this tradition from the perspective of methodology. John McRae terms the approach of treating Chan in terms of its lineages as a "string of pearls" fallacy and advocates a deconstruction of the diagram by a synchronic approach.[4]

In this chapter, I adopt McRae's idea about deconstructing the lineage diagram, but proceed mainly in a philological investigation of historical facts, in order to present a more exact picture of the changing fortunes of the Hongzhou school and the rise of the various houses during the late Tang and Five Dynasties. In our discussions in chapter four, we have seen that the Hongzhou doctrines of "ordinary mind is the Way" and "Buddha-nature manifests in function" drew strong criticism from contemporaries of Mazu and his disciples in the mid-Tang. Furthermore, at the beginning of the late

Tang, during the Huichang reign-period (841–846), the catastrophe of the Huichang persecution of Buddhism occurred. Almost all monasteries were destroyed or removed, and monks and nuns were laicized.[5] Since one of the reasons for the government persecution was the degeneration and violation of the otherworldly spirit of the Buddhist clergy, reflections on their religious doctrines and practices became inevitable in the rehabilitation of Buddhism after the persecution. Both the mid-Tang criticism of the Hongzhou doctrines and the destructive blow of the Huichang persecution urged the successors of the Hongzhou school to reflect on and complement their doctrines. Among the reflections and discussions, two major controversies arose. These controversies in turn resulted in the schism of the Hongzhou school and the rise of various houses.

CONTROVERSIES OVER AND DEVELOPMENT OF THE HONGZHOU DOCTRINE

Based on the tathāgata-garbha theory, Mazu put forward the new doctrines "ordinary mind is the Way" and "Buddha-nature manifests in function" to affirm positively the value of ordinary human life. His unconditional identification of Buddha-nature with the ordinary mind of good and evil, purity and defilement, and truth and delusion attracted the attention of some conservative critics. Huizhong and Zongmi commented sharply that Mazu wrongly regarded the deluded mind as the true mind. These criticisms actually caused some doubts among Chan students. For example, Pei Xiu, who had previously been Zongmi's student, later asked Huangbo Xiyun to which mind the patriarchs referred, the ordinary mind or the sacred, when they said that "this mind is the Buddha."[6] In an encounter dialogue attributed to Zhangjing Huaihui and a student, the latter asked whether the mind transmitted by the patriarchs was the mind of Thusness or the deluded mind, or neither true mind nor deluded mind.[7] This encounter dialogue was possibly created in the late Tang period, and it reflected the same doubt as Pei Xiu's. Out of the responses to those criticisms and doubts, two major controversies were raised during the late Tang period.

The first controversy focused on the relationship between the two propositions, "this mind is the Buddha" and "neither mind nor Buddha." As discussed in chapter three, none of the encounter dialogues involving Mazu's preaching of "neither mind nor Buddha" is authentic. In the *Extended Records of Baizhang*, Baizhang is said to negate both "this mind is the Buddha" and "neither mind nor Buddha" because both are still "in the category of defilement by the dust of doctrine," and "as long as there are verbal formulations, everything is in the realm of affliction and trouble."[8] In addition, one of the central themes in this text is that of "penetrating the three propositions" (*tou sanju guo*).[9] The basic mode of this theme was a threefold negation—nonattachment to all beings and nonbeings, not dwelling in nonattachment, and not making an understanding of nonattachment.[10] This radical apophasis of Mādhyamika dialectic is quite popular in the Buddhist and Taoist texts of the early Tang,[11] but it differs from the more kataphatic stance of Mazu's sermons, and is not found in Zongmi's account of the Hongzhou doctrine. It is more likely that these were modifications by Baizhang's disciples who compiled the discourses.

Huangbo Xiyun, Mazu's second-generation disciple and Baizhang's immediate disciple, advocated the paradoxical proposition that "this mind is the Buddha, and no-mind is the Way."[12] On one hand, he illustrated Mazu's tenet that the ordinary, complete human mind was Buddha-nature: "As sentient beings, this mind is not diminished. As Buddhas, this mind is not increased. . . . The patriarch came from the West to indicate directly that all, complete human beings are Buddhas."[13] On the other hand, he pointed out immediately the emptiness and nonattachment of this mind: "This mind is the mind of no-mind, which departs from all phenomenal appearances."[14] In the preface to *Chuanxin fayao*, Pei Xiu also says Huangbo "transmitted only the one-mind, without any other dharma; whereas the essence of the mind is also empty, and myriad phenomena are all quiescence."[15] Here Huangbo used the concept of the tathāgata-garbha as empty to complement Mazu's "this mind is the Buddha." In the *Śrīmālā Sūtra* and other tathāgata-garbha texts, including the *Awakening of Faith*, the Tathāgata's wisdom of emptiness is explained as twofold—the tathāgata-garbha is empty of either defilements or self-nature, but not empty of either Buddha-dharmas or wholesome qualities that constitute enlightenment.[16] Mazu's "this mind is the Buddha" implies the nonempty quality of the tathāgata-garbha, while Huangbo's complement that "no-mind is the Way" implies the empty quality of the tathāgata-garbha. Put together, this new proposition "this mind is the Buddha, and no-mind is the Way" proposes a dialectical way to eschew the criticism that the Hongzhou school regarded the tathāgata-garbha/Buddha-nature as an eternal entity and viewed the deluded mind as the true mind. In this way Huangbo further developed the Hongzhou doctrine and balanced the tathāgata-garbha thought with the prajñāpāramitā analysis. It provides the ontological foundation for and the basic paradigm of the religious experience of the perplexing "classical" Chan: to be active in daily life yet free from any attachment; to run in the crossroads of markets yet be transcendent as if singing on a high peak.[17]

In the fictional story, "the plum is ripe," when Damei Fachang was informed that Mazu had changed his proposition from "this mind is the Buddha" to "neither mind nor Buddha," Fachang replied, "You can have 'neither mind nor Buddha,' but I would insist on 'this mind is the Buddha.' "[18] The second proposition, "neither mind nor Buddha," was sometimes expressed as "the mind is not the Buddha, and the wisdom is not the Way," or "it is not the mind, not the Buddha, and not a thing." There are ten more encounter dialogues involving the controversy over the comparison between these two propositions.[19] Superficially, these dialogues seem to argue that one proposition was superior to the other, or both were used by Mazu as expedients to guide learners. Nevertheless, the real idea contained in these dialogues was, just like that of Huangbo, to use the second proposition "neither mind nor Buddha" to defend and complement Mazu's "ordinary mind." Thus, the real rivals in this controversy were the critics of the Hongzhou doctrine. Those encounter dialogues were attributed to Mazu or his immediate disciples, including Xitang Zhizang, Funiu Zizai, Nanquan Puyuan, Panshan Baoji, and Dongsi Ruhui. As was proved in the case of Damei Fachang, these dialogues were most likely modified or created by Mazu's second- or third-generation disciples.

The second controversy involved a competitive comparison between the Hongzhou and Shitou doctrines. This controversy started with a fictional story preserved in Yaoshan Weiyan's entry in the *ZTJ*, which is extraordinary in both length and content. As discussed in chapter two, although Yaoshan did visit Shitou, he studied with Mazu for nearly twenty years, and therefore had a much closer relationship with him than with Shitou. However, in this entry, he is described as Shitou's disciple exclusively. Moreover, the entry strangely includes a long story about Daowu Yuanzhi and Yunyan Tansheng. The two were said to be brothers who had been separated for a long time and met again at the Baizhangsi. After learning from Baizhang for one year, Daowu went to visit Yaoshan and became his disciple. One day, he sent a letter to Yunyan, in which he said: "Shitou is a genuine-gold store, and Jiangxi a convenience store." "Genuine-gold store" (*zhenjin pu*) referred to true Buddhist teaching, while "convenience store" (*zahuo pu*) was obviously used to derogate the Hongzhou school. The story then relates that when the letter arrived even Baizhang thought Daowu's criticism was valid, so Yunyan left Baizhang to become Yaoshan's disciple. Later, when Yunyan planned to visit Guishan Lingyou, Daowu again stopped him.[20] As Ui Hakuju indicates, Daowu's secular surname was Zhang, and Yunyan's secular surname was Wang, so the two were not brothers; Daowu actually studied with Baizhang Fazheng, not Baizhang Huaihai.[21] This story is full of legendary color and is obviously a later creation. It is notable that this is not the only instance of the metaphor of "genuine gold." In Qingyuan Xingsi's entry in the *ZTJ*, we again find it in another made-up encounter-dialogue story: Shenhui visited Qingyuan, and asked, "Is there any genuine gold in your place to be given to others?" Qingyuan answered, "Supposing there is one, if I give it to you, where are you going to take it?"[22] Here "genuine gold" again refers to true Buddhist teaching. The two stories were obviously created by the Shitou line, but by whom and when?

The answer may be found in Yangshan Huiji's (807–883) response to these stories. Yangshan preached in one of his sermons: "Shitou is a genuine-gold store, and my place is a convenience store. If someone comes to seek a general item, I will pick it up and give it to him. If someone comes to seek genuine gold, I will also give it to him."[23] Yangshan accepted the metaphors of "genuine-gold store" and "convenience store," but attached to the latter a positive interpretation, saying that his teaching was more flexible as he used different expedients, either "genuine gold" or "general merchandise," to guide learners. Referring to the argument that both propositions of the Hongzhou school, "the mind is the Buddha" and "neither mind nor Buddha," were expedients for guiding learners, we can see that this controversy about "genuine gold" was simply a continuation of the first controversy, with the criticisms about the Hongzhou school's deviation from Buddhist tenets as their common background.

As observed in chapter three, Yangshan was one of the forerunners of mature encounter dialogue; hence, his discourses are relatively datable. The story about Daowu and Yunyan and the story about Shenhui and Qingyuan, in which the metaphor of "genuine gold" is seen, must have been created earlier than or contemporary to Yangshan, as his sermon was obviously a retort to this metaphor. Since Dongshan Liangjie (807–869) was Yunyan's disciple and also the first to elevate Shitou's teaching and attributed himself to the Shitou line exclusively (see the next section), we have reason to assume that it was he who created those stories and started the controversy.

THE SCHISM OF THE HONGZHOU SCHOOL AND THE RISE OF THE SHITOU LINE AND VARIOUS HOUSES: DECONSTRUCTING THE GENEALOGY

During the late Tang and Five Dynasties, various houses of Chan Buddhism sprang up, among which some major houses claimed to be successors of Shitou. Since the Song dynasty, historians of Chan Buddhism have all described a genealogical diagram of two lines and five houses after the sixth patriarch Huineng, as seen in Table 3.

This traditional genealogy is now challenged by two historical facts. First, although Shitou was nearly as famous as Mazu during his lifetime,[24] he and his disciples did not form an influential lineage during the mid-Tang period.

TABLE 3. Traditional Chan Genealogy after the Sixth Patriarch Huineng

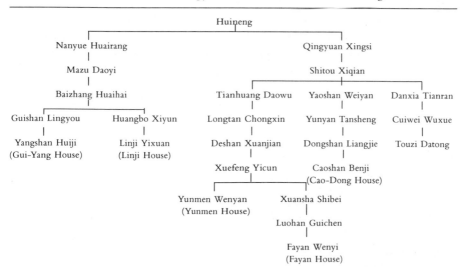

As discussed in chapter five, in several epitaphs for Chan monks written from 818 to 841, in reference to the Huineng line, only two lineages/schools, the Hongzhou and the Heze, are listed, whereas the Shitou is not mentioned at all. In Zongmi's works about Chan Buddhism, when he discussed the four or seven major lineages/schools, he did not mention the Shitou except when he talked about the ten major and minor branches/lineages/schools.[25] Thus, before the Huichang persecution of Buddhism, the Shitou had not been regarded as a major branch of the Huineng line. The other fact is that the two masters, Yaoshan Weiyan and Tianhuang Daowu, to whom the three houses of the Shitou line traced themselves, actually learned from both Mazu and Shitou, and Yaoshan had a much closer relationship with the former.[26] Therefore, they should not be ascribed to the Shitou line exclusively.

Du Jiwen and Wei Daoru assert that the rise of the Shitou line may be attributed to the ZTJ with its obvious sectarian inclination toward this school.[27] Xu Wenming assumes that the disciples of Yunju Daoying (d. 902), who was Yaoshan's third-generation disciple, were the first to claim that they came from the Shitou line.[28] According to early sources, however, this assertion of lineage can be traced to a much earlier date.

The Silla monk Yŏŏm (862–930) came to China in 892 and learned from Yunju Daoying. His epitaph reads: "Under Caoxi, the most excellent disciples were named Huairang and Xingsi. Xingsi's heir was Xiqian, Xiqian's heir Weiyan, Weiyan's heir Tansheng, Tansheng's heir Liangjie, Liangjie's heir Daoying, Daoying's heir the great master."[29] Another Silla monk Iŏm (870–936) came to China in 896 and also learned from Yunju. His epitaph again reads:

> There were only two excellent disciples [of Huineng], namely Huairang and Xingsi, whose successors have multiplied in great numbers. The one who inherited Huairang was Daji, and the one who inherited Xingsi was Shitou. Shitou passed [his teachings] to Yaoshan, Yanshan to Yunyan, Yunyan to Dongshan, Dongshan to Yunju, and Yunju to the great master.[30]

According to these epitaphs, Xu Wenming suggests that it was the disciples of Yunju who first ascribed themselves to the Shitou line. However, the Korean monks' assertion of their common line precisely reveals that this assertion must have come from their common mentor, Yunju.

Yet Yunju was not the first to do so but just passed on the idea of his mentor, Dongshan Liangjie. In Caoshan Benji's biography in the SGSZ, there is an important statement that has been almost totally ignored:

> At the beginning of the Xiantong reign-period, the Chan school sprang up, and this tendency started from Dagui. As for Shitou and Yaoshan, their names were unknown to the public. Fortunately, Dongshan pitied the situation and elevated Shitou's teaching. Learners

went to study with him, and the learning became a common practice, just like that of Confucius and his disciples in the Zu-Si area.[31]

Dagui referred to Guishan Lingyou, the first founder of the Gui-Yang house. According to this statement, in about 860, the Mazu-Baizhang-Guishan line prevailed in the Chan mainstream, while the names of Shitou Xiqian and Yaoshan Weiyan were unknown to the public; it was Dongshan Liangjie (807–869) who first elevated Xiqian's teaching and made the Shitou-Yaoshan line prosperous. The Northern Song monk Huihong also said, "In the past, I read the discourses preserved at Dongshan, and found that the line of Chan master Wuben (i.e., Dongshan) had aimed to deify and expound Shitou's teaching."[32] Huihong seems to have read some materials that were not included in the popular lamp histories, and found that Dongshan and his successors had deliberately elevated Shitou's teaching.

Looking at the rise of the various houses during the late Tang period, *SGSZ*'s record becomes more creditable. As early as about 820, Lingyou built a monastery at Daguishan. He gathered more than one thousand followers, and even set certain rules for his order. Except for the brief period of the Huichang persecution, he taught at the mountain until he died in 853. During this long period of about thirty years, "the master was regarded as number one among Buddhist preachers all over the country."[33] After Lingyou passed away, his three major disciples, Yangshan Huiji, Xiyuan Da'an, and Xiangyan Zhixian, continued to exert important influence in the Chan school.[34]

In 852, two years before Lingyou's death, Dongshan Liangjie built his monastery at Xinfengshan (i.e., Dongshan).[35] Around that time Linji Yixuan (d. 867) became popular in the north. Surely, as described in the *SGSZ*, at the beginning of the Xiantong reign-period (860) when Dongshan was becoming active, the Guishan house had already firmly built its reputation. Facing this strongly established Guishan house in neighboring Hunan and the growing Linji house in Hebei, it is highly possible that, in order to build an independent, distinct house, Dongshan deliberately elevated Shitou's teaching, broke away from the Hongzhou line, and attributed himself to the Shitou line exclusively, ignoring the fact that Yaoshan studied with Mazu for a long period. The alleged story that Shitou learned from Huineng for a while could have been useful to Dongshan in claiming his line as the orthodox heir of Huineng.[36] The criticism of the Hongzhou doctrine in the mid-Tang period must also have been an important factor that pushed Dongshan away from the Hongzhou line or caused him to accept Shitou's teaching as superior to Mazu's, despite the fact that he also learned from Wuye Lingmo, Mazu's disciple.[37] As discussed in the previous section, Yaoshan's long entry in the *ZTJ* presents Yaoshan as Shitou's disciple exclusively, and it also includes the legends of Yunyan and Daowu, in which the metaphors of "genuine-gold store" and "convenience store" are put forward and the teachings of Mazu, Baizhang, and Guishan are depreciated. Those fabricated stories in this entry end with the generation of Dongshan's mentor. Thus, it is highly possible that Dongshan fabricated these stories when he elevated Shitou's teaching in the early Xiantong period.

In the late Tang, along with Dongshan's separation from the Hongzhou line, another branch of Yaoshan also attached itself to the Shitou line. The Silla monk Hyŏnhwi (879–941) came to China in 906 and learned from Jiufeng Daoqian (d. 923), who, like Yunju, was Yaoshan's third-generation disciple. Hyŏnhwi's epitaph also emphasizes that "Huineng's descendents divided into two lines: the first was named Huairang, and the second was named Xingsi."[38] In this genealogy passed on from Hyŏnhwi, the Southern school was again clearly divided into two lines; this implied that his line had already broken from the former and attached itself to the latter. This separation was probably conducted by Shishuang Qingzhu (807–888), Daoqian's mentor. Shishuang had a close relationship with Dongshan, and went to stay at Shishuangshan in 868, a time when various houses were arising. Shishuang's house was actually regarded as a major house in the Five Dynasties and early Song (see later). Hence, he was probably influenced by Dongshan to break away from the Hongzhou line and ascribe himself to the Shitou line in order to establish his own distinctive house.

The Yunmen and Fayan houses, two houses that arose in the Five Dynasties, were the successors of Xuefeng Yicun. When did this line begin to connect with Shitou? In Xuefeng's *Discourse Record*, he already declares himself to be the successor of Shitou.[39] However, the initial connection seems to have begun with Xuefeng's mentor Deshan Xuanjian (782–865). Deshan's biographies in the *ZTJ* and *SGSZ* are quite similar. Both state that because Deshan heard that Longtan Chongxin was Shitou's second-generation disciple, he moved to Longtan and studied with him for more than thirty years. At the beginning of the Xiantong reign-period (860), Xue Tingwang, Prefect of Langzhou, invited Xuanjian to stay at Deshan. Xuanjian gathered about five hundred followers and passed away in the sixth year of Xiantong (865).[40] Since the compilers of the *ZTJ* indicated that the biography was based on Deshan's epitaph written by the monk Yuanhui soon after his death, we can infer that the *SGSZ* biography must also have been based on the same epitaph, so both texts are reliably datable. We can assume that Deshan was the first to ascribe the Tianhuang-Longtan line exclusively to Shitou, and the time was likely during the early Xiantong period when he stayed at Deshan and gathered a great number of followers. His turning to the Shitou line may also have been inspired by Dongshan's elevation of Shitou's teaching at the same time, along with his own ambition to establish a distinctive house. His house was actually regarded as a major house during the Five Dynasties and early Song (see later).

At about the same time, Danxia Tianran's second-generation disciple Touzi Datong (819–914) also broke away from the Hongzhou line. The Silla monk Ch'anyu (869–958) came to China in 892 and learned from Datong. The epitaph for Ch'anyu claims that Datong was "the heir-apparent of Shitou's dharma-grandson Cuiwei Wuxue."[41] This lineage account must have been passed on from his mentor. Datong established his own monastery at Touzishan in the Tongchengxian of Shuzhou (in present-day Anhui) during the Qianfu-Zhonghe reign-periods (874–884). Thus, following the successors of Yaoshan and Tianhuang, Danxia's successors also broke away from the Hongzhou line and attached themselves to the Shitou line.

It should be noted that in Qingyuan Xingsi's biography in the *CDL*, Emperor Xizong (r. 873–888) is said to have conferred on him the posthumous title Hongji (Great Relieving) and to his stūpa the title Guizhen (Returning to True Nature).[42] Before this, Xingsi had been an obscure figure. For example, Zongmi mentioned Huairang occasionally in his works, but never mentioned Xingsi. Emperor Xizong's bestowal signaled the official acknowledgment of the Qingyuan-Shitou line, which was obviously the result of the lineage assertions made by Dongshan, Shishuang, Deshan, and Touzi during the reigns of Emperors Yizong and Xizong.

Having clarified the historical reality of the division of the Hongzhou and Shitou lines, we can now proceed to examine the traditional designation of the Five Houses. The Chan tradition has held that during the late Tang and Five Dynasties, five houses were derived from the two major lines, namely the Gui-Yang, Linji, Cao-Dong, Yunmen, and Fayan. However, when examining early sources carefully, we find that this tradition is also problematic. Fayan Wenyi says in his *Zongmen shigui lun* (Treatise on the Ten Regulations of the School):

> The two branches [of Jiangxi and Shitou] derived various factions respectively. Each of these factions dominates a region and derives numerous streams. For example, there are the [factions of] the Deshan, Linji, Gui-Yang, Cao-Dong, Xuefeng, and Yunmen, each of which has its own house strategies and ranked remarks [of encounter dialogue].[43]

Thus, to Fayan who was active in the late Five Dynasties, there had been six major houses: Deshan, Linji, Gui-Yang, Cao-Dong, Xuefeng, and Yunmen. If his own Fayan house is added, the number is then seven. By the early Song, when Yang Yi (974–1020) wrote the preface for Fenyang Shanzhao's (ca. 946–ca. 1023) discourse records, he named ten houses: Jiangxi, Shitou, Nanquan, Zhaozhou, Dongshan, Yangshan, Xuefeng, Yunmen, Huangbo, and Linji.[44] Shanzhao himself listed seven houses: Mazu, Dongshan, Shishuang, Gui-Yang, Shitou-Yaoshan, Xuefeng-Dizang, and Linji.[45] Shanzhao's disciple Shishuang Chuyuan commented on seven house styles: Fayan-Fadeng,[46] Yunyan-Dongshan, Xuefeng-Xuansha, Guishan-Yangshan, Daowu-Shishuang, Muzhou-Yunmen, and Linji-Deshan.[47] If we omit the mid-Tang masters and lineages, we can see that the people of the late Five Dynasties to early Song in general acknowledged eight major houses of the late Tang to Five Dynasties period: Gui-Yang, Cao-Dong, Deshan, Linji, Shishuang, Xuefeng, Yunmen, and Fayan. According to these sources, Suzuki Tetsuo asserts that the designation of the

Five Houses had not been fixed by the early Song, but was finalized in mid-Northern Song texts, such as Jinshan Tanying's *Genealogies of the Five Houses* (*Wujia zongpai*) and Heshan Huifang's discourse records.[48]

The reasons for the origination and prosperity of so many houses during the late Tang and Five Dynasties can be observed from four perspectives. First, the controversies over the Hongzhou doctrine and the schism of the Hongzhou school triggered competitions for orthodoxy and legitimacy between Chan masters; hence, those who were the earliest to change their lineage assertions, such as Dongshan, Deshan, and Shishuang, succeeded in establishing their own houses/lineages. Like their mid-Tang predecessors, many Chan masters of this period learned from more than one mentor.[49] This fact also indicates that lineage assertions were often accompanied by the will to claim orthodoxy for their own houses.

Second, during the Huichang persecution, almost all Buddhist monasteries were destroyed. After the catastrophe, the late-Tang rulers adopted a post-persecution policy of granting laymen the unrestricted right to build monasteries in villages and sponsor the ordination of monks and nuns.[50] The decentralizing forces that accompanied the decline of the Tang and the emergence of the Five Dynasties and Ten Kingdoms further allowed local authorities to build or sponsor constructions of monasteries. Many Chan monks of Mazu line seized this chance to follow their mid-Tang predecessors in building numerous monasteries and cloisters with the clear denomination "Chan."[51] These self-built and self-administered monasteries and cloisters became institutional bases for gathering large numbers of followers and establishing houses. It was not by accident that most of the founders of the houses were the "opening mountain" patriarchs of monasteries. Then, along with the successive abbotships of these monasteries held by Chan monks, a new concept of monastery genealogy (*shidai*) emerged.[52] These regional Chan establishments and movements became a major force through which the official institutionalization of Chan monasteries during the Northern Song was precipitated.

Third, after the severe destruction of Buddhist scriptures in the two successive catastrophes—the Huichang persecution and Huang Chao rebellion—"those schools like the Tiantai and Huayan which were heavily dependent on textual exegesis for the explication of their doctrines experienced a sharp decline from which they never fully recovered."[53] As discussed in chapter five, during the mid-Tang, the polemical claim of the Chan school as a special transmission without relying on scriptures by Mazu's first-generation disciples was interpreted as a major doctrine of the Chan school by Mazu's second-generation disciples. Then, during the late Tang and Five Dynasties, in the context of the general decline of the scholastic traditions, this interpretation was generally accepted and practiced by Chan monks and became a theoretical framework for the iconoclastic, radical aspect of encounter dialogue. The image of Yaoshan Weiyan changed from a diligent preacher of Buddhist scriptures to an iconoclastic pioneer who "always forbade others to read scriptures."[54] Encounter dialogue rapidly reached high maturity. Students began to ask their masters about their "house style" (*jiafeng* or *menfeng*),[55] which referred to the unique rhetorical and pedagogical style of encounter dialogue established by each house. It actually became the hallmark of each house, as Yongming Yanshou said, "The masters bestowed [their teachings] for the dharma, without sparing their house styles. There was no question they could not answer. When there were doubts, they solved all of them"; "They only wanted to keep their house styles tough and radical, and the questions and answers sharp and novel."[56] Fayan Wenyi actually identified several houses by their "house styles."[57] The identification of house identity with house style conveys an important message: the various houses of the late Tang and Five Dynasties differed in encounter-dialogue styles, but doctrinally they still followed the basic tenets of the Hongzhou school.

Fourth and most importantly, under the surface of the vigorous rise of various houses lay the strong motif of striving for the orthodoxy of the Huineng line or the so-called Southern Chan, which triumphed completely in the Chan movement after the persecution. This competition is displayed clearly in the epitaphs of Yangshan Huiji, the second founder of the Gui-Yang house, and Xuefeng Yicun, who founded his own house and was the patriarch of both the Yunmen and Fayan houses. Yangshan Huiji founded his own monastery at Yangshan in about 866, the seventh year of the Xiantong period,[58] soon after Dongshan and Deshan attached themselves to the Shitou line. Yangshan redefined the implication of the metaphors about the "genuine-gold store" and "convenience store" in order to refute Dongshan's depreciation of the Hongzhou doctrine, as discussed in the previous section. He and his disciples further openly claimed him as the orthodox heir of the Huineng line. His epitaph written by Lu Xisheng in 895 reads: "According to the secret prophecies of India, after Bodhidharma entered China, there should be seven generations (*ye*), like grass (*cao*) having its upper part removed. Yangshan was a native of Shaozhou, and his secular surname was Ye. Upwardly, he followed the sixth patriarch to become the seventh generation."[59] This statement must have been based on Yangshan's story or that of his disciples. "The secret prophecies of India" refers to the prophecies forged by the compiler(s) of the *Baolin zhuan*. As mentioned in chapter one, the original prophecies in the *Baolin zhuan* were lost, but fortunately they are preserved in the *ZTJ*, in which the phrase "like grass (*cao*) having its upper part removed" is found.[60] In the *ZTJ*, this prophecy is explained as referring to Shitou with the reasoning that no grass could grow on a rock (*shitou*).[61] However, Yangshan and his disciples explained it in another way: if the upper part of the character *cao* was removed, the character became *zao* (early), which was homophonic with Shao, Yangshan's hometown. His secular surname was Ye, and one of the meanings of this character is "generation." Yangshan and his disciples oddly claimed him to be the seventh patriarch who directly inherited Huineng's teaching. In the epitaph for Yangshan Guangyong, Yangshan's disciple, Song Qiqiu also says, "After Caoxi passed away, Yangshan rose. Caoxi was the marrow, while Yangshan was the bone. Caoxi was void, while Yangshan was solid."[62] Obviously Yangshan and his disciples claimed they were the orthodox line of the sixth patriarch, and their rivals were the newly proclaimed branches of the Shitou line.

To this claim, Xuefeng Yicun and his disciples made an immediate retort. Xuefeng built his own cloister at Xuefeng in 870 and gathered more than fifteen hundred followers. His epitaph written by Huang Tao in 908 states: "From Caoxi, different lineages were derived. Who inherited the Southern line? By one word, he [Xuefeng] became the best; for six generations, he was regarded as the most outstanding one."[63] Surely Xuefeng and his disciples also had the ambition to become recognized as the most orthodox house after Huineng.

The criticism of the Hongzhou doctrine in the mid-Tang, and possibly the impact of the Huichang persecution of Buddhism as well, led to reflections and controversies on the Hongzhou doctrine among Chan masters in the late Tang. These reflections and controversies brought about new lineage assertions. Dongshan Liangjie, Deshan Xuanjian, Shishuang Qingzhu, and Touzi Datong, who were successors of Tianhuang, Yaoshan, and Danxia, broke away from the Hongzhou line and attached themselves to the Shitou line exclusively. As a result, the tradition of the two great lineages after Huineng was retrospectively created. From the late Tang to Five Dynasties, this dynamic process of division, further triggered by the impetus of striving for orthodoxy of the Southern Chan and the establishment of many new monasteries and cloisters headed by Chan masters, gave birth to various houses, among which were eight major ones—Gui-Yang, Linji, Cao-Dong, Deshan, Xuefeng, Shishuang, Yunmen, and Fayan. The designation of the Five Houses—Gui-Yang, Linji, Cao-Dong, Yunmen, and Fayan—was not fixed until the mid-Northern Song, and represented the current state of the Northern Song Chan after the rise and fall of the various houses. Thus, the traditional Chan genealogy of two lines and five houses is deconstructed by historical reality, and further studies of Chan history surely should apply new frameworks of narration.

APPENDIX

ANNOTATED TRANSLATION OF MAZU DAOYI'S DISCOURSES

CONVENTIONS OF TRANSLATION AND ANNOTATION

1. This translation contains only authentic or relatively datable discourses of Mazu Daoyi, including six sermons and four dialogues, as discussed in chapter three.

2. The text used for each sermon or dialogue is the earliest, or most complete, or most reliable chosen from six early texts: *Quan Zaizhi wenji, Zutang ji, Zongjing lu, Song gaoseng zhuan, Jingde chuandeng lu,* and *Tiansheng guangdeng lu.* Unless there are obvious errors, I do not make collations in order to present the original state of the texts. When a correction is necessary, I use parentheses to indicate words that should be deleted and brackets to indicate words that should be added. Corresponding early texts and major textual differences are indicated in the notes.

3. In the notes I adduce extensively Zongmi's works and discourses of Mazu's first- and second-generation disciples from stele inscriptions and other reliably datable Tang texts to verify the authenticity of Mazu's sermons and dialogues.

4. Five modern works or translations, Yanagida Seizan's "Goroku no rekishi: Zen bunken no seiritsushiteki kenkyū," Iriya Yoshitaka's *Baso no goroku,* Julian Pas's translation of *The Recorded Sayings of Ma-tsu,* Cheng Chien's *Sun-face Buddha: The Teaching of Ma-tsu and the Hung-chou School of Chan,* and Robert Buswell's translation of Zongmi's *Chan Chart* (in *The Korean Approach to Zen: The Collected Works of Chinul,* 265–81) are consulted throughout this translation and will not be indicated individually in the notes.

SERMON 1 (*ZJL, T.* 48: 1.418b/c, 24.550c)

1

The great master Mazu in Hongzhou preached: The great master Bodhidharma came from South India to China only to transmit the Mahāyāna dharma of one-mind.[1] He used the *Laṅkāvatāra-sūtra* to certify the minds of all sentient beings, lest they not believe in that dharma of one-mind. The *Laṅkāvatāra-sūtra* says: "In the Buddha's discourses, the mind is the essence,[2] and no-gate is the dharma-gate." Why, in Buddha's discourses, is the mind the essence? In Buddha's discourse of mind, the mind and the Buddha are identical. What I am speaking right now is exactly the mind-discourse. Therefore, [the sūtra] says, "In Buddha's discourses, the mind is the essence."[3]

洪州馬祖大師云: 達磨大師從南天竺國來, 唯傳大乘一心之法, 以 "楞伽經" 印眾生心, 恐不信此一心之法. "楞伽經" 云: "佛語心為宗, 無門為法門." 何故 "佛語心為宗?" 佛語心者, 即心即佛, 今語即是心語. 故云 "佛語心為宗."

2

"No-gate is dharma-gate" means that if one understands that the original nature is empty, there is not a single dharma. Nature itself is the gate; as nature is formless, there is also no gate. Therefore, [the sūtra] says, "No-gate is dharma-gate." It is also called the empty gate or the phenomenal gate. Why is it so? Emptiness is the emptiness of dharma-nature (dharmatā), and the phenomenal is the phenomenal of dharma-nature. [Dharma-nature] is without form and sign, so it is called emptiness; [its functions] of knowing and seeing are endless, so it is called the phenomenal. Therefore, [the sūtra] says, "The phenomenal of the Tathāgata is endless, and so is his wisdom."[4] From where all dharmas are engendered, there are again countless samādhi-gates, which are far away from internal and external clinging of knowledge and affections. They are also called gate of absolute-holding or gate of bestowal,[5] which means not to think all internal and external dharmas of good and evil. Thus, they all are gates of various perfections (pāramitā). The physical-body (rūpakāya) Buddha is the function of the true-form Buddha.[6] The sūtra says, "All the thirty-two marks and eighty signs are engendered from the thinking of the mind."[7] This is also called the flame of dharma-nature or the exploit of dharma-nature.[8] When the Boddhisattva cultivates Buddhist wisdom (prājñā), the flame [of wisdom] burns out all internal and external things of the triple world, within which not a single blade of grass is damaged because all dharmas are the same as the [true] form. Therefore, the sūtra says, "Do not destroy the idea of a self; all things are of a single form."[9]

"無門為法門" 者, 達本性空, 更無一法. 性自是門, 性無有相, 亦無有門. 故云: "無門為法門." 亦名空門, 亦名色門. 何以故? 空是法性空, 色是法性色. 無形相故謂之空, 知見無盡故謂之色. 故云: "如來色無盡, 智慧亦復然." 隨生諸法處, 復有無量三昧門, 遠離內外知見情執. 亦名總持門, 亦名施門. 謂不念內外善惡諸法, 乃至皆是諸波羅蜜門. 色身佛是實相佛家用. 經云: "三十二相八十種好, 皆從心想生." 亦名法性家焰, 亦法性功勳. 菩薩行般若時, 火燒三界內外諸物盡, 於中不損一草葉, 為諸法如相故. 故經云: "不壞於身, 而隨一相."

3

Now that you know that self-nature is the Buddha, you walk, abide, sit, and lie in all time-periods, without ever attaining one single dharma. Even the "Tathatā" (Thusness) does not belong to the category of all names and is also without no-name. Therefore, the sūtra says, "The wisdom does not admit of existence and nonexistence."[10] Do not seek within or without, just letting original nature be free, and also without the mind of letting nature be free. The sūtra says, "Various bodies produced at will, I say they are the mind-capacity."[11] This is the mind of no-mind and the capacity of no-capacity. No-name is true name, and no-seeking is true seeking.[12]

今知自性是佛, 於一切時中, 行住坐臥, 更無一法可得. 乃至真如, 不屬一切名, 亦無無名. 故經云: "智不得有無." 內外無求, 任其本性, 亦無任性之心. 經云: "種種意生身, 我說為心量." 即無心之心, 無量之量. 無名為真名, 無求是真求.

4

The sūtra says, "Those who seek the dharma should seek nothing."[13] Outside of the mind there is no other Buddha; outside of the Buddha there is no other mind.[14] Do not grasp good; do not reject evil. Do not rely on both sides of purity and defilement.[15] All dharmas are without self-nature, and the triple world is [made of] mind only (cittamātra).[16] The sūtra says, "The densely arrayed myriad phenomena are the impressions of the unique dharma."[17] Whenever you see the phenomenal, you see the mind. The mind does not exist by itself; its existence is due to the phenomenal. The phenomenal does not exist by itself; its existence is due to the mind.[18] Therefore, the sūtra says, "Seeing the phenomenal is seeing the mind."[19]

經云: "夫求法者, 應無所求." 心外無別佛, 佛外無別心. 不取善, 不(作) [捨]惡, 淨穢兩邊, 俱不依[怙]. 法無自性, 三界唯心. 經云: "森羅及萬像, 一法之所印." 凡所見色, 皆是見心. 心不自心, 因色故心. 色不自色, 因心故色. 故經云: "見色即是見心."

5

If you understand this matter, you can at any time wear clothes, eat food, freely and unrestrainedly following your destiny.[20]

汝若悟此事了, 但随时著衣吃饭, 任运腾腾.

SERMON 2 (*ZJL, T.* 48: 14.492a)

6

The great master Mazu preached: If you want to recognize the mind, that which is speaking is your mind. This mind is called the Buddha, and it is also the dharma-body (dharmakāya) Buddha of true-form, and is called the Way as well.[21] The sūtra says, "[The Buddha] has numerous names in the three great countless kalpas,[22] which are named according to conditions and situations."[23] For example, the maṇi pearl changes in accord with the colors [it contacts].[24] When it contacts the color blue, it becomes blue; when it contacts the color yellow, it becomes yellow, though its essence lacks coloration.[25] The finger does not touch by itself, the knife does not cut by itself, and the mirror does not reflect by itself. Each is named according to the causes that appear in specific conditions.

馬祖大師云: 汝若欲識心, 祇今語言, 即是汝心. 喚此心作佛, 亦是實相法身佛, 亦名為道. 經云: "有三阿僧祇百千名號, 隨世應處立名." 如隨色摩尼珠, 觸青即青, 觸黃即黃, 體非一切色. 如指不自觸, 如刀不自割, 如鏡不自照, 隨緣所見之處, 各得其名.

7

This mind is as long-lived as space. Even though you transmigrate to multiple forms in the six ways of transmigration, this mind never has birth and death. Since the sentient beings do not realize their self-mind, they falsely raise deluded feelings and receive retribution for various karmas. They are confused in their original nature, and falsely cling to the matters of the world. The body of four elements (mahābhūta) currently has birth and death, but the nature of the numinous mind actually has no birth or death. Now you realize this nature, which is called longevity, and also called the longevity-measure of the Tathāgata and the motionless nature of fundamental emptiness. All sages of the past and future recognize this nature only as the Way.[26]

此心與虛空齊壽. 乃至輪迴六道, 受種種形, 即此心未曾有生, 未曾有滅. 為眾生不識自心, 迷情妄起, 諸業受報. 迷其本性, 妄執世間風息. 四大之身, 見有生滅, 而靈覺之性, 實無生滅. 汝今悟此性, 名為長壽, 亦名如來壽量, 喚作本空不動性. 前後諸聖, 祇會此性為道.

8

Now seeing, listening, sensing, and knowing are fundamentally your original nature, which is also called original mind. It is not that there is a Buddha other than this mind.[27] This mind originally existed and exists at present,[28] without depending on intentional creation and action; it was originally pure and is pure at present, without waiting for cleaning and wiping. Self-nature attains nirvāṇa; self-nature is pure; self-nature is liberation; and self-nature departs [from delusions]. It is your mind-nature, which is originally the Buddha, and you do not have to seek the Buddha from somewhere else.[29] You are the diamond-samādhi by yourself, without again intending to attain samādhi by concentration. Even though you attain it by concentration and meditation, you do not reach the supreme.[30]

今見聞覺知, 元是汝本性, 亦名本心. 更不離此心別有佛. 此心本有今有, 不假造作; 本淨今淨, 不待瑩拭. 自性涅槃, 自性清淨, 自性解脫, 自性離故. 是汝心性, 本自是佛, 不用別求佛. 汝自是金剛定, 不用更作意凝心取定. 縱使凝心斂念作得, 亦非究竟.

SERMON 3 (*ZJL, T.* 48: 49.707b)

9

The great master Mazu preached: If these things are perceived by the mind—the places one has passed by in this life, his own fields and house, and his parents and brothers, the mind actually does not go there. Do not think that the mind goes there because one sees these things. The mind-nature originally does not come or go, and it is also without rising or extinction.[31]

馬祖大師云: 若此生所經行之處, 及自家田宅處所、父母兄弟等, 舉心見者, 此心本來不去. 莫道見彼事, 則言心去. 心性本無來去, 亦無起滅.

SERMON 4 (*CDL*, 28.6b–7b)

10

The Chan master Daji Daoyi in Jiangxi preached to the assembly:[32] The Way needs no cultivation, just not defiling it. What is defilement? When you have a mind of birth and death and an intention of creation and action, all these are defilement. If you want to know the Way directly, then ordinary mind is the Way.[33] What is an ordinary mind? It means no intentional creation or action, no right or wrong, no grasping or rejecting, no terminable or permanent, no profane or holy.[34] The sūtra says, "Neither the practice of ordinary men, nor the practice of sages—that is the practice of the Bodhisattva."[35] Now all these are just the Way: walking, abiding, sitting, lying, responding to conditions, and handling matters.[36] The Way is the dharma-realm (dharmadhātu). None of the marvelous functions, which are numerous as the sands of the Ganges, falls outside the dharma-realm. If it is not so, how could we speak of the dharma-gate of mind-ground? How could we speak of the inextinguishable lamp? All dharmas are mind dharmas, and all names are mind names. The myriad dharmas arise from the mind, and the mind is the essence of the myriad dharmas.

江西大寂道一禪師示眾云: 道不用修, 但莫污染. 何爲污染? 但有生死心, 造作趣向, 皆是污染. 若欲直會其道, 平常心是道. [何]謂平常心? 無造作, 無是非, 無取捨, 無斷常, 無凡無聖. 經云: "非凡夫行. 非賢聖行. 是菩薩行." 只如今行住坐臥, 應機接物, 盡是道. 道即是法界. 乃至河沙妙用, 不出法界. 若不然者, 云何言心地法門? 云何言無盡燈? 一切法皆是心法, 一切名皆是心名. 萬法皆從心生, 心爲萬法之根本.

11

The sūtra says, "Realizing the mind and reaching the fundamental source, therefore, one is called a monk (śramaṇa)."[37] The names are equal, the meanings are equal, and all dharmas are equal. They are pure and unconfused. Within the Buddhist gate, if you attain freedom at any time, when establishing dharma-realm, all are dharma-realms; when establishing Thusness, all are Thusness; when establishing the absolute, all dharmas are the absolute; when establishing the phenomenal, all dharmas are phenomena. Mentioning one, thousands can be inferred. The absolute and the phenomenal are without difference; both are wonderful functions. There is no other principle, and all are because of the revolving of the mind. For example, though there are many reflections of the moon, the real moon is not manifold. Though there are many springs of water, the nature of water is not manifold. Though there are myriad phenomenal appearances in the universe, the space is not manifold. Though there are many principles being spoken of, the unobstructed wisdom is not manifold.[38] Whatever is established comes from the one-mind. One can construct it or sweep it away; either way is a wonderful function, and the wonderful function is oneself. It is not that there is a place to stand where one leaves the Truth, but the very place where one stands is the Truth and the essence of oneself.[39] If it is not so, then who is one?

經云: "識心達本[源], 故號[為]沙門." 名等義等, 一切諸法皆等, 純一無雜. 若於教門中, 得隨時自在, 建立法界, 盡是法界. 若立眞如, 盡是眞如. 若立理, 一切法盡是理. 若立事, 一切法盡是事. 舉一千從, 理事無別, 盡是妙用, 更無別理, 皆由心之迴轉. 譬如月影有若干, 眞月無若干. 諸源水有若干, 水性無若干. 森羅萬象有若干, 虛空無若干. 道理有若干, 無礙慧無若干. 種種成立, 皆由一心也. 建立亦得, 埽蕩亦得, 盡是妙用, 妙用盡是自家. 非離眞而有, 立處即眞, 立處盡是自家體. 若不然者, 更是何人?

12

All dharmas are the Buddha's dharma, and all dharmas are liberation. Liberation is Thusness, and all dharmas never leave Thusness. Walking, abiding, sitting, and lying—all these are inconceivable function, which does not wait for a timely season. The sūtra says, "In every place there is the Buddha."[40] The Buddha is the Merciful One and has wisdom.[41] He is good in understanding the conditions, and able to break the net of all sentient beings' doubts and free them from the bondages of existence and nonexistence. All feelings of the ordinary and the sacred are ended, and all men and dharmas are empty. He turns the incomparable wheel, transcending number and measure. His activities are unobstructed, and he penetrates both the absolute and the phenomenal. As clouds appear in the sky suddenly and then disappear without leaving any trace, or as writing on water, the great nirvāṇa has neither birth nor death. In bondage it is called tathāgata-garbha; free from bondage it is called Great dharma-body (dharmakāya).[42] Dharma-body is boundless, and its essence neither increases nor decreases. It can be large or small, and square or round. Responding to things, it manifests itself in [many] shapes, like the reflections of the moon in water.[43] It functions constantly without establishing a root.[44] It does not exhaust action, and does not cling to nonaction.[45] Action is the function of nonaction, and nonaction is the dependence of action. It does not cling to dependence, as [the sūtra] says, "Like the void it is without any dependence."[46]

一切法皆是佛法, 諸法即解脫. 解脫者即眞如, 諸法不出於[真]如. 行住坐臥, 悉是不思議用, 不待時節. 經云: "在在處處, 則爲有佛." 佛是能仁, 有智慧, 善機情, 能破一切衆生疑網, 出離有無等縛. 凡聖情盡, 人法俱空, 轉無等輪, 超於數量. 所作無礙, 事理雙通. 如天起雲, 忽有還無, 不留礙迹, 猶如畫水成文. 不生不滅, 是大寂滅. 在纒名如來藏, 出纒名大法身. 法身無窮, 體無增減. 能大能小, 能方能圓. 應物現形, 如水中月. 滔滔運用, 不立根栽. 不盡有爲, 不住無爲. 有爲是無爲家用, 無爲是有爲家依. 不住於依, 故云如空無所依.

13

There are the aspect of the mind subject to birth and death, and the aspect of the mind as Thusness.[47] The mind as Thusness is like a clear mirror that reflects images. The mirror symbolizes the mind, and the images symbolize various dharmas. If the mind grasps various dharmas, it gets involved in external causes and conditions, and is therefore subject to birth and death. If the mind does not grasp various dharmas, it is as Thusness. The Śrāvaka (Hearer) perceives Buddha-nature by auditory perception, while the Bodhisattva perceives Buddha-nature by visual perception.[48] He understands its nonduality, which is called equal nature. The nature is without differentiation, but its functions are different. In ignorance it functions as consciousness; in awakening it functions as wisdom. To follow the absolute is enlightenment; to follow the phenomenal is ignorance. When ignorant, it is the ignorance of one's own original mind; when awakened, it is the awakening of one's own original nature. Once awakened, one is awakened forever, never again becoming ignorant. As when the sun rises, it is incompatible with darkness; when the sun of wisdom rises, it does not go together with the darkness of afflictions. If you understand the mind and the phenomenal appearance, deluded thought will not originate.[49] If deluded thought does not originate, this is the acceptance of the nonproduction of dharmas.[50] [It] originally existed and exists at present. It does not depend on the cultivation of the Way and seated meditation. Neither cultivation nor seated meditation—this is the pure Chan (dhyāna) of Tathāgata.[51] If you now understand this reality, you will truly not create any karma. Following your destiny, passing your life, with one cloak or one robe, wherever sitting or standing, it is always with you. Observing the precepts (śīna), you accumulate pure karma. If you can be like this, why are you concerned about not understanding? All people, you have been standing for a long time; take care.[52]

心生滅義, 心眞如義. 心眞如者, 譬如明鏡照像. 鏡喻於心, 像喻諸法. 若心取法, 即涉外因緣, 即是生滅義. 不取諸法, 即是眞如義. 聲聞聞見佛性, 菩薩眼見佛性. 了達無二, 名平等性, 性無有異, 用則不同. 在迷爲識, 在悟爲智. 順理爲悟, 順事爲迷. 迷即迷自家本心, 悟即悟自家本性. 一悟永

悟, 不復更迷. 如日出時, 不合於冥. 智慧日出, 不與煩惱暗俱. 了心及境界,
妄想即不生.　妄想既不生,　即是無生法忍.　本有今有,　不假修道坐禪.
不修不坐, 即是如來清淨禪. 如今若見此理, 真正不造諸業. 隨分過生, 一
衣一衲, 坐起相隨. 戒行增薰, 積於淨業. 但能如是, 何慮不通. 久立諸人珍
重.

SERMON 5 (*GDL*, *XZJ* 135: 8.652a–653a)

14

Someone asked, "What is the cultivation of the Way?" The master replied,
"The Way does not belong to cultivation. If you speak of any attainment
through cultivation, whatever is accomplished through cultivation will again
decay, just the same as the Śrāvaka (Hearer). If you speak of no-cultivation,
then you will be the same as an ordinary man." He asked again, "What kind
of knowledge should one have in order to understand the Way?" The master
replied, "Self-nature is originally perfectly complete. If only one is not hindered
by either good or evil things, he is called a man who cultivates the Way.
Grasping good and rejecting evil, contemplating emptiness and entering
concentration—all these belong to intentional creation and action. If one seeks
further outside, he strays farther away.[53] Just put an end to all mental calcula-
tions of the triple world. If one originates a single deluded thought, this is
the root of birth and death in the triple world. If one simply lacks a single
thought, then he excises the root of birth and death and obtains the supreme
treasure of the dharma-king. Since countless kalpas, the deluded thoughts of
ordinary man—flattery, deception, self-intoxication, and arrogance—have
formed the one body. Therefore, the sūtra says, 'It is only by many dharmas
that this body is aggregated. When arising, it is only dharmas arising; when
extinguishing, it is only dharmas extinguishing.'[54] When the dharma arises, it
does not say 'I arise'; when the dharma extinguishes, it does not say 'I extin-
guish.' The former thought, the later thought, and the present thought—all
successive moments of thought do not wait for one another, and all successive
moments of thought are quiescent and extinct.[55] This is called the ocean-seal
samādhi, which contains all dharmas.[56] As hundreds and thousands of streams
together return to the great ocean, they are all called seawater. If one lingers
in the single taste, then all tastes are imbibed.[57] Flowing into the ocean, all
streams are mixed. As if one bathes in the water of the great ocean, he uses
the water of all streams."

　　問: "如何是修道?" 師云: "道不屬修. 即言修得, 修成還壞, 即同聲聞.
若言不修, 即同凡夫." 云: "作何見解, 即得達道?" 師云: "自性本來具足, 但
於善惡事上不滯, 喚作修道人. 取善捨惡, 觀空入定, 即屬造作. 更若向外
馳求, 轉疎轉遠. 但盡三界心量, 一念妄想, 即是三界生死根本. 但無一念,
即除生死根本, 即得法王無上珍寶. 無量劫來, 凡夫妄想, 諂曲邪偽, 我慢
貢高, 合為一體. 故經云: '但以眾法, 合成此身. 起時唯法起, 滅時唯法滅.'
此法起時不言我起, 滅時不言我滅. 前念後念中念, 念念不相待, 念念寂滅.

喚作海印三昧, 攝一切法. 如百千異流, 同歸大海, 都名海水. 住於一味, 即攝眾味. 住於大海, 即混諸流. 如人在大海水中浴, 即用一切水."

15

Therefore, the Śrāvaka is awakened, and yet still ignorant; the ordinary man is ignorant about awakening. The Śrāvaka does not know that the sacred mind originally has no position, cause, fruition, or stage, and because of the deluded thought of mental calculation, he cultivates causes and attains fruition, abiding in the samādhi of emptiness. Passing through the eighty thousand and twenty thousand kalpas,[58] although he is awakened, his awakening is ignorant. In the view of the Bodhisattvas, this is like the suffering of the hell, sinking into emptiness and clinging to quiescence, without seeing Buddha-nature. If those sentient beings who are of superior quality unexpectedly meet a good, learned master and gain understanding under his instructions, they will be awakened suddenly to their original nature, without ever passing through stages and positions. Therefore, the sūtra says, "The ordinary man has a changeable, returnable mind, while the Śrāvaka has not."[59] It is in contrast to ignorance that one speaks of awakening. Since originally there is no ignorance, awakening also need not be established. Since limitless kalpas, all sentient beings have never left the samādhi of dharma-nature, and they have always abided in the samādhi of dharma-nature. Wearing clothes, eating food, talking and responding, making use of the six senses, all activities are dharma-nature.[60] If one does not know to return to the source, he follows names and seeks forms, delusively raising ignorant feelings, and creating various kinds of karmas. If one can reflect within by one single thought, the complete mind becomes sacred mind.

所以聲聞悟迷, 凡夫迷悟. 聲聞不知, 聖心本無地位因果階級, 心量妄想, 脩因證果, 住於空定, 八萬劫二萬劫, 雖即已悟卻迷. 諸菩薩觀, 如地獄苦, 沈空滯寂, 不見佛性. 若是上根眾生, 忽爾遇善知識指示, 言下領會, 更不歷於階級地位, 頓悟本性. 故經云: "凡夫有返覆心, 而聲聞無也." 對迷說悟, 本既無迷, 悟亦不立. 一切眾生, 從無量劫來, 不出法性三昧, 長在法性三昧中. 著衣喫飯, 言談祇對, 六根運用, 一切施為, 盡是法性. 不解返源, 隨名逐相, 迷情妄起, 造種種業. 若能一念返照, 全體聖心.

16

All of you should understand your own mind respectively, and do not remember my words. Even if I speak of as many principles as the sands of the Ganges, the mind does not increase; and if I speak of nothing, the mind does not decrease. If I can talk about it, it is your mind; if I cannot, it is still your mind. Even if I could multiply my body, radiate light, or manifest the eighteen transformations, it is still better to return me to my own ashes. Ashes that have been sprinkled are without power, which are like the Śrāvaka who falsely cultivates cause and attains fruition. Ashes that have not been sprinkled are powerful, which are like the Bodhisattva whose karmas of the Way are pure and mature, without being defiled by any evil.[61] If one wants to preach the Tathāgata's expedient teachings of the tripiṭaka, he will not be able to finish the sermon even passing through as many kalpas as the sands of the Ganges. It is just like a chain that is never broken. If you understand the sacred mind, there is never anything else. You have been standing for a long time; take care.

汝等諸人, 各達自心, 莫記吾語. 縱饒說得河沙道理, 其心亦不增. 總說不得, 其心亦不減. 說得亦是汝心, 說不得亦是汝心. 乃至(今)[分]身放光, 現十八變, 不如還我死灰來. 淋過死灰無力, 喻聲聞妄修因證果. 未淋過死灰有力, 喻菩薩道業純熟, 諸惡不染. 若說如來權教三藏, 河沙劫說不可盡, 猶如鉤鏁, 亦不斷絕. 若悟聖心, 總無餘事. 久立珍重.

SERMON 6 (QUAN DEYU, "DAOYI STŪPA," *QUAN ZAIZHI WENJI*, 28.2a)

17

[The master] often said, "The Buddha is not far away from people, but is realized in the mind. Though the dharma is not attached to anything, every phenomenon one has contact with is Thusness. How could it have many side roads to retard learners? Therefore, the more Kuafu and Kaigou sought, the more far away the things they sought were.[62] Yet the diamond and ghee are right in the mind."[63]

嘗曰: "佛不遠人, 即心而證. 法無所着, 觸境皆如. 豈在多岐, 以泥學者. 故夸父喫訴, 求之愈踈. 而金剛醍醐, 正在方寸."

DIALOGUE 1 DAZHU HUIHAI'S FIRST VISIT TO MAZU (DAZHU'S ENTRY IN THE *CDL*, 6.3b–4a)

18

When [Dazhu Huihai] first came to Jiangxi to visit Mazu, Mazu asked, "Where do you come from?" The master [Dazhu] answered,[64] "From the Dayunsi in Yuezhou." Mazu asked, "What is your intention to come here?" He answered, "I come to seek the Buddha-dharma." Mazu said, "Without looking at your own treasure, why do you abandon your home and wander about? Here I do not have a single thing. What kind of Buddha-dharma are you looking for?" Thereupon the master bowed, and asked, "What is Huihai's own treasure?" Mazu replied, "That which is asking me right now is your treasure. It is perfectly complete and lacks nothing. You are free to use it. What is the need to seek outside?" Upon hearing these words, the master realized his original mind, beyond knowing and feeling. Overjoyed, he bowed and thanked him.[65] After serving Mazu as a disciple for six years, because his preceptor was old, he returned to take care of him. Thereupon he obscured his activities and presented himself as dull-witted and dumb. He wrote by himself the *Treatise on the Essential Teaching of Suddenly Entering into Enlightenment,* in one *juan*.[66] Xuanyan, his dharma-nephew, stole it and went to Jiangxi to present it to Mazu. After reading the treatise, Mazu told the assembly, "In Yuezhou there is a great pearl, whose perfect brilliance shines freely without obstruction."

[大珠慧海] 初至江西參馬祖. 祖問曰: "從何處來?" 曰: "越州大雲寺來." 祖曰: "來此擬須何事?" 曰: "來求佛法." 祖曰: "自家寶藏不顧, 拋家散走作什麼? 我遮裏一物也無, 求甚麼佛法?" 師遂禮拜, 問曰: "阿那箇是慧海自家寶藏?" 祖曰: "即今問我者是汝寶藏, 一切具足, 更無欠少, 使用自在, 何假向外求覓?" 師於言下自識本心, 不由知覺, 踊躍禮謝. 師事六載後, 以受業師年老, 遽歸奉養. 乃晦跡藏用, 外示癡訥. 自撰 "頓悟入道要門論" 一卷, 被法門師姪玄晏竊出江外, 呈馬祖. 祖覽訖, 告眾云: "越州有大珠, 圓明光透自在, 無遮障處也."

DIALOGUE 2 FENZHOU WUYE'S FIRST VISIT TO MAZU (*SGSZ*, 11.247–48)

19

Later, [when Wuye] heard that Daji in Hongzhou was the leader of the Chan school, he went especially to see him and pay his respects. Wuye was more than six *chi* tall and stalwart like a standing mountain. When he watched, he beheld with a fixed gaze; and his voice was like [the sound of] a bell. As soon as he saw Wuye, Daji thought he was special. He smiled and said, "What a lofty Buddha hall! But no Buddha is inside of it." Then Wuye respectfully knelt down, and said, "As for the literature of the three vehicles, I have already roughly understood their meanings. I heard that the teaching of the Chan school is that 'this mind is the Buddha,' but I am really unable to understand it." Daji replied, "This very mind that doesn't understand is it, without any other thing. When people do not understand, they are ignorant; when they understand, they are awakened. Being ignorant, they are the sentient beings; being awakened, they are the Buddha.[67] The Way is not apart from the sentient beings; how can there again be any other Buddha? This is like making a fist with one's hand—the whole fist is the hand." Upon hearing these words, Wuye was awakened suddenly. He wept and told Daji, "Formerly I thought the Buddhist Way is far away, and I had to make efforts for many kalpas to realize it. Today for the first time I know that the true form of dharma-body is originally complete within oneself. All the myriad dharmas are produced from the mind. They only have names, without any reality." Daji said, "So it is, so it is! The nature of all dharmas is without birth and death,[68] and all dharmas are fundamentally empty and quiescent.[69] The sūtra says, 'From the beginning all dharmas are always in the form of extinction.'[70] [The sūtra] says again, 'It is a house of ultimate emptiness and quiescence.'[71] [The sūtra] also says, 'Emptiness is the seat of all dharmas.'[72] That is to say that all Buddhas and Tathāgatas abide in the place of nonabiding. If one knows this, he abides in the house of emptiness and quiescence and sits on the dharma-seat of emptiness. Whether lifting his foot or putting it down, one does not leave the place of enlightenment.[73] Upon hearing the words, one understands immediately, again without any gradual stages. This is the so-called ascending the mountain of nirvāṇa without moving the foot."

[無業] 後聞洪州大寂禪門之上首, 特往瞻禮. 業身逾六尺, 屹若山立, 顧必凝睇, 聲仵洪鐘. 大寂一見異之, 笑而言曰: "巍巍佛堂, 其中無佛." 業於是禮跪而言曰: "至如三乘文學, 粗窮其旨. 嘗聞禪門即心是佛, 實未能了." 大寂曰: "只未了底心即是, 別物更無. 不了時, 即是迷. 若了, 即是悟. 迷即眾生, 悟即是佛. 道不離眾生, 豈別更有佛. 亦猶手作拳, 拳全手也." 業言下豁然開悟, 涕淚悲泣, 向大寂曰: "本謂佛道長遠, 勤苦曠劫, 方始得成. 今日始知法身實相, 本自具足, 一切萬法, 從心所生, 但有名字, 無有實者." 大寂曰: "如是如是, 一切法性不生不滅, 一切諸法本自空寂. 經云: '諸法從本來常自寂滅相.' 又云: '畢盡空寂舍.' 又云: '諸法空為座.' 此即諸佛如來住此無所住處. 若如是知, 即住空寂舍, 坐空法座, 舉足下足, 不離道場. 言下便了, 更無漸次. 所謂不動足而登涅槃(上) [山]者也."

DIALOGUE 3 TAKING WINE AND MEAT (MAZU'S ENTRY IN THE *CDL*, 6.3b)

20

The pure-handed Commissioner in Hongzhou asked, "To take wine and meat or not to do it, which is correct?" The master replied, "If you, the Vice Censor-in-chief, take them, it is [the use of] your salary. If you don't, it is your blessing."

洪州廉使問曰: "弟子喫酒肉即是? 不喫即是?" 師云: "若喫是中丞祿, 不喫是中丞福."

DIALOGUE 4 SUN-FACE BUDDHA AND MOON-FACE BUDDHA (MAZU'S ENTRY IN THE *ZTJ*, 14.308)

21

The master was going to pass away tomorrow. That evening, the abbot asked, "The Reverend's health has not been in good condition. How is the Reverend feeling these days?" The master replied, "Sun-face Buddha, Moon-face Buddha."[74]

師明晨遷化, 今日晚際, 院主問: "和尚四體違和, 近日如何?" 師曰: "日面佛, 月面佛."

NOTES

INTRODUCTION

1. Xu Shen (ca. 58–ca. 147), *Shuowen jiezi* (Beijing: Zhonghua, 1963), 151; Yu Xingwu and Yao Xiaoshui, eds., *Jiagu wenzi gulin* (Beijing: Zhonghua, 1996), no. 2041. See Albert Welter, "The Problem with Orthodoxy in Zen Buddhism: Yongming Yanshou's Notion of *zong* in the *Zongjing lu* (Records of the Source Mirror)," *Studies in Religion* 31.1 (2002): 7–8.

2. Tang Yongtong, "Lun Zhongguo fojiao wu 'shizong'," *Zhexue yanjiu* 3 (1962): 47–54; idem, "Zhongguo fojiao zongpai wenti bulun," *Beijing daxue xuebao* 5 (1963): 1–18; Mano Shōjun, *Bukkyō ni okeru shū kannen no seiritsu* (Kyoto: Risōsha, 1964), 234–96; Hirai Shun'ei, *Chūgoku hannya shisōshi kenkyū: Kichizō to Sanron gakuha* (Tokyo: Shunjūsha, 1976), 27–57; and Stanley Weinstein, "Schools of Buddhism: Chinese Buddhism," in *Encyclopedia of Religion*, ed. Mircea Eliade (New York: Macmillan, 1987), 2: 482–87.

3. Mano, *Bukkyō ni okeru shū kannen no seiritsu*, 209–11; John Jorgensen, "The 'Imperial' Lineage of Ch'an Buddhism: The Role of Confucian Ritual and Ancestor Worship in Ch'an's Search for Legitimation in the Mid-T'ang Dynasty," *Papers on Far Eastern History* 35 (1987): 89–133; and T. Griffith Foulk, "The Ch'an *Tsung* in Medieval China: School, Lineage, or What?" *The Pacific World*, New Series 8 (1992): 18–31.

4. Jorgensen, " 'Imperial' Lineage of Ch'an Buddhism," 89–133.

5. Hirakawa Akira, *A History of Indian Buddhism: From Śākyamuni to Early Mahāyāna*, trans. and ed. Paul Groner (Honolulu: University of Hawaii Press, 1990), 83–86.

6. Étienne Lamotte, *History of Indian Buddhism: From the Origins to the Śaka Era*, trans. Sara Webb-Boin and Jean Dantinne (Louvain-Paris: Peeters Press, 1988), 517–23.

7. *Mohe zhiguan*, *T.* 46: 1.1a/b. See Hu Shi, "Heze Shenhui dashi zhuan" (1929), in *Hu Shi ji*, ed. Huang Xianian (Beijing: Zhongguo shehui kexue, 1995), 73; and Andō Toshio, *Tendaigaku: Konpon shisō to sono tenkai* (Tokyo: Heirakuji shoten, 1968), 7.

8. Bernard Faure, *The Will to Orthodoxy: A Critical Genealogy of Northern Chan Buddhism* (Stanford: Stanford University Press, 1997), 9.

9. The other five groups are represented respectively by Sengchou (480–560), Sengshi (476–563), Zhicui (d. after 577), Huisi (515–577) and Zhiyi (538–597), and

Huizan (536–607). See Chen Jinhua, "An Alternative View of the Meditation Tradition in China: Meditation in the Life and Works of Daoxuan (596–667)," *T'oung Pao* 88.4–5 (2002): 345–67, 384–85.

10. For a detailed discussion of the relationship between lineage and orthodoxy in Buddhist tradition, see Albert Welter, "Lineage," in *Encyclopedia of Buddhism*, ed. Robert E. Buswell, Jr. (New York: Macmillan, 2004), 461–65.

11. Weinstein uses "full-fledged school" to designate the first type of tradition/ lineage; see his "Schools of Buddhism," 484.

12. Foulk argues that only groups that were made up of real persons can be defined as schools; see his "Ch'an *Tsung* in Medieval China," 19. However, as all lineages of Chan Buddhism were made up of both legendary and real persons, including those defined by Foulk as schools, such as the Northern and the Heze, this definition is insignificant. The real value of his argument is not terminological but methodological: when studying a lineage or school, we must first distinguish the real members from the fictitious ancestors in its genealogy and then study the two parties from different perspectives—discussing the actual formation, doctrines, and practices of the first party and indicating the symbolic claim of authority implied in the second party.

13. Hu emphasizes that Chan can be understood only within its historical context, and modern historians must strive to reconstruct that history. In contrast, Suzuki argues that if one looks for history in Zen (Chan), one misses the point, because the essence of Zen is timeless truth based on an experience free of history. See Hu, "Ch'an/Zen Buddhism in China: Its History and Method," *Philosophy East and West* 3.1 (1953): 3–24; Suzuki, "Zen: A Reply to Hu Shih," ibid.: 25–46.

14. Bernard Faure, *The Rhetoric of Immediacy: A Cultural Critique of Chan/Zen Buddhism* (Princeton: Princeton University Press, 1992), 55.

15. For example, see Yanagida Seizan, *Shoki zenshū shisho no kenkyū* (Kyoto: Hōzōkan, 1967; reprint, vol. 6 of *Yanagida Seizan shu*, 2001), 17–18; idem, "The 'Recorded Sayings' Texts of Chinese Ch'an Buddhism," trans. John McRae, in *Early Chan in China and Tibet*, ed. Whalen Lai and Levis R. Lancaster (Berkeley: Asian Humanities Press, 1983), 193–94, 198; John C. Maraldo, "Is There Historial Consciousness within Ch'an?" *Japanese Journal of Religious Studies* 12.2–3 (1985): 141–72; Dale S. Wright, "Historical Understanding: The Ch'an Buddhist Transmission Narratives and Modern Historiography," *History and Theory* 31.1 (1992): 37–46; and Heinrich Dumoulin, *Zen Buddhism: A History. Vol. 1. India and China*, trans. James W. Heisig and Paul Knitter (rev. ed., New York: Macmillan, 1994), xvii–xxiii.

16. The term "encounter dialogue" is a translation of the Chinese/Japanese term *jiyuan wenda/kien mondō*, the special type of dialogue that is said to take place between Chan masters and students. It was first used by McRae in his translation of Yanagida's article, "'Recorded Sayings' Texts," 185–205.

17. Foulk posits that as "the hagiographies and discourse records of the T'ang Ch'an masters in the generations following Hui-neng survive only in late collections (none dating before 952) and do not appear among contemporary T'ang materials discovered in Tun-huang or preserved in Japan," those texts were no more than a body of religious mythology created by Song Chan monks to serve polemical, ritual, and didactic functions in the world of Song Chan. Mario Poceski thinks that Foulk is overstating his case and indicates that among the three main types of narrative discourse found in Chan discourse records and "transmission of lamp" histories—namely, biographical

sketches, sermons, and encounter dialogues—the first two are basically compilations of original Tang texts. However, Poceski also asserts that none of the encounter dialogues was written before the mid-tenth century, and reaches a similar conclusion that those dialogues are important only for understanding the Song Chan tradition. John McRae posits that the encounter-dialogue activities and events did not actually happen in the eighth through tenth centuries, but were instead the retrospective recreation of Song-dynasty Chan devotees. See Foulk, "Myth, Ritual, and Monastic Practice in Sung Ch'an Buddhism," in *Religion and Society in T'ang and Sung China*, ed. Patricia B. Ebrey and Peter N. Gregory (Honolulu: University of Hawaii Press, 1993), 149–50; Poceski, "The Hongzhou School of Chan Buddhism during the Mid-Tang Period" (Ph.D. diss., University of California, Los Angeles, 2000), 48–59, 123–25; idem, "Mazu yulu and the Creation of the Chan Records of Sayings," in *The Zen Canon: Understanding the Classic Texts*, ed. Steven Heine and Dale Wright (New York: Oxford University Press, 2004), 72–75; and McRae, *Seeing through Zen: Encounter, Transformation, and Genealogy in Chinese Chan Buddhism* (Berkeley: University of California Press, 2003), 19, 120–21.

18. For example, see Foulk, "Myth, Ritual, and Monastic Practice in Sung Ch'an Buddhism," 149–50; McRae, *Seeing through Zen*, 19, 120–21.

19. Those inscriptions are preserved in Liu Xihai (d. 1853), ed., *Haidong jinshi yuan*, in *Shike shiliao congshu*, ser. 1, no. 21 (Taibei: Yiwen, 1966); *QTW*; Lu Xinyuan (1834–1894), ed. *Tang wen shiyi*, in vol. 11 of *QTW*; Chōsen sōtokufu, ed., *Chōsen kinseki sōran* (Keijō: Chōsen sotokufu, 1919).

20. Zanning acknowledges in his preface that he has made use of biographies and stele inscriptions written in previous centuries; see his *Song gaoseng zhuan* (Beijing: Zhonghua, 1987), 1 (hereafter cited as *SGSZ*). This is also affirmed by Zhipan (fl. 1258–1269) in his *Fozu tongji* (*T.* 49: 43.400a), and can be easily proven from extant original inscriptions. For example, at the end of the biography of Yangqi Zhenshu, Zanning states that the monk Zhixian wrote the epitaph for Zhenshu. Fortunately, the original stele is extant, and a copy of the epitaph is also preserved in the *Quan Tangwen*, ed. Dong Gao (1740–1818) et al. (1814; reprint, Beijing: Zhonghua, 1983), 919.10b–11a (hereafter cited as *QTW*). By comparing the three texts—the original stele inscription (Zhou Shaoliang and Zhao Chao, eds., *Tangdai muzhi huibian xuji* [Shanghai: Shanghai guji, 2001], 913), the *QTW* copy, and the *SGSZ*—we find that the biography cites the epitaph almost verbatim. About Zanning's use of early sources, see also Chou Yi-liang, "Tantrism in China," *Harvard Journal of Asiatic Studies* 8.3–4 (1945): 250.

21. Jing and Yun, *Zutang ji* (Changsha: Yuelu shushe, 1996; hereafter cited as *ZTJ*).

22. Daoyuan, *Jingde chuandeng lu* (*SBCK*; hereafter cited as *CDL*).

23. For example, see Yün-hua Jan (i.e., Ran Yunhua), "Tsung-mi: His Analysis of Ch'an Buddhism," *T'oung Pao* 8 (1972): 2–3; Maraldo, "Is There Historical Consciousness within Ch'an," 156–58; Peter Gregory, *Tsung-mi and the Sinification of Buddhism* (Princeton: Princeton University Press, 1991), 15–16.

24. For a detailed comparison, see the Appendix.

25. See Dale Wright, *Philosophical Meditations on Zen Buddhism* (Cambridge: Cambridge University Press, 1998), 1–19. Another text, *Wanling lu* (Records of Wanling), also acknowledges Pei Xiu as the compiler. However, in his preface to the *Chuanxin fayao*, Pei Xiu clearly states that the text includes Huangbo's teachings in both Hongzhou

and Wanling (*T*. 48: 1.379b/c). Moreover, the *Wanling lu* contains some mature encounter dialogues, which did not appear until the late Tang; it even uses the Song-dynasty term, "gong'an" (ancient case). Yanagida infers that it was compiled by Huangbo's disciples ("Goroku no rekishi: Zen bunken no seiritsushiteki kenkyū," in vol. 2 of *Yanagida Seizan shū*, 373). It must also have been reshaped in later times.

26. Modern scholars in general regard this text as an indigenous Chinese composition.

27. Of course, in the view of modern critical Buddhists, the genuineness of the Hongzhou doctrine is questionable, as it was related to the problematic tathāgatagarbha theory. For detailed discussion, see chapter four.

28. The designations "early Chan" and "Song-dynasty Chan" have been generally used. Ran Yunhua, Robert Buswell, and John McRae suggest the designation "middle Chan"; see Ran, "Tsung-mi: His Analysis of Ch'an Buddhism," 4; Buswell, *The Korean Approach to Zen: The Collected Works of Chinul* (Honolulu: University of Hawaii Press, 1983), 39; and McRae, *Seeing through Zen*, 11–21. McRae also designates the practitioners surrounding Bodhidharma and Huike as "proto-chan."

29. This term appears several times in Daoxuan's *Xu Gaoseng zhuan*, but in this text it means "Chan master," referring to those who practice seated meditation or dhūta (mortification). See Yanagida, *Shoki zenshū shisho no kenkyū*, 447–49.

30. Ennin, *Nittō shinkyu seikyō mokuroku, T*. 55: 1.1083b; *Liuzu Tanjing*, ed. Yang Zengwen (Beijing: Zongjiao wenhua, 2001), 1.

31. *Shenhui heshang chanhua lu*, ed. Yang Zengwen (Beijing: Zhonghua, 1996), 15.

32. For example, Li Yong, "Dazhao chanshi taming," *QTW*, 262.3b; *Lengqie shizi ji, T*. 85: 1.1286c; *Shenhui heshang chanhua lu*, 45; and *Lidai fabao ji* (Record of the Dharma Jewel through the Ages), *T*. 51: 1.195c.

33. Foulk asserts that prior to the mid-tenth century only Zongmi mentioned "Chanzong" in his texts ("Ch'an *Tsung* in Medieval China," 25). This assertion is not well documented. In Chengguan's (738–839) two annotations to the *Huayan jing* (*Avatamsaka-sūtra*) written in about 784–790, he used this term frequently, and in some places he clearly indicated "the six patriarchs of Chanzong" or "the Chanzong transmitted from Bodhidharma"; see his *Da fangguang fo huayanjing shu, T*. 35: 47.859c, 2.512b–c, 15.609b; and *Da fangguang fo huayanjing shu yanyi chao, T*. 36: 8.62a/b, 20.156c, 29.224a, 33.256a, 37.284a, 37.284b, 47.370a, 74.586c, 80.625b, 76.601a. In the Dunhuang manuscript *Dunwu dasheng zhengli jue* (P. 4646, S. 2672), a document about the Tibetan debate that happened in 792–794 (some scholars date it in 780–782), the term "Chanzong" appears four times; see Paul Demiéville, *Le concile de Lhasa* (Paris: Press Universitaires de France, 1952), 24, 39, 119, 177; and Yanagida, *Shoki zenshū shisho no kenkyū*, 454–55. In Huangbo's *Chuanxin fayao*, this term also appears several times; see Sekiguchi Shindai, *Zenshū shishōshi* (Tokyo: Sankibō Busshorin, 1964), 217. In many stele inscriptions written for Chan monks during this period, the term was generally used; for example, Mazu's stūpa inscription written by Quan Deyu (761–818) in 791 and Zhangjing Huaihui's (757–816) epitaph by the same writer in 817 (*Quan Zaizhi wenji, SBCK*, 28.1a–3a, 18.13a–4b); in an inscription inscribed on the back of Bodhidharma's stele written in 806, Li Chaozheng named Bodhidharma as "the first patriarch of Chanzong" (*QTW*, 998.1a). See also *QTW*, 390.2a, 510.7b, 721.13a, 790.22b, 813.21a, 869.13a. Ennin's diary uses "Chanmen zong" to differentiate Chan monks from those of other schools; see Edwin O. Reischauer, trans., *Ennin's Diary: The*

Recorder of a Pilgrimage to China in Search of the Law (New York: Ronald Press, 1955), the fourteenth day of the tenth month in 838, and the fifteenth day of the first month in 840; and Yanagida, *Shoki zenshū shisho no kenkyū*, 456–57. In Eun's catalog dated 847 (*T.* 55: 1.1091b), a text titled "Chanzong [xue]maizhuan" (Blood-Lineage Transmission of the Chan School) is recorded.

CHAPTER ONE

1. For example, see Ui Hakuju, *Zenshūshi kenkyū* (1939; reprint, Tokyo: Iwanami shoten, 1966), 377–96; Suzuki Tetsuo, *Tō Godai zenshūshi* (Tokyo: Sankibō busshorin, 1985), 369–75; Nishiguchi Yoshio, "Baso no denki," *Zengaku kenkyū* 63 (1984): 111–46; He Yun, "Mazu Daoyi pingzhuan," *Shijie zongjiao yanjiu* (1989) 1: 19–29; Cheng Chien (i.e., Mario Poceski), *Sun-Face Buddha: The Teaching of Ma-tsu and the Hung-chou School of Ch'an* (Berkeley: Asian Humanities Press, 1992), 14–29; and Poceski, "Hongzhou School," 126–83.

2. *SGSZ*, 10.221–23. At the end of the biography, Zanning mentions this epitaph. This indicates his use of the original source, which is a convention throughout the book (see Introduction).

3. *Quan Zaizhi wenji (SBCK)*, 28.1a–3a.

4. "Mazu chanshi sheli shihan tiji," copied by Chen Baiquan, "Mazu chanshi shihan tiji yu Zhang Zongyan tianshi kuangji," *Wenshi* 14 (1982): 258.

5. *ZTJ*, 14.304–309; *CDL*, 4.1b–3b.

6. For example, some fragments of the *Baolin zhuan* are also seen in Mazu's entries in the *ZTJ* and *CDL*. See Shiina Kōyū, "*Horinden* itsubun no kenkyū," *Komazawa daigaku Bukkyō gakubu ronshū* 11 (1980): 249; and idem, "*Horinden* makikyū makijū no itsubun," *Sōgaku kenkyū* 22 (1980): 191–98. See also Tokiwa Daijō, *Shina Bukkyō no kenkyū* (Tokyo: Shunjūsha, 1943), 282–85; and Yanagida, *Shoki zenshū shisho no kenkyū*, 235, 252, 319, 390–91. Regarding the creation of the *Baolin zhuan*, see chapter five.

7. For a detailed discussion of these sources, see chapter three.

8. For a detailed discussion of this text, see chapter three.

9. Ouyang Xiu (1007–1072), *Xin Tang shu* (Beijing: Zhonghua, 1975), 42.1081. "Daoyi Stūpa" (28.1a) states that Mazu's family lived in Deyang for many generations, and both *ZTJ* (14.304) and *CDL* (6.25a) say that Mazu was a native of Shifang in Hanzhou.

10. *Quan Zaizhi wenji*, 28.1a.

11. *SGSZ*, 10.221.

12. See Iriya Yoshitaka, *Baso no goroku* (Kyoto: Zenbunka kenkyūjo, 1984), 2.

13. *Quan Zaizhi wenji*, 28.1b; *SGSZ*, 10.221; *ZTJ*, 14.304, 2.41. The "Daoyi Stūpa" says that Mazu chose to become a monk because he regarded the nine schools of Chinese thought and the six classics of Confucian as inadequate. According to this, Poceski asserts that Mazu must have come from an upper-class family and received classical education ("Hongzhou School," 134–37). However, what Quan Deyi said was a cliché of monk epitaphs and should not be taken as fact without other supporting material. On the contrary, judging from the fact that Mazu began his monastic life when he was still a child, he must have come from a lower-class and poor family.

14. The two Dunhuang manuscripts of *Lidai fabao ji* (comp. ca. 774–779) give different years for Chuji's death: S. 516 records it as 736, and P. 2125 as 732 (*T.* 51: 1.184c). The hagiography of Chuji in the *SGSZ* (20.507–8), which is quite different from the *Lidai fabao ji*, says that Chuji's family name was Zhou, and he lived from 648 to 734. Since many Tang sources refer to Chuji as Reverend Tang, the account of the *Lidai fabao ji* is generally considered more reliable.

15. *Quan Zaizhi wenji*, 28.2a.

16. *SGSZ*, 10.222.

17. Zongmi, *Zhonghua chuan xindi chanmen shizi chengxitu*, *XZJ* 110: 1.867b (hereafter cited as *Chan Chart*). This text was originally titled *Pei Xiu shiyi wen*, and the title was changed to *Chanmen shizi chengxitu* when it was compiled into Zongmi's *Daosu chouchang wenji* by his disciples soon after he passed away; see Ishii Shūdō, "Shinpuku-ji bunko shozō no Hai kyū shūi mon no honkoku," *Zengaku kenkyū* 60 (1981): 71–104; and Ran Yunhua, "Heishuicheng chanjuan 'Chengxitu' yanjiu," in *Qingzhu Pan Shichan xiansheng jiuzhi huadan Dunhuangxue tekan*, ed. Liu Cunren (Taibei: Wenjin, 1996), 75–87.

18. *Lidai fabao ji*, *T.* 50: 1.185a. *SGSZ* (19.488) gives different dates of 680–756.

19. *SGSZ*, 19.486.

20. *Lidai fabao ji*, *T.* 50: 1.184c–5a. See Yanagida, ed., *Shoki no zenshi*, vol. 2, *Rekidai hōbōki* (Tokyo: Chikuma shobō, 1976), 151–52; Yu Xianhao, *Tang cishi kao quanbian* (Hefei: Anhui daxue, 2000), 222.2947; and Gregory, *Tsung-mi*, 38–40.

21. Ui has pointed out that Mazu was not Wuxiang's disciple (*Zenshūshi kenkyū*, 380).

22. Zongmi, *Yuanjue jing dashu chao*, *XZJ* 14: 3.556a.

23. *CDL*, 4.2b.

24. Yanagida, *Shoki zenshū shisho no kenkyū*, 338–39.

25. Suzuki, *Tō Godai zenshūshi*, 369.

26. Ziwen, ed., *Foguo Yuanwu Zhenjue chanshi xinyao*, *XZJ* 120: 1.702b; and Shaotan, ed., *Wujia zhengzong zan*, *XZJ* 135: 1.907b. See Yanagida, *Shoki zenshū shisho no kenkyū*, 347–48.

27. See Nishiguchi, "Baso no denki," 119.

28. *QTW*, 780.3b.

29. Zongmi, *Yuanjue jing dashu chao*, *XZJ* 14: 3.557a.

30. *Xin Tang shu*, 40.1027.

31. Yue Shi, *Taiping huanyu ji (SKQS)*, 146.16b.

32. See Ishikawa Rikisan, "Baso zen keisei no ichisokumen," *Sōgaku kenkyū* 13 (1971): 106.

33. Zongmi, *Chan Chart*, *XZJ* 110: 1.867b.

34. Qisong, *Chuanfa zhengzong ji*, *T.* 51: 7.750a.

35. *Quan Zaizhi wenji*, 28.1b; and Zhang Zhengfu (752–834), "Hengzhou Boresi Guanyin dashi beiming bingxu," *QTW*, 619.2a.

36. See Hu's letter to Yanagida, in *Hu Shi ji*, 335.

37. *QTW*, 619.2b; and Shiina Kōyū, "*Horinden* itsubun no kenkyū," 248. Dao'an's epitaph written by Song Dan is poorly preserved in the *QTW*. Fortunately, the *Tangwen*

xushi (3.13b–18a) recopied a quite complete version from the original stele. His biography in the *SGSZ* (18.452–54) lists his name as Hui'an and gives a different family name and dates of birth and death. These sources state that he was Hongren's disciple; however, since he was much older than Hongren according to these sources, his date of birth and early biography are in considerable doubt. For detailed discussions of Dao'an, see McRae, *Northern School*, 56–59; and Faure, *Will to Orthodoxy*, 100–105.

38. "Songshan . . . [three characters missing] gu dade Jingzang chanshi shentaming bingxu," *Jinshi cuibian*, ed. Wang Chang, *XXSKQS*, 87.15a–16b.

39. *QTW*, 619.2a. See also Zongmi, *Yuanjue jing dashu chao, XZJ* 14: 1.278c; *SGSZ*, 9.200; and Chen Tianfu (fl. 1164), *Nanyue zongsheng ji*, in *Wanwei biezang* (Reprint, Nanjing: Jiangsu guji, 1984), 49: 2.9b.

40. *Nanyue zongsheng ji*, 2.10a/b, Fig. 6. It is still acknowledged as a historical site, and is called either the Mazu hermitage, or Chuanfayuan, or Terrace of Polishing Mirror. See Tokiwa Daijō, *Shina bukkyō shiseki tōsaki* (Tokyo: Ryūginsha, 1938), 78. The last name came from the story of Mazu's first meeting with his master.

41. *CDL*, 5.14b.

42. *ZTJ*, 3.87–88; *CDL*, 5.14a/b.

43. For a detailed discussion of the emergence and evolution of encounter dialogue, see chapter three.

44. See Shiina, "*Horinden* itsubun no kenkyū," 248.

45. For a detailed discussion about the creation of this text, see chapter five.

46. *SGSZ*, 9.207.

47. Ibid., 10.226.

48. Ibid., 11.254. See Nishiguchi, "Baso no denki," 127.

49. *SGSZ*, 11.253.

50. Tang Ji, "Gonggongshan Xitang chishi Dajue chanshi chongjian Dabaoguangta beiming," preserved in *Ganxian zhi*, ed. Chu Jingxin et al. (1872; reprint, Taibei: Chengwen chuban gongsi, 1975); and *Fuzhoufu zhi*, ed. Xie Huang et al. (1872; reprint, Taibei: Chengwen chuban gongsi, 1975). See Ishii Shūdō, "Kōshūshū ni okeru Saidō Chizō no ichi ni tsuite," *Indogaku Bukkyōgaku kenkyū* 20.1 (1978): 280–84. Suzuki Tetsuo cites Ouyang Fu's *Jigu qiuzhen xubian* to conjecture that Tang Ji must be Tang Zhi; see his *Tō Godai no zenshū: Konan Kōsei hen* (Tokyo: Daitō shuppansha, 1984), 173–75. However, the stele inscription found by Ouyang Fu was not the original but one recopied by a Song monk, Juexian, so it might contain some scribal errors. Yu Xianhao (*Tang cishi kao*, 161.2335–36) cites the rubbing copy of the Tang epitaph for Sun Fangshao preserved in the Shanghai Library, which mentions Tang Ji as the Prefect of Qian prefecture. In addition, Fu Xuancong, Zhang Chenshi, and Xu Yimin cite the "Zaixiang shixi biao" in the *Xin Tang shu*, in which the names of Tang Ji's cousins are recorded as Tang Chi and Tang Fu, both characters "chi" and "fu" with a "hand" constituent; see their *Tang Wudai renwu zhuanji ziliao zonghe suoyin* (Beijing: Zhonghua shuju, 1982), 55. Therefore, Tang Ji must be the correct name. The biography of Xitang in the *SGSZ* (10.223), which was based on Xitang's epitaph written by Li Bo (773–831), gives the years of his birth and death as 735 and 814, and states that he followed Mazu on Fojiling in Jianyang. If we accept this record, then Zhizang was only eight years old when he followed Mazu in Jianyang in 742. It is not likely that an eight-

year-old child left his home in Qianzhou and went far away to the mountains in Jianyang. Thus, Tang Ji's writing seems to be more reasonable.

51. See Nishiguchi, "Baso no denki," 128.

52. *Quan Zaizhi wenji*, 28.1b.

53. *SGSZ*, 10.221.

54. *Guangxu fuzhoufu zhi*, 83.4b, 4.37b.

55. Both *ZTJ* (14.313–14) and *CDL* (6.8a/b) record that before he became a monk, Huizang was a hunter. One day, he drove some deer through Mazu's hermitage, and was enlightened by Mazu. Considering the fact that Huizang later became the abbot of Shigongsi, this event likely happened in Shigong, and he should be considered a native of that place.

56. *SGSZ*, 9.200; this hagiography is based on the epitaph for Huairang written by Gui Deng (754–820). *CDL* (5.15a) says Huairang died on the eleventh day.

57. Cited by Yu Jing in his "Shaozhou Yuehuashan Huajiesi chuanfa zhuchi ji," *Wuxi ji (SKQS)*, 9.8a/b. See also *ZTJ*, 4.102; *CDL*, 14.6b. *ZTJ* records Huilang's name as Huiming, which may be a scribal error.

58. *Quan Zaizhi wenji*, 28.1b. The version in *QTW* (501.15b) misreads Qianzhou as Chuzhou.

59. *Tang cishi kao*, 49.601, 161.2327–28. Nishiguchi has pointed out that Prefect Pei was Pei Xu, but he surmises without convincing evidence that Pei was Prefect of Qianzhou in the years 765–766 ("Baso no denki," 129–35). Qianzhou was also called Nankangjun, so the Chan sources often mention Nankang as a place where Mazu stayed. From 742 to 758, the Tang government abolished the label *zhou* (prefecture) and replaced it with *jun* (commandery). According to this, Suzuki assumes that Mazu stayed in Qianzhou during 742–758 (*Tō Godai zenshūshi*, 382). However, the people of the Tang and later eras always felt free to use either *zhou* or *jun* when mentioning a place and were not restricted by the short-term change.

60. *Xin Tang shu*, 41.1069.

61. *Ganxian zhi*, 51.9b–10a, 4.1b–3b.

62. *ZTJ*, 4.102; *CDL*, 14.6a/b.

63. Chen Xu, "Tang Hongzhou Baizhangshan gu Huaihai chanshi taming," *QTW*, 446.4b–7a.

64. *SGSZ*, 11.245; *CDL*, 7.5a.

65. Wudeng was from Weishixian of Bianzhou (in present-day Henan), but he lived in Qianzhou because his father held office there (*SGSZ*, 11.253; *CDL*, 7.11b).

66. Lu Jianqiu (789–864) said that Qi'an was from Haitingjun. See his "Hangzhou Yanguanxian Haichangyuan chanmen dashi tabei," *QTW*, 733.21a–3a. The *SGSZ* (11.261) records that Qi'an was from Haimenjun. However, neither Haiting nor Haimen existed in the Tang, and the Haimenxian in the Song was then still included in Hailing. See *Xin Tang shu*, 41.1052; and Wang Cun (1023–1101), *Yuanfeng jiuyu zhi* (Beijing: Zhonghua, 1984), 5.196–99. Thus, Qi'an was probably from Hailing.

67. Zongmi, *Yuanjue jing dashu chao*, *XZJ* 14: 3.557a.

68. *Xin Tang shu*, 42.1088; and *Yuanfeng jiuyu zhi*, 10.495. Subordinated prefectures were established for the purpose of keeping the minorities subdued, with the chiefs of the minorities as prefects.

69. *Hu Shi ji*, 298.

70. He Yun, "Mazu Daoyi pingzhuan," 19.

71. *Xin Tang shu*, 37.963.

72. See Ran, "Tsung-mi: His Analysis of Ch'an," 46.

73. *Chan Chart, XZJ* 110: 1.866a. These errors might instead have been made by later copyists.

74. *Quan Zaizhi wenji*, 28.1b; and Xitang Zhizang's biography in the *SGSZ*, 10.223. *Lisuo* means *zhisuo*, the place where an administrative center was located. Original Tang texts usually use "li" to replace "zhi" in order to prevent any mention of Emperor Gaozong's (r. 649–683) name, Li Zhi. Poceski misunderstands "lisuo" as the "official residence" of Lu Sigong; see his "Hongzhou School," 167. The *Xin Tang shu* (41.1067–68) informs us that the administrative center of Hongzhou was in Nanchangxian, which "was originally named Yuzhang. . . . In the first year of the Baoying reign-period [762], Yuzhang was changed to Zhongling. During the Zhenyuan reign-period [785–804], the name changed again." Thus, during the Dali period, the district was called Zhongling. Since Hongzhou was also called Yuzhangjun, Chan records sometimes mention Hongzhou, sometimes Yuzhang. Ui misunderstands them as two places where Mazu stayed in turn (*Zenshūshi kenkyū*, 389–91).

75. *Tang cishi kao*, 157.2254.

76. *SGSZ*, 10.222.

77. *Tang cishi kao*, 157.2255. Nishiguchi surmises that Bao Fang, Pei Xu, and Mazu might have been punished for disobeying the imperial order ("Baso no denki," 138–40). This assumption is not supported by any evidence, and is a misinterpretation of the sources.

78. The *Shishi jigu lüe* (*T.* 49: 3.829c) by Jue'an (b. 1286) states, "In the fourth year of Dali [769] of Emperor Daizong, [Daoyi's] name was registered at the Kaiyuansi in Zhongling. At that time, Commissioner Lu Sigong heard his fame and highly admired him." According to this, Nishiguchi says that Mazu first went to the Kaiyuansi in 769 ("Baso no denki," 139). However, the *Shishi jigu lüe* is a Yuan dynasty text that cannot be relied on alone, and the statement that "at that time Commissioner Lu Sigong . . ." is not exact because Lu was not in Hongzhou in 769.

79. This edict is not seen in other early sources. However, during the early years of his reign (779–782), upon the appeals of several officials, Emperor Dezong did determine to purge Buddhist clergies. See Weinstein, *Buddhism under the T'ang*, 89–91.

80. *SGSZ*, 11.251, 256.

81. Zongmi, *Chan Chart, XZJ* 110: 1.866a.

82. "Stone Case Inscription," 248; "Daoyi Stūpa," *Quan Zaizhi wenji*, 28.1a; Yao Xuan (968–1020), *Tangwen cui* (*SBCK*), 64.11a. But the *QTW* version of the "Daoyi Stūpa" (501.16a) states that Mazu died in the second year of Zhenyuan (786). This must be a scribal error. See Chen Yuan, *Shishi yinian lu* (1923; reprint, Yangzhou: Jiangsu Guangling guji keyinshe, 1991), 176.

83. *Quan Zaizhi wenji*, 28.2a.

84. *ZTJ*, 14.309.

85. *CDL*, 6.3b.

86. "Stone Case Inscription," 258.

87. *ZTJ*, 14.308. The lifespan of Sun-face Buddha is said to be one thousand eight hundred years, while that of Moon-face Buddha is only one day and one night; see the *Buddhanāma-sūtra (Foming jing)*, *T.* 14: 7.154a; and Iriya, *Baso no goroku*, 16. For the reliability of this dialogue, see chapter three. Poceski asserts that Mazu was made abbot of the Kaiyuansi ("Hongzhou School," 176). This assertion lacks any evidence and is incorrect, as the epitaph by Baoji says only that "[Mazu's] name was registered at the Kaiyuansi in Zhongling" (*SGSZ*, 10.222).

88. *SGSZ*, 10.222.

89. "Stone Case Inscription," 258; *Quan Zaizhi wenji*, 28.2a/b. It was very common during the Tang for a monk to choose a mountain as the site for his stūpa. Nishiguchi proposes that Mazu might have moved to Shimenshan around 785 since he disobeyed the imperial order during the Jianzhong reign-period ("Baso no denki," 142). This is a misunderstanding of the sources.

90. Zanning states in the *SGSZ* (10.223), "Now, [Daoyi's] portrait-hall is still extant in Haihunxian." Jianchang was called Haihun in the Han (Li Jifu, *Yuanhe junxian tuzhi*, 28.670). It became a custom and ritual to worship a deceased master in a portrait-hall in the Tang; see Chou, "Tantrism in China," 288; Wendi Adamek, "Imaging the Portrait of a Chan Master," in *Chan Buddhism in Ritual Context*, ed. Bernard Faure (London and New York: RoutledgeCurzon, 2003), 36–73; Foulk and Robert H. Sharf, "On the Ritual Use of Chan Portraiture in Medieval China," ibid., 74–150.

91. *SGSZ*, 10.222–23; *ZTJ*, 14.309; *CDL*, 6.3b. These sources say only that the title was conferred during the Yuanhe period; however, in Quan Deyu's "Tang gu Zhangjingsi Baiyan dashi beiming bingxu" (*Quan Zaizhi wenji*, 18.13a–14b) written in 817, this title is already mentioned. Emperor Xianzong summoned Mazu's disciples Zhangjing Huaihui and Xingshan Weikuan to court in 808 and 809 respectively; see Quan Deyu's same inscription and Bai Juyi's (772–846) "Chuanfatang bei," in *Bai Juyi ji jianjiao*, ed. Zhu Jincheng (Shanghai: Shanghai guji, 1988), 41.2690–91. This marks the beginning of the emperor's interest in the Hongzhou school. Therefore, the title may have been conferred between 808 and 817.

92. Wang Qinruo et al., eds., *Cefu yuangui* (Reprint, Taibei: Qinghua, 1967), 52.579a. See Yanagida, "Goroku no rekishi," 461. According to Yu Xianhao (*Tang cishi kao*, 157.2261), Li Xian was Surveillance Commissioner of Jiangxi that year.

93. In the Yuan edition of the *CDL* (*T.* 51: 6.246c), an anonymous note is added to the end of Mazu's entry. It states the reconstruction and renaming of the monastery and attributes the writing of the characters to Pei Xiu (791–864). The *ZTJ* (14.309) also records that Grand Councillor Pei wrote the *zhuan* characters. Grand Councillor Pei refers to Pei Xiu, who held this office during the reign of Xuanzong. However, according to Yu Xianhao (*Tang cishi kao*, 157.2263–64), Pei Xiu was Surveillance Cmmissioner of Jiangxi from 841 to 843, and Pei Chou from 849 to 850. Thus, it must be Pei Chou who ordered the reconstructions and wrote the characters in 850. The anonymous note does not mention the bestowal of the stūpa's title, but considering the facts that all early sources record the title as "Grand Adornment," and that it

was rededicated that year, it must have been retitled at the same time. The *Cefu yuangui* (52.581a) records that in 847 there was an imperial order to rebuild all monasteries destroyed during the Huichang persecution. Hence, it is also possible that the reconstruction of the Baofengsi and Mazu's stūpa began in that year and was finished in 850.

CHAPTER TWO

1. *ZTJ*, 14.309.

2. *SGSZ*, 11.256.

3. *Quan Zaizhi wenji*, 28.2b.

4. *ZTJ*, 14.309; *CDL*, 6.3b. Guishan Lingyou (771–853), one of Baizhang Huaihai's disciples, said that Mazu had eighty-four great disciples; see *Hongzhou Baizhangshan Dazhi chanshi [Huaihai] yulu*, in *Sijia yulu, Wujia yulu* (*Shike goroku, Goke goroku*), ed. Yanagida (Kyoto: Chūben shuppansha, 1983), 1.2b. Huangbo Xiyun (d. ca. 850), another disciple of Baizhang, said, "Under the great master Ma, eighty-eight sat in the halls of the Way" (*ZTJ*, 16.364). However, the reliability of these two discourses is problematic.

5. Yanagida, "Goroku no rekishi," 335–44.

6. Nukariya Kaiten, *Zengaku shisōshi* (1923; reprint, Tokyo: Meicho kankōkai, 1969), vol. 1, 497–525; Chen Yuan, *Shishi yinian lu*, 5.143–44; and Ui Hakuju, *Daini zenshūshi kenkyū* (1941; reprint, Tokyo: Iwanami shoten, 1966), 458–60.

7. Ge Zhaoguang, *Zhongguo chansixiang shi: Cong Liushiji dao jiushiji* (Beijing: Beijing daxue, 1996), 298–300.

8. *ZTJ*, 4.94–95; *CDL*, 14.3b.

9. *SGSZ*, 9.208. At the end of the biography, Zanning states that Liu Ke wrote an epitaph for Daowu during the Changqing reign-period (821–824).

10. Cited by Huihong in *Linjian lu*, 1.15a.

11. *XZJ* 110: 1.869a/b.

12. Fu Zai's surname *fu*, the character with a "grass" constituent, is written as *fu*, the character with a "bamboo" constituent, in *Quan Tangshi, QTW,* and some other texts. According to the epitaph of Fu Zai's wife, it should be the former. See Cen Zhongmian, *Cen Zhongmian shixue lunwenji* (Beijing: Zhonghua, 1990), 688.

13. *SGSZ*, 10.231–32.

14. *QTW*, 691.1a.

15. *T.* 49: 15.615a.

16. *ZTJ*, 4.94; *CDL*, 14.3b.

17. *CDL*, 14.4a.

18. *ZTJ*, 4.94–95; *CDL*, 14.4a.

19. See chapter three for detailed discussion of this point.

20. Daowu's entry in the *Wudeng huiyuan* cites this epitaph, saying: "He has three Dharma descendents, namely Huizhen, Wenbi, and Youxian." See Puji (1179–1253), ed., *Wudeng Huiyuan* (Beijing: Zhonghua, 1984), 7.370. Huang Zongxi (1610–1695) already indicated this mistake; see his *Nanlei wen'an*, in *Nanlei ji (SKQS)*, 4.25a.

21. *ZTJ*, 4.92; *CDL*, 30.8a; Shengyen, trans., *Faith in Mind* (Taibei: Fagu wenhua, 1999), 6. The title of this verse refers to the Taoist text on alchemy attributed to Wei Boyang in the Han dynasty.

22. *Linjian lu*, 1.15a. See Nukariya, *Zengaku shisōshi*, vol. 1, 497–98.

23. *XZJ* 113: 1.4a.

24. Cited by Zhizhao in his *Rentian yanmu* (Eyes of Humans and Gods), *T.* 48: 5.328c. In his *Famen chugui* (1667), Jingfu argued that Zhang Shangying converted to Buddhism after he was twenty years old and paid attention to the differentiation of Chan schools only in old age. Because Zhang was only eighteen when Tanying died, it was not possible for him to get the epitaph from Tanying (*XZJ* 147: 1.685b–86a). However, Zhang Shangying and Lü Xiaqing might have found the text in Tanying's book, like Huihong, and Juemengtang simply did not describe the event clearly. Jiang Wu identifies Juemengtang as Mengtang Tan'e (1285–1373); see his "Orthodoxy, Controversy, and the Transformation of Chan Buddhism in Seventeenth-Centuy China" (Ph.D. diss., Harvard University, 2002), 38. However, in the preface, the author calls the Song dynasty "our august dynasty"; therefore, he was a Song monk and not Tan'e who was born in the Yuan dynasty.

25. Cited by Tongrong (1593–1661) in the *Wudeng yantong mulu*, *XZJ* 139: 1.9b.

26. Chen Yuan argues that because both Tanying and Huihong still attributed the Yunmen house to Shitou in their works, the record in the *Linjian lu* is questionable (*Shishi yinian lu*, 5.143). However, the record in the *Linjian lu* was cited repeatedly in the Song and Yuan periods; hence, it must not be a forgery. Although Tanying and Huihong accepted the epitaph as authentic, they did not necessarily change the traditional lineage. For example, though Puji said in his note to Tianhuang's entry in the *Wudeng huiyuan* that Tianwang Daowu should be listed as Mazu's disciple, he did not actually do so in the text. The Qing monk Daning said that this note was added by Yehai Ziqing when he reprinted *Wudeng huiyuan* in the Yuan dynasty ("Famen chugui youxu," in *Famen chugui*, 689b). However, this note already appears in the Baoyou edition of *Wudeng huiyuan* printed in the Song dynasty, so it must be Puji's original note; see Chen Yuan, *Zhongguo Fojiao shiji gailun* (Shanghai: Shanghai shudian, 1999), 81–82.

27. *Wudeng huiyuan*, 7.369–70; *T.* 49: 7.651a/b; *QTW*, 713.3a–4a.

28. For summaries of those controversies, see Nukariya, *Zengaku shisōshi*, vol. 1, 497–525; Chen Yuan, *Shishi yinian lu*, 5.143–44; Ui, *Daini zenshūshi kenkyū*, 458–60; Suzuki, *Tō Godai zenshūshi*, 430–31; and Jiang Wu, "Orthodoxy, Controversy, and the Transformation of Chan Buddhism in seventeenth-century China," 109–78.

29. *Rentian yanmu*, 333c.

30. *CDL*, 10.6a.

31. *ZTJ*, 17.390.

32. Li Kang, *Duyi zhi (SKQS)*, 1.12a/b; and Qian Yi, *Nanbu xinshu (SKQS)*, 10.9b–10a.

33. Qiu Xuansu's "Poem of Goddess Temple" was engraved in the Goddess temple in Kuizhou, and his title was Prefect of Kuizhou. This inscription was still to be seen in the Song dynasty; see Ouyang Xiu (1007–1072), *Jigu lu (SKQS)*, 8.9a; Chen Si, *Baoke congbian (SKQS)*, 19.4b; and Wang Xiangzhi, *Yudi beiji mu (SKQS)*, 4.23a.

34. All Jingnan Military Commissioners during the Zhenyuan-Yuanhe reign-periods are recorded in the *Jiu Tang shu* and other Tang sources, but Qiu Xunsu's name does not appear; see Yu Xianhao, *Tang cishi kao*, 195.2678–71.

35. Nukariya and Ui have already indicated this; see *Zengaku shisōshi*, 525; and *Daini zenshūshi kenkyū*, 460.

36. For example, see Ge Zhaoguang, *Zhongguo chansixiang shi*, 299.

37. *ZTJ*, 4.95–102; *CDL*, 14.4b–6a.

38. *SGSZ*, 11.250–51.

39. Du Jiwen and Wei Daoru, *Zhongguo chanzong tongshi* (Nanjing: Jiangsu guji, 1993), 276–77.

40. See Liu Zongyuan (773–819), "Hengshan Zhongyuan dalüshi taming," *Liu Zongyuan ji* (Beijing: Zhonghua shuju, 1972), 7.173.

41. About Shencou, see *SGSZ*, 16.391; about Weiyan, see later.

42. Duan Chengshi, *Youyang zazu (SKQS)*, 3.15a/b; also cited by Li Fang (925–996) et al., eds., *Taiping guangji (SKQS)*, 83.10a/b.

43. See Yu, *Tang cishi kao*, 48.559.

44. The *ZTJ* adds the detail that the brows of the Abbot of the Huilinsi were burned when he wanted to warm himself by the fire as well. This must be a later embellishment.

45. See Chen Shangjun, ed., *Quan Tangshi xushi*, in vol. 2 of *Quan Tangshi bubian* (Beijing: Zhonghua, 1992), 24.1006–10. But Chen omits one of the poems recorded in the *ZTJ*.

46. *ZTJ*, 4.102–110; *CDL*, 14.6b–9b; and *SGSZ*, 17.423–24.

47. Yao Xuan (968–1020), ed., *Tangwen cui (SKQS)*, 62.4a–5b. This epitaph is also included in Zuxiu, *Longxing fojiao biannian tonglun* (*XZJ* 130: 24.658b–660a); Nianchang, *Fozu lidai tongzai* (*T.* 49: 16.629a/c); and *QTW*, 536.12b–5a. The last text copies the *Tangwen cui* text verbatim.

48. *Sijia yulu, Wujia yulu*, 1.15a–6a.

49. *Dahui Pujue chanshi yulu, T.* 47: 23.907b.

50. For example, Ui, *Daini zenshūshi kenkyū*, 425; and Yinshun, *Zhongguo chanzongshi* (Shanghai: Shanghai shudian, 1992), 420.

51. See Xu Wenming, "Yaoshan Weiyan de zongxi he chanfeng," in *Shiji zhijiao de Tansuo* (Beijing: Beijing shifan daxue, 2000), 151–66.

52. Wang Pu (922–982), *Tang huiyao* (Beijing: Zhonghua, 1955), 76.1390; Wang Qinruo (962–1025) et al., ed., *Cefu yuangui (SKQS)*, 644.12b–13a; Song Minqiu (1019–1079), ed., *Tang dazhaoling ji (SKQS)*, 106.22b–23a; and Xu Song (1781–1848), *Dengke ji kao* (Beijing: Zhonghua, 1984), 20.722. See Yanagida, *Goroku no rekishi*, 327; and Suzuki Tetsuo, *Tō Godai no zenshū: Konan Kōsei hen* (Tokyo: Daitō shuppansha, 1984), 53–54.

53. See Suzuki, *Tō Godai no zenshū*, 53.

54. The *ZTJ* says he died on the sixth day of the eleventh month, and the *CDL* says he died in the second month; these might be errors attributable to miscopying.

55. Yinshun, *Zhongguo chanzong shi*, 420.

56. *Bai Juyi ji*, 41.2690–91.

57. See Lin Bao (fl. 806–820), *Yuanhe xingcuan* (Beijing: Zhonghua, 1994), 4.494.

58. Xu Wenming surmises that this master might be Hongzheng, Puji's disciple ("Yaoshan Weiyan de zongxi he chanfeng," 154–55).

59. See Wang Xiangzhi, *Yudi jisheng (SKQS)*, 30.9a.

60. Xu Wenming already mentions this point ("Yaoshan Weiyan de zongxi he chanfeng," 159).

61. *ZTJ*, 4.104, 110.

62. Peng Dingqiu (1645–719) et al., eds., *Quan Tangshi* (1707; reprint, Beijing: Zhonghua, 1960), 492.5571.

63. T. H. Barrett already presumes that, if the epitaph for Yaoshan written by Tang Shen is authentic, Yaoshen's meetings with Li Ao are not reliable. For a detailed discussion, see his *Li Ao: Buddhist, Taoist, or Neo-confucian* (Oxford: Oxford University Press, 1992), 51–57.

64. *CDL*, 8.1a/b; Yanagida's list, no. 98, 132. Yanagida notes this repetition.

65. *CDL*, 8.1a/b; Yanagida's list, no. 96, 128.

66. *CDL*, 8.1b; Yanagida's list, no. 127, 146.

67. See Chen, *Shishi yinian lu*, 219.

68. Both the *ZTJ* (15.346) and *CDL* mistake Wuliao as Mazu's disciple.

69. *ZTJ*, 14.311; Yanagida's list, no. 145.

70. *QTW*, 446.6b.

71. Zhao Mingcheng, *Jinshi lu (SKQS)*, 9.18b–9a.

72. Wang Xiangzhi, *Yudi bei jimu (SKQS)*, 2.3a.

73. *QTW*, 713.12b.

74. *Linjian lu*, 1.58b. See Ui Hakuju, *Daisan zenshūshi kenkyū* (1942; reprint, Tokyo: Iwanami shoten, 1966), 25–26; and Suzuki, *Tō Godai no zenshū*, 143–44. Ishii Shūdō says that Fazheng and Niepan heshang must be two monks who held the abbotship of the Baizhangsi successively, but he does not give any convincing evidence; see his "Hyakujō shingi no kenkyū," *Komazawa daigaku zenkenkyūjo nenpō* 6 (1995): 15–53.

75. *CDL*, 6.1b; Yanagida's list, no. 16.

76. See Dayi's epitaph by Wei Chuhou (773–829), *QTW*, 715.25b.

77. *CDL*, 8.1b; Yanagida's list, no. 133.

78. *ZTJ*, 15.347.

79. *CDL*, 7.1b; Yanagida's list, no. 76.

80. See Sekiguchi, *Zenshū shisōshi*, 316–19.

81. *ZTJ*,15.347–78; Yanagida's list, no. 151.

82. *CTL*, 10.13a.

83. *CDL*, 8.15a; Yanagida's list, no. 113.

84. *ZTJ*, 5.123.

85. Yanagida's list, no. 153.

86. *ZTJ*, 4.94; *CDL*, 5.24a.

87. *ZTJ*, 18.396.

88. See *Xin Tang shu*, 59.1530; and Chao Gongwu, *Junzhai dushuzhi houzhi (SKQS)*, 2.69b–70a. For a detailed discussion of Li Fan's apprenticeship with Mazu and his work, see chapter three.

CHAPTER THREE

1. McRae, "The Antecedents of Encounter Dialogue in Chinese Ch'an Buddhism," 54–70; and idem, *Seeing through Zen*, 83–98.

2. *QTW*, 319.13b, 320.3b.

3. *QTW*, 755.20a. McRae has mentioned this dialogue as an antecedent of encounter dialogue; see his *Northern School*, 96; and "Antecedents of Encounter Dialogue," 60.

4. Duan Chengshi, *Youyang zazu xuji (SKQS)*, 4.2a. Duan then cited Qiyu's words that "A novice monk of eight years can recite it, but a monk of one hundred years cannot practice it" as the provenance of Jingshan's words. Duan's citation was from the *Zazhuan* by Emperor Yuan of the Liang Dynasty (r. 552–555), and it is also seen in the *Fayuan zhulin (SKQS)*, 37.9b.

5. *ZTJ*, 3.66; *CDL*, 4.12b–13a. See Yanagida, *Goroku no rekishi*, 473.

6. This is recognized at the end of the biography, *SGSZ*, 11.249.

7. *SGSZ*, 11.247.

8. *QTW*, 715.23a/b.

9. See chapter two.

10. Zongmi, *Chanyuan zhuquanji duxu*, *T*. 48: 1.399c, 400a.

11. This collection is no longer extant except the preface. About the fact that Zongmi actually compiled this work, see Yün-hua Jan (Ran Yunhua), "Two Problems Concerning Tsung-mi's Compilation of Ch'an-tsang," *Transactions of the International Conference of Orientalists in Japan* 19 (1974): 37–47; and Gregory, *Tsung-mi*, 322–23.

12. Li Zunxu, *Tiansheng Guangdeng lu*, *XZJ* 135: 8.652a–53a (hereafter cited as *GDL*). Mazu's sermons are relatively authentic; see next section.

13. *SGSZ*, 9.209.

14. *Horinden yakuchu*, 429.

15. See Dale Wright, "The Huangbo Literature," in *Zen Canon*, ed. Heine and Wright, 113–17, 125–29.

16. See Shiina Kōyū, "*Horinden* itsubun no kenkyū," 248.

17. *Horinden yakuchu*, 89, 97, 101, 120, 124–25, 165, 182, 277, 285–86, 429.

18. *Liuzu Tanjing*, 59.

19. *Chan Chart*, *XZJ* 110: 1.866b–67a.

20. *QTW*, 813.9b.

21. *QTW*, 870.15a. See also Huihong, the biography of Guangyong in the *Chanlin sengbao zhuan (SKQS)*, 2b–4a.

22. Da'an's stūpa inscription by Yunming, copied by Ishii Shūdō, "Isan kyōdan no dōkō ni tsuite—Hukushū Daian no shinjinki no shōkai ni chinande," *Indogaku bukkyōgaku kenkyū* 27.1 (1978): 90–96.

23. Da'an's biography in the *SGSZ*, 12.281–82. Zanning mentions Cui Yin's writing of Da'an's epitaph at the end of the biography, and the content of the biography is quite similar to the stūpa inscription. The *Baoke congbian* also records a "Dagui Yansheng chanshi bei" (Epitaph of Chan Master Dagui Yansheng) by Cui Yin (*SKQS*, 19.23a). See Ishii, "Isan kyōdan no dōkō ni tsuite," 96.

24. *ZTJ*, 14.314.

25. Weibai (fl. 1101), *Dazangjing gangmu zhiyao lu*, in *Dazheng xinxiou fabao zongmulu* (reprint, Taibei: Xinwenfeng, 1985), 2.770b. For studies on *Shengzhou ji*, see Yanagida, *Shoki zenshū shisho no kenkyū*, 394–404; and Tanaka Ryōshō, *Tonkō zenshū bunken no kenkyū* (Tokyo: Taitō shuppansha, 1983), 121–34.

26. See Nianchang, *Fozu lidai tongzai*, T. 49: 9.551a.

27. *Dazheng xinxiou fabao zongmulu*, 2.770b.

28. *QTW*, 869.12b. Guanxi's entry in the *ZTJ* (20.451) also records this couplet.

29. *ZTJ*, 20.451.

30. *Chōsen kinseki sōran*, v. 1, 157–62.

31. Yicun, "Nanti taming bingxu," in *Quan Tangwen bubian*, ed. Chen Shangjun, 116.1444.

32. For example, Kim Chongŏn, "[Ko]ryo-guk Kwangju Hŭiyanghyŏn ko Baekgyesan Okryong-sa chesi Tongjin taesa Poun chi t'ap pyŏngsŏ," dated 949, *Haidong jinshi yuan buyi*, 1.28a–34a; idem, "Koryŏ-guk Kwangju Hyemok-san Kodal-wŏn ko kuksa chesi Wŏnjong taesa Hyejin chi t'ap pi'myŏng pyŏngsŏ," dated 958, *Chōsen kinseki sōran*, vol. 1, 207–15; Lei Yue, "Kuangzhen dashi taming," dated 958, *Tangwen shiyi*, 48.9a; Han Xizai, "Xuanji chanshi bei," dated 962, *QTW*, 877.15b–18b; and Chen Shouzhong, "Da Han Shaozhou Yunmenshan Dajue chansi Daciyun Kuangsheng Hongming dashi beiming bingxu," dated 964, *QTW*, 892.6b–7a.

33. See Yanagida, " 'Recorded Sayings' Texts," 185–205; and idem, *Goroku no rekishi*, 23–36.

34. *Goroku no rekishi*, 23.

35. See Huihong, *Linjian lu*, XZJ 148: 1.591a; Huikong (1096–1158), *Dongshan Huikong chanshi yulu*, XZJ 120: 1.297b; and You Mao (1127–1194), *Suichutang shumu (Congshu jicheng chubian)*, 19.

36. For a detailed study of the editions of the *Sijia lu*, see Shiina Kōyū, "Baso shike roku no shobon," *Zenbunka kenkyūjo kiyō* 24 (1998.12): 161–81.

37. Ding Bing, *Shanben shushi cangshuzhi* (Beijing: Zhonghua, 1990), 22: 5a/b.

38. Zhongguo guji shanben shumu bianji weiyuanhui, ed., *Zhongguo guji shanben shumu: Zibu* (Shanghai: Shanghai guji, 1994), no. 11108.

39. The Japanese edition of the *Sijia yulu* dated 1684, which was based on a Ming edition, also includes Yang Jie's preface. Following this preface are a few words explaining that it was copied from an old edition (*Sijia yulu, Wujia yulu*, 2b). In addition, in this same edition, behind the *Huangbo Duanji chanshi Wanling lu*, there is a mind-verse attributed to Pei Xiu and also a postscript dated 1048 by a Chan monk named

Tianzhen. These are not found in the edition preserved in the Nanjing Library, and might have been copied from the Yuan-edition *CDL* (*T*. 51: 9.273a).

40. As Yang Jie called Huinan "The old Nan of Jicui" in his preface, Yanagida asserts that this text must have been compiled around 1066, when Huinan built and named his hermitage Jicui (*Goroku no rekishi*, 476). However, Yang Jie might have used "Jicui" simply as an appellation.

41. See Poceski, "Mazu yulu," 57–62. All the texts of the *Mazu yulu* cited in this chapter are from the *Sijia yulu*, *Wujia yulu*, 1.4a–16b.

42. *ZTJ*, 14.304, 308.

43. *Goroku no rekishi*, 290–320.

44. This statistic is based on the annotations to the translation of Mazu's discourses in the Appendix.

45. Poceski has noted the conservative style of Mazu's sermons; see his "Mazu yulu," 59–60.

46. Including Mazu's dialogue with the abbot of Kaiyuansi, which is included in the biographical section.

47. *Baso no goroku*, 50. See also Yanagida, "'Recorded Sayings' Texts," 193.

48. *QTW*, 446.5b.

49. *ZTJ*, 14.307.

50. *CDL*, 6.2b.

51. Ibid., 6.3b–4a.

52. Ibid., 28.8b.

53. Ibid., 6.7b–8a.

54. *Zhenzhou Linji Huizhao Chanshi yulu*, *T*. 47: 1.505a/b.

55. *ZTJ*, 14.307–308; *CDL*, 7.2b.

56. *CDL*, 7.6b.

57. *ZTJ*, 4.101.

58. *Baso no goroku*, 67.

59. *SGSZ*, 11.259–60. Zanning indicates Jiang's authorship at the end of the biography. The epitaph is titled "Dameishan Chang chanshi huanyuan bei" and still existed in the Southern Song; see *Baoke congbian (SKQS)*, 13.23b; *Baoke leibian (SKQS)*, 5.39a.

60. *ZTJ*, 15.336.

61. *CDL*, 8b–9a.

62. Iriya believes the version in the *ZTJ* to be the original; see *Baso no goroku*, 70. However, a careful comparison of this version with the biography in the *SGSZ* displays the obviously fictitious color of the former.

63. *ZTJ*, 15.344–45. However, Wuye's entry in the same text is almost the same as the *SGSZ* version.

64. *ZJL*, *T*. 48: 98.942c–43a; *CDL*, 8.2a.

65. Poceski has already compared the *Mazu yulu* version with that of the *SGSZ* ("Mazu yulu," 67–72). However, his analysis and conclusions are different from mine.

66. *CDL*, 6.3a.

67. *ZTJ*, 15.348; *CDL*, 8.18a.

68. *Pang jushi yulu*, *XZJ* 120: 1.55a.

69. *ZJL*, T. 48: 92.919b; *CDL*, 28.21a.

70. *CDL*, 6.2b.

71. Ibid., 6.2b.

72. Ibid., 8.8a.

73. Ibid., 6.3b.

74. See Jia, *Jiaoran nianpu*, 107.

75. About the date of the letter, see Jia, *Jiaoran nianpu*, 104–107. In this visit, Lingche became familiar with the Hongzhou school, and later he even wrote the preface to the *Baolin zhuan*. For detailed discussion of Lingche's relationship with the Hongzhou school, see chapter five.

76. *ZTJ*, 14.308.

77. See chapter five for a detailed discussion.

78. Iriya, *Baso no goroku*, 120–214. This number has subtracted four repetitions with the *Mazu yulu*.

79. *GDL*, *XZJ* 135: 8.655a.

80. *ZTJ*, 15.333.

81. See chapter two.

82. *XZJ* 136: 4.493b–94a. Yanagida and Iriya have noted these two layered fabrications; see *Goroku no rekishi*, 358–59; *Baso no goroku*, 169.

83. *ZTJ*, 14.306.

84. *ZTJ*, 14.307–308; *CDL*, 6.3b.

85. *GDL*, 8.655a. This event is first found in Baizhang's entry in the *CDL*.

86. *GDL*, 8.655a–56a.

87. *Chongwen zongmu (Yueyatang congshu)*, 4.82b, 84b.

88. *Tongzhi (SKQS)*, 67.72b.

89. *Song shi (SKQS)*, 205.9a, 10a, 12b.

90. *CDL*, 6.3b–4a. In 738 many Dayunsi built by Empress Wu were converted to Kaiyuansi; however, there is evidence that some Dayunsi continued to exist. See Weinstein, *Buddhism under the T'ang*, 168, n. 20.

91. Yanagida, "'Recorded Sayings' Texts," 194–97.

92. Yanagida, "'Recorded Sayings' Texts," 197. See also Faure, *Will to Orthodoxy*, 69, 179.

93. Suzuki, *Tō Godai zenshūshi*, 352–53, 359–63. Ran Yunhua also indicates that the "jianxing" concept in the *Dunwu yaomen* is quite close to Shenhui's concept; see his "Lun Tangdai chanzong de jianxing sixiang," in *Cong Yindu fojiao dao Zhongguo fojiao*, 133–37.

94. *CDL*, 6.3b–7a.

95. *ZTJ*, 14.310–11.

96. *CDL*, 28.8b–17b.

97. *ZTJ*, 14.309–11.

98. *ZJL*, *T.* 48: 85.883a, 98.946b.

99. One of these dialogues, Dazhu Huihai's first visit to Mazu, is discussed in the section titled "Discourse Records Attributed to Mazu."

100. *QTW*, 446.5b.

101. *T.* 55: 1.1101a.

102. *T.* 48: 15.494c, 98. 944c.

103. *Chongwen zongmu*, 4.84a.

104. Huihong, "Ti Baizhang Chang Chanshi suobian Dazhi guanglu," in *Shimen wenzi chan (SBCK)*, 25.14a/b. See Yanagida, *Goroku no rekishi*, 360; and idem, " 'Recorded Sayings' Texts," 191–92.

105. *Shimen wenzi chan (SBCK)*, 25.14a/b.

106. *Goroku no rekishi*, 25, 360–61.

107. Suzuki Tetsuo has noted this theme; see his "Hyakujō kōroku ni mirareru shisō," *Indogaku bukkyōgaku kenkyū* 46.2 (1998): 67.

108. Zezangzhu, *Gu zunsu yulu*, 1.10–13.

109. For a detailed discussion, see chapter six.

110. *Chongwen zongmu*, 4.81b.

111. *Xin Tang shu*, 49.1531.

112. Chao Gongwu, *Junzhai dushu zhi (SKQS)*, 3b.21a. In addition, the *Suichutang shumu* records *Pang jushi shi* (Poems of Lay Buddhist Pang; *SKQS*, 54b); the *Tong zhi* records *Pang jushi ge* in one *juan*, *Pang jushi yulu* in one *juan*, and *Pang Yun shiji* in three *juan* (*SKQS*, 67.46a, 47a). See Shiina Kōyū, *Sō Gen-ban zenseki no kenkyū*, 415, 421, 423, 432.

113. The *Junzhai dushu zhi* says that he was from Xiangyang. Since he lived in Xiangyang in his later time (*ZTJ*, 15.348), Chao Gongwu might have mistaken it as his native place. In the Ming edition of *Pang jushi yulu* (printed during the Chongzhen reign-period, 1628–1644), there is a preface by Wumingzi, which states that Pang was from Xiangyang, and his father was the Prefect of Hengzhou. This account has no earlier support, and therefore is not credible.

114. The compilation of this text is attributed to Commissioner Yu Di (d. 818), who was the Commissioner of Xiangzhou from 798 to 808 (*Tang cishi kao*, 189.2589). However, as the first part of the text is a later collection (see below), this attribution is also not authentic.

115. Chen Shangjun adds seven more verses collected from the *ZJL*, *Wanshan tonggui ji*, and *Xutang heshang yulu*; see vol. 2 of the *Quan Tangshi xushi*, 21.971–73.

116. *ZTJ*, 15.348.

117. *CDL*, 8.18a.

118. See the section entitled "Discourse Records Attributed to Mazu."

119. For a detailed discussion of this idea, see chapter four.

120. *SGSZ*, 11.259–60.

121. See Yanagida, "'Recorded Sayings' Texts," 197.

122. *ZTJ*, 15.335–6; *CDL*, 7.8b–9b.

123. *ZJL*, *T*. 48: 23.543c, 98.944c. One of the sermons is also seen in the *CDL*, 7.9a/b. The *ZJL* includes one more sermon (98.945a) and the *CDL* one more dialogue (7.7b), neither of which is included in the *Fachang yulu*.

124. See the section entitled "Discourse Records Attributed to Mazu", and chapter six.

125. *T*. 55: 1.1106c.

126. *SGSZ*, 11.249.

127. *Tangwen cui*, 62.5b.

128. *Tangdai muzhi huibian xuji*, 913.

129. *QTW*, 501.11a.

130. Preserved in Ch'ŏnch'aek, *Sŏnmun pojang nok*, *XZJ* 113: 1.990b. Muyŏm's treatise is not extant, and the *Sŏnmun pojang nok* was compiled in 1293.

131. *QTW*, 715.23a–24b.

132. *QTW*, 733.22a.

133. *Bai Juyi ji*, 41.2691–92.

134. *SGSZ*, 10.233.

135. *SGSZ*, 11.250. For a detailed discussion of these dialogues, see chapter two.

136. *ZJL*, *T*. 48: 98.943b.

137. *T*. 55: 1.1084b.

138. *Xin Tang shu*, 59.1530.

139. *Junzhai dushuzhi houzhi (SKQS)*, 2.69b–70a.

140. Chao Jiong, *Fazang suijin lu (SKQS)*, 1.25b–26a, 2.12a/b; *Daoyuanji yao (SKQS)*, 2.5a. According to these fragments, we know that chapter 11 of the book was about "inspiring the nature of mind essential," chapter 12 was about "showing the body of motionless," chapter 13 was about "understanding the truth of awakening from dreams," and chapter 14 was about "entering the quiescence of listening and meditation."

CHAPTER FOUR

1. This statistic is based on the annotations to the translation of Mazu's discourses in the Appendix.

2. Modern scholars in general regard this text as an indigenous Chinese composition written during the sixth century.

3. Buswell claims that this text was composed by the Korean monk Pŏmnang around 685; see his *The Formation of Ch'an Ideology in China and Korea*, 164–76.

4. For example, see Nukariya, *Zengaku shisōshi*, 436–37.

5. *Tō Godai zenshūshi*, 376–77, 383–84.

6. Baozhi's verses were created by Mazu's disciples; see chapter five.

7. The character "bie," separate, does not appear in the original title of this text, but was added in certain Japanese editions and listings. See Yanagida, *Shoki zenshū shisho no kenkyū*, 219.

8. See Yanagida, *Shoki zenshū shisho no kenkyū*, 219–52. Suzuki further posits that, although Daoyi at the beginning of his career taught that "this mind is the Buddha," after he moved to Hongzhou he used an alternative proposition "neither mind nor Buddha," in order to fend off attacks from outside the Chan circle and to correct abuses inside the school; see his *Tō Godai zenshūshi*, 377–82. However, this proposition is not seen in Mazu's sermons; it appears in the *Extended Discourses of Baizhang* and some encounter dialogues created in the late Tang, and was used to ward off criticism of Mazu's teaching. For detailed discussions of this proposition, see chapters three and six.

9. *Lengqie shizi ji*, *T*. 85: 1.1288a. In another place, the text again cites an expression from the *Mañjuśrībhāsita-mahāpārajñāpramitā-sūtra* (*Wenshushili suoshuo moheboreboluomi jing*): "The mind that is aware of the Buddha is the Buddha" (*T*. 85: 1.1286c). See Yanagida, *Shoki no zenshi I, Ryōka shiji ki, Den hōbō ki* (Tokyo: Chikuma shobō, 1971), 225; and *Pan Guiming, Zhongguo chanzong sixiang licheng* (Beijing: Jinri Zhongguo chubanshe, 1992), 49.

10. *Shenhui heshang chanhua lu*, 12; and Zongmi, *Yuanjue jing dashu chao*, *XZJ* 14: 3.558b.

11. *CDL*, 28.9a; Appendix, Sermon 4.10.

12. *SGSZ*, 12.247; Appendix, Dialogue 2.19.

13. *GDL*, *XZJ* 135: 8.652a; Appendix, Sermon 5.14.

14. Yanagida has indicated that Mazu's "ordinary mind" refers to the complete mind including both ignorance and enlightenment; see his *Mu no tankyū: Chūgoku zen* (Tokyo: Kadokawa shoten, 1969), 153, 157.

15. *Chan Chart, XZJ* 110: 1.870b; Buswell, *Korean Approach to Zen*, 266.

16. *CDL*, 28.1b–3a.

17. See Nukariya, *Zengaku shisōshi*, 163; Yanagida, *Shoki zenshū shisho no kenkyū*, 161–63; Yinshun, *Zhongguo chanzongshi*, 264; Ishii Shūdō, "Nanyō Echū no nanpō shūshi no hihan ni tsuite," *Chūgoku no bukkyo to bunka: Kamata Shigeo hakushi kanreki kinen ronshū* (Tokyo: Daizō shuppansha, 1988), 315–44; and idem, "Nansōzen no tongo shisō no tenkai: Kataku Shine kara Kōshūshū e," *Zenbunka kenkyūjo kiyō* 20 (1990): 136–38.

18. *Chan Chart, XZJ* 110: 1.875a/b.

19. *ZJL*, *T*. 48: 1.418b; Appendix, Sermon 1.1. Huangbo Xiyun also emphasized this transmission; see *Chuanxin fayao*, *T*. 48: 1.379c, 381b.

20. In the *Laṅkāvatāra-sūtra* (*T*. 16: 1.519a) and *Awakening of Faith* (*T*. 32: 1.576a), one-mind is equivalent to the tathāgata-garbha. See Fazang, *Dasheng qixin lun yiji*, *T*. 44: 2.251b–c.

21. See Takasaki Jikidō, *Nyoraizō shisō no keisei: Indo Daijō Bukkyō shisō kenkyū* (Tokyo: Shunjūsha, 1974), 3–13; idem, *Nyoraizō shisō* (Tokyo: Shunjūsha, 1988), 6–7; Hirakawa Akira et al, eds. *Nyoraizō shisō* (Tokyo: Shunjūsha, 1982), 2–3; Florin G. Sutton, *Existence and Enlightenment in the Laṅkāvatāra-sūtra* (Albany: State University of New York Press, 1991), 51–78; and Brian Brown, *The Buddha Nature: A Study of the Tathāgata-garbha and Ālayavijñāna* (Delhi: Motilal Banarsidass Publishers, 1991), 249.

22. *CDL*, 28.7b; Appendix, Sermon 4.14.

23. *CDL*, 6.3b; Appendix, Dialogue 1.18.

24. *ZJL*, *T.* 48: 14.492a; Appendix, Sermon 2.6.

25. See Takasaki, *Nyoraizō shisō no keisei*, 3–13; idem, *Nyoraizō shisō*, 6–7; and Hirakawa et al, *Nyoraizō shisō*, 2–3.

26. *T.* 16: 7.556b; Suzuki, trans., *Laṅkāvatāra Sūtra*, 190.

27. *T.* 16: 7.556b; Suzuki, *Laṅkāvatāra Sūtra*, 190.

28. *T.* 32: 1.576a/c. See Gregory, "The Problem of Theodicy in the *Awakening of Faith.*" *Religious Studies* 22.1 (1986): 72; idem, *Tsung-mi*, 179–81; and Buswell, *Formation of Ch'an Ideology*, 82–83.

29. *CDL*, 28.7b; Appendix, Sermon 4.13.

30. The metaphor of mirror and image implies the Yogācāra doctrine of the "great perfect mirror wisdom" (*da yuanjing zhi;* Sanskrit ādarśana-jñāna), which represents the transformation of the ālayavijñāna. See *T:* 45: 2.521c. This metaphor appears frequently in early Chan literature in a much simpler form and implication. See McRae, *Northern School*, 144–47.

31. *SGSZ*, 11.247–48; Appendix, Dialogue 2.19.

32. *SGSZ*, 10.233.

33. *T.* 16: 1.484b; *T.* 16: 2.523b; Suzuki, *Laṅkāvatāra Sūtra*, 42.

34. *Awakening of Faith, T.* 32: 1.576c; Gregory, *Trung-mi*, 161.

35. See Whalen Lai, "Chan Metaphors: Waves, Water, Mirror, and Lamp," *Philosophy East and West* 29 (1979): 244–48.

36. See Takasaki, *Study of the Ratnagotravibhāga*, 26–31.

37. *ZJL*, *T.* 48: 14.492a; Appendix, Sermon 2.7.

38. *CDL*, 28.12b; *SGSZ*, 11.249; *QTW*, 919.10b.

39. *CDL*, 28.1a/b.

40. See Matsumoto Shirō, "The Doctrine of Tathāgata-garbha Is Not Buddhist," in *Pruning the Bodhi Tree: The Storm over Critical Buddhism*, ed. James B. Hubbard and Paul L. Swanson (Honolulu: University of Hawaii Press, 1997), 165–73; and idem, "Critiques of Tathāgata-garbha Thought and Critical Buddhism," *Komazawa daigaku Bukkyō gakubu ronshū* 33 (2002): 360–78.

41. *CDL*, 28.7b; Appendix, Sermon 4.13.

42. *ZJL*, *T.* 48: 14.492a; Appendix, Sermon 2.8.

43. *T.* 32: 1.576b. See Gregory, "The Problem of Theodicy in the Awakening of Faith," 74; Buswell, *Formation of Ch'an Ideology*, 83–84; and Jacqueline Stone, *Original Enlightenment and the Transformation of Medieval Japanese Buddhism* (Honolulu: University of Hawaii Press, 1999), 5–6.

44. *GDL, XZJ* 135: 8.652a–653a; Appendix, Sermon 5.15.

45. *Chan Chart, XZJ* 110: 1.875b.

46. *CDL*, 28.6b; Appendix, Sermon 4.10.

47. Zongmi, *Chan Chart, XZJ* 110: 1.871a; *Chan Preface, T.* 48: 1.402c; *Yuanjue jing dashu chao, XZJ* 14: 3.557b; Buswell, *Korean Approach to Zen*, 267.

48. See Robert Sharf, "On Pure Land Buddhism and Ch'an/Pure Land Syncretism in Medieval China," *T'oung Pao* 88.4–5 (2002): 301–309. As Sharf summarizes in the article, the term *nianfo* covers a variety of practices and can be translated as "recollection of the Buddha," "contemplation of the Buddha," "recitation of the name(s) of the Buddha," "invocation of the Buddha," and so on.

49. See McRae, *Northern School*, 136–44, 207–209; and Faure, *Will to Orthodoxy*, 58–74.

50. See chapter one.

51. Among the schools of preclassical Chan, the Heze had begun to criticize seated meditation, and the Baotang master Wuzhu was particular in his rejection of all forms of Buddhist ritual and religious practice. See Faure, *Will to Orthodoxy*, 73–74; and Yanagida, "The *Li-tai Fa-pao Chi* and the Ch'an Doctrine of Sudden Awakening," 39–41.

52. Faure, *Will to Orthodoxy*, 69.

53. Kim Yŏng, "Silla-guk Muju Kaji-san Porim-sa si Pojo Sŏnsa yŏngt'ap pi'myŏng pyŏngsŏ," *Haidong jinshi yuan*, 1.33a–34a; and Ch'oe Chi-wŏn (857–928?), "Tae Tang Silla-guk ko Pong'amson-sa kyosi Chijŭng taesa Chŏkcho chi t'ap pi'myŏng pyŏngsŏ," *Haidong jinshi yuan*, 2.16b–17a.

54. *CDL*, 28.7b; Appendix, Sermon 4.13.

55. *T*. 16: 3.505b.

56. *T*. 16: 5.618c–19a.

57. *Ratnagotravibhāga (Jiujing yisheng baoxing lun)*, *T*. 31: 3.824a/b; and Takasaki, *A Study of the Ratnagotravibhāga*, 167–69. See William Grosnick, "Non-origination and Nirvāṇa in the Early Tathāgata-garbha Literature," *Journal of the International Association of Buddhist Studies* 4.2 (1981): 33–43.

58. *GDL, XZJ* 135: 8.652a; Appendix, Sermon 5.14.

59. *Shenhui heshang chanhua lu*, 39, 50, 79. For an inspiring discussion on the apophatic and kataphatic discourse of Buddhism, see Robert M. Gimello, "Apophatic and Kataphatic Discourse in Mahāyāna: A Chinese View," *Philosophy East and West* 26.2 (1976): 117–36.

60. By contrast, Mazu's non-origination might have been influenced by the Northern school's "linian" (detachment from thought). This term is quite ambiguous in the Northern school texts. Shenhui and Zongmi interpreted it as detaching oneself from false thoughts; but it can also be interpreted as the mind is always already detached from all thoughts, as two other Northern school terms "budong" (immobility) and "buqinian" (without originating thought) suggest. See Robert B. Zeuschner, "The Concept of *li nien* ('being free from thinking') in the Northern Line of Ch'an Buddhism," in *Early Ch'an in China and Tibet*, ed. Lai and Lancaster, 131–48; and Faure, *Will to Orthodoxy*, 42–45, 111. Mazu's lay disciple Li Fan actually advocated "budong" in his *Xuansheng qulu* (Chao Jiong, *Fazang suijin lu*, 2.12a/b; and *Daoyuanji yao*, 2.5a).

61. *GDL, XZJ* 135: 8.652a/b; Appendix, Sermon 5.14, 15.

62. Yanagida, *Mu no tankyū*, 167.

63. *GDL, XZJ* 135: 8.653a; Appendix, Sermon 5.15.

64. *CDL*, 28.7b; Appendix, Sermon 4.13.

65. *CDL*, 6.6a.

66. Zongmi, *Yuanjue jing dashu chao, XZJ* 14: 3.557a; *Chan Chart, XZJ* 110: 1.870b.

67. Yanagida, *Mu no tankyū*, 145.

68. *CDL*, 28.7a; Appendix, Sermon 4.11.

69. *ZJL, T.* 48: 14.492a; Appendix, Sermon 2.7. A large part of this sermon is also attributed to Qingyuan Xingsi in the same book, *T.* 48: 97.940b. Considering Zongmi's attack (see later), this sermon should be attributed to Mazu. See Yanagida, "Goroku no rekishi," 490.

70. Yanagida, *Shoki zenshū shisho no kenkyū*, 406–407.

71. *CDL*, 3.4b.

72. Buswell, "'Short-cut' Approach of K'an-hua Meditation," 341.

73. Fazang, *Huayan jing tanxuan ji, T.* 35: 16.405a/c; *Xiu Huayan aozhi wangjin huanyuan guan, T.* 45: 1.637b/c.

74. Fazang, *Huayan jing tanxuan ji, T.* 35: 16.405c–406a; *Dasheng qixinlun yiji, T.* 44: 1.243c; *Huayan youxin fajie ji, T.* 45: 1.644c; *Huayan yisheng jiaoyi fenqi zhang, T.* 45: 2.484c–85b. See Kobayashi Jitsugen, "Jijimuge to jirimuge: shōki to no kanren ni oite," *Bukkyōgaku kenkyū* 16–17 (1959): 105–18; Francis H. Cook, "Fa-tsang's Treatise on the Five Doctrines: An Annotated Translation" (Ph.D. diss., University of Wisconsin, 1970), 218–12; idem, *Hua-yen Buddhism: The Jewel Net of Indra* (University Park: Pennsylvania State University Press, 1977), 56–74; Yoshizu Yoshihide, *Kegonzen no shisōshi no kenkyū* (Tokyo: Daitō shuppansha, 1985), 135–36; and Gregory, *Tsung-mi*, 157–58.

75. *CDL*, 28.1b.

76. *Chan Chart, XZJ* 110: 1.872a–74b. See Gregory, *Tsung-mi*, 236–44.

77. Yanguan's epitaph by Lu Jianqiu, *QTW*, 733.22b.

78. See chapter two.

79. *Guishan jingce, QTW*, 919.6b.

80. *Xin Tang shu*, 59.1530.

81. Chao Jiong, *Fazang suijin lu*, 2.12a/b; and *Daoyuanji yao*, 2.5a.

82. *ZTJ*, 14.320.

83. Sharf cites the regulations in the *Chanyuan qinggui* (1103) and other texts and Yongming Yanshou's practice to verify that the ritual practice of *nianfo* continued in Chan establishments ("On Pure Land Buddhism and Ch'an/Pure Land Syncretism," 309–14.

84. For a detailed discussion, see chapter five.

85. For example, see McRae, "Encounter Dialogue and the Transformation in Ch'an," in *Paths to Liberation: The Mārga and Its Transformations in Buddhist Thought*, ed. Robert Buswell and Robert Gimello (Honolulu: University of Hawaii Press, 1992), 357.

86. The term "dharma-eye" contains a central idea of Mazu's disciples as expressed in the *Baolin zhuan*; see chapter five.

87. *ZTJ*, 4.98–101; *CDL*, 30.18a–19a.

88. *ZTJ*, 14.314–15.

89. *CDL*, 30.19b–20a.

90. Ibid., 30.19a.

91. *ZJL, T.* 48: 14.492a; Appendix, Sermon 2.8.

92. For example, *ZTJ*, entry of Danxia Tianran, 4.100; entry of Dongshan Liangjie, 6.142–43, entry of Changsha Jingcen, 17.384; entry of Zhaozhou Congshen, 18.394; and entry of Yangshan Huiji, 18.412. See Wu Yansheng, *Chanzong zhexue xiangzheng* (Beijing: Zhonghua shuju, 2001), 224–31.

93. Ouyang Xi, "Hongzhou Yungaishan Longshouyuan Guanghua dashi baolu beiming," *QTW*, 869.12b. Guanxi's entry in the *ZTJ* (20.451) also records this couplet.

94. *Zhenzhou Linji Huizhao chanshi yulu, T.* 47: 1.498a.

95. See Andrew Rawlinson, "The Ambiguity of the Buddha-nature Concept in India and China," in *Early Ch'an in China and Tibet*, 259–80.

96. Of course to modern critical Buddhists, the genuineness of the Hongzhou doctrine is questionable as it was related to the problematic tathāgata-garbha theory.

97. *Chan Chart, XZJ* 110: 1.870a; *Yuanjue jing dashu chao, XZJ* 14: 3.557a; Buswell, *Korean Approach to Zen*, 267.

CHAPTER FIVE

1. See Weinstein, *Buddhism under the T'ang*, 61–62.

2. Sima Guang, *Zizhi tongjian*, 224.7196–97. See Weinstein, *Buddhism under the Tang*, 77–89.

3. See chapter one.

4. Yanagida, *Shoki zenshū shisho no kenkyū*, 351–65.

5. Zhiju is also recorded as Huiju or Faju in various early sources. See Yanagida, *Shoki zenshū shisho no kenkyū*, 351–52. Early sources record that Zhiju discussed the verses attributed to the Indian patriarchs with an Indian monk named Shengchi Sanzang in Caoxi, and Lingche (746–816) wrote the preface. Yanagida points out that the "Indian monk" was obviously a fantasy used to claim authority for the stories of the Indian patriarchs.

6. Yanagida, *Shoki zenshū shisho no kenkyū*, 360.

7. "Tang gu Zhangjingsi Baiyan dashi beiming bingxu," *Quan Zaizhi wenji*, 18.14a.

8. The *Baolin zhuan* we can see today includes only *Juan* 1, 2, 3, 4, 5, 6, and 8. The eighth *juan* ends with the biography of Sengcan, the third patriarch. However, scholars in general agree that the main body of the text should hold the twenty-eight Indian patriarchs and the six Chinese patriarchs. See Tokiwa Daijō, *Horinden no kenkyū* (Tokyo: Tōhō bunka kenkyūjo, 1934); and Yanagida, *Shoki zenshū shisho no kenkyū*, 365–80, 405–18. In addition, according to the prophecy of the twenty-seventh patriarch Prajñātāra and Narendrayaśas cited in the *ZTJ* (2.39–45) and fragments of the *Baolin zhuan*, the tenth *juan* is most likely the biography of Huineng, and it may have included narratives about Shenxiu, Huineng's several disciples, and Mazu Daoyi, his third-

generation disciple. See Shiina Kōyū, "*Horinden* itsubun no kenkyū," *Komazawa daigaku Bukkyō gakubu ronshū* 11 (1980): 248. In the *ZTJ* (2.44), there is also a prophecy about Shitou Xiqian. However, it is still uncertain if this was contained in the original *Baolin zhuan* or a later addition; see Yanagida, *Shoki zenshū shisho no kenkyū*, 363.

9. *Horinden yakuchu*, 1.30–31.

10. See Tei Shiken, "Hōrinden ni okeru shōbōgenzō no imi," *Sogaku kenkyū* 131 (1989): 246–51.

11. Yanagida, *Shoki zenshū shisho no kenkyū*, 351–65, 380–83, 405–18.

12. See Jia, *Jiaoran nianpu*, 1.

13. About the monk-poet Lingche and the author of the preface to the *Baolin zhuan* being the same person, see Tozaki Tetsuhiko, "*Horinden* no josha Reitetsu to shisō Reitetsu," *Bukkyō shigaku kenkyū* 30.2 (1987): 28–55.

14. See Jiaoran, "Zeng Bao zhongcheng shu," *Zhou shangren ji (SBCK)*, 9.10a–11b; Quan Deyu, "Song Lingche shangren Lushan hui gui Wozhou xu," *Quan Zaizhi wenji*, 38.6b–7a; and Jia, *Jiaoran nianpu*, 104–107.

15. Quan Deyu wrote the epitaph for Huaihui, and wrote "Song Lingche shangren Lushan hui gui Wozhou xu" for Lingche.

16. See Tang Yongtong, *Han Wei liang Jin Nanbeichao fojiaoshi* (1928; reprint, Shanghai: Shanghai shudian, 1991), 28.

17. Huaihui's biography in the *SGSZ* (10.227), which is based on the epitaph written by Jia Dao, states that a scholar named Liu Ji showed his respects to Huaihui, and the two discussed and certified the Chan doctrine mutually.

18. Benjue, *Shishi tongjian*, *XZJ* 131: 10.950b.

19. *Quan Zaizhi wenji*, 18.13a/b.

20. Bai Juyi, "Chuanfatang bei," *Bai Juyi ji*, 41.2690–92.

21. Hu Shi, "Bai Juyi shidai de chanzong shixi," in *Hu Shi ji*, 36–39.

22. Xu Wenming, "Hu Shi 'Bai Juyi shidai de chanzong shixi' zhimiu," *Yuanxue* 6 (1995): 369–77.

23. *Horinden yakuchu*, 299–304, 442. See also Yanagida, *Shoki zenshū shisho no kenkyū*, 374–76.

24. "Tang Zhongyue shamen shi Faru chanshi xingzhuang," in *Jinshi xubian*, ed. Lu Yaoyu, *XXSKQS*, 6.5b–7b. See Yanagida, *Shoki zenshū shisho no kenkyū*, 335–46.

25. For a detailed description of the process, see Philip B. Yampolsky, *The Platform Sūtra of the Sixth Patriarch* (New York: Columbia University Press, 1967), 3–57.

26. Zhang Yue, "Tang Yuquansi Datong chanshi beiming bingxu," *QTW*, 231.1a–4b.

27. See Hu Shi, "Lengqiezong kao," *Hu Shi ji*, 174–80; Yanagida, *Shoki zenshū shisho no kenkyū*, 4–5; Faure, *Will to Orthodoxy*, 147–48, 158–59; and McRae, *Northern School*, 28–29.

28. See Chappell, "Teachings of the Fourth Ch'an Patriarch Tao-hsin," 95; and Buswell, *Formation of Ch'an Ideology*, 148–49.

29. *Will to Orthodoxy*, 6.

30. "Teachings of the Fourth Ch'an Patriarch Tao-hsin," 95.

31. *Shenhui heshang chanhua lu*, 73; *Liuzu Tanjing*, 15.

32. *Liuzu Tanjing*, 78–79. In the epitaph for Ehu Dayi, Wei Chuhou (773–829) also says that the successors of Shenhui "use the *Platform Sūtra* to transmit their lineage," *QTW*, 715.22a.

33. About the robe transmission in Shenhui's discourses, the *Platform Sūtra*, and the *Lidai fabao ji*, and its symbolic implication, see Wendi Adamek, "Robes Purple and Gold: Transmission of the Robe in the *Lidai fabao ji*," *History of Religions* 40.1 (2000): 58–81.

34. In the *Baolin zhuan*, Śākyamuni gave his robe to Mahākāśyapa and asked him to transmit it to Maitreya, the future Buddha. Accordingly, after transmitting the mind-dharma to the second patriarch, Ānanda, Mahākāśyapa took the robe and went to Mt. Cock's Foot to await the birth of Maitreya. Later Simhabhiksu, the twenty-fourth patriarch, also passed his robe to Basiasita, but he stressed that it was only to be used as a sign to deal with a belief crisis because the disciple was going to spread the teaching to a foreign country. As a result, the twenty-fifth patriarch again discontinued the robe transmission when the crisis was over. When Bodhidharma transmitted his robe to Huike, he said it was used as a proof that he came from a foreign country. See *Horinden yakuchu*, 73, 80, 291, 350, 381. There are many versions of the legend that the Buddha entrusted to Mahākāśyapa the transmission of the robe to Maitreya, and *Baolin zhuan*'s narrative comes from Xuanzang's (602–664) *Da Tang xiyu ji* (Grand Tang-Dynasty Account of the Western Regions). See Jonathan Silk, "The Origins and Early History of the Mahāratnakūṭa Tradition of Mahāyāna Buddhism with a Study of the Ratnarāśisūtra and Related Materials" (Ph.D. diss., University of Michigan, 1994), 61; and Adamek, "Robes Purple and Gold," 74.

35. The compiler(s) of the *Baolin zhuan* coined the term "dharma-eye of mind-ground" (*xindi fayan*) to connote this meaning more clearly. This term is seen in the story of Mazu's first meeting with Huairang, which first appeared in the *Baolin zhuan* and is preserved in the *ZTJ* (3.87); see Shiina, "*Horinden* itsubun no kenkyū," 248.

36. The Dunhuang-version *Platform Sūtra* contains some mind-verses, but they were only attributed to the six Chinese patriarchs. Because of the emphasis on the *Diamond Sūtra* and the robe, these verses are not as important as those in the *Baolin zhuan*.

37. Cited by Muyŏm (800–888), Magu Baoche's Silla disciple, in his "Musŏlt'o ron," preserved in *Sŏnmen pojang nok*, ed. Ch'ŏnch'l'aek, *XZJ* 113: 1.990b. A fragment of this treatise is also preserved in the *ZTJ*, 17.380.

38. *Quan Zaizhi wenji*, 18.14a.

39. The various branches of early Chan already emphasized the ineffability of Truth and enlightenment experience, an idea clearly expressed in the *Laṅkāvatāra-sūtra* (see Suzuki, *Studies in the Laṅkāvatāra Sūtra*, 274). It was said that when Bodhidharma transmitted the *Laṅkāvatāra-sūtra* to Fachong, he said that language was not important and should be forgotten (Daoxuan, *Xu Gaoseng zhuan*, T. 50: 25.666a). Northern School texts such as Faru's biography, *Langqie shizi ji*, and *Chuan fabao ji* further illustrate this idea (*Jinshi xubian*, 6.5b–7b; T. 85: 1.1289b, 1.1291a; see Yanagida, *Shoki zenshū shisho no kenkyū*, 39, 58; and Faure, *Will to Orthodoxy*, 139–41). In Shenhui's discourses and the *Platform Sūtra*, the phrase "transmitting mind with mind" even appeared (*Shenhui heshang chanhua lu*, 7; *Liuzu Tanjing*, 15). However, since early Chan still marked their transmission of certain sūtras, the idea of Chan lineage as "a special

transmission of the Buddha's mind/enlightenment without relying on writings" had not yet emerged.

40. Muyŏm, "Musŏlt'o ron," *Sŏnmun pojang nok, XZJ* 113: 1.990a/b. See Buswell, *Korean Approach to Zen*, 14.

41. *Chuanxin fayao, T*. 48: 1.382a.

42. *Chuanxin fayao, T*. 48: 1.379b.

43. See T. Griffith Foulk, "Sung Controversies Concerning the 'Separate Transmission' of Chan," in *Buddhism in the Sung*, ed. Peter N. Gregory and Daniel Getz (Honolulu: University of Hawaii Press, 1999), 236.

44. *Haedong ch'iltae rok*, in *Sŏnmun pojang nok*, ed. Ch'ŏnchl'aek, *XZJ* 113: 2.997a.

45. *Haedong ch'iltae rok*, in *Sŏnmun pojang nok, XZJ* 113: 1.991a. In Chinese sources, the first appearance of this phrase is in the biography of Linji Yixuan (d. 867) attributed to his disciple Yanzhao, which is included in the *Linji lu, T*. 47: 1.506c. Since this text was compiled in the Song, later additions and modifications are inevitable.

46. *ZJL, T*. 48: 1.418b; Appendix, Sermon 1.1.

47. *ZTJ*, 2.39–45; and Shiina, "*Horinden* itsubun no kenkyū," 248–49.

48. See Yanagida, *Shoki zenshū shisho no kenkyū*, 415–16.

49. Bai Juyi, "Chuanfatang bei," *Bai Juyi ji*, 41.2690–91.

50. See Chŏljung's (826–900) epitaph by Ch'oe Ŏnhwi (868–944), *Chōsen kinseki sōran*, 1: 157–62; and Simhŭi's (855–923) epitaph by Pak Sŭng'yŏng (d. 924), *Haidong jinshi yuan*, 2.31b–32a.

51. *CDL*, 29.1b–8b.

52. Zongmi, *Yuanjue xiuduoluo liaoyi jing lüeshu, T*. 39: 2.545a; idem, *Yuanjue jing dashu shiyi chao, T*. 14: 2.494a; *Chuanxin fayao, T*. 48: 1.383b/c; and *ZJL, T*. 48: 1.421b, 98.941c. The poem was collected by Chen Shangjun in the *Quan Tangshi xushi*, 59.1737. The six couplets have not been noted by scholars.

53. Ouyang Xun (557–641) et al., *Yiwen leiju* (Shanghai: Shanghai guji, 1981), 77.1321–22; and Huijiao (497–554), *Gaoseng zhuan* (Beijing: Zhonghua, 1992), 10.394–98.

54. For a complete study of Baozhi's life and legend, see Makita Tairyō, "Hōshi oshō den kō: Chūgoku ni okeru bukkyō reiken juyō no ichi keitai," *Tōhō gakuhō* 26 (1956): 64–89.

55. Yang Xuanzhi (fl. 528–547), *Luoyang qielan ji, T*. 51: 4.1014b.

56. See Wang Zhongmin, *Dunhuang yishu lunwen ji* (Taibei: Mingwen shuju, 1985), 160–61, 313–26. Based on these discussions, Chen Shangjun includes those verses in his *Quan Tangshi xushi*, 59.1729–38.

57. *Luoyang qielan ji, T*. 51: 4.1014b; Wei Shou (506–572), *Wei shu (SKQS)*, 13.19a–23b; and *Fayuan zhulin, T*. 53: 91.956a/b.

58. The Tang literati Duan Chengshi already confused the two as one; see his *Youyang zazu (SKQS)*, 3.10b.

59. "Eulogy of the Twelve Time-Periods," no. 3. See also "Eulogy of Fourteen Classes," nos. 3, 6, 8, 9.

60. "Eulogy of Fourteen Classes," no. 1. See also "Encomium of Mahāyāna," nos. 3, 8, and "Eulogy of Fourteen Classes," nos. 2, 4.

61. "Eulogy of Twelve Time-Periods," no. 12.

62. *Chan Chart, XZJ* 110: 1.870b.

63. *Gu zunsu yulu*, 2.23.

64. "Encomium of Mahāyāna," no. 7.

65. "Eulogy of Fourteen Classes," no. 5.

66. The hagiography of Foku Weize in the *SGSZ* (10.229) records: "He wrote 'Explanation on the Titles of Baozhi['s Works]' in twenty-four sections." According to this record, Weize was also involved in the works attributed to Baozhi. Weize was a successor of the Niutou school, and the doctrines of Niutou and Hongzhou had some common features. However, as the idea of "immutable Buddha-nature" and the metaphor of wheat flour and its products are found only in the Hongzhou literature, those verses must have been composed by Hongzhou monks.

67. *Horinden yakuchu*, 8.370–72.

68. *ZTJ*, 2.40.

69. *Gu zunsu yulu*, 2.23, 29.

70. *T.* 55: 1.1089a.

71. *T.* 55: 1.1100c.

72. *Fozu tongji, T.* 49: 10.202b.

73. Hu Shi, "Suowei 'Yongjia zhengdao ge'," in vol. 3 of the *Hu Shi wencun*, 4.541–54.

74. Ui, *Daini zenshūshi kenkyū*, 275–81.

75. Faure, *Will to Orthodoxy*, 52.

76. Nie, "'Zhengdao ge' zuozhe kao," *Zongjiaoxue yanjiu* 1 (1999): 131–37.

77. *SGSZ*, 12.247; Appendix, Dialogue 1.18.

78. *ZJL, T.* 48: 1.418c; Appendix, Sermon 1.4.

79. *ZJL, T.* 48: 1.418c; Appendix, Sermon 1.3.

80. *Chan Preface, T.* 48: 2.402c.

81. For the translation of the song, see Sheng-yen, *The Sword of Wisdom* (Taibei: Dharma Drum, 1999), 19–31.

82. *CDL*, 28.7a; Appendix, Sermon 3.10.

83. Ui, *Daini zenshūshi kenkyū*, 278–79.

84. *T.* 55: 1.1075b, 1.1077b, 1.1084b, 1.1089a, 1.1093c, 1.1101a.

85. *ZTJ*, 3.86; *SGSZ*, 8.184; *CDL*, 5.15a/b.

86. In an epitaph written in 780 (*QTW*, 917.15b), Jiaoran states that Xuanjue was Shenhui's confrere.

87. Shiina, "*Horinden* itsubun no kenkyū," 248.

88. *T.* 48: 1.380b, 383b–c.

89. *T.* 48: 1.385b, 387a.

90. *ZTJ*, 2.54; *T.* 48: 31.594c.

91. *Liuzu Tanjing*, 13–14.

92. See Yampolsky, *Platform Sūtra of the Sixth Patriarch*, 94.

93. The *Chuanxin fayao* also cites two mind-verses, which are attributed to Śākyamuni and the Twenty-third Patriarch respectively, from the *Baolin zhuan* (*T.* 48: 1.383a, 383c; *Horinden yakuchu*, 1.31; 5.279). See Mizuno Kogen, "Denhōge no seiritsu ni tsuite," *Sōgaku kenkyū* 2 (1960.1): 37.

94. According to a citation in Yangshan's entry in the *ZTJ*, Yanagida surmises that this change first happened in the *Baolin zhuan*,; see his *Shoki zenshū shisho no kenkyū*, 411–12.

95. *ZTJ*, 2.42, 54.

96. *CDL*, 6.14b–15b.

97. *SGSZ*, 10.236–37. The *Chixiu Baizhang qinggui* (Pure Regulations of Baizhang Compiled under Imperial Order) compiled by Dongyang Dehui (fl. 1329–1336) in the Yuan dynasty includes a "Gu qinggui xu" (Preface to the Old Pure Regulations) by Yang Yi (974–1020) dated in 1004 (*T.* 48: 8.1157a). This preface copies the *CDL* text almost verbatim, even mistakenly including some notes by later commentators, and it is not seen in Yang Yi's *Wuyi xinji*. As Zanning cited the same text in the *SGSZ*, this text could not have been written by Yang Yi in 1004.

98. *Xin Tang shu*, 59.1529.

99. For more detailed discussions of the content of the *Chanmen guishi*, see Martin Collcutt, "The Early Ch'an Monastic Rule: *Ch'ing Kuei* and the Shaping of Ch'an Community Life," in *Early Ch'an in China and Tibet*, 165–84; and Foulk, "Ch'an School and Its Place in the Buddist Monastic Tradition," 328–79.

100. For earlier studies, see Ui, *Daini zenshūshi kenkyū*, 375–95; Ōishi Shuyū, "Ko shingi ni tsuite," *Zengaku kenkyū* 44 (1953): 81–88; Yanagida, "Chūgoku zenshū shi," 58–60; Kagamishima Genryū, "Hyakujō shingi no seiritsu to sono igi," *Aichi gakuin daigaku zenkenkyūjo kiyo* 6 & 7 (1976): 117–34.

101. Kondō Ryōichi, "Hyakujō shingi no seiritsu to sono genkei," *Hokaidō Komazawa Daigaku kenkyū kiyo* 3 (1968): 19–48; and idem, "Hyakujō shingi seiritsu no yōin," *Indo tetsugaku bukkyōgaku* 2 (1987): 231–46.

102. Yifa, *The Origins of Buddhist Monastic Codes in China* (Honolulu: University of Hawaii Press, 2002), 28–35. Foulk and Poceski also indicate that the monastic regulations described in the *Chanmen guishi* were based on traditional Buddhist codes explained in the Vinaya texts and practiced in medieval monasteries. See Foulk, "'Ch'an School'," 388; and Poceski, "Hongzhou School," 435–36.

103. Ishii Shūdō, "Hyakujō kyōdan to Isan kyōdan," *Indogaku bukkyōgaku kenkyū* 41.1 (1992): 106–11; idem, "Hyakujo kyōdan to Isan kyōdan (zoku)," *Indogaku bukkyōgaku kenkyū* 42.1 (1993): 289–95; and idem, "Hyakujō shingi no kenkyū," *Komazawa daigaku zenkenkyūjo nenpō* 6 (1995): 15–53.

104. Foulk, "'Ch'an School'," 366–79; and idem, "Myth, Ritual, and Monastic Practice in Sung Ch'an Buddhism," 150, 156–59. Poceski follows Foulk's argument, but he set the creation of the Baizhang legend earlier in the late Tang to Five Dynasties; see his "Hongzhou School," 38.

105. *T.* 48: 8.1157a.

106. *Baoke leibian (SKQS)*, 5.16a.

107. *T.* 48: 8.1157a.

108. *Baoke leibian*, 5.16a. The *Chixiu Baizhang qinggui* records the date as the third day of the tenth month (*T.* 48: 8.1157a).

109. Baizhang's stūpa inscription, *QTW*, 446.7a.

110. Huang Jin (1277–1357), "Baizhangshan Dazhi shousheng chansi tianxia shibiaoge ji," *T.* 48: 8.1157b.

111. A few scholars have noticed this text, including Kagamishima Genryū, Ishii Shūdō, and Yifa. However, they have not paid much attention to it. See Kagamishima, "Hyakujō shingi no seiritsu to sono igi," 117–34; Ishii, "Hyakujō shingi no kenkyū," 24; and Yifa, *Origins of Buddhist Monastic Codes in China*, 34.

112. *QTW*, 446.6b.

113. See chapter two for a detailed discussion.

114. *Linjian lu (SKQS)*, 1.58b.

115. *QTW*, 713.12b.

116. *SGSZ*, 10.236; Yue Shi, *Taiping huanyu ji (SKQS)*, 106.13b–14a.

117. *QTW*, 446.6a.

118. In the *Fengxinxian zhi* (comp. 1871), Lü Maoxian and Shuai Fangwei cite an old gazetteer to indicate this date (16.32b).

119. *SGSZ*, 10.237.

120. The *Fengxinxian zhi* (4.64a) records that the name-tablet of the Baizhangsi was bestowed by Emperor Xuanzong (846–859) because he once visited the monastery as a monk before he ascended the throne. However, all the legends about Emperor Xuanzong's association with Chan monks are obviously fictitious.

121. Gernet, *Buddhism in Chinese Society*, 43–44.

122. The *Chixiu Baizhang qinggui* (*T.* 48: 3.1130b) declares that the abbot should be elected by the assembly and approved by official authority.

123. See Weinstein, *Buddhism under the T'ang*, 93–94, 119, 128–29.

124. *ZTJ*, 14.317.

125. Poceski, "Hongzhou School," 404–408.

126. We know that there was also no ownership of such lands during Baizhang Huaihai's tenure because, if there had been, the regulations would have mentioned how to deal with the lands.

127. *QTW*, 446.6a.

128. Reischauer, trans., *Ennin's Diary*, 131, 150.

129. Yifa, *Origins of Buddhist Monastic Codes in China*, 3–52.

130. Guishan's epitaph by Zheng Yu, *QTW*, 820.23a–27a; Yu Jing, "Lushan Chengtian Guizong chansi chongxiu ji," 7.4b; and Lin Hongyan (fl. 1639), ed., *Xuefeng Zhenjue chanshi yulu*, *XZJ* 119: 2.972b–73b. See Ishii, "Hyakujō shingi no kenkyū," 47–50; and Poceski, "Hongzhou School," 414–21.

131. *XZJ* 111; *Xuefeng Zhenjue chanshi yulu*, *XZJ* 119: 2.972b–73b.

132. *Xuefeng Zhenjue chanshi yulu*, *XZJ* 119: 2.973b.

133. For detailed discussions of Guishan's admonitions and Xuefeng's regulations, see Poceski, "Hongzhou School," 418–22, 456–92.

134. See chapter two, Table 1.

135. See Shiina Kōyū, "Shotō zensha no ritsuin kyojū ni tsuite," *Indogaku bukkyōgaku kenkyū* 17.2 (1969): 325–27.

136. Yunmen's epitaph by Chen Shouzhong, *QTW*, 892.4a–12b.

137. Chengyu, "Shushan Baiyun chanyuan ji," *QTW*, 920.17a–22a.

138. Ren Guang, "Tang Linchuanfu Chongrenxian Dizang pu'an chanyuan beiming," *QTW*, 869.3b–5b.

139. Lu Yuanhao, "Xianju dong Yong'an chanyuan ji," *QTW*, 869.8b–11a.

140. Han Xizai, "Xuanji chanshi bei," *QTW*, 877.15b–18b.

141. *Chunxi Sanshan zhi (SKQS)*, 38.8a.

142. Da'an's stūpa inscription by Yunming, copied by Ishii Shūdō, "Isan kyōdan no dōkō ni tsuite," 90–96; and *Chunxi Sanshan zhi*, 34.13b–14a.

143. *Chunxi Sanshan zhi*, 34.14b–15a.

144. Bai Juyi, "Wozhoushan Chanyuan ji," *Bai Juyi ji*, 68.3684–85.

145. *Yanyou Siming zhi (SKQS)*, 17.11a–15a.

146. *SGSZ*, 13.311–12.

147. Ibid., 12.289–90.

148. Li Yue, "Ruifeng Yong'an Zhushan chanyuan ji," in *Quan Tangwen bubian*, ed. Chen Shangjun, 112.1400–1401.

149. *SGSZ*, 13.305.

150. Shen Jian, "Da Tang Shuzhou Huatingxian Gutinglinshi xinchuang Fayun chansi ji," *QTW*, 792.21b–22a; *Baoke leibian*, 6.14a.

151. "Chi Changxing wanshou chanyuan die," *Jinshi cuibian*, *XXSKQS*, 119.44a/b.

152. Liu Congyi, "Da Zhou Guangci chanyuan ji," *Jinshi cuibian*, 121.16a–17a; and "Guangci chanyuan chandie," *Jinshi cuibian*, 121.7a/b.

153. For a discussion of the official institutionalization of Chan monasteries, see Foulk, "Myth, Ritual, and Monastic Practice in Sung Ch'an Buddhism," 147–208.

154. See Suzuki, *Tō Godai zenshūshi*, 394–414.

155. *ZTJ*, 14.318; Huihong, *Linjian lu*, 1.58b; *CDL*, 25.24a. See Ishii Shūdō, "Hyakujō shingi no kenkyū," *Komazawa daigaku zenkenkyūjo nenpō* 6 (1995): 38.

156. *CDL*, 24.20a.

157. *CDL*, 20.18b–19a, 25.24a–25a. See Ishii, "Hyakujō shingi no kenkyū," 39.

158. *Tō Godai zenshūshi*, 394–414.

159. *ZTJ*, 14.318.

160. See chapter three.

161. The geographical whereabouts of many of these disciples are described in Suzuki's *Tō Godai no zenshū* and *Tō Godai zenshūshi*.

162. Huijian's epitaph by Xu Dai, in *Xi'an beilin quanji*, ed. Gao Xia (Guangzhou: Guangdong jingji, 1999), 2: 20.2056–78. See Ran Yunhua, "'Tang gu Zhaoshengsi dade

Huijian Chanshi bei' kao," in *Cong Yindu fojiao dao Zhongguo fojiao* (Taibei: Dongda, 1995), 145–74.

163. *Chan Chart, XZJ* 110: 1.867b. Hu Shi doubted the reliability of Zongmi's record; see his "Ba Pei Xiu de Tang gu Guifeng Dinghui chanshi fabei," *Hu Shi ji*, 304–305. However, scholars have in general accepted Zongmi's record as historical fact; for example, see Ui, *Zenshūshi kenkyū*, 235–38; Ran Yunhua, "Chanzong diqizu zhizheng de wenxian yanjiu," *Zhongguo wenhua yanjiusuo xuebao* 6 (1997): 417–37.

164. See Dayi's epitaph by Wei Chuhou, *QTW*, 715.22a–26a. The epitaph indicates that Huo Xianming was the Commander of the Shence Army of the Right then, and Huo was in this post in 796–798 (*Jiu Tang shu*, 184.4766).

165. Li Chaozheng, "Chongjian Chanmen diyizu Putidamo dashi beiyin wen," *QTW*, 998.1a–3b.

166. *CDL*, 6.9a–10b.

167. *ZTJ*, 14.326; *Bai Juyi ji*, 41.2690–92; and Huairang's biography in the *SGSZ*, 9.200. This biography was based on the epitaph written by Gui Deng.

168. See Huineng's epitaph by Liu Zongyuan, *Liu Zongyuan ji*, 6.149–52. Liu Yuxi (772–842) said that the bestowal happened in 816; see the epitaph he written for Huineng, in *Liu Yuxi ji jianzheng*, ed. Qu Tuiyuan (Shanghai: Shanghai guji, 1989), 4.105. Since the first epitaph gives the day and month, and the second was written three years later, the first seems more exact.

169. See chapter one.

170. Huairang's epitaph by Zhang Zhengfu, *QTW*, 619.1a–3a. According to Yu Xianhao (*Tang cishi kao*, 2134), Zhang was Surveillance Commissioner of Hunan from the eighth year to the eleventh year of Yuanhe. The stele inscription gives the eighteenth year of Yuanhe, but the Yuanhe period had only fifteen years, and Huaihui died in the tenth year. In his *Longxing fojiao biannian tonglun* (*XZJ* 130: 16.584a), Zuxiu cites this stele inscription and records its date as the tenth year of Yuanhe.

171. *SGSZ*, 9.200.

172. *SGSZ*, 9.200.

173. Ouyang Xiu, *Jigu lu (SKQS)*, 9.14.

174. Huaihui's biography in the *SGSZ*, 10.227. This biography was based on Huaihui's epitaph written by Jia Dao (779–843).

175. Weikuan's biography in the *SGSZ*, 10.228.

176. Bai Juyi, "Chuanfatang bei," *Bai Juyi ji*, 41.2692.

177. *SGSZ*, 10.223, 10.236–37. However, in Xitang's epitaph written by Tang Ji, the bestowal happened in 824 (50.2b).

178. *QTW*, 715.22a/b.

179. Ibid., 731.23b.

180. *Chan Chart, XZJ* 110: 1.870a–72a; *Yuanjue jing dashu chao, XZJ* 14: 3.554a–59a; *Chan Preface, T.* 48: 1.400c.

181. *QTW*, 743.13b.

CHAPTER SIX

1. Hu Shi, "Yu Liutian Shengshan lun chanzongshi shu," in *Hu Shi ji*, 336–37.

2. Du Jiwen and Wei Daoru, *Zhongguo chanzong tongshi*, 274–80.

3. Suzuki, *To Godai zenshūshi*, 428–29.

4. McRae, *Northern School*, 7–8, 252–53; and idem, *Seeing through Zen*, 9–21.

5. See Weinstein, *Buddhism under the T'ang*, 114–36.

6. *Chuanxin fayao, T.* 48: 1.383a.

7. *CDL*, 7.3b.

8. Zezangzhu, *Gu zunsu yulu*, 13–14; Thomas Cleary, *The Five Houses of Zen* (Boston: Shambhala, 1997), 13.

9. Suzuki Tetsuo has noted this theme; see his "Hyakujō kōroku ni mirareru shisō," *Indogaku bukkyōgaku kenkyū* 46.2 (1998): 67.

10. *Gu zunsu yulu*, 10–13.

11. In Taoist texts it is called "twofold mystery" (*chongxuan*). For detailed discussions, see Timothy H. Barrett, "Taoist and Buddhist Mysteries in the Interpretaiton of the *Tao-te ching*," *Journal of the Royal Asiatic Society* 1 (1982): 35–43; and Robert H. Sharf, *Coming to Terms with Chinese Buddhism: A Reading of the Treasure Store Treatise* (Honolulu: University of Hawaii Press, 2002), 61–71.

12. *Wanling lu, T.* 48: 1.384b. Although this text may contain later additions and creations (see Introduction), the idea "no-mind" is actually implied in the *Chuanxin fayao* (*T.* 48: 1.379c, 381c).

13. *Chuanxin fayao, T.* 48: 1.379c, 383a.

14. Ibid., *T.* 48: 1.380a/b.

15. Ibid., *T.* 48: 1.379b.

16. *T.* 12: 1.221c, 32: 1.576a.

17. The masters of the Niutou school also advocated "no-mind"; see Yanagida and Tokiwa Gishin, *Zekkanron: Eibun yakuchū, genbun kōtei, kokuyaku* (Kyoto: Zenbunka kenkyūjo, 1976), Chinese, 87b; English, 5. However, since they did not relate "no-mind" to "one-mind" or "ordinary mind," their "no-mind" was a thorough apophasis of Madhyamaka thought. Zongmi was critical of the fact that the masters of the Niutou school did not recognize the nonempty aspect of the mind, but "assumed that the intrinsically enlightened nature is likewise empty and that there is nothing to be cognized" (*Chan Chart, XZJ* 110: 1.871a). See Gregory, *Tsung-mi*, 234–36.

18. See chapter three.

19. See Suzuki, *To Godai zenshushi*, 384–88.

20. *ZTJ*, 4.106.

21. Ui, *Daisan zenshūshi kenkyū*, 2, 23–26.

22. *ZTJ*, 3.70.

23. *ZTJ*, 18.400; *CDL*, 11.4a.

24. Liu Ke said in Shitou's epitaph, "Daji was the great master in Jiangxi, while Shitou was the great master in Hunan. Learners traveled between the two places; if

someone did not see both masters, he was regarded as ignorant." See Shitou's biography in the *SGSZ*, 9.209.

25. *Chan Chart*, *XZJ* 110: 1.870a–72a; *Yuanjue jing dashu chao*, *XZJ* 14: 3.554a–59a; *Chan Preface*, *T.* 48:1.400c.

26. For detailed discussions, see chapter two.

27. Du and Wei, *Zhongguo chanzong tongshi*, 280.

28. Xu Wenming, "Cao-Dong zong guizong Qingyuan yixi de yuanyin chuxi," *Pumen xuebao* 2 (2001): 126–36.

29. Yŏŏm's epitaph by Ch'oe Ŏnhwi, *Haidong jinshi yuan*, 3.8a/b.

30. Iŏm's epitaph by Ch'oe Ŏnhwi, *Haidong jinshi yuan*, 3.1b.

31. *SGSZ*, 13.308.

32. Huihong, "Ji Xihu yeyu," in *Shimen wenzi chan (SKQS)*, 24.19a.

33. Lingyou's epitaph written by Zheng Yu in 866 (*QTW*, 820.23a–27a) and his biography in the *SGSZ* (11.264), which was based on the epitaph written by Lu Jianqiu (789–864) soon after his death.

34. Huiji's epitaph written by Lu Xisheng in 895, *QTW*, 813.8a–10a.

35. Yu Jing, "Yunzhou Dongshan Puli chanyuan chuanfaji," in *Wuxi ji (SKQS)*, 9.14a–18a. See Ishii Shūdō, *Sōdai zenshūshi no kenkyū* (Tokyo: Daitō shuppansha, 1987), 410–13.

36. *SGSZ*, 9.208–209.

37. Yu Jing, "Yunzhou Dongshan Puli Chanyuan chuanfaji, " *Wuxi ji (SKQS)*, 15b. Liangjie's entries in the *ZTJ* (6.139) and *SGSZ* (12.280) states that he also studied with Nanquan Puyuan.

38. Hyŏnhwi's epitaph by Ch'oe Ŏnhwi, *Haidong jinshi yuan*, 3.33b–34a.

39. *Xuefeng Zhenjue chanshi yulu*, *XZJ* 119: 2.960a.

40. *ZTJ*, 5.129–31; *SGSZ*, 12.275. Xue Tingwang was written as Xue Yanwang in these two texts. I follow the records in the *Xin Tang shu*; see Yu Xianhao, *Tang cishi kao*, 173.2500.

41. Ch'anyu's epitaph by Kim Chongŏn, *Chōsen kinseki sōran*, vol. 1, 209.

42. *CDL*, 5.13b.

43. *Zongmen shigui lun*, *XZJ* 110: 1.878b.

44. Chuyuan, ed., *Fenyang Wude chanshi yulu*, *XZJ* 120: 1.85a.

45. *Fenyang Wude chanshi yulu*, *XZJ* 120: 2.142b–43a.

46. Fadeng Taiqin was Fayan's disciple; see *CDL*, 25.19b–20a.

47. Muzhou Daozong was also Yunmen's mentor; see Yunmen's epitaph by Chen Shouzhong, *QTW*, 892.6b–7b. Huinan, ed., *Shishuang Chuyuan chanshi yulu*, *XZJ* 120: 1.185b–86a.

48. Huihong, *Linjian lu*, *XZJ* 148: 1.592a; *Heshan Fang chanshi yulu*, *XZJ* 120: 1.268a/b. See Suzuki, *Tō Godai zenshūshi*, 428–29.

49. For example, in addition to Deshan Xuanjian, Xuefeng Yicun also studied with Furong Lingxun, Mazu's second-generation disciple (Xuefeng's epitaph by Huang Tao,

QTW, 826.5b); and in addition to Xuefeng Yicun, Yunmen Wenyan also studied with Muzhou Daozong, Mazu's third-generation disciple.

50. See Weinstein, *Buddhism under the T'ang*, 141, 144–46.

51. For a detailed discussion, see chapter five.

52. See Suzuki, *Tō Godai zenshūshi*, 394–414; and chapter five.

53. Weinstein, *Buddhism under the T'ang*, 147–50.

54. *ZTJ*, 4.104, 110.

55. See Suzuki, *To Godai zenshūshi*, 402–407.

56. *ZJL*, *T*. 48: 93.923c, 25.520b.

57. *Zongmen shigui lun*, *XZJ* 110: 1.878b–79b.

58. According to Xinghua Cunjiang's epitaph written by Gongsheng Yi in 889 (*QTW*, 813.19a), when Huiji had just founded his monastery at Yangshan, Cunjiang visited him; soon Cunjiang left Yangshan to attend his master Linji Yixuan, who died the next year. Yixuan died in 867; thus, Cunjiang visited Huiji in about 866.

59. *QTW*, 813.9a.

60. *ZTJ*, 2.44. This prophecy is also possibly a later addition; see Yanagida, *Shoki zenshū shisho no kenkyū*, 363.

61. *ZTJ*, 2.44.

62. *QTW*, 870.16a/b. The saying "Caoxi was void" may represent the understanding of the story of Huineng by late-Tang Chan monks.

63. *QTW*, 826.8b–9a.

APPENDIX

1. The phrase "dharma of one-mind" appears in the *Dasheng qixin lun* (*The Awakening of Faith*; *T*. 32: 1.576a) and some sūtras. The *Laṅkāvatāra-sūtra* says, "One-mind is named tathāgata-garbha" (*Ru Lengqie jing*, *T*. 16: 1.519a). Fazang also identified one-mind with tathāgata-garbha; see his *Dasheng qixin lun yiji*, *T*. 44: 2.251b–c.

2. Zongmi said, "[The Hongzhou school] meant to follow the *Laṅkāvatāra-sūtra*, which states: '. . . In the Buddha's discourses, the mind is the essence'." 意准 "楞伽經" 云: ". . . 佛語心" (*Yuanjue jing dashu chao, XZJ* 14: 3.557a; *Chan Chart, XZJ* 110: 1.870a). This expression does not actually appear in any of the three extant Chinese translations of the *Laṅkāvatāra-sūtra*. The phrase "Yiqie foyu xin" 一切佛語心 (The essential of all the Buddha's discourses) is the subtitle of Guṇabhadra's translation (*Lengqie abaduoluo baojing, T*. 16: 1.480a, 489a, 497c, 505b), and it also appears once in the text of the same version (*T*. 16: 1.484a). In this phrase, however, "xin" does not mean "mind" but "essential." It seems that Mazu deliberately explained it as "mind."

3. The *Chuanxin fayao* records, "Since the great master Bodhidharma arrived in China, he only said one-mind and only transmitted one dharma. He used the Buddha to transmit the Buddha, without talking about other Buddhas; he used the dharma to transmit the dharma, without talking about other dharmas. The dharma is the ineffable dharma, and the Buddha is the unattainable Buddha: it is the pure mind of fundamental source." 自達摩大師到中國, 唯說一心, 唯傳一法. 以佛傳佛, 不說餘佛; 以法傳法, 不說餘法. 法即不可說之法, 佛即不可取之佛, 乃是本源清淨心也; "The Buddhas

and all the sentient beings are just one-mind, and there is no other dharma. . . . This mind is the Buddha, and the Buddha is the sentient being." 諸佛與一切眾生, 唯是一心, 更無別法. . . . 此心即是佛, 佛即是众生 (T. 48: 1.381b, 379c). Passage 1 is also seen in the ZTJ (14.304), CDL (6.2a), GDL (8.651b), and Mazu yulu (1.5b), with some textual differences. The most important difference is that at the beginning of the other three texts there is an additional sentence, which reads, "All of you should believe that your mind is the Buddha, and this mind is the Buddha-mind." 汝等諸人各信自心是佛, 此心即是佛心.

4. This quotation appears in the Śrīmālādevī-simhanāda-sūtra (Shengman shizihou yisheng dafangguang jing), T. 12: 1.217a; and the Mahāratnakūṭa-sūtra (Da baoji jing), T. 11: 119.673a.

5. Zongchi 總持 is a Chinese translation of dhāraṇī, which means absolute memory aids to hold or support something in the mind, and also refers to formulas, spells, and incantations. Mazu used it in the first meaning. Shimen 施門 is the abbreviation of bushimen 布施門 (gate of bestowal); see the Avatamsaka-sūtra (Da fangguang fo huayan jing), T. 9: 6.435a; T. 10: 4.17b, 14.74b; and the Da baoji jing, T. 11: 54.318b.

6. The true-form Buddha refers to the dharma-body (dharmakāya) Buddha.

7. The thirty-two marks and eighty signs are the physical characteristics of the Buddha. This sentence is a paraphrased quotation from the Sukhāvatīvyūha-sūtra (Guan Wuliangshoufo jing), which reads: "When you think of the Buddha in your mind, the mind is the thirty-two marks and eighty signs." 汝等心想佛時, 是心即是三十二相八十隨形好 (T. 12: 1.343a); or the Suvikrāntavikrami-paripricchā-prajñāpāramitā-sūtra (Shengtianwang bore boluomi jing), which reads, "The thirty-two marks and eighty signs manifest along with the sentient beings' conception" 三十二相八十種好, 隨眾生意如是現之 (T. 8: 7.723a).

8. The word jia 家 is used as an auxiliary, like the word de 的 (of).

9. This quotation is from the Vimalakīrti-sūtra (Weimojie suoshuo jing), T. 14: 1.540b.

10. This quotation is from the Laṅkāvatāra-sūtra (Lengqie abaduoluo baojing, T. 16: 1.480a, 480b; and Ru Lengqie jing, T. 16: 1.590c).

11. This quotation is from the Laṅkāvatāra-sūtra (Lengqie abaduoluo baojing), T. 16: 3.500b.

12. Some parts of Passages 2 and 3 are also cited as Qingyuan Xingsi's discourses in the ZJL, T. 48: 97.940b. As Xingsi was an obscure figure during his lifetime, all extant discourses attributed to him are not authentic.

13. This quotation appears in several sūtras, with some minor differences; see the Vimalakīrti-sūtra (Weimojie suoshuo jing), T. 14: 2.546a; Mahāprajñāpāramitā-sūtra (Da bore boluomiduo jing), T. 7: 571.948a); Shengtianwang bore boluomi jing, T. 8: 5.711c. It is also seen in the Ratnagotravibhāga (Jiujing yisheng baoxing lun), T. 45: 1.146a.

14. The Extended Discourses of Dazhu Huihai reads, "A monk asked, 'Who is the Buddha?' The master answered, 'Apart from the mind there is no Buddha.'" 僧問: "何者是佛?" 師曰: "離心之外即無有佛" (CDL, 28.16b). Ganquan Zhixian said, "If one can realize his own mind, outside of the mind there is no other Buddha, and outside of the Buddha there is no other mind." 若能識自心, 心外更無別佛, 佛外無別心 (ZJL, T. 48: 98.943b). The Chuanxin fayao records, "This mind is the Buddha; there is

no other Buddha, and there is also no other mind." 此心即是佛, 更无别佛, 亦无别心 (*T*. 48: 1.380a).

15. Zhangjing Huaihui's epitaph written by Quan Deyu records Huaihui's words as thus: "Neither dismiss the phenomenal to accord the mind, nor reject defilement to obtain purity." 非遣境以會心, 非去垢以取淨 (*Quan Zaizhi wenji*, 18.14a). Tianhuang Daowu's biography in the *SGSZ*, which is based on the epitaph written by Fu Zai, records Daowu's words as thus: "Defilement and purity stay together, as water and wave share the same substance." 垢淨共住, 水波同體 (*SGSZ*, 10.233). Bai Juyi recorded his conversations with Xingshan Weikuan as follows: "My second question was this: 'If there is not a distinction, in what way does one cultivate his mind?' The master answered, 'The mind originally is not damaged. How should it be repaired? Regardless of defilement or purity, all one needs is not to originate the thought.' My third question was this: 'Truly defilement should not be thought about, but is it right not to think about purity?' The master said, 'It is like the fact that no one single object can be put into one's eyes. Though bits of gold are valuable, if they are put into one's eyes, they still cause illness.' " 第二問云: "既無分別, 何以修心." 師曰: "心本無損傷, 云何要修理. 無論垢與淨, 一切勿起念." 第三問云: "垢即不可念, 淨無念可乎?" 師曰: "如人眼睛上, 一物不可住; 金屑雖珍貴, 在眼亦為病." (*Bai Juyi ji*, 41.2691–92)

16. The expression "The triple world is [made of] mind only" appears in the *Laṅkāvatara-sutra (Lengqie abaduoluo baojing*, *T*. 16: 2.489c; and *Dasheng ru Lengqie jing*, *T*. 16: 7.555b, *T*. 16: 5.618a); and the *Huayan jing, T*. 10: 54.288c. It is also seen in the *Mūlajāta-hridayabhūmi-dhyāna-sūtra (Dasheng bensheng xindiguan jing)*, *T*. 3: 8.327a/b; however, this sūtra was translated in 810 (*Jiu Tang shu*, 149.4020), after Mazu passed away.

17. This quotation is from the *Faju jing* (*T*. 85: 1.1435a), which is generally regarded as an indigenous Chinese composition.

18. The *Shaoshi liumen* 少室六門 reads, "The phenomenal does not exist by itself; its existence is due to the mind. The mind does not exist by itself; its existence is due to the phenomenal." 色不自色, 由心故色. 心不自心, 由色故心 *(T*. 48: 1.370c). A same expression is also found in *Damo dashi wuxing lun* 達磨大師悟性論, *XZJ* 110: 1.817a.

19. This quotation is unidentified. The passage is also seen in the *ZTJ* (14.304), *CDL* (6.2a), *GDL* (8.651b), and *Mazu yulu* (1.5b), with some textual differences. A part of this passage is also cited as Nanyue Huairang's discourse in the *ZJL*, *T*. 48: 97.940b. Since Huairang was an obscure figure during his lifetime, all the extant discourses attributed to him are questionable.

20. When the *ZJL* cites this passage, it only mentions a certain "ancient virtuous" (*gude* 古德); but according to similar passages in the *ZTJ* (14.304), *CDL* (6.2a/b), *GDL* (8.652a), and *Mazu yulu* (1.6a), as well as Zongmi's summary of the Hongzhou doctrine (see later), this passage must be Mazu's discourse. In the other four texts this passage is much longer, and reads: "You can speak at any time. The phenomenal is the absolute, and they are without obstruction. The fruit of perfect enlightenment (bodhi) is also like this. Whatever arises in the mind is called the phenomenal. If you know the phenomenal is empty, then production is non-production. If you understand this meaning, you can at any time wear clothes, eat food, and nourish the sacred embryo. Freely following your destiny to pass the time, how can you again have anything to do? Having received my teaching, you listen to my verse: 'The mind-ground is spoken of

at any time, / But perfect enlightenment (*bodhi*) is just tranquil. Both the phenomenal and absolute are without obstruction, / And production is non-production.' " 汝但隨時言說, 即事即理, 都無所礙. 菩提道果, 亦復如是. 於心所生, 即名為色, 知色空故, 生即不生. 若了此意, 乃可隨時著衣喫飯, 長養聖胎, 任運過時, 更有何事. 汝受吾教, 聽吾偈曰: 心地隨時說, 菩提亦只寧. 事理俱無礙, 當生即不生. In the *ZTJ, CDL, GDL,* and *Mazu yulu,* this passage and other two passages that correspond to Passage 1 and 4 form a sermon. However, as some scholars have indicated, in the *Baolin zhuan,* from the Indian patriarchs to Mazu, every patriarch was attributed a mind-verse (see Mizuno Kogen, "Denhōge no seiritsu ni tsuite," 23). The passage previously cited also contains a mind-verse; thus, the sermon recorded in these four texts is quite possibly a citation from the *Baolin zhuan,* especially when noting the fact that Mazu's entry in the *ZTJ* was based on this text (see chapter one) and this is the only sermon contained in that entry. It is likely that this sermon was changed by the compiler(s) of the *Baolin zhuan,* and therefore it is different from the *ZJL* version to a large extent. The *Extended Discourses of Dazhu Huihai* reads, "You just do not see the nature, but it is not that there is no nature. Now you see [the activities] of wearing clothes, eating food, walking, abiding, sitting, and lying. Facing these but not recognizing them, you can be called a fool." 汝自不見性, 不可是無性. 今見著衣吃飯, 行住坐臥, 對面不識, 可謂愚迷 (*CDL,* 28.12b–13a). Zongmi summarized the Hongzhou doctrine as follows: "Neither excising [evil] nor cultivating [good], but freely following one's destiny and being spontaneous in all situations: this is called liberation. The nature is like space which is neither increasing nor decreasing. How can we assume to complement it? If you at any time and any place cease making kalpa and keep mental tranquility, your sacred embryo will grow and its natural wonder will become manifest. This is true enlightenment, true cultivation, and true realization." 不斷不修, 任運自在, 名為解脫. 性如虛空, 不增不減, 何假添補. 但隨時隨處, 息業養神, 聖胎增長, 顯發自然神妙. 此即是為真悟真修真證也 (*Chan Preface, T.* 48: 2.402c).

21. The *Extended Records of Baizhang* reads, "So long as all actions and activities, speaking, being mute, crying, and laughing, these are all the Buddha's wisdom." 但是一切舉動施為, 語默啼笑, 儘是佛慧 (*Gu zunsu yulu,* 2.30). Zongmi said that the masters of the Hongzhou school preached: "Consequently, we know that what is capable of speech and activity must be Buddha-nature." 故知能言語動作者必是佛性 (*Chan Chart, XZJ* 110: 1.870b); "Now that what is capable of speech, activity, greed, hatred, compassion, toleration, the performance of good or evil actions, the corresponding retribution of happiness or suffering, and so forth, is your Buddha-nature." 即今能語言動作, 貪嗔慈忍, 造善惡, 受苦樂等, 即汝佛性 (*Chan Preface, T.* 48: 2.402c).

22. The three great countless (asamkhyeya) kalpas are the three timeless periods of a bodhisattva's progress to Buddhahood.

23. This is a paraphrased quotation from the *Laṅkāvatāra-sūtra (Lengqie abaduoluo baojing, T.* 16: 4.506b; and *Dasheng ru Lengqie jing, T.* 16: 5.615c).

24. Maṇi is a general name for jewel, gem, precious stone, pearl, and so on. The *Laṅkāvatāra-sūtra* reads, "It is like the maṇi that manifests colors according to the mind." 亦如摩尼, 隨心現色 (*Dasheng ru Lengqie jing, T.* 16: 2.598c).

25. Zongmi stated, "For example, there is a maṇi pearl that is perfectly round, pure, luminous, and untarnished by any shade of color. As its essence is luminous, when it comes into contact with external objects it can reflect all different shades of color. These shades of color may have individual differences, but the luminous pearl is never

altered. Although there are hundreds and thousands of different colors that the pearl may reflect, let us take the color black that is opposed to the luminous pearl as a metaphor, to illustrate the fact that although the numinous, bright knowledge and vision are the exact opposite of the darkness of ignorance, it is nevertheless of the same single essence. When the pearl reflects the color black, its entire substance becomes completely black; its luminosity is no longer visible. If ignorant children or country bumpkins then happened to see it, they would immediately think that it was a black pearl. . . . There is another type of person who points out, 'It is precisely this blackness itself that is the luminous pearl. The essence of that luminous pearl can never be seen. If someone wants to know what the luminous pearl is, it is precisely that blackness and precisely all the different colors like blue and yellow.' Such a position will cause the fools who have firm faith in these words either to remember only the shade of blackness or to recognize all the different shades as being the luminous pearl. . . . (The view of the Hongzhou school is parallel to this. The term 'fools' refers to successors of this school)." 如一摩尼珠, 唯圓淨明, 都無一切差別色相. 以體明故, 對外物時, 能現一切差別色相. 色相自有差別, 明珠不曾變易. 然珠所現色, 雖有百千般, 今且取與明珠相違之黑色, 以況靈明知見, 與黑暗無明, 雖即相違, 而是一體. 謂如珠現黑色時, 徹體全黑, 都不見明. 如癡孩子, 或村野人見之, 直是黑珠. . . . 復有一類人, 指示云: "即此黑暗便是明珠. 明珠之體, 永不可見. 欲得識者, 即黑便是明珠, 乃至青黃種種皆是. 致令愚者的信此言, 專記黑相, 或認種種相為明珠. . . . (洪州見解如此也. 言愚者, 彼宗後學也). See *Chan Chart*, *XZJ* 110: 1.872a–3a.

26. Fenzhou Wuye's biography in the *SGSZ* (11.249), which is based on the epitaph written by Yang Qian, records Wuye's words: "Your nature of seeing, listening, sensing, and knowing is as long-lived as space, without birth or death." 汝等見聞覺知之性, 與太虛同壽, 不生不滅. Yangqi Zhenshu's epitaph written by Zhixian records his words: "The fundamental source of all the numinous minds assumes its name as the Buddha. Even though the body is exhausted and the shape disappears, it never perishes; even though the metal melts and the stone smashes, it forever exists." 群靈本源, 假名為佛, 體竭形消而不滅, 金流(樸)[璞]散而常存 (*QTW*, 919.10b; *SGSZ*, 10.235). The *Extended Discourses of Dazhu Huihai* reads, "The body is originated by the nature; when the body dies, how can one say that the nature perishes?" 身因性起, 身死豈言性滅(*CDL*, 28.12b). The *Chuanxin fayao* records, "Since beginningless time, this nature of numinous mind is as long-lived as space; it is never born and never dies." 此靈覺性無始以來, 與虛空同壽, 未曾生未曾滅 (*T.* 48: 381a). The *Extended Discourses of Nanyang Huizhong* cites a wandering Chan practitioner's words as follows: "Learned people in that quarter show the learners directly that this mind is the Buddha, which means enlightenment. . . . The body has birth and death, but the mind-nature has never had birth or death since beginningless time. When a body is born or dies, it is like a dragon transforming its bones, a snake sloughing off its skin, or a man leaving his old house. Thus, the body is transitory, but the nature is eternal." 彼方知識直下示學人, 即心是佛, 佛是覺義. . . . 此身即有生滅, 心性無始以來, 未曾生滅. 身生滅者, 如龍換骨, 蛇脫皮, 人出故宅. 即身是無常, 其性常也 (*CDL*, 28.1a/b). Scholars in general agree that "learned people in that quarter" refers to the masters of the Hongzhou school; see chapter four.

27. The wandering Chan practitioner's words cited in the *Extended Discourses of Nanyang Huizhong* also states that the masters of the Hongzhou school preached: "You now possess the entire nature of seeing, listening, sensing, and knowing. This nature is adept in the raising of eyebrows and the twinkling of eyes. It freely functions every-

where through one's body: when it strikes the head, the head knows it; when it strikes the foot, the foot knows it. Hence, it is called the correct, complete knowing. Apart from it, there is no other Buddha." 汝今悉具見聞覺知之性, 此性善能揚眉瞬目, 去來運用, 遍於身中. 挃頭頭知, 挃腳腳知, 故名正遍知. 離此之外, 更無別佛. Upon hearing this, Huizhong criticized: "If we take seeing, listening, sensing, and knowing to be Buddha-nature, Pure Reputation [i.e., Vimalakīrti] should not say that the dharma is separate from seeing, listening, sensing, and knowing. If one practices seeing, listening, sensing, and knowing, then these are seeing, listening, sensing, and knowing, not seeking the dharma." 若以見聞覺知為佛性者, 淨名不應云法離見聞覺知. 若行見聞覺知, 是則見聞覺知, 非求法也 (CDL, 28.1b). In addition, in Bodhidharma's entry in the CDL (T. 51: 3.218b), which must have been copied from the Baolin zhuan, there is a dialogue between Boluoti, who is said to have been awakened by Bodhidharma, and an Indian King. The King asked, "Where is [Buddha-]nature?" Boluoti replied, "[Buddha-]nature manifests in function." He then recited a verse: "In an embryo it is the body; in society it is called a man; in eyes it is called seeing; in ears it is called listening; in noses it smells odor; in mouth it speaks; in hands it grabs; in feet it runs; it manifests itself in all worlds that are as numerous as the sands of the Ganges; and it is embodied within a molecule. Those who understand know it is Buddha-nature, while those who do not understand call it essential soul." [王]云: "性在何處?" 曰: "性在作用." . . . 波羅提即說偈曰: "在胎為身, 處世名人, 在眼曰見, 在耳曰聞, 在鼻辨香, 在口談論, 在手執捉, 在足運奔. 遍現俱該沙界, 收攝在一微塵. 識者知是佛性, 不識喚作精魂."

28. The Mahāparinirvāṇa-sūtra (Da boniepan jing 大般涅槃經) has a famous verse of "[Buddha-nature] originally existed but does not exist at present" (benyou jinwu 本有今無; T. 12: 27.524b).

29. The Extended Discourses of Dazhu Huihai records, "The master said, 'The mind is the Buddha; you need not use the Buddha to look for the Buddha. The mind is the dharma; you need not use the dharma to look for the dharma. . . . The nature is originally pure, without waiting for cultivation and completion." 師曰: "心是佛, 不用將佛求佛. 心是法, 不用將法求法. . . . 性本清淨, 不待修成" (CDL, 28:9a/b). The Extended Records of Baizhang states, "From ancient to present, the Buddha is just a man, and a man is just the Buddha. It is also the samādhi meditation. You need not use meditation to enter meditation; you need not use Chan to think of Chan; you need not use the Buddha to look for the Buddha." 自古至今, 佛祇是人, 人祇是佛. 亦是三昧定. 不用將定入定, 不用將禪想禪, 不用將佛覓佛 (Gu zunsu yulu, 1.16). The Chuanxin fayao records, "The nature is the mind, the mind is the Buddha, and the Buddha is the dharma. When one thought departs the true [essence], this is delusion. One cannot use the mind to look for the mind, use the Buddha to look for the Buddha, or use the dharma to look for the dharma." 性即是心, 心即是佛, 佛即是法. 一念離真, 皆為妄想. 不可以心更求於心, 不可以佛更求於佛, 不可以法更求於法 (T. 48: 1.381a/b). Zongmi summarized the Hongzhou teaching of no-cultivation as follows: "Since the principles of awakening are all spontaneous and natural, the principles of cultivation should accord with them. One should neither arouse his intention to excise evil, nor arouse his intention to cultivate the Way. The Way is the mind; one cannot use the mind to cultivate the mind. Evil too is the mind; one cannot use the mind to excise the mind. One who neither excises evil nor cultivates good, but freely follows his destiny and is spontaneous in all situations, is called a liberated man. There is no dharma that can bind and no Buddha that can be attained. The mind is like space that is neither increasing nor decreasing. How can we presume to

supplement it? Why is this? There is not one dharma that can be found outside the mind-nature; hence, cultivation means simply to let the mind be free." 既悟解之理, 一切天真自然. 故所修行理, 宜順此, 而乃不起心斷惡, 亦不起心修道. 道即是心, 不可將心還修於心; 惡亦是心, 不可將心還斷於心. 不斷不造, 任運自在, 名為解脫人. 無法可拘, 無佛可作, 猶如虛空不增不減, 何假添補. 何以故? 心性之外, 更無一法可得故, 故但任心即為修也 (*Chan Chart, XZJ* 110: 1.871a; see also *Chan Preface*, T. 48: 2.402c; *Yuanjue jing dashu chao, XZJ* 14: 3.557b).

30. Some parts of Sermon 2 are also cited as Qingyuan Xingsi's discourses in the *ZJL*, T. 48: 97.940b. As previously mentioned, none of the discourses attributed to Xingsi is authentic.

31. In the *ZJL*, after this passage there are more sentences that illustrate the same idea. Yanagida Seizan thinks that these are also Mazu's discourses (*Goroku no rekishi*, 319–21). However, these sentences are obviously Yanshou's explanation of Mazu's discourse.

32. Daji, Great Quiescence, is Mazu's posthumous title.

33. The *Extended Discourses of Dazhu Huihai* records, "Someone asked: 'How can one attain Buddhahood?' The master answered, 'You do not need to abandon the mind of sentient beings, just not to defile the self-nature'" 問: "'云何得作佛去?' 師曰: '不用舍眾生心, 但莫污染自性'"; "[The monk] asked again, 'What is cultivation?' The master answered, 'If you do not defile the self-nature, this is cultivation'" [僧]又問: "如何是修行?" 師曰: "但莫污染自性, 即是修行" (*CDL*, 28.14a/b). The *Extended Records of Baizhang* records, "It is also said that the Way of Chan needs no cultivation, just not to defile it." 又云禪道不用修, 但莫污染 (*Gu zunsu yulu*, 1.16).

34. Zongmi summarized the Hongzhou doctrine as thus: "The essence of Buddha-nature is free of the whole range of differentiation, and yet it can produce the whole range of differentiation. That its essence is devoid of differentiation means that this Buddha-nature is neither holy nor profane, neither cause nor effect, and neither good nor evil. It has neither form nor sign, neither root nor abiding; and, finally, it is neither Buddha nor sentient being." 佛性體非一切差別種種, 而能造作一切差別種種. 體非種種者, 謂此佛性非聖非凡, 非因非果, 非善非惡, 無色無相, 無根無住, 乃至無佛無眾生也 (*Chan Chart, XZJ* 110: 1.870b).

35. This quotation is from the *Vimalakīrti-sūtra* (*Weimojie suoshuo jing*), T. 14: 2.545b.

36. Yanguan Qi'an's stupa inscription written by Lu Jianqiu records Yanguan's words: "Walking, abiding, sitting, and lying—all these are at the place of enlightenment." 行住坐臥, 皆是道場 (*QTW*, 733.22a). The *Extended Discourses of Dazhu Huihai* reads, "To those who understand the Way, walking, abiding, sitting, and lying are the Way" 會道者行住坐臥是道; "Walking, abiding, sitting, and lying—all these are the functioning of your nature." 行住坐臥, 並是汝性用 (*CDL*, 28.14b, 17b).

37. This quotation is from the *Madhyametyukta-sūtra* (*Zhong benqi jing*), T. 4: 1.153c. *Shi xin* 識心 (realizing the mind) is originally written as *xi xin* 息心 (appeasing the mind). The *Chuanxin fayao* records, "When his body and mind are in natural condition, one reaches the Way and realizes the mind. Since he reaches the fundamental source, he is called a monk." 身心自然, 達道識心. 達本源故號為沙門 (T. 48: 1.382c).

38. The *Vimalakīrti-sūtra* reads, "Ānanda, you see there are many Buddha-lands, but the space is not manifold. In the same way, you see there are many physical bodies of

Buddhas, but their unobstructed wisdom is not manifest." 阿難. 汝見諸佛國土地有若干, 而虛空無若干也. 如是見諸佛色身有若干耳, 其無礙慧無若干也 (*Weimojie suoshuo jing, T.* 14: 3.554a).

39. The *Zhao lun* 肇論 (Treatise of Sengzhao) reads, "It is not that there is a place to stand where one leaves the Truth, but the very place where one stands is the Truth." 非離真而立處, 立處即真也 (*T.* 45: 1.153a).

40. The *Mahāvaipulya-mahāsamnipāta-sūtra* (*Da fangdeng daji jing*) reads, "In every place, there is the Buddha." 在在處處, 有佛世尊 (*T.* 13: 39.264b).

41. Nengren 能仁, the Merciful One, is an early, incorrect interpretation of Śākyamuni, but probably indicating his character.

42. This is a paraphrased quotation from the *Śrīmālā Sūtra*, which reads, "If one has no doubt with the tathāgata-garbha that is in the bondage of the storehouse of boundless afflictions, he will have no doubt with the dharma-body that is out of the bondage of the storehouse of boundless afflictions." 若於無量煩惱藏所纏如來藏不疑惑者, 於出無量煩惱藏法身亦無疑惑 (*T.* 12: 1.221b).

43. This sentence appears in the *Suvarṇa-prabhāsa-uttamarāja-sūtra* (*Jinguangming jing, T.* 16: 2.344b; and *Hebu jinguangming jing, T.* 16: 5.385b).

44. The word *genzai* 根栽 is written as *genmiao* 根苗 in the *GDL* (8.654b). Both *zai* and *miao* mean seedling; *genzai* and *genmiao* are synonyms, meaning root and seedling or simply root.

45. Although the text does not indicate it, this sentence is a quotation from the *Vimalakīrti-sūtra* (*Weimojie suoshuo jing*), *T.* 14: 3.554b.

46. This line appears in a verse in the *Huayan jing, T.* 10: 51.273a. It is also seen in a few other sūtras: *Vimalakīrti-sūtra* (*Weimojie suoshuo jing*), *T.* 14: 1.538a; *Daśasahasrikā-prajñapāmitā-sūtra* (*Xiaopin bore boluomi jing*), *T.* 8: 5.558c; *Da baoji jing, T.* 11: 62.360b; *Mahākāśagarbha-bodhisattva-paripṛicchā-sūtra* (*Daji daxu Kongzang pusa suowen jing*), *T.* 13: 7.640c.

47. This idea is based on the famous two aspects of one-mind in the *Awakening of Faith, T.* 32: 1.584c.

48. This is a paraphrased quotation from the *Da boniepan jing*, which reads, "There is the visual perception: all Buddhas and the Bodhisattvas of the tenth stage perceive Buddha-nature by visual perception. There is again the auditory perception: all sentient beings and the Bodhisattvas of the ninth stage perceive Buddha-nature by auditory perception." 復有眼見, 諸佛如來十住菩薩眼見佛性. 復有聞見, 一切眾生乃至九地聞見佛性 (*T.* 12: 25.772c). However, in another place the same sūtra says that the Bodhisattvas of the tenth stage perceive Buddha-nature by auditory perception (*T.* 12: 25.772b).

49. This sentence comes from a verse in the *Laṅkāvatāra-sūtra* (*Lengqie abaduoluo baojing*), *T.* 16: 3.505b.

50. This idea is based on the *Laṅkāvatāra-sūtra*, which reads, "Departing from the deluded thought of discrimination in one's mind, one will attain acceptance of the non-production [of dharmas]." 离心意意识妄分别想, 獲無生忍 (*Dasheng ru Lengqie jing, T.* 16: 5.618c–19a).

51. The pure Chan of Tathāgata is the highest among the four kinds of dhyāna expounded in the *Laṅkāvatāra-sūtra* (*Lengqie abaduoluo baojing*), *T.* 16: 2.492a.

52. This sermon is also seen in the *GDL* (8.653b–54b) and *Mazu yulu* (1.7b–9b).

53. Zongmi summarized: "The idea of the Hongzhou school is that . . . the total essences of greed, hatred, or delusion, the performance of good and evil actions, and the corresponding retribution of happiness or suffering of bitterness are all Buddha-nature." 洪州意者 . . . 全體貪嗔癡, 造善造惡, 受樂受苦, 此皆是佛性 (*Chan Chart*, *XZJ*, 110: 1.870b; see also *Yuanjue jing dashu chao*, *XZJ* 14: 1.557a; *Chan Preface*, *T.* 48: 2.402c).

54. This quotation is from the *Vimalakīrti-sūtra (Weimojie suoshuo jing)*, *T.* 14: 2.545a.

55. *Nian* 念 is a Chinese translation for Sanskrit smṛti, a moment or a thought. The *Vimalakīrti-nirdeśa-sūtra* reads, "All dharmas arise and are extinguished without abiding, like an illusion or a flash of lightning. All dharmas do not wait for one another and do not abide for even a single moment of thought." 一切法生滅不住, 如幻如電. 諸法不相待, 乃至一念不住 (*T.* 14: 2.541b). The *Baozang lun* 寶藏論 (Treasure Store Treatise) reads, "All dharmas are successive moments of thought and do not wait for one another." 諸法念念, 各不相待 (*T.* 45: 1.144b).

56. "Ocean-seal" is a metaphor that symbolizes that the Buddha's wisdom is like the ocean in which all phenomena are reflected. According to the Huayan tradition, the Buddha entered the ocean-seal samādhi immediately following his enlightenment, and in the ocean-seal samādhi he preached the *Huayan jing*.

57. This is a paraphrased quotation from the *Vajrasamādhi-sūtra (Jingang sanmei jing)*, which reads, "The true meaning of the single taste can be compared to that of the one ocean: there is not one of the myriad of streams that does not flow into it. Elder! The tastes of all the dharmas are just like those streams: while their names and classifications may differ, the water is indistinguishable. Once [those streams] have flowed into the ocean, [the seawater] then absorbs all those streams. If one lingers in the single taste, then all tastes are imbibed." 一味實義如一大海, 一切眾流無有不入. 長者. 一切法味猶彼眾流, 名數雖殊, 其水不異. 若住大海, 則括眾流. 住於一味, 則攝諸味. See Buswell, *Formation of Ch'an Ideology*, 233.

58. There are four stages in which the Śrāvaka cultivates cause and attains fruition: the first is the eighty thousand kalpas; the second the sixty thousand kalpas; the third the forty thousand kalpas; and the fourth the twenty thousand kalpas.

59. This quotation is from the *Vimalakīrti-sūtra*, which reads, "The ordinary man can be changed and return to Buddhist dharma, while the Śrāvaka cannot." 凡夫於佛法有返復, 而聲聞無也 (*Weimojie suoshuo jing*, *T.* 14: 2.549b).

60. Zongmi summarized: "The idea of the Hongzhou school is that the arising of mind, the activity of thought, the snapping of the fingers, the twinkling of the eyes, and all actions and activities are the functioning of Buddha-nature's total essence." 洪州意者, 起心動念, 彈指動目, 所作所為, 皆是佛性全體之用 (*Chan Chart*, *XZJ* 110: 1.870b; see also *Yuanjue jing dashu chao*, *XZJ* 14: 3.557a).

61. When the Śrāvaka achieves relative nirvāṇa, he is disposed of supernatural power and is able to perform certain physical transformations. He can stop his existence in the triple world by entering into the "flame-samādhi" that destroys body and mind and thus annihilates the root of all afflictions, like ashes being totally extinguished by water. To the Mahāyāna opinion, however, the nirvāṇa thus attained is a sterile emptiness. "Ashes that have been sprinkled" refers to this kind of emptiness, and "ashes that

have not been sprinkled" refers to the true, dynamic emptiness of the Bodhisattva, who enters nirvāṇa without annihilating afflictions.

62. Kuafu was a legendary demigod, who competed with the Sun in a race and died of thirst halfway through; see *Shanhai jing (SKQS)*, 8.2b. Kaigou was a legendary man of unusual strength, who was sent by the Yellow Emperor to seek for the Mysterious Pearl but never found it; see *Zhuangzi zhu (SKQS)*, 5.3b.

63. In many sūtras, the taste of ghee is likened to the perfect Buddhist teaching.

64. This dialogue appears in Dazhu Huihai's entry in the *CDL*; hence, it uses "master" to refer to Dazhu.

65. The *Extended Discourses of Dazhu Huihai* records, "I, the poor priest, heard that the Reverend in Jiangxi said, 'Your own treasure is perfectly complete; you are free to use it and do not need to seek outside.' From that moment onward, I have ceased from [my seeking]." 貧道聞江西和尚道: "汝自家寶藏一切具足, 使用自在, 不假外求." 我從此一時休去 (*CDL*, 28.8b).

66. The *Chongwen zongmu* (*Yueyatang congshu*, 4.82b) records this text; hence, we know that it was current during the Northern Song. The *Tong zhi* (*SKQS*, 67.72b) and the *Song shi* (*SKQS*, 205.9a, 10a, 12b) also record it. This text is likely the *Extended Discourses of Dazhu Huihai* preserved in *Juan* 28 of the *CDL*; for a detailed discussion, see chapter three.

67. The *Extended Discourses of Dazhu Huihai* reads, "Being awakened, they are the Buddha; being ignorant, they are called the sentient beings." 悟即是佛, 迷號眾生 (*CDL*, 28.17a).

68. This expression appears in the *Dafangdeng daji jing*, T. 13: 10.61b.

69. A similar expression, "All dharmas are empty and quiescent" 一切諸法皆悉空寂, appears in many sūtras.

70. This quotation is from the *Saddharmapuṇḍarīka-sūtra (Miaofa lianhua jing*, T. 9: 1.8b; and *Tianpin miaofa lianhua jing*, T. 9: 1.141b).

71. This quotation comes from a verse in the *Vimalakīrti-sūtra (Weimojie suoshuo jing)*, T. 14: 2.549c.

72. This quotation is from the *Saddharmapuṇḍarīka-sūtra (Miaofa lianhua jing*, T. 9: 4.32a; and *Tianpin miaofa lianhua jing*, T. 9: 4.166c).

73. This is a paraphrased quotation from the *Vimalakīrti-sūtra (Weimojie suoshuo jing)*, T. 14: 1.543a.

74. The lifespan of Sun-face Buddha is said to be eighteen hundred years, while the lifespan of Moon-face Buddha is only one day and one night. See the *Buddhanāma-sūtra (Fo shuo foming jing)*, T. 14: 7.154a.

GLOSSARY

(For the names of Mazu's immediate disciples, see Table 1)

anxin 安心
Bai Juyi 白居易
Baimasi 白馬寺
Baiyun chanyuan 白雲禪院
Baizhang Fazheng 百丈法政
Baizhang guanglu 百丈廣錄
Baizhang guangyu 百丈廣語
Baizhang Weizheng 百丈惟政
Baizhangshan heshang yaojue 百丈山
　和尚要決
Bao Fang 鮑防
Bao gong 寶公
Bao Ji 包佶
Baofengsi 寶峰寺
Baoyou 寶祐
Baozhi 寶誌
Beishu heshang 桿樹和尚
benjing jinjing 本淨今淨
benjue 本覺
benlai mianmu 本來面目
benlairen 本來人
Bianzhou 汴州
bielu 別錄
Boluoti 波羅提
Buddhasena 佛馱先那 (佛大先)
bujue 不覺
Can tong qi 參同契
Caoshan Benji 曹山本寂
Caoxi chanshi zhengdao ge 曹溪禪
　師證道歌

Changlexian 長樂縣
Changsongshan 長松山
Changsongsi 長松寺
Changxing wanshou chanyuan 長興
　萬壽禪院
Chanmen guishi 禪門規式
Chanmen miyao jue 禪門秘要訣
Ch'anyu 璨幽
Chaozhou 潮州
*Chizhou Nanquan Puyuan heshang
　[guang]yu* 池州南泉普願和尚
　[廣]語
Chongjingsi 崇敬寺
Chongrenxian 崇仁縣
Chongxian 重顯
Chu sanzang ji 出三藏記
Chuji 處寂
Chuzhou 處州
Cui Congzhi 崔從質
Cui Yin 崔胤
Cuiwei Wuxue 翠微無學
Cuiyan chanyuan 翠巖禪院
Da Tang xiyu ji 大唐西域記
Dache 大徹
Dagui Yansheng chanshi bei 大潙延
　聖禪師碑
Dahui 大慧
Daji 大寂
Dajian 大鑒
Dajue chansi 大覺禪寺

177

Dajue 大覺
Dameishan Chang chanshi huanyuan bei 大梅山常禪師還源碑
Danxiashan 丹霞山
Danyangxian 丹陽縣
Daowu Yuanzhi 道吾圓智
Daoxing ge 道性歌
Daozhi 道智
Dapuci baoguo chanyuan 大普慈報國禪院
Dasheng zan 大乘贊
Daxuanjiao chanshi 大宣教禪師
Dayun heshang yaofa 大雲和尚要法
Dayunsi 大雲寺
Dazhi 大智
Dazhuangyan 大莊嚴
Dechunsi 德純寺
Dehui 德煇
Dharmada 達摩達
dili 地利
dinghui deng 定慧等
Dizang pu'an chanyuan 地藏普安禪院
Dongjin chanyuan 東津禪院
Dongshan Liangjie 洞山良价
Dunwu rudao yaomen lun 頓悟入道要門論
Fadeng Taiqin 法燈泰欽
Faju 法炬
Fanyun 梵雲
faxi 法系
Fayan shizi zhuan 法眼師資傳
fayao 法要
Fayun chansi 法雲禪寺
Fayun chanyuan 法雲禪院
Fazheng chanshi bei 法正禪師碑
feixin feifo 非心非佛
Fenyang Shanzhao 汾陽善昭
Fenzhou Dada Wuye guoshi [guang]yu 汾州大達無業國師[廣]語
Fojiling 佛蹟嶺
Foku Weize 佛窟遺則
Forifeng 佛日峰

Foxing ge 佛性歌
Fu Zai 符載
Furong Lingxun 芙蓉靈訓
Fuzhou 福州
Fuzhou 撫州
Ganquan heshang yuben 甘泉和尚語本
Ganxian 贛縣
gengchen 庚辰
Gonggongshan 龔公山
Gu qinggui xu 古清規序
Guangci chanyuan 廣慈禪院
Guangtai chanyuan 光泰禪院
guangyu 廣語
Guannan Daochang 關南道常
Guanxi Zhixian 灌溪志閑
guanxin 觀心
Gui Deng 歸登
Guishan Lingyou 溈山靈祐
Guizhen 歸真
Haedong ch'iltae rok 海東七代錄
Haihunxian 海昏縣
Hailingxian 海陵縣
Haimenjun 海門郡
Haimenxian 海門縣
Haitingjun 海汀郡
Han 韓
Hanzhou 漢州
Henanfu 河南府
Hengshan 衡山
Hengtong 恒通
Hengyangxian 衡陽縣
Hengyuesi 衡嶽寺
Heshan Huifang 禾山慧方
Hongji 弘濟
Hongren 弘忍
Hongzheng 弘正
Hongzhou 洪州
Huangbo Xiyun 黃檗希運
Huatingxian 華亭縣
Hui 惠
Hui'an 惠安
Huibao 慧寶
Huicong 惠從
Huijian 慧堅

Huijing 惠靜
Huiju 慧炬
Huiming 惠明
Huinan 惠南
Huisi 慧思
Huiyun 惠雲
Huizan 慧瓚
Huizhao 惠照
Huizhen 惠真
Huizhen 慧真
Huzhou 湖州
Huzhou 虎州
Hyŏnhwi 玄暉
Hyŏnuk 玄昱
Iŏm 利嚴
jia 家
Jian daoxing ge 見道性歌
Jianchangxian 建昌縣
Jiang Ji 江積
Jiangxi Daji Daoyi chanshi [guang]yu 江西大寂道一禪師[廣]語
Jiangxian 絳縣
Jiangxidao 江西道
Jiangzhou 江州
Jiangzhou 絳州
jianxing 見性
Jianyangxian 建陽縣
Jianzhou 建州
Jiaoran 皎然
jiaowai biechuan 教外別傳
Jigu qiuzhen xubian 集古求真續編
jimizhou 羈縻州
Jincheng 金城
Jing'anxian 靖安縣
Jingshan Faqin 徑山法欽
Jingzhao Huayansi 京兆華嚴寺
Jingzhaofu 京兆府
Jingzhou 荊州
Jiran 寂然
Jiufeng Daoqian 九峰道虔
Jiufeng zhenguo chanyuan 九峰鎮國禪院
Jōjin 成尋
juan 卷
Judun 居遁

Juexian 覺顯
jun 郡
Kaiyuansi 開元寺
Kuaijixian 會稽縣
Kuizhou 夔州
Langzhou 朗州
Lao'an 老安
Letansi 泐潭寺
Li Ao 李翱
Li Bi 李泌
Li Chang 李常
Li Fan 李繁
Li Jian 李兼
Li Xian 李憲
Li Xun 李遜
Li Zhi 李治
Li Zhifang 李直方
lianshi 廉使
lianshuai 連帥
Lingche 靈徹
Linghu Chu 令狐楚
lisuo 理所
Liu Gongquan 柳公權
Liu Ji 劉濟
Liu Ke 劉軻
Liu Yan 劉晏
Liyangjun 澧陽郡
Liyangxian 澧陽縣
Lizhou 澧州
Lizhou Yaoshan Weiyan heshang [guang]yu 澧州藥山惟儼和尚 [廣]語
Longchengxian 隴城縣
Longtan Chongxin 龍潭崇信
Longxingsi 龍興寺
Lu Chui 陸倕
Lu Jianqiu 盧簡求
Lu Sigong 路嗣恭
Lü Xiaqing 呂夏卿
Luohansi 羅漢寺
Luoyang 洛陽
Ma Boji 馬簸箕
Masu 馬素
Mazu Daoyi 馬祖道一
Mazu faku 馬祖法窟

Mengtang Tan'e 夢堂曇噩
Miaojue 妙覺
Miaoxie 妙葉
Mimoyan heshang 秘魔巖和尚
Mingjue 明覺
Mingyueshan 明月山
Mingzhao 明照
Mingzhou 明州
Musang 無相
Musŏlt'o ron 無舌土論
Muyŏm 無染
Muzhou Daozong 睦州道蹤
Nan'anxian 南安縣
Nanchangxian 南昌縣
Nanjun 南郡
Nankangjun 南康郡
Nanyang Huizhong 南陽慧忠
Nanyangxian 南陽縣
Nanyue Huairang 南嶽懷讓
Narendrayaśas 那連耶舍
Niaoke 鳥窠
Niepan heshang 涅槃和尚
Niutou Huizhong 牛頭惠忠
Ouyang Fu 歐陽輔
Pang jushi ge 龐居士歌
Pang jushi shi 龐居士詩
Pang Yun shiji 龐蘊詩偈
Pei Chou 裴儔
Pei Xiu shiyi wen 裴休拾遺問
Pei Xiu 裴休
Pei Xu 裴謂
pingchangxin 平常心
Pōmil 梵日
Pŏmnang 法朗
Prajñātāra 般若多羅
Puji 普寂
Qiang 羌
Qianzhou 虔州
Qianzhou 乾州
Qinghua chanyuan 清化禪院
Qingzhou 清畫
Qinzhou 秦州
Qiren 契任
Qishan 棲山
Qiyu 耆域

Quan Deyu 權德輿
Quan yantieshi 權鹽鐵使
Quanfu 全付
Quanzhou Huizhong 泉州惠忠
Quanzhou 泉州
Qujiangxian 曲江縣
renhe 人和
renyun 任運
Rudao anxin yao fangbian famen 入道安心要方便法門
Rudao yaomen lun 入道要門論
rulai zhongxing 如來種姓
rulaizang 如來藏
Runzhou 潤州
San Tendai Godai san ki 參天台五臺山記
sanxue deng 三學等
Sanzang Qianna 三藏揵那
Sengchou 僧稠
Sengshi 僧實
Shandao 善導
Shaoshan Huanpu 韶山寰普
Shaozhou 韶州
Shengchi Sanzang 勝持三藏
Shengrui chanyuan 聖瑞禪院
Shengwen 聲聞
Shengzhou ji 聖胄集
Shenxing 神行
shidai 世代
Shi'erchen ge 十二辰歌
Shi'ershi song 十二時頌
Shifangxian 什邡縣
shijue 始覺
Shimenshan 石門山
Shishan chanyuan 十善禪院
Shishuang Qingzhu 石霜慶諸
Shisike song 十四科頌
Shitou Xiqian 石頭希遷
shouxin 守心
Shouxun 守勳
Shushan Kuangren 疎山匡仁
Shuzhou 舒州
Sishi'erzhang jing 四十二章經
Songzixian 松滋縣
Sun Fangshao 孫方紹

Tang Chi 唐持

Tang Fu 唐扶

Tang Zhi 唐枝

Tanying 曇穎

Tanzhao 曇照

Tiangushan 天谷山

tianshi 天時

Tiantaishan 天台山

Tianwang Daowu 天王道悟

Tianzhen 天真

Tianzhufeng 天柱峰

Tongchengxian 桐城縣

tou sanju guo 透三句過

Toūi 道義

Touzi Datong 投子大同

Toyun 道允

Wang Kangju 王康琚

Wangmu Xiaoran 王姥翛然

Wei Boyang 魏伯陽

Weijin 惟勁

Weishixian 尉氏縣

Wenbi 文賁

Wozhoushan chanyuan 沃洲山禪院

Wu Yihuang 武翊黃

wu yiwu 無一物

Wujia zongpai 五家宗派

Wumingzi 無名子

wunian 無念

Wushan 巫山

wushi 無事

wuxiu 無修

wuzhu 無住

Xiangyang 襄陽

Xiantong yanqing chanyuan 咸通延慶禪院

Xicao 希操

Xichen 希琛

xin shengmie men 心生滅門

xin Zhenru men 心真如門

xindi famen 心地法門

Xinfengxian 信豐縣

xing zai zuoyong 性在作用

Xingchang 行常

Xinghua Cunjiang 興化存獎

Xinglu nan 行路難

xinglu 行錄

xingzhuang 行狀

Xitang heshang ji 西唐和尚偈

Xiyuan Da'an 西院大安

Xu Baolin zhuan 續寶林傳

Xuanlang 玄朗

Xuanmen shengzhou ji 玄門聖冑集

Xuanwei 玄偉

Xuanzang 玄奘

Xue Tingwang 薛庭望

Xue Yanwang 薛延望

Xuefeng Yicun 雪峰義存

Yang Jie 楊傑

Yang Qian 楊潛

Yang Wuling 楊於陵

Yang Yi 楊億

Yangshan Guangyong 仰山光湧

Yangshan Huiji 仰山慧寂

Yangzhou 揚州

Yanlingxian 延陵縣

Yanshou chanyuan 延壽禪院

Yanzhao 延沼

yaojue 要訣

Yaoshan Keqiong 藥山可瓊

yaoyu 要語

Yehai Ziqing 業海子清

Yingtian xuefeng chanyuan 應天雪峰禪院

yixin 一心

yixing sanmei 一行三昧

Yizhou 益州

Yong'an chanyuan 永安禪院

Yongchang chanyuan 永昌禪院

Yongjia ji 永嘉集

Yongjia Xuanjue 永嘉玄覺

Yongjia zhengdao ge 永嘉證道歌

Yǒǒm 麗嚴

youxian 幽閒

Yuan 圓

Yuanchang 圓暢

Yuanhui 元會

Yuanjue 緣覺

Yuanzheng 圓證

yuben 語本

Yulu zhi yu 語錄之餘

yulu 語錄
Yungai Huaiyi 雲蓋懷溢
Yunmen Wenyan 雲門文偃
Yunyan Tansheng 雲岩曇晟
Yuquansi 玉泉寺
Yuyaoxian 余姚縣
Yuzhangjun 豫章郡
Yuzhou 渝州
Zaixiang shixi biao 宰相世系表
zan 贊
Zanghuan 藏奐
Zazhuan 雜傳
Zeng Weiyan shi 贈惟儼師
Zhang Shangying 張商英
Zhangqiu Jianqiong 章仇兼瓊
Zhaojue 招覺
Zhaozhou Congshen 趙州從諗
Zheng Yin 鄭絪
Zheng Yuqing 鄭餘慶
Zhengdao ge 證道歌
zhengtong 正統
zhengzong 正宗
Zhi gong ge 志公歌

Zhicui 智璀
Zhiguang 智廣
Zhiju 智炬
Zhijue 智覺
Zhishen 智詵
zhisuo 治所
Zhiyi 智顗
Zhonglingxian 鍾陵縣
Zhongzhou 忠州
zhuan 篆
Zhufang menren canwen yulu 諸方門
　人參問語錄
zijia baozang 自家寶藏
zijia benxin 自家本心
zijia benxing 自家本性
Zizhou 資州
zong 宗
zongxi 宗系
Zuishangsheng foxing ge 最上乘佛
　性歌
Zuisheng lun 最勝輪
zushi chan 祖師禪

BIBLIOGRAPHY

INSCRIPTIONS

Bai Juyi 白居易 (772–846). "Chuanfatang bei" 傳法堂碑 (819). *Bai Juyi ji jianjiao*, ed. Zhu Jincheng, 41.2690–92.

———. "Tang Jiangzhou Xingguosi lüdade Cou gong [Shencou, 744–817] tajieming bingxu" 唐江州興果寺律大德湊公 [神湊] 塔碣銘並序 (817). *Bai Juyi ji jianjiao*, 41.2701–702.

———. "Wozhoushan chanyuan ji" 沃洲山禪院記 (832). *Bai Juyi ji jianjiao*, 68.3684–85.

Chen Shouzhong 陳守中. "Da Han Shaozhou Yunmenshan Dajue chansi Daciyun kuangsheng hongming dashi [Wenyan, 864–949] beiming bingxu" 大漢韶州雲門山大覺禪寺大慈雲匡聖宏明大師 [文偃] 碑銘並序 (964). *QTW*, 892.4a–12b.

Chen Xu 陳詡. "Tang Hongzhou Baizhangshan gu Huaihai [749–814] chanshi taming" 唐洪州百丈山故懷海禪師塔銘 (818). *QTW*, 446.4b–7a.

Chengyu 澄玉. "Shushan Baiyun chanyuan ji" 疎山白雲禪院記. *QTW*, 920.17a–22a.

Ch'oe Chi-wŏn 崔致遠 (857–928?). "Yu Tang Silla-guk ko Chiri-san Ssanggye-sa kyosi Chin'gam sŏnsa [Haeso, 774–850] pi'myŏng pyŏngsŏ" 有唐新羅國故知異山雙谿寺教諡真鑒禪師 [慧昭] 碑銘並序 (887). In *Haidong jinshi yuan*, ed. Liu Xihai, 1.37a–44a; *Tangwen shiyi*, ed. Lu Xinyuan, 44.1a–7a; *Chōsen kinseki sōran*, ed. Chōsen sōtokufu, vol. 1, 66–72.

———. "Yu Tang Silla-guk ko yangjo kuksa kyosi Taenanghye hwasang [Muyŏm, 800–888] Baek'wŏlbogwang chi t'ap pi'myŏng pyŏngsŏ" 有唐新羅國故兩朝國師教諡大朗慧和尚 [無染] 白月葆光之塔碑銘並序 (890). *Haidong jinshi yuan*, 2.1a–14a; *Tangwen shiyi*, 44.7a–19b; *Chōsen kinseki sōran*, vol. 1, 72–83.

———. "Tae Tang Silla-guk ko Pong'amsan-sa kyosi Chijŭng taesa [Tohŏn, 824–882] Chŏkcho chi t'ap pi'myŏng pyŏngsŏ" 大唐新羅國故鳳巖山寺教諡智證大師 [道憲] 寂照之塔碑銘並序 (924). *Haidong jinshi yuan*, 2.15a–23b; *Tangwen shiyi*, 19b–28a; *Chōsen kinseki sōran*, vol. 1, 88–97.

Ch'oe Ha 崔賀. "Muju Tongri-san Taean-sa Chŏk'in sŏnsa [Hyech'ŏl, 785–861] pisong pyŏngsŏ" 武州桐裏山大安寺寂忍禪師 [慧徹] 碑頌並序 (872). *Chōsen kinseki sōran*, vol. 1, 116–19.

Ch'oe Inyŏn 崔仁滾. "Silla-guk ko yangjo kuksa kyosi Nang'gong taesa [Haengchŏk, 832–916] Baekwŏlsŏun chi t'ap pi'myŏng pyŏngsŏ" 新羅國故兩朝國師教諡朗空大師 [行寂] 白月棲雲之塔碑銘並序 (917). *Haidong jinshi yuan*, 2.23b–29b; *Chōsen kinseki sōran*, vol. 1, 181–86.

Ch'oe Ŏnhwi 崔彥撝 (868–944). "Koryŏ-guk ko Muwigap-sa Sŏn'gak taesa [Hyŏngmi, 864–917] P'yŏngwang'yŏng t'ap pi'myŏng pyŏngsŏ" 高麗國故無為岬寺先覺大師 [逈微] 遍光靈塔碑銘並序 (ca. 918). *Haidong jinshi yuan*, 3.35b–40b; *Tangwen shiyi*, 70.5a–9b; *Chōsen kinseki sōran*, vol. 1, 170–74.

———. "Yu Tang Silla-guk Sa[cha]-san [Hŭngnyŏng-sŏnwŏn] kyosi Chinghyo taesa [Chŏljung, 826–900] Poin chi t'ap pi'myŏng pyŏngsŏ" 有唐新羅國師 [子] 山 [興寧禪院] 教諡澄曉大師 [折中] 寶印之塔碑銘並序 (924). *Chōsen kinseki sōran*, vol. 1, 157–62.

———. "Yu Tang Koryŏ-guk Haeju Sumi-san Kwang jo-sa ko kyosi Chinch'ŏl sŏnsa [Iŏm, 870–936] Powŏlsŭngkong chi t'ap pi'myŏng [pyŏngsŏ]" 有唐高麗國海州須彌山廣照寺故教諡真澈禪師 [利嚴] 寶月乘空之塔碑銘[並序] (937). *Haidong jinshi yuan*, 3.1a–7a; *Tangwen shiyi*, 69.4a–9b; *Chōsen kinseki sōran*, vol. 1, 125–30.

———. "Koryŏ-guk Miji-san Poje-sa ko kyosi Taegyŏng taesa [Yŏŏm, 862–930] Hyŏngi chi t'ap pi'myŏng pyŏngsŏ" 高麗國彌智山菩提寺故教諡大鏡大師 [麗嚴] 玄機之塔碑銘並序 (939). *Haidong jinshi yuan*, 3.7b–11b; *Tangwen shiyi*, 69.17b–21b; *Chōsen kinseki sōran*, vol. 1, 130–34.

———. "Koryŏ-guk Myŏngju Pohyŏn-san Chijang-sŏnwŏn ko kuksa Nangwŏn taesa [Kaech'ŏng, 835–930] Ochin chi t'ap pi'myŏng pyŏngsŏ" 高麗國溟州普賢山地藏禪院故國師朗圓大師 [開清] 悟真之塔碑銘並序 (940). *Haidong jinshi yuan*, 3.12a–16b; *Tangwen shiyi*, 70.1a–5a; *Chōsen kinseki sōran*, vol. 1, 140–44.

———. "Yu Chin Koryŏ[guk] chung'wŏnpu ko Kaech'ŏn-san Chŏngt'o-sa kyosi Pŏpgyŏng taesa [Hyŏnhwi, 879–941] Chadŭng chi t'ap pi'myŏng pyŏngsŏ" 有晉高麗 [國] 中原府故開天山淨土寺教諡法鏡大師 [玄暉] 慈燈之塔碑銘並序 (943). *Haidong jinshi yuan*, 3.22b–30b; *Tangwen shiyi*, 69.9b–17b; *Chōsen kinseki sōran*, vol. 1, 150–56.

"Chi Changxing wanshou chanyuan die" 敕長興萬壽禪院牒 (932). *Jinshi cuibian*, ed. Wang Chang, *XXSKQS*, 119.44a/b.

Dugu Ji 獨孤及 (715–767). "Shuzhou Shangusi Juejita Sui gu Jingzhi chanshi beiming bingxu" 舒州山谷寺覺寂塔隋故鏡智禪師碑銘並序 (772). *QTW*, 390.21b–24b.

Fazheng 法正 (d. 819) et al. "Huaihai chanshi tabei yinmian ji" 懷海禪師塔碑陰面記 (818). In *Chixiu Baizhang qinggui*, ed. Dehui, *T*. 48: 8.1157a.

Feng Yansi 馮延巳 (ca. 903–960). "Kaixian chanyuan beiji" 開先禪院碑記 (954). *QTW*, 876.14a–17b.

"Fengxue Qizu Qianfeng baiyun chanyuan yinmian ji" 風穴七祖千峰白雲禪院陰面記. *Quan Tangwen you zaibu* 全唐文又再補, in *Quan Tangwen bubian*, ed. Chen Shangjun, 9.2378.

Fu Zai 符載 [pseud.]. "Jingzhou chengdong Tianhuangsi Daowu [727–808] chanshi bei" 荊州城東天皇寺道悟禪師碑. *Fozu lidai tongzai*, ed. Nianchang, *T*. 49: 15.615a; *QTW*, 691.1a.

Gongsheng Yi 公乘億. "Weizhou gu chandade Jianggong [Cunjiang, d. 925] tabei" 魏州故禪大德獎公 [存獎] 塔碑 (889). *QTW*, 813.19a.

"Guangci chanyua chandie" 廣慈禪院殘牒 (953). *Jinshi cuibian*, *XXSKQS*, 121.7a/b.

Han Xizai 韓熙載 (902–970). "Xuanji chanshi [Yinwei, 886–961] bei" 玄寂禪師 [隱微] 碑 (962). *QTW*, 877.15b–18b.

Hu Di 胡的. "Da Tang gu Taibai chanshi [Guanzong, 721–809] taming bingxu" 大唐故太白禪師 [觀宗] 塔銘並序 (815). *Tangdai muzhi huibian*, ed. Zhou Shaoliang and Zhao Chao, 1971–72.

Huang Jin 黃溍 (1277–1357). "Baizhangshan Dazhi shousheng chansi tianxia shibiaoge ji" 百丈山大智壽聖禪寺天下師表閣記 (1336). *T.* 48: 1157a–c.

Huang Tao 黃滔 (b. ca. 840). "Fuzhou Xuefengshan gu Zhenjue dashi [Yicun, 822–908] beiming" 福州雪峰山故真覺大師 [義存] 碑銘 (908). *QTW*, 826.5a–9a.

Huikong 慧空. "Da Tang dongdu Hezesi mo gu diqizu guoshi dade [Shenhui, 684–758] yu Longmen baoyingsi longshoufu jian shentaming bingxu" 大唐東都荷澤寺歿故第七祖國師大德 [神會] 于龍門寶應寺龍首腹建身塔銘並序 (765). *Tangdai muzhi huibian xuji*, ed. Zhou Shaoliang and Zhao Chao, 690.

I Mongyu 李夢遊. "Koryŏ-guk Sangju Hŭiyang-san Pong'am-sa wangsa chŭngsi Chŏngjin taesa [kyŏng'yang, 878–956] Wŏn'o chi t'ap pi'myŏng pyŏngsŏ" 高麗國尚州曦陽山鳳岩寺王師贈諡靜真大師 [競讓] 圓悟之塔碑銘並序 (965). *Haidong jinshiyuan*, 4.3b–16a; *Chōsen kinseki sōran*, vol. 1, 196–207.

Jia Su 賈餗 (d. 835). "Yangzhou Hualinsi Dabei chanshi [Yuntan, 709–816] beiming bingxu" 揚州華林寺大悲禪師 [雲坦] 碑銘並序 (825). *QTW*, 731.23a–26a.

Jiaoran 皎然 (ca. 720-ca. 793). "Tang Huzhou Fochuansi gu dashi [Huiming, 697–780] taming bingxu" 唐湖州佛川寺故大師[惠明]塔銘並序 (780). *QTW*, 917.15a–b.

Kim Chongŏn 金廷彦. "[Ko]ryo-guk Kwangju Hŭiyanghyŏn ko Baekgye-san Okryong-sa chesi Tongjin taesa [Kyŏngbo, 869–948] Poun chi t'ap pyŏngsŏ" [高]麗國光州晞陽縣故白雞山玉龍寺制諡洞真大師 [慶甫] 寶雲之塔並序 (ca. 949). *Haidong jinshi yuan buyi*, 1.28a–34a; *Chōsen kinseki sōran*, vol. 1, 189–94.

———. "Koryŏ-guk Kwangju Hyemok-san Kodal-wŏn ko kuksa chesi Wŏnjong taesa [Ch'anyu, 869–958] Hyejin chi t'ap pi'myŏng pyŏngsŏ" 高麗國廣州慧目山高達院故國師制諡元宗大師 [璨幽] 慧真之塔碑銘並序 (958). *Chōsen kinseki sōran*, vol. 1, 207–15.

Kim Hŏnjŏng 金獻貞. "Haedong ko Sinhaeng [d. 779] sŏnsa chi pi pyŏngsŏ" 海東故神行禪師之碑並序 (813). *Haidong jinshi yuan*, 1.27a–31a; *Chōsen kinseki sōran*, vol. 1, 113–16.

Kim Yŏng 金穎. "Silla-guk Muju Kaji-san Porim-sa si Pojo sŏnsa [Ch'ejŭng, 804–880] yŏngt'ap pi'myŏng pyŏngsŏ" 新羅國武州迦智山寶林寺諡普照禪師 [體澄] 靈塔碑銘並序 (883). *Haidong jinshi yuan*, 1.32a–36b; *Tangwen shiyi*, 68.20a–24b; *Chōsen kinseki sōran*, vol. 1, 60–64.

———. "[Silla-guk] . . . [two characters missing] kangpu Wŏl'am-san Wŏlgwang-sa chosi Wŏnnang sŏnsa [Taet'ong, 816–883] Taebosŏngwang yŏngt'ap pi pyŏngsŏ" [新羅國] . . . 江府月巖山月光寺詔諡圓朗禪師 [大通] 大寶禪光靈塔碑並序 (890). *Chōsen kinseki sōran*, vol. 1, 83–86.

Lang Su 郎肅. "Ganquanyuan seng Xiaofang taji" 甘泉院僧曉方塔記 (871). *Tangdai muzhi huibian*, 2452.

Lei Yue 雷嶽. "Kuangzhen dashi [Wenyan, 864–949] taming" 匡真大師 [文偃] 塔銘 (958). *Tangwen shiyi*, 48.5b–10b.

Li Chaozheng 李朝正. "Chongjian chanmen diyizu Putidamo dashi beiyin wen" 重建禪門第一祖菩提達摩大師碑陰文 (806). *QTW*, 998.1a–3b.

Li Chong 李充. "Da Tang dongdu Jing'aisi gu kafa lintan dade Fawan [724–790] chanshi taming bingxu" 大唐東都敬愛寺故開法臨檀大德法玩禪師塔銘並序 (791). *Tangdai muzhi huibian*, 1863.

Li Hua 李華 (715–766). "Jingzhou Nanquan Dayunsi gu Lanruo heshang [Huizhen, 673–751] bei" 荊州南泉大雲寺故蘭若和尚 [惠真] 碑 (751). *QTW*, 319.11a–14b.

———. "Runzhou Helinsi gu Jingshan dashi [Xuansu, 668–752] beiming" 潤州鶴林寺故徑山大師 [玄素] 碑銘 (752). *QTW*, 320.12a–16b.

Li Jifu 李吉甫 (758–814). "Hangzhou Jingshansi Dajue chanshi [Faqin, 714–792] beiming bingxu" 杭州徑山寺大覺禪師 [法欽] 碑銘並序 (793). *QTW*, 512.17a–21a.

Li Shangyin 李商隱 (ca. 813–858). "Tang Zizhou Huiyijingshe Nanchanyuan Sizhengtang beiming bingxu" 唐梓州慧義精舍南禪院四證堂碑銘並序 (853). *QTW*, 780.1a–7a.

Li Siyuan 李嗣源 (867–933). "Qianfeng chanyuan chi" 千峰禅院敕. *Quan Tangwen bubian*, 96.1186.

Li Yong 李邕 (678–747). "Dazhao chanshi [Puji, 651–739] taming" 大照禪師 [普寂] 塔銘 (742). *QTW*, 262.3b–10a.

Li Yue 李約. "Ruifeng Yong'an Zhushan chanyuan ji" 瑞峰永安竹山禪院記 (970). *Quan Tangwen bubian*, 112.1400–1401.

Liangyue 良說. "Da Tang Beiyue Huijusi jiansi gu chanshi [Zhili, 688–774] shendao yingtang jidebei bingxu" 大唐北嶽慧炬寺建寺故禪師 [智力] 神道影堂紀德碑並敘 (805). *Baqiongshi jinshi buzheng xubian, XXSKQS*, 34.173a–74b.

Lin Cheng 林澂. "Tang Fuzhou Anguo chanyuan xian kaishan Zongyi dashi [Shibei, 835–908] beiwen bingxu" 唐福州安國禪院先開山宗一大師 [師備] 碑文並序 (930). *Fuzhou Xuansha Zongyi dashi guanglu, XZJ* 126: 3.399b–402b.

Lingyao 靈曜. "Huijusi seng Zhili yidebei" 慧炬寺僧智力遺德碑 (799). *Baqiongshi jinshi buzheng xubian, XXSKQS*, 33.166a/b.

Liu Congyi 劉從义. "Da Zhou Guangci chanyuan ji" 大周廣慈禪院記 (955). *Jinshi cuibian, XXSKQS*, 121.16a–17a.

Liu Zongyuan 柳宗元 (773–819). "Caoxi diliuzu cishi Dajian chanshi [Huineng, 638–713] bei" 曹溪第六祖賜諡大鑒禪師 [惠能] 碑 (815). *Liu Zongyuan ji*, 6.149–52.

———. "Hengshan Zhongyuan dalüshi [Xicao] taming" 衡山中院大律師 [希操] 塔銘. *Liu Zongyuan ji*, 7.173–74.

Lu Jianqiu 盧簡求 (789–864). "Hangzhou Yanguanxian Haichangyuan chanmen dashi [Qi'an, ca. 752–842] tabei" 杭州鹽官縣海昌院禪門大師 [齊安] 塔碑 (843). *QTW*, 733.21a–23a.

Lu Xisheng 陸希聲. "Yangshan Tongzhi dashi [Huiji, 807–883] taming" 仰山通智大師 [慧寂] 塔銘 (895). *QTW*, 813.8b–10a.

Lu Yuanhao 陸元浩. "Xianjudong Yong'an chanyuan ji" 仙居洞永安禪院記 (932). *QTW*, 869.8b–11a.

"Mazu chanshi sheli shihan tiji" 馬祖禪師舍利石函題記 (791). Chen Baiquan 陳柏泉. "Mazu chanshi shihan tiji yu Zhang Zongyan tianshi kuangji" 馬祖禪師石函

題記與張宗演天師壙記, *Wenshi* 文史 14 (1982): 258; *Quan Tangwen zaibu* 全唐文再補, in *Quan Tangwen bubian*, 2149.

Ouyang Xi 歐陽熙. "Hongzhou Yungaishan Longshouyuan Guanghua dashi [Huaiyi, 847–934] baolu beiming" 洪州雲蓋山龍壽院光化大師 [懷溢] 寶錄碑銘 (934). *QTW*, 869.11b–14b.

Pak Sŭng'yŏng 朴昇英 (d. 924). "Yu Tang Silla-guk ko kuksa si Chin'gyŏng taesa [Simhŭi, 855–923] Powŏlnŭng'gong chi t'ap pi'myŏng pyŏngsŏ" 有唐新羅國故國師諡真鏡大師 [審希] 寶月淩空之塔碑銘並序 (924). *Haidong jinshi yuan*, 2.30b–35a; *Tangwen shiyi*, 68.9b–14a; *Chōsen kinseki sōran*, vol. 1, 97–101.

Pei Xiu 裴休 (791–864). "Guifeng chanshi [Zongmi, 780–841] beiming bingxu" 圭峰禪師 [宗密] 碑銘並序 (855). *QTW*, 743.12b–17b.

Qiji 齊己 (864–ca. 943). "Lingyunfeng Yongchang chanyuan ji" 淩雲峰永昌禪院記 (917). *QTW*, 921.4a–5b.

Qiu Xuansu 邱玄素 [pseud.]. "Tianwang Daowu chanshi bei" 天王道悟禪師碑. *QTW*, 713.3a–4a.

Quan Deyu 權德輿 (761–818). "Tang gu Hongzhou Kaiyuansi Shimen Daoyi [709–788] chanshi taming bingxu" 唐故洪州開元寺石門道一禪師塔銘並序 (791). *Quan Zaizhi wenji*, 28.1a–3a.

———. "Tang gu Zhangjingsi Baiyan dashi [Huaihui, 757–816] beiming bingxu" 唐故章敬寺百岩大師 [懷暉] 碑銘並序 (817). *Quan Zaizhi wenji*, 18.13a–14b.

Ren Guang 任光. "Tang Linchuanfu Chongrenxian Dizang pu'an chanyuan beiming" 唐臨川府崇仁縣地藏普安禪院碑銘. *QTW*, 872.3b–5b.

Shen Jian 沈珹. "Da Tang Shuzhou Huatingxian Gutinglinshi xinchuang Fayun chansi ji" 大唐蘇州華亭縣顧亭林市新創法雲禪寺記 (860). *Jiangsu tongzhi gao* 江蘇通志稿, in vol. 2 of *Sui Tang Wudai shike wenxian quanbian* 隋唐五代石刻文獻全編, 156b–57a, Beijing: Beijing tushuguan chubanshe, 2003; *QTW*, 792.21b–22a.

Sikong Tu 司空圖 (837–908). "Xiangyan zhanglao [Zhixian] zan" 香岩長老 [智閑] 贊. *QTW*, 808.8b.

Son So 孫紹. "Yu Tang Koryŏ-guk Muju ko Tongri-san Taean-sa kyosi Kwangja taesa [Yunda, 864–945] pi'myŏng pyŏngsŏ" 有唐高麗國武州故桐裏山大安寺教諡廣慈大師 [允多] 碑銘並序 (950). *Haidong jinshi yuan*, 3.44a–47b; *Tangwen shiyi*, 70.9b–12b; *Chōsen kinseki sōran*, vol. 1, 174–79.

Song Dan 宋儋. "Da Tang Songshan Huishansi gu dade Dao'an [584–708] chanshi bei bingxu" 大唐嵩山會善寺故大德道安禪師碑並序 (727). *QTW*, 396.12a–14b; *Tangwen xushi*, 3.13b–18a.

Song Qiqiu 宋齊邱 (887–959). "Yangshan Guangyong [850–938] zhanglao taming ji" 仰山光湧長老塔銘記 (944). *QTW*, 870.14b–16b.

"Songshan . . . [three characters missing] gu dade Jingzang [775–746] chanshi shentaming bingxu" 嵩山 . . . 故大德淨藏禪師身塔銘並序 (746). *Jinshi cuibian*, *XXSKQS*, 87.15a–16b; *QTW*, 997.10a–11a.

Tang Ji 唐技. "Gonggongshan Xitang chishi Dajue chanshi [Zhizang, 738–817] chongjian Dabaoguangta beiming" 龔公山西堂敕諡大覺禪師 [智藏] 重建大寶光塔碑銘 (864). In *Ganxian zhi* 贛縣志, ed. Chu Jingxin 褚景昕 et al., 1872, reprint, Taibei: Chengwen chuban, 1975; and *Fuzhoufu zhi* 撫州府志, ed. Xie Huang 謝煌 et al., 1876, reprint, Taibei: Chengwen chuban, 1975.

Tang Shen 唐伸. "Lizhou Yaoshan gu Weiyan [744–827] dashi beiming bingxu" 澧州藥山故惟儼大師碑銘並序 (835). *Tangwen cui*, 62.4a–5b; *QTW*, 536.12b–15a.

"Tang Zhongyue shamen shi Faru [638–689] chanshi xingzhuang" 唐中岳沙門釋法如禪師行狀 (689). *Jinshi cuibian*, 6.5b–7b; *Tangwen shiyi*, 67.16b–18b.

Wang Feng 王諷. "Zhangzhou Sanping dashi [Yizhong, 782–872] beiming bingxu" 漳州三平大師 [義忠] 碑銘並序 (872). *QTW*, 791.8a–9b.

Wei Chuhou 韋處厚 (773–829). "Xingfusi neidaochang gongfeng dade Dayi [746–818] chanshi beiming" 興福寺內道場供奉大德大義禪師碑銘 (818). *QTW*, 715.22a–26a.

Wu Yihuang 武翊黃. "Baizhangshan Fazheng [d. 819] chanshi beiming" 百丈山法正禪師碑銘. *QTW*, 713.12b (*QTW* attributes this work to Liu Gongquan 柳公權).

Xu Dai 徐岱. "Tang gu Zhaoshengsi dade Huijian [719–792] chanshi beiming bingxu" 唐故招聖寺大德慧堅禪師碑銘並序 (806). *Xi'an beilin quanji* 西安碑林全集, ed. Gao Xia 高峽, vol. 2, 20.2056–78. Guangzhou: Guangdong jingji, 1999.

Xu Lun 徐綸. "Da Zhou Zezhou Yangchengxian Longquan chanyuan ji" 大周澤州陽城縣龍泉禪院記 (952). *Shanyou shike congbian, XXSKQS*, 10.36b–39a.

Yicun 義存 (822–908). "Nanti taming bingxu" 難提塔銘並序 (903). *Quan Tangwen bubian*, 116.1444.

"Yu Chin Koryŏ-guk Yong'am-san Oryong-sa ko wangsa kyosi Pŏpgyŏng taesa [Kyŏng'yu, 871–921] Pojohye'gwang chi t'ap pi'myŏng pyŏngsŏ" 有晉高麗國龍巖山五龍寺故王師教諡法鏡大師 [慶猷] 普照慧光之塔碑銘並序 (944). *Haidong jinshi yuan*, 3.31a–35a; *Tangwen shiyi*, 70.13b–16b; *Chōsen kinseki sōran*, vol. 1, 162–66.

余靖 (1000–1064). "Lushan Chengtian Guizong chansi chongxiu ji" 廬山承天歸宗禪寺重修記. *Wuxi ji* 武溪集, *SKQS*, 7.4b.

———. "Yunzhou Dongshan Puli chanyuan chuanfaji" 筠州洞山普利禪院傳法記. *Wuxi ji*, 9.14a–18a.

———. "Shaozhou Yuehuashan Huajiesi chuanfa zhuchi ji" 韶州月華山花界寺傳法住持記. *Wuxi ji*, 9.8a/b.

Yu Xifan 虞希範. "Fengxue Qizu Qianfeng baiyun chanyuan ji" 風穴七祖千峰白雲禪院記 (950). *Quan Tangwen you zaibu* 全唐文又再補, in *Quan Tangwen bubian*, 7.2346.

Yunming 允明. "Tang Fuzhou Yanshou chanyuan gu Yansheng dashi [Da'an, 793–883] tanei zhenshen ji" 唐福州延壽禪院故延聖大師 [大安] 塔內真身記 (884). Copied by Ishii Shūdō, "Isan kyōdan no dōkō ni tsuite: Hukushū Daian no shinjinki no shōkai ni chinande" 潙山教團の動向について：福州大安の "真身記" の紹介に因んで, *Indogaku bukkyōgaku kenkyū* 印度學佛教學研究 27.1 (1978): 90–96.

Zhang Shangying 張商英 (1043–1122). "Suizhou Dahongshan Lingfengsi Shifang chanyuan ji" 隨州大洪山靈峰寺十方禪院記 (1102). *Hubei jinshi zhi* 湖北金石志, ed. Zhang Zhongxin 張仲炘, in *Lidai shike shiliao huibian* 歷代石刻史料彙編, series 3, vol. 4, 322–23, Beijing: Beijing tushuguan chubanshe, 2000; *Zimen jingxun* 緇門警訓, ed. Rujin 如巹, *T*. 48: 10.1096a–97a.

———. "Xinzhou Dingxiangxian xinxiu Dadi heshang tayuan ji" 忻州定襄縣新修打地和尚塔院記 (1090). *Shanyou shike congbian* 山右石刻叢編, *XXSKQS*, 15.26a/b.

Zhang Yue 張說 (667–731). "Tang Yuquansi Datong chanshi [Shenxiu, ca. 606–706] beiming bingxu" 唐玉泉寺大通禪師 [神秀] 碑銘並序 (706). *QTW*, 231.1a–4b.

Zhang Zhengfu 張正甫 (752–834). "Hengzhou Boresi Guanyin dashi [Huairang, 677–744] beiming bingxu" 衡州般若寺觀音大師 [懷讓] 碑銘並序 (815). *QTW*, 619.1a–3a.

Zheng Yu 鄭愚. "Tanzhou Daguishan Tongqingsi Dayuan chanshi [Lingyou, 771–853] beiming bingxu" 潭州大溈山同慶寺大圓禪師 [靈祐] 碑銘並序 (866). *QTW*, 820.23a–27a.

Zhiben 智本. "Baiyansi fengchi zaixiu chongjian fatang ji" 百岩寺奉敕再修重建法堂記 (854). *Tangwen xushi*, 8.10b–13a.

Zhixian 至閑. "Da Tang Yuanzhou Pingxiangxian Yangqishan gu Zhenshu [d. 820] dashi taming" 大唐袁州萍鄉縣楊岐山故甄叔大師塔銘 (832). *Tangdai muzhi huibian xuji*, 913; *QTW*, 919.10b–11a.

OTHER PRIMARY WORKS

Bai Juyi 白居易 (772–846). *Bai Juyi ji jianjiao* 白居易集箋校, ed. Zhu Jincheng 朱金城. 6 vols. Shanghai: Shanghai guji chubanshe, 1988.

Baizhang guanglu 百丈廣錄. *Sijia lu; Gu zunsu yulu.*

Baoke leibian 寶刻類編. *SKQS.*

Baozang lun 寶藏論. Attributed to Sengzhao 僧肇 (384–414). *T.* 45, 1857.

Benjue 本覺. *Shishi tongjian* 釋氏通鑒. *XZJ* 131.

Caoxi dashi biezhuan 曹溪大師別傳. *XZJ* 146.

Chao Gongwu 晁公武 and Zhao Xibian 趙希弁. *Junzhai dushu zhi. Houzhi. Kaoyi. Fuzhi* 郡齋讀書志. 後志. 考異. 附志. *SKQS.*

Chao Jiong 晁迥 (951–1034). *Fazang suijin lu* 法藏碎金錄. *SKQS.*

———. *Daoyuanji yao* 道院集要. *SKQS.*

Chen Shangjun 陳尚君, ed. *Quan Tangshi bubian* 全唐詩補編. 3 vols. Beijing: Zhonghua shuju, 1992.

———. *Quan Tangwen bubian* 全唐文補編. 3 vols. Beijing: Zhonghua shuju, 2005.

Chen Si 陳思. *Baoke congbian* 寶刻叢編. *SKQS.*

Chen Tianfu 陳田夫. *Nanyue zongsheng ji* 南嶽總勝集. *Wanwei biezang* 宛委別藏. Nanjing: Jiangsu guji chubanshe, 1984.

Chengguan 澄觀 (738–839). *Da fangguang fo huayanjing shu* 大方廣佛華嚴經疏. *T.* 35, 1735.

———. *Da fangguang fo huayanjing suishu yanyi chao* 大方廣佛華嚴經隨疏演義鈔. *T.* 36, 1736.

Ch'ŏnch'aek 天頙. *Sŏnmun pojang nok* 禪門寶藏錄 (1293). *XZJ* 113.

Chongwen zongmu 崇文总目. *Yueyatang congshu* 粵雅堂叢書.

Chōsen sōtokufu 朝鮮總督府, ed. *Chōsen kinseki sōran* 朝鮮金石總覽. 2 vols. Keijō: Chōsen sotokufu, 1919.

Chuyuan 楚圓, ed. *Fenyang Wude chanshi yulu* 汾陽無德禪師語錄. *XZJ* 120.

Collcutt, Martin. "The Early Ch'an Monastic Rule: Ch'ing kuei and the Shaping of Ch'an Community Life." *Early Ch'an in China and Tibet*, ed. Lai and Lancaster, 165–84.

Da baoji jing 大寶積經 (*Mahāratnakūṭa-sūtra*). *T.* 11, 310.

Da boniepan jing 大般涅槃經 (*Mahāparinirvāṇa-sūtra*). Trans. Tanwuchen 曇無讖 (385–433). *T.* 12, 374.

Da bore boluomiduo jing 大般若波羅密多經 (*Mahāprajñāpāramitā-sūtra*). Trans. Xuanzang 玄奘 (596–664). *T.* 5–7, 220.

Da fangdeng daji jing 大方等大集經 (*Mahāvaipulya-mahāsamnipāta-sūtra*). *T.* 13, 397.

Da fangdeng Rulaizang jing 大方等如來藏經 (*Tathāgatagarbha-sūtra*). Trans. Buddhabhadra (359–429). *T.* 16, 666.

Da fangguang fo huayan jing 大方廣佛華嚴經 (*Avatamsaka-sūtra*). Trans. Buddhabhadra. *T.* 12, 279.

Da zhidu lun 大智度論. Trans. Kumārajīva. *T.* 25, 1509.

Dahui Pujue chanshi [Zonggao, 1089–1163] yulu 大慧普覺禪師 [宗杲] 語錄. *T.* 47, 1998a.

Daji daxu Kongzang pusa suowen jing 大集大虛空藏菩薩所問經 (*Mahākāśagarbha-bodhisattva-paripṛicchā-sūtra*). *T.* 13, 404.

Dai Nihon zokuzōkkyō 大日本續藏經. Ed. Nakano Tatsue 中野達慧. 150 vols. Kyoto: Zōkyō shoin, 1905–1912. Reprint, Taibei: Xinwenfeng chuban gongsi, 1988.

Daning 大寧. "Famen chugui youxu" 法門鋤宄又序. In *Famen chugui*, by Jingfu.

Daocheng 道誠, ed. *Shishi yaolan* 釋氏要覽 (1019). *T.* 54, 2127.

Daoshi 道世 (d. 684), ed. *Fayuan zhulin* 法苑珠林. *T.* 53, 2122.

Daoxuan 道宣 (596–667). *Xu Gaoseng zhuan* 續高僧傳. *T.* 50, 2060.

———. *Guang Hongming ji* 廣弘明集. *T.* 52, 2103.

Daoyuan 道原. *Jingde chuandeng lu* 景德傳燈錄. *SBCK* (*Sibu congkan* 四部叢刊); *T.* 51, 2076.

Dasheng bensheng xindiguan jing 大乘本生心地觀經 (*Mūlajāta-hṛidayabhūmi-dhyāna-sūtra*). *T.* 3, 159.

Dasheng qixin lun 大乘起信論. *T.* 32, 1666.

Dasheng ru Lengqie jing 大乘入楞伽經 (*Laṅkāvatāra-sūtra*). *T.* 16, 762.

Dasheng wusheng fangbian men 大乘無生方便門. *T.* 85, 2834.

Dazhu Huihai 大珠慧海. *Dunwu rudao yaomen lun* 頓悟入道要門論. *XZJ* 110.

Deqing 德清 (1546–1623). *Lushan Guizongsi zhi* 盧山歸宗寺志. In vol. 16 of *Zhongguo fosi zhi congkan* 中國佛寺誌叢刊, ed. Bai Huawen 白化文. Yangzhou: Jiangsu guangling guji keyinshe, 1992.

Ding Bing 丁丙 (1832–1899). *Shanben shushi cangshuzhi* 善本書室藏書志. Beijing: Zhonghua shuju, 1990.

Dong Gao 董誥 (1740–1818) et al., eds. *Quan Tangwen* 全唐文. 20 vols. 1814. Reprint, Beijing: Zhonghua shuju, 1983.

Dongshan Huikong [1096–1158] chanshi yulu 東山慧空禪師語錄. *XZJ* 120.

Du Fei 杜朏. *Chuan fabao ji* 傳法寶記. *T.* 85, 2838.

Duan Chengshi 段成式 (d. 863). *Youyang zazu* 酉陽雜俎. *SKQS.*

———. *Youyang zazuxuji* 酉陽雜俎續集. *SKQS.*

Enchin 圓珍 (814–891). *Nihon biku Enchin nittō guhō mokuroku* 日本比丘圓珍入唐求法目錄. *T.* 55, 2172.

———. *Chishō daishi shōrai mokuroku* 智證大師請來目錄 (859). *T.* 55, 2173.

Ennin 圓仁 (794–864). *Nittō shinkyu seikyō mokuroku* 入唐新求聖教目錄 (847). *T.* 55, 2167.

———. *Nihon goku Shōwa gonin nittō guhō mokuroku* 日本國承和五年入唐求法目錄 (838). *T.* 55, 2165.

———. *Jikō daishi zaitō sōshin roku* 慈覺大師在唐送進錄 (840). *T.* 55, 2166.

———. *Nittō guhō junrei gyōki* 入唐求法巡禮行記 (838–847). Tokyo: Chūō kōronsha, 1990.

Eun 惠運. *Eun zenji shōrai kyōhō mokuroku* 惠運禪師將來教法目錄 (847). *T.* 55, 2168a.

Fayan Wenyi chanshi yulu 法眼文益禪師語錄. *T.* 47, 1991.

Fazang 法藏 (643–712). *Dasheng qixin lun yiji* 大乘起信論義記. *T.* 44, 1846.

———. *Huayan yisheng jiaoyi fenqi zhang* 華嚴一乘教義分齊章. *T.* 45, 1866.

———. *Huayan youxin fajie ji* 華嚴遊心法界記. *T.* 45, 1877.

———. *Huayan jing tanxuan ji* 華嚴經探玄記. *T.* 35, 1733.

———. *Xiu Huayan aozhi wangjin huanyuan guan* 修華嚴奧旨妄盡還源觀. *T.* 45, 1876.

Fo shuo buzeng bujian jing 佛說不增不減經 (*Anūnatvāpūrnatva-nirdeśa*). Trans. Bodhiruci. *T.* 16, 668.

Fo shuo faju jing 佛說法句經. *T.* 85, 2901.

Fo shuo foming jing 佛說佛名經 (*Buddhanāma-sūtra*). *T.* 14, 440.

Fo shuo guan Wuliangshoufo jing 佛說觀無量壽佛經 (*Sukhāvatīvyūha-sūtra*). *T.* 12, 365.

Fo shuo Weimojie jing 佛說維摩詰經 (*Vimalakīrti-nirdeśa-sūtra*). Trans. Zhiqian 支謙. *T.* 14, 475.

Foxing lun 佛性論. *T.* 31, 1610.

Fuzhou Xuansha Zongyi dashi [Shibei, 835–908] guanglu 福州玄沙宗一大師 [師備] 廣錄. *XZJ* 126.

Guanxin lun 觀心論 (*Poxiang lun* 破相論). *T.* 85, 2833.

Hebu jinguangming jing 合部金光明經 (*Suvarṇa-prabhāsa-uttamarāja-sūtra*). *T.* 16, 664.

Heshan [Hui]fang chanshi yulu 禾山 [慧] 方禪師語錄. *XZJ* 120.

Horinden yakuchu 寶林傳譯注. Ed. Tanaka Ryōshō 田中良昭. Tokyo: Naiyama shoten, 2003.

Hu Pinzhi 胡聘之. *Shanyou shike congbian* 山右石刻叢編. In vols. 907–908 of *XXSKQS.*

Huang Yongwu 黃永武, ed. *Dunhuang baozang* 敦煌寶藏. 140 vols. Taibei: Xinwenfeng chuban gongsi, 1981–1986.

Huangboshan Duanji chanshi wanling lu 黃檗山斷際禪師宛陵錄. *T.* 48, 2012b.

Huihong 慧洪 (1071–1128). *Chanlin sengbao zhuan* 禪林僧寶傳. *SKQS.* 137.

———. *Linjian lu* 林間錄. *XZJ* 148.

———. *Shimen wenzi chan* 石門文字禪. *SBCK.*

Huijiao 慧皎 (497–554). *Gaoseng zhuan* 高僧傳. Beijing: Zhonghua shuju, 1992.

Huinan 惠南 (1002–1069), ed. *Jiangxi Mazu Daoyi chanshi yulu* 江西馬祖道一禪師語錄. *Sijia lu; Sijia yulu, Wujia yulu; XZJ* 119.

———. *Sijia lu.* Preserved in Nanjing Library.

———. *Shishuang Chuyuan chanshi yulu* 石霜楚圓禪師語錄. *XZJ* 120.

Jiaoran (ca. 720–ca. 793). *Zhou shangren ji* 晝上人集. *SBCK.*

Jing 靜, and Yun 筠, eds. *Zutang ji* 祖堂集 (952). 1245. Reprint, Changsha: Yuelu shushe, 1996.

Jingfu 淨符. *Famen chugui* 法門鋤宄 (1667). *XZJ* 147.

Jingang sanmei jing 金剛三昧經 (*Vajrasamādhi-sūtra*). *T.* 9, 273.

Jingjue 淨覺 (683–ca. 750). *Lengqie shizi ji* 楞伽師資記. *T.* 85, 2837.

Jinguangming jing 金光明經 (*Suvarṇa-prabhāsa-uttamarāja-sūtra*). *T.* 16, 663.

Jiujing yisheng baoxing lun 究竟一乘寶性論 (*Ratnagotravibhāga Mahāyānottaratantra-śāstra*). *T.* 31, 1611.

Jizang 吉藏 (549–623). *Dasheng xuanlun* 大乘玄論. *T.* 45, 1853.

Jue'an 覺岸 (b. 1286). *Shishi jigu lüe* 釋氏稽古略. *T.* 49, 2037.

"Juemengtang chongjiao wujia zongpai xu" 覺夢堂重校五家宗派序. In *Rentian yanmu*, by Zhizhao.

Lengqie abaduoluo baojing 楞伽阿跋多羅寶經 (*Laṅkāvatāra-sūtra*). Trans. Gunabhadra (394–468). *T.* 16, 670.

Li Fang 李昉 (925–996) et al., eds. *Taiping guangji* 太平廣記. 10 vols. Beijing: Zhonghua shuju, 1961.

Li Jifu. *Yuanhe junxian tuzhi* 元和郡縣圖志. 2 vols. Beijing: Zhonghua shuju, 1983.

Li Kang 李亢. *Duyi zhi* 獨異志. *SKQS.*

Li Zunxu 李遵勗 (988–1038). *Tiansheng guangdeng lu* 天聖廣燈錄 (1036). *XZJ* 135.

Liang Kejia 梁克家 (1128–1187). *Chunxi Sanshan zhi* 淳熙三山志. *SKQS.*

Lidai fabao ji 歷代法寶記. *T.* 51, 2075.

Lin Bao 林寶 (fl. 806–820). *Yuanhe xingcuan* 元和姓纂. 3 vols. Beijing: Zhonghua shuju, 1994.

Lin Hongyan 林弘衍 (fl. 1639), ed. *Xuefeng Zhenjue chanshi [Yicun] yulu* (1639) 雪峰真覺禪師 [義存] 語錄. *XZJ* 119.

Lingyou 靈祐 (771–853). *Guishan jingce* 溈山警策 (c. 850). *XZJ* 111; *QTW*, 919.3b–7b.

Liu Xihai 劉喜海 (d. 1853), ed. *Haidong jinshi yuan* 海東金石苑. 4 vols. *Shike shiliao congshu*, ser. 1, no. 21. Taibei: Yiwen yinshuguan, 1966.

Liu Xu 劉昫 (888–947) et al. *Jiu Tang shu* 舊唐書. 16 vols. Beijing: Zhonghua shuju, 1975.

Liu Yuxi 劉禹錫 (772–842). *Liu Yuxi ji jianzheng* 劉禹錫集箋證, ed. Qu Tuiyuan 瞿蛻園. 3 vols. Shanghai: Shanghai guji chubanshe, 1989.

Liu Zongyuan 柳宗元 (773–819). *Liu Hedong ji* 柳河東集. 2 vols. Shanghai: Shanghai renmin chubanshe, 1974.

Liuzu Tanjing 六祖壇經. Ed. Yang Zengwen 楊曾文. Beijing: Zongjiao wenhua chubanshe, 2001.

Lu Jihui 陸繼煇, ed. *Baqiongshi jinshi buzheng xubian* 八瓊室金石補正續編. In vols. 899–901 of *XXSKQS*.

Lu Xinyuan 陸心源 (1834–1894), ed. *Tangwen shiyi* 唐文拾遺. In vol. 11 of *QTW*.

———. *Tangwen xushi* 唐文續拾. In vol. 11 of *QTW*.

Lu Yaoyu 陸耀遹 (1774–1836). *Jinshi xubian* 金石續編. In vol. 893 of *XXSKQS*.

Lu Zengxiang 陸增祥 (1816–1882). *Baqiongshi jinshi buzheng* 八瓊室金石補正. In vols. 896–899 of *XXSKQS*.

Lü Maoxian 呂懋先, and Shuai Fangwei 帥方蔚, eds. *Fengxinxian zhi* 奉新縣志 (1871). In ser. 3, vol. 43 of *Zhongguo difangzhi jicheng* 中國地方志集成. Nanjing: Jiangsu guji chubanshe, 1996.

Miaofa lianhua jing 妙法蓮華經 (*Saddharmapundarīka-sūtra*). Trans. Kumārajīva. *T.* 9, 202.

Mingzhou Dameishan Chang chanshi yulu 明州大梅山常禪師語錄. In *Kanazawa bunko shiryō zensho: Butten 1, zenseki hen* 金澤文庫資料全書—佛典, 第一卷, 禪籍篇.

Nianchang 念常. *Fozu lidai tongzai* 佛祖歷代通載 (ca. 1341). *T.* 49, 2036.

Ouyang Xiu 歐陽修 (1007–1072). *Xin Tang shu* 新唐書. 20 vols. Beijing: Zhonghua shuju, 1975.

———. *Jigu lu* 集古錄. *SKQS*.

Ouyang Xun 歐陽詢 (557–641) et al, eds. *Yiwen leiju* 藝文類聚. Shanghai: Shanghai guji chubanshe, 1981.

Pang jushi yulu 龐居士語錄. *XZJ* 120.

Pei Xiu 裴休 (ca. 787–860), ed. *Huangboshan Duanji chanshi chuanxin fayao* 黃檗山斷際禪師傳心法要. *T.* 48, 2012a.

Peng Dingqiu 彭定求 (1645–1719) et al., eds. *Quan Tangshi* 全唐詩. 25 vols. 1707. Reprint, Beijing: Zhonghua shuju, 1960.

Puji 普濟 (1179–1253), ed. *Wudeng Huiyuan* 五燈會元. 3 vols. Beijing: Zhonghua shuju, 1984.

Qian Yi 錢易. *Nanbu xinshu* 南部新書. *SKQS*.

Qisong 契嵩 (1007–1072). *Chuanfa zhengzong ji* 傳法正宗記. *T.* 51, 2078.

Quan Deyu 權德輿 (761–818). *Quan Zaizhi wenji* 權載之文集. *SBCK*.

Ru Lengqie jing 入楞伽經 (*Laṅkāvatāra-sūtra*). *T.* 16, 671.

Saichō 最澄 (767–822). *Dengyō daishi shōrai Osshū roku* 傳教大師將來越州錄. *T.* 55, 2160.

Sengzhao 僧肇 (384–414). *Zhaolun* 肇論. *T.* 45, 1859.

Shanhai jing 山海經. *SKQS*.

Shanqing 善卿. *Zuting shiyuan* 祖庭事苑 (1108). *XZJ* 113.

Shaotan 紹曇. *Wujia zhengzong zan* 五家正宗贊 (1254). *XZJ* 135.

Shengman shizihou yisheng dafangguang jing 勝鬘師子吼一乘大方廣經 (*Śrīmālādevī-simhanāda-sūtra*). Trans. Gunabhadra. *T.* 12, 353.

Shengtianwang bore boluomi jing 勝天王般若波羅蜜經 (*Suvikrāntavikrami-paṭipricchā-prajñāpāramitā-sūtra*). *T.* 8, 231.

Shenhui [684–758] heshang chanhua lu 神會和尚禪話錄. Ed. Yang Zengwen. Beijing: Zhonghua shuju, 1996.

Shenqing 神清 (d. 820). *Beishan lu* 北山錄. *T.* 52, 2113.

Shoulengyan jing 首楞嚴經 (*Śuraṅgama-sūtra*). *T.* 19, 945.

Sijia yulu, Wujia yulu (*Shike goroku, Goke goroku*) 四家語錄, 五家語錄. Ed. Yanagida Seizan. Kyoto: Chūben shuppansha, 1983.

Sima Guang 司馬光 (1019–1086). *Zizhi tongjian* 資治通鑒. 20 vols. Beijing: Zhonghua shuju, 1971.

Song Minqiu 宋敏求 (1019–1079), ed. *Tang dazhaoling ji* 唐大詔令集. *SKQS.*

Taishō shinshū daizōkyō 大正新修大藏經. 100 vols. Ed. Takakusu Junjirō 高楠順次郎 (1866–1945) and Watanabe Kaigyoku 渡邊海旭. Tokyo: Taishō issaikyō kankōkai, 1924–1932. Reprint, Taibei: Xinwenfeng chuban gongsi, 1983–1985.

Tanzhou Guishan Lingyou chanshi yulu 潭州溈山靈祐禪師語錄. *T.* 48, 1989.

Tianpin miaofa lianhua jing 添品妙法蓮華經 (*Saddharmapundarīka-sūtra*). *T.* 9, 264.

Tongrong 通容 (1593–1661). *Wudeng yantong mulu* 五燈嚴統目錄. *XZJ* 139.

Tuotuo 脫脫 (1314–1355) et al. *Songshi* 宋史. 40 vols. Beijing: Zhonghua shuju, 1985.

Wang Chang 王昶 (1725–1807), ed. *Jinshi cuibian* 金石萃編. In vols. 886–891 of *XXSKQS.*

Wang Cun 王存 (1023–1101). *Yuanfeng jiuyu zhi* 元豐九域志. 2 vols. Beijing: Zhonghua shuju, 1984.

Wang Pu 王溥 (922–982). *Tang huiyao* 唐會要. 3 vols. Beijing: Zhonghua shuju, 1955.

Wang Qinruo 王欽若 (d. 1025) et al., eds. *Cefu yuangui* 冊府元龜. 20 vols. Taibei: Qinghua shuju, 1967.

Wang Xiangzhi 王象之 (*jinshi* 1196). *Yudi bei jimu* 輿地碑記目. *SKQS.*

———. *Yudi jisheng* 輿地紀勝. *SKQS.*

Weibai 惟白 (fl. 1101). *Dazangjing gangmu zhiyao lu* 大藏經綱目指要錄. In *Dazheng xinxiu fabao zongmulu* 大正新修法寶總目錄. Reprint, Taibei: Xinwenfeng, 1985.

———. *Jianzhong jingguo xudeng lu* 建中靖國續燈錄 (1101). *XZJ* 136.

Weimojie suoshuo jing 維摩詰所說經 (*Vimalakīrti-nirdeśa-sūtra*). Trans. Kumārajīva. *T.* 14, 475.

Wenshushili suoshuo mohebore boluomi jing 文殊師利所說摩訶般若波羅蜜經 (*Mañjuśrībhāsita-mahāpārajñāpramitā-sūtra*). *T.* 8, 726.

Wenyi 文益 (885–958). *Zongmen shigui lun* 宗門十規論. *XZJ* 110.

Wu Gang 吳鋼, ed. *Quan Tangwen buyi* 全唐文補遺. 7 vols. Xi'an: San Qin, 1994.

Xiaopin bore boluomi jing 小品般若波羅蜜經 (*Daśasahasrikā-prajñapāmitā-sūtra*). *T.* 8, 227.

Xinxin ming 信心銘. Attributed to Sengcan 僧璨. *T.* 48, 2010.

Xuxiu Siku quanshu 續修四庫全書. Shanghai: Shanghai guji chubanshe, 1995.

Xu Shen 許慎 (ca. 58–ca. 147). *Shuowen jiezi* 說文解字. Beijing: Zhonghua shuju, 1963.

Xu Song 徐松 (1781–1848). *Dengke ji kao* 登科記考. 3 vols. Beijing: Zhonghua shuju, 1984.

Xutang heshang yulu 虛堂和尚語錄. *T.* 48, 2000.

Yang Xuanzhi 楊衒之 (fl. 528–547). *Luoyang qielan ji* 洛陽伽藍記. *T.* 51, 2092.

Yang Yi 楊億 (974–1020). *Wuyi xinji* 武夷新集. *SBCK.*

Yanshou 延壽 (904–975). *Zongjing lu* 宗鏡錄. *T.* 48, 2016.

———. *Wanshan tonggui ji* 萬善同歸集. *T.* 48, 2017.

Yao Xuan 姚鉉 (968–1020), ed. *Tangwen cui* 唐文粹 (1011). *SKQS.*

You Mao 尤袤 (1127–1194). *Suichutang shumu* 遂初堂書目. In *Congshu jicheng chubian* 叢書集成初編.

Yu Xingwu 于省吾, and Yao Xiaoshui 姚孝遂, eds. *Jiagu wenzi gulin* 甲骨文字詁林. 4 vols. Beijing: Zhonghua shuju, 1996.

Yuan Jue 袁桷 (1266–1327). *Yanyou Siming zhi* 延祐四明志. *SKQS.*

Yuanzhou Yangshan Huiji chanshi yulu 袁州仰山慧寂禪師語錄. *T.* 47, 1990.

Yue Shi 樂史 (930–1007). *Taiping huanyu ji* 太平寰宇記. *SKQS.*

Yunmen guanglu 雲門廣錄. *T.* 47, 1988.

Zanning 贊寧 (919–1001). *Da Song sengshi lüe* 大宋僧史略 (ca. 978–999). *T.* 54, 2126.

———. *Song gaoseng zhuan* 宋高僧傳 (988). 2 vols. Beijing: Zhonghua shuju, 1987.

Zeng Zaozhuang 曾棗莊, and Liu Lin 劉琳, eds. *Quan Songwen* 全宋文. Chengdu: Ba Shu shushe, 1994.

Zezangzhu 賾藏主, ed. *Gu Zunsu yulu* 古尊宿語錄. 2 vols. Beijing: Zhonghua shuju, 1994.

Zhao Bufei 趙不悔, and Luo Yuan 羅願 (1136–1184), eds. *Xin'an zhi* 新安志. *SKQS.*

Zhao Mingcheng 趙明誠 (1081–1129), ed. *Jinshi lu* 金石錄. *SKQS.*

Zheng Qiao 鄭樵 (1104–1162). *Tongzhi* 通志. 3 vols. Hangzhou: Zhejiang guji, 1988.

Zhengshou 正守. *Jiatai pudeng lu* 嘉泰普燈錄 (1204). *XZJ* 137.

Zhenzhou Linji Huizhao chanshi yulu 鎮州臨濟慧照禪師語錄. *T.* 47, 1985.

Zhipan 志盤 (fl. 1258–1269). *Fozu tongji* 佛祖統紀. *T.* 49, 2035.

Zhisheng 智昇. *Kaiyuan shijiao lu* 開元釋教錄. *T.* 55, 2154.

Zhiyi 智顗 (538–597). *Guanyin xuanyi* 觀音玄義. *T.* 34, 1726.

———. *Miaofa lianhua jing xuanyi* 妙法蓮華經玄義. *T.* 33, 1716.

———. *Mohe zhiguan* 摩訶止觀. *T.* 46, 1911.

Zhiyou 致祐. "Da Yuan Yuanyou chongkan *Rentian yanmu* houxu" 大元延祐重刊人天眼目後序. In *Rentian yanmu*, by Zhizhao.

Zhizhao 智昭. *Rentian yanmu* 人天眼目 (1188). *T.* 48, 2006.

Zhong benqi jing 中本起經 (Madhyametyukta-sūtra). Trans. Tanguo 曇果 and Kang Mengxiang 康孟祥. *T.* 4, 196.

Zhongguo guji shanben shumu bianji weiyuanhui 中國古籍善本書目編輯委員會, ed. *Zhongguo guji shanben shumu: Zibu* 中國古籍善本書目•子部. Shanghai: Shanghai guji chubanshe, 1994.

Zhonglun 中論 (Mādhyamika-śāstra). Trans. Kumārajīva. *T.* 30, 1564.

Zhou Shaoliang 周紹良, ed. *Quan Tangwen xinbian* 全唐文新編. 22 vols. Changchun: Jilin wenshi chubanshe, 2000.

Zhou Shaoliang, and Zhao Chao 趙超, eds. *Tangdai muzhi huibian* 唐代墓誌彙編. 2 vols. Shanghai: Shanghai guji chubanshe, 1992.

———. *Tangdai muzhi huibian xuji* 唐代墓誌彙編續集. Shanghai: Shanghai guji chubanshe, 2001.

Zhou Xunchu 周勛初, ed. *Tang ren yishi huibian* 唐人軼事彙編. 2 vols. Shanghai: Shanghai guji chubanshe, 1995.

Zisheng 子昇, ed. *Chanmen zhu zushi jisong* 禪門諸祖師偈頌. *XZJ* 66.

Ziwen 子文, ed. *Foguo Yuanwu Zhenjue chanshi xinyao* 佛果圓悟真覺禪師心要. *XZJ* 120.

Zonggao 宗杲 (1089–1163). *Zheng fayan zang* 正法眼藏. *XZJ* 118.

Zongmen liandeng huiyao 宗門聯燈會要. *XZJ* 136.

Zongmi 宗密 (780–841). *Chanyuan zhuquanji duxu* 禪源諸詮集都序. *T.* 48, 2015.

———. *Yuanjue jing dashu chao* 圓覺經大疏鈔. *XZJ* 14.

———. *Zhonghua chuan xindi chanmen shizi chengxi tu* 中華傳心地禪門師資承襲圖. *XZJ* 110.

———. *Da fangguang yuanjue xiuduoluo liaoyi jing lüeshu* 大方廣圓覺修多羅了義經略疏, *T.* 39, 1795.

———. *Yuanjue jing dashu shiyi chao* 圓覺經大疏釋義鈔. *XZJ* 14–15.

Zui shangsheng lun 最上乘論. Attributed to Hongren 弘忍 (602–675). *T.* 48, 2011.

Zuxiu 祖琇. *Longxing fojiao biannian tonglun* 隆興佛教編年通論. *XZJ* 130.

SECONDARY WORKS

Abe Chōichi 阿部肇一. *Zōtei Chūgoku zenshūshi no kenkyū: Seiji shakaishi-teki kōsatsu* 增訂中國禪宗史の研究: 政治社會史的考察. Tokyo: Kenbun shuppan, 1986.

———. *Zenshū shakai to shinkō: Zoku Chūgoku zenshūshi no kenkyū* 禪宗社會と信仰—續中國禪宗史之研究. Tokyo: Kindai bungei sha, 1993.

Adamek, Wendi L. "Issues in Chinese Buddhist Transmission as Seen Through the *Lidai fabao ji* (Record of the Dharma-Jewel through the Ages)." Ph.D. diss. Stanford University, 1997.

————. "Robes Purple and Gold: Transmission of the Robe in the Lidai fabao ji (Record of the Dharma-Jewel through the Ages). *History of Religions* 40.1 (2000): 58–81.

————. "Imaging the Portrait of a Chan Master." In *Chan Buddhism in Ritual Context*, ed. Bernard Faure, 36–73.

App, Urs. "Facets of the Life and Teaching of Chan Master Yunmen Wenyan (864–949)." Ph.D. diss. Temple University, 1989.

————. "The Making of a Chan Recod: Reflections on the History of the *Record of Yunmen*." *Zenbunka kenkyūjo kiyō* 禪文化研究所紀要 17 (1991): 1–9.

Barrett, Timothy H. *Li Ao: Buddhist, Taoist, or Neo-Confucian?* New York: Oxford University Press, 1992.

————. "Taoist and Buddhist Mysteries in the Interpretation of the Tao-te ching." Journal of the Royal Asiatic Society 1 (1982): 35–43.

Berling, Judith. "Bringing the Buddha Down to Earth: Notes on the Emergence of Yü-lu as a Buddhist Genre." *History of Religions* 27.1 (1987): 56–88.

Blofeld, John, trans. *The Zen Teaching of Huang-po on the Transmission of Mind*. New York: Grove Press, 1958.

————. trans. *The Zen Teaching of Instantaneous Awakening*. Leicester: Buddhist Publishing Group, 1987.

Bodiford, William M, ed. *Going forth: Visions on Buddhist Vinaya. Essays Presented in Honor of Professor Stanley Weinstein*. Honolulu: University of Hawaii Press, 2005.

Broughton, Jeffrey L. *The Bodhidharma Anthology: The Earliest Records of Zen*. Berkeley and Los Angeles: University of California Press, 1999.

Brown, Brian Edward. *The Buddha Nature: A Study of the Tathāgatagarbha and Ālayavijñāna*. Delhi: Motilal Banarsidass Publishers, 1991.

Buswell, Robert E., Jr. *The Korean Approach to Zen: The Collected Works of Chinul*. Honolulu: University of Hawaii Press, 1983.

————. *The Formation of Ch'an Ideology in China and Korea: The Vajrasamādhi-Sūtra, a Buddhist Apocryphon*. Princeton: Princeton University Press, 1989.

————. "The 'Short-cut' Approach of K'an-hua Meditation: The Evolution of a Practical Subitism in Chinese Ch'an Buddhism." In *Sudden and Gradual*, ed. Peter N. Gregory, 321–77.

————. ed. *Chinese Buddhist Apocrypha*. Honolulu: University of Hawaii Press, 1990.

————. ed. *Encyclopedia of Buddhism*. 2 vols. New York: Macmillan, 2004.

Buswell, Robert E., Jr., and Robert M. Gimello, eds. *Paths to Liberation: The Mārga and Its Transformations in Buddhist Thought*. Honolulu: University of Hawaii Press, 1992.

Cen Zhongmian 岑仲勉 (1885–1961). *Cen Zhongmian shixue lunwenji* 岑仲勉史學論文集. Beijing: Zhonghua shuju, 1990.

Chang, Chung-yuan, trans. *Original Teachings of Chan Buddhism*. New York: Vintage Books, 1971.

Chappell, David W. "The Teachings of the Fourth Ch'an Patriarch Tao-hsin (580–651)." In *Early Ch'an in China and Tibet*, ed. Whalen Lai and Lewis R. Lancaster, 89–130.

————. ed. *Buddhist and Taoist Practice in Medieval Chinese Society*. Honolulu: University of Hawaii Press, 1987.

Chen, Jinhua. "An Alternative View of the Meditation Tradition in China: Meditation in the Life and Works of Daoxuan (596–667)." *T'oung Pao* 88.4–5 (2002): 332–95.

Ch'en, Kenneth K. S. *Buddhism in China: A Historical Survey*. Princeton: Princeton University Press, 1964.

————. *The Chinese Transformation of Buddhism*. Princeton: Princeton University Press, 1973.

Chen Yuan 陳垣 (1880–1971). *Shishi yinian lu* 釋氏疑年錄. Beijing: Furen daxue, 1923. Reprint, Yangzhou: Jiangsu Guangling guji keyinshe, 1991.

————. *Zhongguo fojiao shiji gailun* 中國佛教史籍概論. 1962. Reprint, Shanghai: Shanghai shudian, 1999.

Cheng Chien (i.e., Mario Poceski). *Sun-Face Buddha: The Teaching of Ma-tsu and the Hung-chou School of Chan*. Berkeley: Asian Humanities Press, 1992.

Cheng, Hsüeh-li. "Zen and San-lun Madhyamika Thought: Exploring the Theoretical Foundation of Zen Teachings and Practices." *Religious Studies* 15 (1979): 343–63.

Chou, Yi-liang (1913–2001). "Tantrism in China." *Harvard Journal of Asiatic Studies* 8.3–4 (1945): 241–332.

Cleary, Thomas, trans. *Sayings and Doings of Pai-chang*. Los Angeles: Center Publications, 1978.

————. trans. *The Flower Ornamant Scripture*, 3 vols. Boston & London: Shambala Publications, 1978.

Collcutt, Martin. "The Early Ch'an Monastic Rule: *Ch'ing Kuei* and the Shaping of Ch'an Community Life." In *Early Ch'an in China and Tibet*, ed. Lai and Lancaster, 165–84.

Conze, Edward. *Buddhism: Its Essence and Development*. New York: Harper and Row, 1959.

————. *Buddhist Thought in India: Three Phases of Buddhist Philosophy*. 1962. Reprint, Ann Arbor: University of Michigan Press, 1967.

Cook, Francis H. "Fa-tsang's Treatise on the Five Doctrines: An Annotated Translation." Ph.D. diss. University of Wisconsin, 1970.

————. *Hua-yen Buddhism: The Jewel Net of Indra*. University Park: The Pennsylvania State University Press, 1977.

Demiéville, Paul. *Le concile de Lhasa: Une controverse sur le quiétisme entre les bouddhistes de l'Inde et de la Chine au VIIIe siècle de l'ère chrétienne*. Paris: Press Universitaires de France, 1952.

————. *Entretiens de Lin-tsi*. Paris: Fayard, 1972.

————. "The Mirror of the Mind." In *Sudden and Gradual*, ed. Gregory, 13–40.

Dudbridge, Glen. *Religious Experience and Lay Society in T'ang China*. Cambridge: Cambridge University Press, 1995.

Du Jiwen 杜繼文, and Wei Daoru 魏道儒. *Zhongguo chanzong tongshi* 中國禪宗通史. Nanjing: Jiangsu guji chubanshe, 1993.

Dumoulin, Heinrich. *Zen Buddhism: A History*. Vol. 1. Trans. James W. Heisig and Paul Knitter. Rev. ed. New York: Macmillan, 1994.

Ebrey, Patricia Buckley, and Peter N. Gregory, eds. *Religion and Society in T'ang and Sung China*. Honolulu: University of Hawaii Press, 1992.

Eckel, Malcom David. *To See the Buddha: A Philosopher's Quest for the Meaning of Emptiness*. Princeton: Princeton University Press, 1992.

Faure, Bernard. "Bodhidharma as Textual and Religious Paradigm." *History of Religious* 25.3 (1986): 187–98.

———. "The Concept of One-Practice Samādhi in Early Ch'an." *Traditions of Meditation in Chinese Buddhism*, ed. Peter N. Gregory, 99–128.

———. *The Rhetoric of Immediacy: A Cultural Critique of Chan/Zen Buddhism*. Princeton: Princeton University Press, 1992.

———. *Chan Insights and Oversights: An Epistemological Critique of Chan*. Princeton: Princeton University Press, 1993.

———. *The Will to Orthodoxy: A Critical Genealogy of Northern Chan Buddhism*. Stanford: Stanford University Press, 1997.

———. ed. *Chan Buddhism in Ritual Context*. London and New York: RoutledgeCurzon, 2003.

Foulk, T. Griffith. "The Ch'an School and Its Place in the Buddist Monastic Tradition." Ph.D. diss. University of Michigan, 1987.

———. "The Ch'an *Tsung* in Medieval China: School, Lineage, or What?" *The Pacific World*, New Series 8 (1992): 18–31.

———. "Myth, Ritual, and Monastic Practice in Sung Ch'an Buddhism." In *Religion and Society in T'ang and Sung China*, ed. Ebrey and Gregory, 147–208.

———. "Sung Controversies Concerning the 'Separate Transmission' of Chan." In *Buddhism in the Sung*, ed. Gregory and Getz, Jr., 220–94.

Foulk, T. Griffith, and Robert H. Sharf. "On the Ritual Use of Chan Portraiture in Medieval China." In *Chan Buddhism in Ritual Context*, ed. Faure, 74–150.

Fu Xuancong 傅璇琮, Zhang Chenshi 張忱石, and Xu Yimin 許逸民, eds. *Tang Wudai renwu zhuanji ziliao zonghe suoyin* 唐五代人物傳記資料綜合索引. Beijing: Zhonghua shuju, 1982.

Gardner, Daniel K. "Modes of Thinking and Modes of Discourse in the Sung: Some Thoughts of the Yü-lu ('Recorded Conversations') Texts." *The Journal of Asian Studies* 50.3 (1991): 574–603.

Gernet, Jacques. *Buddhism in Chinese Society: An Economic History from the Fifth to the Tenth Centuries*. Trans. Franciscus Verellen. New York: Columbia University Press, 1995.

Gimello, Robert M. "Apophatic and Kataphatic Discourse in Mahāyāna: A Chinese View." *Philosophy East and West* 26.2 (1976): 117–36.

———. "The Sudden/Gradual Polarity: A Recurrent Theme in Chinese Thought." *Journal of Chinese Philosophy* 9 (1982): 471–86.

Gimello, Robert M., and Peter N. Gregory, eds. *Studies in Ch'an and Huayen*. Honolulu: University of Hawaii Press, 1983.

Gregory, Peter N. "The Problem of Theodicy in the Awakening of Faith." *Religious Studies* 22.1 (1986): 6–78.

————. *Tsung-mi and the Sinification of Buddhism*. Princeton: Princeton University Press, 1991.

————. *Inquiry into the Origin of Humanity: An Annotated Translation of Tsung-mi's Yüan jen lun with a Modern Commentary*. Honolulu: University of Hawaii Press, 1995.

————. ed. *Traditions of Meditation in Chinese Buddhism*. Honolulu: University of Hawaii Press, 1986.

————. ed. *Sudden and Gradual Approaches to Enlightenment in Chinese Thought*. Honolulu: University of Hawaii Press, 1987.

Gregory, Peter N., and Daniel A. Getz, Jr., eds. *Buddhism in the Sung*. Honolulu: University of Hawaii Press, 1999.

Griffiths, Paul J., and John P. Keenan, eds. *Buddha Nature: A Festschrift in Honor of Minoru Kiyota*. Tokyo: Buddhist Books International, 1990.

Grosnick, William H. "Nonorigination and Nirvāṇa in the Early Tathāgata-garbha Literature." *Journal of the International Association of Buddhist Studies* 4.2 (1981): 33–43.

Hakeda Yoshito, trans. *The Awakening of Faith Attributed to Aśvaghosha*. New York: Columbia University Press, 1967.

He Yun 何雲. "Mazu Daoyi pingzhuan"馬祖道一評傳. *Shijie zongjiao yanjiu* 世界宗教研究 (1989) 1: 19–29.

Heine, Steven, and Dale S. Wright, eds. *The Kōan: Texts and Contexts in Zen Buddhism*. Oxford: Oxford University Press, 2000.

————. *The Zen Canon: Understanding the Classic Texts*. New York: Oxford University Press, 2004.

Hirai Shun'ei 平井俊榮. *Chūgoku hannya shisōshi kenkyū: Kichizō to Sanron gakuha* 中國般若思想史研究: 吉藏と三論學派. Tokyo: Shunjūsha, 1976.

————. "The School of Mount Niu-t'ou and the School of the Pao-T'ang Monastery." Trans. Silvio Vita. *Philosophy East and West* 37.1–4 (1987): 337–72.

Hirakawa Akira. *A History of Indian Buddhism: From Śākyamuni to Early Mahāyāna*. Trans. and ed. Paul Groner. Honolulu: University of Hawaii Press, 1990.

Hirakawa Akira 平川彰, Kajiyama Yūichi 梶山雄一, and Takasaki Jikidō 高崎直道, eds. *Nyoraizō shisō* 如來藏思想. Tokyo: Shunjūsha, 1982.

Hu Shi 胡適 (1891–1962). "Ch'an/Zen Buddhism in China: Its History and Method." *Philosophy East and West* 3.1 (1953): 3–24.

————. *Hu Shi wencun* 胡適文存. Taibei: Yuandong tushu gongsi, 1979.

————. "The Development of Zen Buddhism in China." *Chinese and Political Science Review* 15.4: 475–505.

————. *Hu Shi ji* 胡適集. Ed. Huang Xianian 黃夏年. Beijing: Zhongguo shehui kexue, 1995.

Hubbard, James B., and Paul L. Swanson, eds. *Pruning the Bodhi Tree: The Storm over Critical Buddhism*. Honolulu: University of Hawaii Press, 1997.

Iriya Yoshitaka 入矢義高, trans. *Baso no goroku* 馬祖の語錄. Kyoto: Zenbunka kenkyūjo, 1984.

Ishii Shūdō 石井修道. "Kōshūshū ni okeru Saidō Chizō no ichi ni tsuite" 洪州宗に
おける西堂智藏の位置について. *Indogaku Bukkyōgaku kenkyū* 20.1 (1978):
280–84.

———. "Isan kyōdan no dōkō ni tsuite: Hukushū Daian no shinjinki no shōkai ni
chinande" 溈山教團の動向について: 福州大安の "真身記" の紹介に因んで,
Indogaku bukkyōgaku kenkyū 27.1 (1978): 90–96.

———. "Shinpuku-ji bunko shozō no Hai Kyū shūi mon no honkoku" 真福寺文庫
所藏の "裴休拾遺問" の翻刻. *Zengaku kenkyū* 禪學研究 60 (1981): 71–104.

———. *Sōdai zenshūshi no kenkyū* 宋代禪宗史の研究. Tokyo: Daitō shuppansha,
1987.

———. "Nanyō Echū no nanpō shūshi no hihan ni tsuite" 南陽慧忠の南方宗旨の
批判について. In *Chūgoku no bukkyō to bunka: Kamata Shigeo hakushi kanreki kinen
ronshū* 中國の佛教と文化: 鎌田茂雄博士還暦記念論集, 315–44. Tokyo: Daizō
shuppansha, 1988.

———. "Nansōzen no tongo shisō no tenkai: Kataku Shine kara Kōshūshū e" 南宗
禪の頓悟思想の展開: 荷澤神會から洪州宗へ. *Zenbunka kenkyūjo kiyō* 20 (1990):
101–50.

———. "Hyakujō kyōdan to Isan kyōdan" 百丈教團と溈山教團. *Indogaku bukkyōgaku
kenkyū* 41.1 (1992): 106–11.

———. "Hyakujo kyōdan to Isan kyōdan (zoku)" 百丈教團と溈山教團(續). *Indogaku
bukkyōgaku kenkyū* 42.1 (1993): 289–95.

———. "Hyakujō shingi no kenkyū" 百丈清規の研究. *Komazawa daigaku zenkenkyūjo
nenpō* 駒澤大學禪研究所年報 6 (1995): 15–53.

———. "Igyōshu no seisui (1–6)" 溈仰宗の盛衰 (1–6). *Komazawa daigaku bukkyōgakubu
ronshū* 駒澤大學佛教學部論集 18–22, 24 (1985–1991, 1993).

Ishikawa Rikisan 石川力山. "Baso zen keisei no ichisokumen" 馬祖禪形成の一側面.
Sōgaku kenkyū 宗學研究 13 (1971): 105–10.

———. "Baso zō henka katei" 馬祖像の變化過程. *Indogaku bukkyōgaku kenkyū* 20.2
(1972).

Jia Jinhua 賈晉華. *Jiaoran nianpu* 皎然年譜. Xiamen: Xiamen daxue chubanshe,
1992.

———. "Doctrinal Reformation of the Hongzhou School of Chan Buddhism." *Journal
of International Association of Buddhist Studies* 2001.2: 7–26.

———. "Mazu Daoyi: A Complete Biography." *Taiwan Journal of Religious Studies* 1.2
(2001): 119–50.

———. "Chuanshi Baozhi chanji kaobian" 傳世寶誌禪偈考辨. *Zhongguo chanxue* 中
國禪學 3 (2004): 129–32.

———. "Hongzhouxi de fenhua yu Shitouxi de xingqi: jiegou chanzong chuantong
liangxi wuzong shixitu" 洪州系的分化與石頭系的興起: 解構禪宗傳統兩系五宗
世系圖. *Zhonghua wenshi luncong* 中華文史論叢 78 (2004): 54–97.

———. "The Creation and Codification of Monastic Regulations at Mount Baizhang."
Journal of Chinese Religions 33 (2005): 39–59.

Jia Jinhua, and Fu Xuancong. *Tang Wudai wenxue biannianshi: Wudai juan* 唐五代文學
編年史: 五代卷. Vol. 4 of *Tang Wudai wenxue biannianshi*, ed. Fu Xuancong.
Shenyang: Liaohai chubanshe, 1998.

Jorgensen, John. "The 'Imperial' Lineage of Ch'an Buddhism: The Role of Confucian Ritual and Ancestor Worship in Ch'an's Search for Legitimation in the Mid-T'ang Dynasty." *Papers on Far Eastern History* 35 (1987): 89–133.

Kagamishima Genryū 鏡島元隆. "Hyakujō shingi no seiritsu to sono igi" 百丈清規成立とその意義. *Zen kenkyūjo kiyō* 禪研究所紀要 6 & 7 (1976): 117–34.

Kamata Shigeo 鎌田茂雄. "Chūto no bukkyō no hendō to kokka kenryoku" 中唐の佛教の變動と國家權力. *Tōyō bunka kenkyūjo kiyō* 東洋文化研究所紀要 25 (1961): 201–45.

———. *Chūgoku Kegon shisōshi no kenkyū* 中國華嚴思想史の研究. Tokyo: Tōkyō daigaku shuppankai, 1965.

———. *Chūgoku bukkyō shisōshi kenkyū* 中國佛教思想史研究. Tokyo: Shunjushi, 1967.

———. *Shūmitsu kyōgaku no shisōshiteki kenkyū* 宗密教學の思想史的研究. Tokyo: Tōkyō daigaku shuppankai, 1975.

———. *Chōsen bukkyō shi* 朝鮮佛教史. Tokyo: Tōkyō daigaku shuppankai, 1987.

Kieschnick, John. *The Eminent Monk: Buddhist Ideals in Medieval Chinese Hagiography*. Honolulu: University of Hawaii Press, 1997.

King, Sallie B. *Buddha Nature*. Albany: State University of New York Press, 1991.

Kondō Ryōichi 近藤良一. "Hyakujō shingi no seiritsu to sono genkei" 百丈清規の成立とその原形. *Hokkaidō Komazawa daigaku kenkyū kiyō* 北海道駒澤大學研究紀要 3 (1968): 17–48.

———. "Tōdai zenshō no keizai kiban" 唐代禪宗の經濟基盤. *Nippon Bukkyō gakkai nenpō* 日本佛教學會年報 37 (1972): 137–51.

———. "Hyakujō shingi seiritsu no yōin" 百丈清規成立の要因. *Indo tetsugaku bukkyōgaku* 印度哲學佛教學 2 (1987): 231–46.

Kubo Tsugunari, and Yuyama Akira, trans. *The Lotus Sutra*. Berkeley: Numata Center for Buddhist Translation and Research, 1993.

Kuno Hōryū 久野芳隆. "Ryūdōsei ni tomu Tōdai no zenshū tenseki: Tonkō shutsudo hon ni okeru nanzen hokushū no daihyōteki sakuhin" 流動性に富む唐代の禪宗典籍: 敦煌出土本における南禪北宗の代表的作品. *Shūkyō kenkyū* 14.1 (1937): 117–44.

Lai, Whalen. "Chan Metaphors: Waves, Water, Mirror, and Lamp." *Philosophy East and West* 29 (1979): 243–55.

———. "Ma-tsu Tao-i and the Unfolding of Southern Zen." *Japanese Journal of Religious Studies* 12.2–3 (1985): 173–92.

Lai, Whalen, and Lewis R. Lancaster, eds. *Early Ch'an in China and Tibet*. Berkeley: Asian Humanities Press, 1983.

Lai Yonghai 賴永海. *Zhongguo foxinglun* 中國佛性論. Shanghai: Shanghai renmin chubanshe, 1988.

Lamotte, Étienne. *History of Indian Buddhism: From the Origins to the Śaka Era*. Trans. Sara Webb-Boin and Jean Dantinne. Louvain-Paris: Peeters Press, 1988.

Li Zehou 李澤厚. *Zhongguo gudai sixiangshi lun* 中國古代思想史論. Beijing: Renmin chubanshe, 1986.

Lievens, Bavo. *The Recorded Sayings of Ma-tsu*. Trans. Julian F. Pas. Lewiston: Edwin Mellen Press, 1987.

Lopez, Donald S., Jr., ed. *Buddhist Hermeneutics*. Honolulu: University of Hawaii Press, 1988.

Lü Cheng 呂澂 (1896–1989). *Lü Cheng foxue lunzhu xuanji* 呂澂佛學論著選集. 5 vols. Jinan: Qi Lu shushe, 1991.

Makita Tairyō 牧田諦亮. "Hōshi oshō den kō: Chūgoku ni okeru bukkyō reiken juyō no ichi keitai" 寶誌和尚傳考: 中國にぉける佛教靈驗受容の一形態, *Tōhō gakuhō* 東方學報 26 (1956): 64–89.

Mano Shōjun 真野正順. *Bukkyō ni okeru shū kannen no seiritsu* 佛教にぉける宗觀念の成立. Kyoto: Risōsha, 1964.

Maraldo, John C. "Is There Historial Consciousness within Ch'an?" *Japanese Journal of Religious Studies* 12.2–3 (1985): 141–72.

Matsumoto Shirō 松本史朗. *Zen shisō no hihanteki kenkyū* 禪思想の批判的研究. Tokyo: Daizō shuppan, 1993.

———. "The Doctrine of Tathāgata-garbha Is Not Buddhist." In *Pruning the Bodhi Tree: The Storm over Critical Buddhism*, ed. Hubbard and Swanson, 165–73.

———. "Critiques of Tathāgata-garbha Thought and Critical Buddhism." *Komazawa daigaku Bukkyō gakubu ronshū* 駒澤大學佛教學部論集 33 (2002): 360–78.

McRae, John R. "The Ox-head School of Chinese Ch'an Buddhism: From Early Ch'an to the Golden Age." In *Studies in Ch'an and Hua-yen*, ed. Gimello and Gregory, 169–252.

———. *The Northern School and the Formation of Early Ch'an Buddhism*. Honolulu: University of Hawaii Press, 1986.

———. "Shenhui and the Teaching of Sudden Enlightenment in Early Chan Buddhism." In *Sudden and Gradual*, ed. Gregory, 227–78.

———. "Encounter Dialogue and the Transformation in Ch'an." In *Paths to Liberation: The Marga and Its Transformations in Buddhist Thought*, ed. Buswell and Gimello, 339–69.

———. "Shenhui's Vocation on the Ordination Platform and Our Visualization of Medieval Chinese Ch'an Buddhism." *Annual Report of the Institute for Zen Studies, Hanazono University* 24 (December 1998): 43–66.

———. "The Antecedents of Encounter Dialogue in Chinese Ch'an Buddhism." In *The Kōan: Texts and Contexts in Zen Buddhism*, ed. Heine and Wright, 54–70.

———. *Seeing through Zen: Encounter, Transformation, and Genealogy in Chinese Chan Buddhism*. Berkeley: University of California Press, 2003.

Mizuno Kogen 水野弘元. "Denhōge no seiritsu ni tsuite" 傳法偈の成立について. *Sōgaku kenkyū* 2 (1960.1): 37.

Ng, Yu-kwan. *Tien-t'ai Buddhism and Early Mādhyamika*. Honolulu: University of Hawaii Press, 1993.

Nie Qing 聶清. " 'Zhengdao ge' zuozhe kao" 證道歌作者考. *Zongjiaoxue yanjiu* 宗教學研究 1 (1999): 131–37.

Nishiguchi Yoshio 西口芳男. "Baso no denki" 馬祖の傳記. *Zengaku kenkyū* 63 (1984): 111–46.

Nukariya Kaiten 忽滑谷快天. *Zengaku shisōshi* 禪學思想史. 1923. Reprint, Tokyo: Meicho kankōkai, 1969.

Ogawa Kōkan 小川弘貫. *Chūgoku nyoraizō shisō kenkyū* 中國如來藏思想研究. Tokyo: Bukkyō shorin nakayama shobō, 1976.

Okimoto Katsumi 沖本克己. "Hyakujō shingi to Zenin shingi" 百丈清規と禪院清規. *Indogaku bukkyōgaku kenkyū* 17/2 (1969): 733–75.

———. "Hyakujō kogi ni tsuite" 百丈古規について. *Zenbunka kenkyūjo kiyō* 1 (1980): 51–61.

———. "Rinzai roku ni okeru kyoko to shinjitsu" 臨濟錄におくる虚構と真實. *Zengaku kenkyū* 73 (1995.1): 17–49.

Ōishi Morio 大石守雄. "Ko shingi ni tsuite" 古清規について. *Zengaku kenkyū* 11 (1953): 81–88.

———. "Shingi no kenkyū" 清規の研究. *Zengaku kenkyū* 54 (1964): 109–15.

Pang Guiming 潘桂明. *Zhongguo chanzong sixiang licheng* 中國禪宗思想歷程. Beijing: Jinri Zhongguo chubanshe, 1992.

Poceski, Mario. "The Hongzhou School of Chan Buddhism during the Mid-Tang Period." Ph.D. diss. University of California, Los Angeles, 2000.

———. "Mazu yulu and the Creation of the Chan Records of Sayings." In *The Zen Canon: Understanding the Classic Texts*, ed. Heine and Wright, 53–80.

Power, William. *The Record of Tung-shan*. Honolulu: University of Hawaii Press, 1986.

Ran Yunhua 冉雲華 (Jan, Yün-hua). "Tsung-mi: His Analysis of Ch'an Buddhism." *T'oung Pao* 53 (1972): 1–53.

———. "Two Problems Concerning Tsung-mi's Compilation of Ch'an-tsang." *Transactions of the International Conference of Orientalists in Japan* 19 (1974): 37–47.

———. "Conflict and Harmony in Ch'an Buddhism." *Journal of Chinese Philosophy* 4 (1977): 287–302.

———. *Zongmi* 宗密. Taibei: Dongda tushugongsi, 1988.

———. *Zhongguo chanxue yanjiu lunji* 中國禪學研究論集. Taibei: Dongchu chubanshe, 1990.

———. " 'Tang gu Zhaoshengsi dade Huijian chanshi bei' kao" 唐故招聖寺大德慧堅禪師碑考. *Cong Yindu fojiao dao zhongguo fojiao*, 145–74.

———. *Cong Yindu fojiao dao Zhongguo fojiao* 從印度佛教到中國佛教. Taibei: Dongda chubangongsi, 1995.

———. "Heishuicheng chanjuan 'Chengxitu' yanjiu" 黑水城殘卷 "承襲圖" 研究. In *Qingzhu Pan Shichan xiansheng jiuzhi huadan Dunhuangxue tekan* 慶祝潘石禪先生九秩華誕敦煌學特刊, ed. Liu Cunren 柳存仁 (Taibei: Wenjin, 1996), 75–87.

———. "Chanzong diqizu zhizheng de wenxian yanjiu" 禪宗第七祖之爭的文獻研究, *Zhongguo wenhua yanjiusuo xuebao* 中國文化研究所學報 6 (1997): 417–37.

Rawlinson, Andrew. "The Ambiguity of the Buddha-nature Concept in India and China," in *Early Ch'an in China and Tibet*, ed. Lai and Lancaster, 259–80.

Reischauer, Edwin O., trans. *Ennin's Diary: The Recorder of a Pilgrimage to China in Search of the Law*. New York: Ronald Press, 1955.

Ren Jiyu 任繼愈, ed. *Zhongguo zhexue fazhanshi: Sui Tang* 中國哲學發展史: 隋唐. Beijing: Renmin chubanshe, 1994.

Robinson, Richard H. *Early Mādhyamika in India and China*. 1967. Reprint, Delhi: Motilal Banarsidass, 1995.

Sasaki, Ruth Fuller, trans. *The Recorded Sayings of Ch'an Master Lin-chi Hui-chao of Chen Prefecture*. Kyōto: The Institute for Zen Studies, 1975.

Sasaki, Ruth Fuller et al., trans. *A Man of Zen: The Recorded Sayings of Layman P'ang*. New York: Weatherhill, 1971.

Schlütter, Morten. "Chan Buddhist in Song-Dynasty China (960–1279): The Rise of the Caodong Tradition and the Formation of the Chan School." Ph.D diss. Yale University, 1988.

————. "A Study in the Genealogy of the *Platform Sutra*." *Studies in Central and East Asian Religions* 2 (1989): 53–115.

Sekiguchi Shindai 関口真大. *Zenshū shishōshi* 禪宗思想史. Tokyo: Sankibō Busshorin, 1964.

Sharf, Robert H. *Coming to Terms with Chinese Buddhism: A Reading of the Treasure Store Treatise*. Honolulu: University of Hawaii Press, 2002.

————. "On Pure Land Buddhism and Ch'an/Pure Land Syncretism in Medieval China," *T'oung Pao* 88.4–5 (2002): 282–331.

Sheng-yen, trans. *The Sword of Wisdom*. Taibei: Dharma Drum Corp., 1999.

Shiina Kōyū 椎名宏雄. "Shotō zensha no ritsuin kyojū ni tsuite" 初唐禪者の律院居住について. *Indogaku bukkyōgaku kenkyū* 17.2 (1969): 325–27.

————. "*Horinden* itsubun no kenkyū" 寶林傳逸文の研究. *Komazawa daigaku Bukkyō gakubu ronshū* 11 (1980): 234–57.

————. "*Horinden* makikyū makijū no itsubun" 寶林傳卷九卷十の逸文. *Sōgaku kenkyū* 22 (1980): 191–98.

————. *Sō Gen-ban zenseki no kenkyū* 宋元版禪籍の研究. Tokyo: Daitō shuppansha, 1993.

————. "*Baso shike roku* no shobon" 馬祖四家錄の諸本, *Zenbunka kenkyūjo kiyō* 24 (1998.12): 161–81.

Shim Jae-ryong. *Korean Buddhism: Tradition and Transformation*. Seoul: Jimoondang, 1999.

Shinohara Hisao 篠原壽雄, and Tanaka Ryōshō 田中良昭, eds. *Tonkō butten to zen* 敦煌佛典と禪. Tokyo: Daitō shuppansha, 1980.

Sohaku Ogata. *The Transmission of the Lamp: Early Masters*. Wolfboro: Longwood Academic, 1990.

Stone, Jacqueline. *Original Enlightenment and the Transformation of Medieval Japanese Buddhism*. Honolulu: University of Hawaii Press, 1999.

Sutton, Florin G. *Existence and Enlightenment in the Laṅkāvatāra-sūtra: A Study in the Ontology and Epistemology of the Yogācāra School of Mahāyāna Buddhism*. Albany: State University of New York Press, 1991.

Suzuki Daisetsu (Teitarō) 鈴木大拙 (貞太郎, 1870–1966). "Zen: A Reply to Hu Shih," *Philosophy East and West* 3.1(1953): 25–46.

———. *Suzuki Daisetsu zenshū* 鈴木大拙全集. 32 vols. Tokyo: Iwanami shoten, 1968–1971.

———. trans. *The Laṅkāvatāra Sūtra: A Mahayana Text*. London: Routledge, 1932.

Suzuki Tetsuo 鈴木哲雄. *Tō Godai no zenshū: Konan Kōsei hen* 唐五代の禪宗: 湖南江西篇. Tokyo: Daitō shuppansha, 1984.

———. *Tō Godai zenshūshi* 唐五代禪宗史. Tokyo: Sankibō busshorin, 1985.

———. "Hyakujō kōroku ni mirareru shisō" 百丈廣錄にみられる思想. *Indogaku bukkyōgaku kenkyū* 46.2 (1988): 583–88.

———. *Chūgoku zenshūshi rōnkō* 中國禪宗史論考. Tokyo: Sankibō busshorin, 1999.

Swanson, Paul L. *Foundations of T'ien-t'ai Philosophy: The Flowering of the Two Truths Theory in Chinese Buddhism*. Berkeley: Asian Humanities Press, 1989.

Takasaki Jikidō 高崎直道. *A Study of the Ratnagotravibhāga (Uttaratantra): Being a Treatise on the Tathāgatagarbha Theory of Mahāyāna Buddhism*. Rome: Istituto Italiano per il Medio ed Estremo Oriente, 1966.

———. *Nyoraizō shisō no keisei: Indo Daijō Bukkyō shisō kenkyū* 如來藏思想の形成: インド大乘佛教思想研究. Tokyo: Shunjūsha, 1974.

———. *Nyoraizō shisō* 如來藏思想. Tokyo: Shunjūsha, 1988.

Tanaka Ryōshō 田中良昭. "Shoki zenshū to kairitsu" 初期禪宗と戒律. *Shūgaku kenkyū* 11 (1969): 31–36.

———. "*Genoshoshu to sareru Tonkō bon Daii kyosaku ni tsuite*" 彥和尚集とされる敦煌本大潙警策について. *Indogaku bukkyōgaku kenkyū* 22.2 (1974): 630–35.

———. *Tonkō zenshū bunken no kenkyū* 敦煌禪宗文獻の研究. Tokyo: Taitō shuppansha, 1983.

Tang Yongtong 湯用彤 (1893–1964). *Han Wei liang Jin Nanbeichao fojiaoshi* 漢魏兩晉南北朝佛教史. 1928. Reprint, Shanghai: Shanghai shudian, 1991.

———. "Lun Zhongguo fojiao wu 'shizong'" 論中國佛教無十宗. *Zhexue yanjiu* 哲學研究 3 (1962): 47–54.

———. "Zhongguo fojiao zongpai wenti bulun" 中國佛教宗派問題補論. *Beijing daxue xuebao* 北京大學學報 5 (1963): 1–18.

Tei Shiken 鄭茂煥. "Hōrinden ni okeru shōbōgenzō no imi" 寶林傳 における 正法眼藏の意味. *Sōgaku kenkyū* 131 (1989): 246–51.

Tokiwa Daijō 常盤大定 (1870–1945). *Horinden no kenkyū* 寶林傳の研究. Tokyo: Tōhō bunka kenkyūjo, 1934.

———. *Shina Bukkyō shiseki tōsaki* 支那佛教史蹟踏査記. Tokyo: Ryūginsha, 1938.

Twitchett, Denis. "The Monasteries and the Chinese Economy in Medieval Times." *Bulletin of the School of Oriental and African Studies* 19.3 (1957): 526–49.

———. ed. *The Cambridge History of China, Volume 3: Sui and T'ang China*. 589–906. Part 1. Cambridge: Cambridge University Press, 1979.

Ui Hakuju 宇井伯壽 (1882–1963). *Zenshūshi kenkyū* 禪宗史研究. 1939. Reprint, Tokyo: Iwanami shoten, 1966.

———. *Daini zenshūshi kenkyū* 第二禪宗史研究. 1941. Reprint, Tokyo: Iwanami shoten, 1966.

———. *Daisan zenshūshi kenkyū* 第三禪宗史研究. 1942. Reprint, Tokyo: Iwanami shoten, 1966.

Wang, Youru. *Linguistic Strategies in Daoist Zhuangzi and Chan Buddhism: The Other Way of Speaking*. London and New York: RoutledgeCurzon, 2003.

Wang Zhongmin 王重民 (1903–1975). *Dunhuang yishu lunwen ji* 敦煌遺書論文集. Taibei: Mingwen shuju, 1985.

Watson, Burton, trans. *The Zen Teachings of Master Lin-chi: A Translation of the Lin-chi lu*. Boston: Shambala, 1993.

———, trans. *The Lotus Sūtra*. New York: Columbia University Press, 1993.

———, trans. *The Vimalakīrti Sūtra*. New York: Columbia University Press, 1997.

Weinstein, Stanley. *Buddhism under the Tang*. New York: Cambridge University Press, 1987.

———. "Schools of Buddhism: Chinese Buddhism." In *Encyclopedia of Religion*, ed. Mircea Eliade, vol. 2, 482–87. New York: Macmillan, 1987.

Welter, Albert. *The Meaning of Myriad Good Deeds: A Studey of Yung-ming Yen-shou and the Wan-shan t'ung-kuei chi*. New York: Peter Lang, 1993.

———. "Lineage." *Encyclopedia of Buddhism*, 461–65.

———. "The Problem with Orthodoxy in Zen Buddhism: Yongming Yanshou's Notion of *zong* in the *Zongjin lu* (Records of the Source Mirror)." *Studies in Religion/Science Religieuse* 31.1 (2002): 3–18.

———. "Lineage and Context in the Patriarch's Hall Collection and the Transmission of the Lamp." In *Zen Canon*, ed. Heine and Wright, 137–80.

Wright, Dale S. "Historical Understanding: The Ch'an Buddhist Transmission Narratives and Modern Historiography," *History and Theory* 31.1 (1992): 37–46.

———. "The Discourse of Awakening: Rhetorical Practice in Classical Chan Buddhism." *Journal of the American Academy of Religion* 61.1 (1993): 23–40.

———. *Philosophical Meditations on Zen Buddhism*. Cambridge: Cambridge University Press, 1998.

Wu, Jiang. "Orthodoxy, Controversy, and the Transformation of Chan Buddhism in Seventeenth-century China." Ph.D. diss. Harvard University, 2002.

Xu Wenming 徐文明. "Hu Shi 'Bai Juyi shidai de chanzong shixi' zhimiu" 胡適 "白居易時代的禪宗世系" 指謬. *Yuanxue* 原學 6 (1995): 369–77.

———. "Yaoshan Weiyan de zongxi he chanfeng" 藥山惟儼的宗系和禪風. In *Shiji zhijiao de Tansuo* 世紀之交的探索, 151–66. Beijing: Beijing shifan daxue chubanshe, 2000.

———. "Cao-Dong zong guizong Qingyuan yixi de yuanyin chuxi" 曹洞宗歸宗青原一系的原因初析. *Pumen xuebao* 普門學報 2 (2001): 126–36.

Yampolsky, Philip B. *The Platform Sūtra of the Sixth Patriarch*. New York: Columbia University Press, 1967.

Yanagida Seizan 柳田聖山. *Shoki zenshū shisho no kenkyū* 初期禪宗史書の研究. Kyoto: Hōzōkan, 1967; reprint, vol. 6 of *Yanagida Seizan shu*.

———. *Mu no tankyū: Chūgoku zen* 無の探求: 中國禪. Tokyo: Kadokawa shoten, 1969.

————. *Shoki no zenshi, vol. 1, Ryōka shiji ki, Den hōbō ki* 初期の禪史 I: 楞伽師資記·傳法寶記. Tokyo: Chikuma shobō, 1971.

————. "Chūgoku zenshū shi" 中國禪宗史. In *Zen no rekishi: Chūgoku* 禪の歴史: 中國, ed. Nishitani Keiji 西谷啓治, 7-108. Tokyo: Chikuma shobō, 1974.

————. "The *Li-Dai Fa-Pao Chi* and the Ch'an Doctrine of Sudden Awakening." Trans. Carl W. Bielefeldt. In *Early Ch'an in China and Tibet*, 13–50.

————. "The 'Recorded Sayings' Texts of the Chinese Ch'an School." Trans. John R. McRae. In *Early Ch'an in China and Tibet*, 185–205.

————. "Goroku no rekishi: Zen bunken no seiritsushiteki kenkyū" 語錄の歴史: 禪文獻の成立史的研究. *Tōhō gakuhō* 57 (1985): 211–663; reprint, *Zen bunken no kenkyū* 禪文獻の研究, vol. 2 of *Yanagida Seizan shū*.

————. *Yanagida Seizan shū* 柳田聖山集. Kyoto: Hōzōkan, 2001.

Yanagida Seizan and Tokiwa Gishin 常盤義伸. *Zekkanron: Eibun yakuchū, genbun kōtei, kokuyaku* 絕觀論: 英文譯注·原文校定·國譯. Kyoto: Zenbunka kenkyūjo, 1976.

Yang Zengwen 楊曾文. *Tang Wudai chanzongshi* 唐五代禪宗史. Beijing: Zhongguo shehui kexue chubanshe, 1999.

Yifa. *The Origins of Buddhist Monastic Codes in China: An Annotated Translation and Study of the Chanyuan qinggui.* Honolulu: University of Hawaii Press, 2002.

Yinshun 印順. *Rulaizang zhi yanjiu* 如來藏之研究. Taipei: Zhengwen chubanshe, 1981.

————. *Zhongguo chanzong shi* 中國禪宗史. 1971. Reprint, Shanghai: Shanghai shudian, 1992.

Yoshizu Yoshihide 吉津宜英. *Kegonzen no shisōshiteki kenkyū* 華嚴禪の思想史的研究. Tokyo: Daitō shuppansha, 1985.

Yu Xianhao 郁賢皓. *Tang cishi kao quanbian* 唐刺史考全編. 5 vols. Hefei: Anhui daxue chubanshe, 2000.

Zeuschner, Robert B. "The Concept of li nien ('being free from thinking') in the Northern Line of Ch'an Buddhism," in *Early Ch'an in China and Tibet*, 131–48.

Zürcher, Erik. *The Buddhist Conquest of China: The Spread and Adaptation of Buddhism in Early Medieval China.* 2 vols. Leiden: Brill, 1959.

INDEX

absolute/phenomena paradigm. *See* doctrine of Hongzhou Chan

actualized enlightenment (*benjue*). *See* enlightenment

Adamek, Wendi L., 140n90, 157nn33–34

An Lushan rebellion, 11, 18, 21, 24, 27, 58, 83

anxin (pacifying the mind), 74, 76, 79, 81

apophasis, 75, 108, 164

Avatamsaka-sūtra (Da fangguang fo huayan jing), 167n5, 168n16, 173n46

Awakening of Faith in Mahāyāna (Dasheng qixin lun), 6, 67, 70–73, 78, 151n20, 152n34, 166n1, 173n47

Bai Juyi, 5, 48 65, 104, 140n91, 144n56, 150n133, 156n20, 158n49, 162n144, 163n167, 163n176

Baizhang Fazheng (Baizhang Weizheng, Niepan heshang), 7, 31, 95, 98, 100, 102–3, 144n74. *See also* monastic regulations of Baizhangsi

Baizhang guanglu. See *Extended Records of Baizhang*

Baizhang Huaihai, 7, 16, 26, 31, 33, 53, 80, 111 table 3, 113; conferral of posthumous title (Dazhi chanshi or Chan Master Great Wisdom), 98; conferral of stūpa title (Da baosheng lun or Great Wheel of Treasure and Superiority), 98; extolled in encounter dialogues,

54–56, 59–60; examination of Baizhang's discourses, 62. *See also* Baizhangsi; *Chanmen guishi; Extended Records of Baizhang;* monastic regulations of Baizhangsi

Baizhang Weizheng. *See* Baizhang Fazheng

Baizhangsi (Baizhang monastery): abbots, 31, 33 table 1, 96, 98–99, 102; bestowal of imperial name-tablet, 99, 161n120; date of establishment, 98. See also *Chanmen guishi;* monasteries of Chan; monastic regulations of Baizhangsi; monastic regulations of Chan

Bao Fang, 18, 83

Bao Ji, 11, 57–58

Baofengsi (Baofeng monastery), 19

Baolin zhuan (Chronicle of the Baolin Monastery): claim of orthodoxy, 86–89; edition and fragments, 155–56n8; encounter stories of enlightenment, 50; genealogy, 86–89; original title (*Fayan shizi zhuan*), 84–85; true author (Zhangjing Huaihui), 84–86

Baotang school, 2, 86–87

Baoxing lun. See *Ratnagotravibhāga*

Baozang lun (Treasure Store Treatise), 174n55

Baozhi, 6–7; Bao gong (Master Bao) being another person, 90; biographical sources, 89–90, 158nn53–54; rhyming scheme of

209